Derrida, Kristeva, and the Dividing Line

COMPARATIVE LITERATURE AND CULTURAL STUDIES
VOLUME 5
GARLAND REFERENCE LIBRARY OF THE HUMANITIES
VOLUME 2078

COMPARATIVE LITERATURE AND CULTURAL STUDIES
JONATHAN HART, *Series Editor*

Derrida, Kristeva, and the Dividing Line

An Articulation of Two Theories of Difference

Juliana de Nooy

Garland Publishing, Inc.
A member of the Taylor & Francis Group
New York and London
1998

Library of Congress Cataloging-in-Publication Data

de Nooy, Juliana.
    Derrida, Kristeva, and the dividing line : an articulation of two theories
of difference / by Juliana de Nooy.
        p.   cm. — (Garland reference library of the humanities ; v. 2078.
Comparative literature and cultural studies ; v. 5)
    Includes bibliographical references and index.
    ISBN 0-8153-2571-1 (hc : alk. paper)
    1. Derrida, Jacques, 1930– —Contributions in criticism. 2. Kristeva,
Julia, 1941– —Contributions in criticism. 3. Criticism. I. Title. II. Series:
Garland reference library of the humanities ; v. 2078. III. Series: Garland
reference library of the humanities. Comparative literature and cultural
studies ; v. 5.
PN81.D397   1998
801'.95—dc21   98-15871
                                                             CIP

Cover art copyright © Barbara Penrose.

Printed on acid-free, 250-year-life paper
Manufactured in the United States of America

Goethe's *Weltliteratur*—a discussion of literature as a whole rather than a partisan interest in those who are in or out of favour, and how that literature relates to other arts as well as to philosophical, historical, and cultural contexts—lies behind this series. A comparative study of literature in different contexts will be the focus of each volume. The series, whose authors and scope are international, will be pluralistic, and include disparate points of view. Its only criterion is the quality of the work. Here, comparative studies will include the comparison of literary texts, as well as cross-disciplinary and theoretical inquiries. The books in this series will explore the crossing of linguistic and cultural boundaries in comparative literature, and its increasingly close relation to or overlap with cultural studies. This comparative literature will not compare European languages and literatures alone, but will also address East-West, minority, gender, and aboriginal issues. One of the goals of the Comparative Literature and Cultural Studies series is to increase consciousness or self-consciousness about methods and ideological assumptions while fostering a better understanding of specific literary, historical, and cultural texts. The volumes that constitute the series should help to improve the dialogue between theory and practice in comparative studies. Comparative literature and cultural studies are closely related, and the uniqueness of this series is that it is the only one, to my knowledge, that explores the boundaries between them. Both disciplines emphasize popular culture, visual arts, and the sociology of literature. Here cultural studies, which is also connected to cultural history, is meant as something changing, perhaps widening, its intellectual appeal. Although comparative literature and cultural studies have interesting origins, the volumes will not all be "true" to those origins. Some will be revisionary. While the Birmingham School was instrumental in contributing to cultural studies in the English-speaking world, the study of culture has undergone important changes and controversies. Another aim of this series will be to contribute to this changing debate on literature and culture. In the global village these cultural, historical, and literary comparisons may help to engender new ways of seeing in the university and the various societies in which it finds itself. How the contributors construct their visions will be, although part of a cooperative enterprise, an individual matter.

Jonathan Hart

Contents

Abbreviations

WORKS BY DERRIDA

Dis	*Dissemination*
FL	"Force of Law: The Mystical Foundation of Authority"
HAS	"How to Avoid Speaking: Denials"
LG	"The Law of Genre"
LI	*Limited Inc*
MP	*Margins of Philosophy*
OG	*Of Grammatology*
PC	*The Post Card*
Pos	*Positions*
TP	*The Truth in Painting*
UG	"Ulysses Gramophone: Hear Say Yes in Joyce"
WD	*Writing and Difference*
TI	"TITLE (to be specified)"

WORKS BY KRISTEVA

BS	*Black Sun*
DL	*Desire in Language*
JG	"Joyce 'The Gracehoper' or the Return of Orpheus"
KR	*The Kristeva Reader*
NMS	*New Maladies of the Soul*
PH	*Powers of Horror*
PL	*Polylogue*
Révolution	*La Révolution du langage poétique* (untranslated chapters)
RPL	*Revolution in Poetic Language*

Σ	*Sèméiotiké*
SNR	*Sens et Non-sens de la Révolte*
TL	*Tales of Love*

Acknowledgments

I am very grateful to Peter Cryle, whose questions and comments on each chapter made this a better book. I am also indebted to Peter Cowley, co-author of Chapter 8, for research assistance, indexing, and advice on translations. My thanks to Jean-Louis Houdebine for his supervision of the thesis from which this book evolved and to Anne Freadman for invaluable advice on its reorientation for publication in English. I should also like to thank Anne for her feedback on some of the chapters.

Jonathan Hart, my editor, offered welcome advice, and many others (particularly from the Department of Romance Languages, University of Queensland) contributed to the work through discussions and seminars, by offering insights into uptakes of Derrida and Kristeva, and by reading drafts and offering support. Thanks are due to Keith Atkinson, Siobhan Brownlie, Deirdre Gilfedder, Barbara Hanna, Joe Hardwick, John Macarthur, Janis McKauge, Guy Pigerre, Elizabeth Ruinard and Bronwyn Statham.

The award of a University of Queensland New Staff Research Grant assisted greatly with the completion of the book.

Introduction

"Compare and contrast," they used to ask on the old examination papers. But how can you compare two theories of the production of difference? What conception of difference do you use to go about it? Any search for a dividing line between Derrida and Kristeva already engages with their preoccupations and their practices of division. How then can the juxtaposition of these practices be conceived? As a face-to-face encounter, a confrontation? Is there indeed encounter as such, or rather a gap, a hiatus? Could it be a dialectic? Or a *différance*? Should it be thought of in terms of Kristeva's work . . . or Derrida's? The articulation of the two becomes a question not only of subject matter but of methodology.

This book is a reading of a set of discursive encounters and non-encounters between the two bodies of text signed Derrida and Kristeva. Its starting point now appears in the final chapter concerning uptakes: I was intrigued by the wide variation in the ways in which the two are taken up at various times and places and in various disciplines and debates. I was particularly struck by the range of readings of the relation between the two. Both these theorists have made an enormous impact throughout the humanities with their theories of signification, their understandings of identity and difference, and their analyses of literary and theoretical texts.[1] But the connections made between the theories differ widely according to the temporal, geographical and disciplinary position of the reader. Kristeva and Derrida have often been cited side by side and their theories used interchangeably (particularly during the seventies and eighties to denote a certain "French post-structuralism" or "French feminism," or in debates over essentialism). Elsewhere, their theories are regularly opposed to one another (in queer theory for example and Judith Butler's work in particular) or viewed as dissimilar (in the visual arts). In yet other contexts, they have tended to be regarded as more clearly separated by the disciplines of philosophy and psychoanalysis (in France, for instance, where the notion of the interdisciplinary perhaps rests on a premise of firmer boundaries between disciplines than in Anglophone countries). Strangely, however, although the theories have sometimes been regarded as more or less indistinguishable and sometimes as simply incompatible, there has been no real debate about their relation to one another. Certainly no detailed study has existed of the ways in which the texts might be read together. The relation or lack of one has tended to be assumed rather than argued.

One particular kind of relation is, however, regularly explored: introductions to Kristeva's work commonly explain it in terms of Derrida's influence. Kristeva is often said to appropriate Derrida's work, and her theory is explained in terms of its reliance on and departure from Derrida's. It is highly unusual, on the other hand, to find Derrida's work situated in relation to Kristeva's or indeed to find references to Kristeva in introductions to Derrida's work. This book poses the question differently. It avoids the paradigm of influence and its inevitable anxieties in favor of a series of active engagements between the theories. After all, although Derrida started publishing a few years before Kristeva and although his philosophical project was consolidated somewhat earlier than hers, for the last thirty years both have been writing prolifically. It seems to me that their texts have more and more interesting things to say to and about each other and their objects than a one-way expression of debt.

This book, then, connects—and disconnects—the work of Derrida and Kristeva in other ways. It goes beyond the naive question of whether the theories are simply the same or different, compatible or incompatible. It aims at establishing precisely how Kristeva's and Derrida's writings may be articulated, tracing intersections and divergences, parallels and discontinuities between them.

However the book will not arrive at a single, simple, unambiguous answer to the question of how the theories of Kristeva and Derrida fit together. The first reason for this is that they are not fixed entities but shifting sets of practices. The proper names "Derrida" and "Kristeva" are not self-identical. Each holds together a set of texts, but neither is itself held together in any permanent way. Depending on which of those texts are foregrounded, the names tend to function differently. If I

regularly need to refer to "two" theories-theorists-practices, neither of
these two is an undivided, homogeneous entity and I have constantly
had to resist the temptation to synthesize the texts into two streamlined
theories with neat edges. We can take the corpora as convenient
ensembles, but we must recognize that they each contain divisions,
internal tensions, shifts of emphasis. There are developments and
discontinuities in each corpus, Kristeva's somewhat more obvious than
Derrida's, and this means that it is often necessary to mark which
particular Derrida or Kristeva is being referred to. Although the book is
not set up historically, as a reading of their development, time is
inscribed in each chapter, and each chapter mobilizes a Kristeva and a
Derrida attached to specific texts.

The second reason for not arriving at a once-and-for-all model for
the relation between Kristeva and Derrida is that discursive conditions
(genre, discipline, speaking position)—not to mention methodology
and conceptions of difference—affect the articulation of the two. In
particular, as the book demonstrates, a Derridean reading of the relation
between the two is unlikely to coincide with a Kristevan interpretation.
I gave caricatural examples above of readings of the relation whereby
the theories of Kristeva and Derrida are said to be indistinguishable,
incompatible, antagonistic, or unrelated. These resemble the disparate
descriptions of the elephant by the six blind men of Indostan: they are
all valid in a limited way, but none of them gives the whole picture.
Unlike the case of the elephant, however, in the articulation of the
theories there is no whole picture. Although we can remove our
blindfolds and investigate thoroughly from a number of positions, we
cannot find a place to stand outside the preoccupations of Derrida's and
Kristeva's work (self, other, language, the history of Western thought)
to give an objective, comprehensive overview of their relation. It is as if
we were part of the elephant. Every account of the two has something
at stake and involves a particular conception of limits and difference.
Every snapshot intervenes. The questions being asked, the reasons for
invoking Kristeva and Derrida determine the politics of alliance and
opposition.

This book therefore abandons all pretence at a global presentation
of the complete Kristeva and Derrida, read together without remainder.
It makes no attempt to account for all their texts or all aspects of their
work in an exhaustive exposition. Instead it is unashamedly but
strategically selective. It relinquishes the dream of total mastery in

favor of calculating the variations in distance between objects in movement.[2]

If discursive sites determine how Derrida and Kristeva can be put together, then we need to choose specific sites in order to articulate the textual practices. The texts studied are texts that I feel have a great deal to say to each other. Some of the most productive connections come from the sixties and seventies. This was a time when a number of arguments that have continued to underpin the work of Derrida and Kristeva were spelt out in the most detail. This was also the time when both contributed to the journal *Tel Quel* and wrote on a common corpus of literary and philosophical texts. But then again the work of the *Tel Quel* team was never homogeneous. An analysis of the texts from this period shows points of proximity and of rupture. It can lead us to discover where discontinuities in the discourse(s) of post-structuralism have been papered over to political ends. Texts from the eighties and nineties are also studied. These sometimes seem to bear little relation to each other at first glance. Here close attention to the texts can find where parallels have been masked by institutional divides.

The questions around which these texts are articulated concern self and other, identity and difference (in Parts I and II), and literature (in Part III). Many readers come to Derrida and Kristeva through feminism. Although feminist concerns have shaped the focus of this book, they are not its focal point. This is for two reasons. Firstly, the implications and uses of Derrida and Kristeva for feminism(s) exceed the dimensions of a few chapters. This is a subject deserving a book of its own. And this is a future project. Secondly, the analysis of the production of difference in the two theories and the reading of a relation of difference between the two theories not only has payoffs for feminism but seems to me to be a precondition for undertaking such a project. It highlights the problems of too quickly assimilating or dissociating the practices of the two in disciplines where difference counts.

The specific sites of articulation shift from chapter to chapter. If Kristeva and Derrida are to be seen as other to each other, a first step is to investigate the notion of otherness. Chapter 1 is a juxtaposition of two attempts to discover a breach in the limits of thought and of Western experience, to gain limited access to that which is irreducibly and ungraspably other.

Chapter 2 looks at the possibility of telling the difference between the ways in which Derrida and Kristeva "tell" difference: it examines their efforts to account for the production of difference and identity. Both theorists undermine the notion of a clear-cut binary opposition neatly separating same and other but also refuse the idea of resolving oppositions into a third term of synthesis. Instead they multiply the dividing line to find identity within difference and difference within identity. However, apparently similar notions—like Kristevan ambiguity and Derridean undecidability—do not coincide. This raises the question posed at the beginning of this introduction: given that Derrida and Kristeva each theorize difference, how can we conceive of, tell or describe the difference between?

Part II takes this question further and investigates a couple of options. Chapter 3 examines the textual encounters between the two theorists that occur in the form of references to one another's work. In *Positions*, Derrida states that he has "always subscribed" to Kristeva's project and that the two theories are not in conflict with each other. He studiously avoids contradicting Kristeva's notion of contradiction. Kristeva, on the other hand, in *Revolution in Poetic Language*, clearly distances herself from Derrida's deconstructive work and argues energetically against his theory of *différance*. Although institutional and political issues are involved here and the theories shift with regard to each other over time, I suggest that the reading of the relation between the two sets of writings is largely dependent on the reader's understanding of oppositional structures and that the way in which the two theories are sometimes used together already relies on a conception of difference that is often not explicit.

From the patterns that emerge from these cross-references, we can extrapolate cross-readings. Chapter 4 mimics Derridean practice to indicate the way in which Kristeva's theory can be absorbed into deconstruction. Without arguing against Kristeva, it can be demonstrated that what she terms the "semiotic" and the "symbolic" modes are complicitous, that they are a pair of terms among others, subordinated to the movement of "différance," the symbolic merely a deferred moment of the semiotic. Little more than a change of emphasis is needed to show how Kristeva too challenges the primacy of speech over writing and introduces the notions of gap, interval and mark to defer any conception of "Being as presence." The Kristevan subject is reinterpreted in terms of "effects of subjectivity"; her dialectic fits the logic of the supplement. Although such a reading hijacks Kristeva's work, it does not contradict it, merely turns it back on itself.

But Kristeva could never accept this reading: in contrast with these assimilating moves, the Kristevan strategy is one of attack and defense. Chapter 5 thus takes the form of direct speech—dialogue and debate. My Kristevan reading of Derrida's work focuses on what it sees as an abdication of the subject, a denial of heterogeneity, a precious philosophical game played within metalanguage, never coming to grips with a radical otherness that cannot be recuperated by language and intelligence. Parallel to the accusation of the denial of heterogeneity is what Kristeva interprets as the denial of Law, of the power of the social structure and of communicative language: in this way, having no anchoring, the subject cannot struggle against power and Law but is condemned to drift in a void.

If Part I reads the two writers on their own terms, then Part II reads them decidedly against the grain. In this way, it is possible to discover what is at stake in articulating the two and to identify the issues and debates that are likely to produce alliances and ruptures between them in the way they are invoked by others.

Part III zooms out from the focus on difference to hinge Derrida and Kristeva together around literary texts. Over the last thirty years, the bulk of Kristeva's writing has analyzed works of literature, and, according to Derrida himself, literature has been a constant interest in his work.[3] The literary text is a privileged object of their attention, but it is often pushed to the background in readings of their work. They are frequently read for their philosophical propositions. And yet their reading practices are the basis for such propositions, are indeed inseparable from them. For in their writings they are always reading texts, frequently literary ones. Part III asks what it means to read with these two and to read them together. Rather than distilling propositions, it follows the moves they make and examines how they go about that process we call reading.

Chapter 6 starts by asking to what extent and how Kristeva and Derrida distinguish between the literary and the non-literary. Interestingly, in both cases, the concept of literature relies on a certain relation to the law. Chapter 7 studies texts on Sollers, Mallarmé, Genet, Artaud, and Joyce to find out how Derrida and Kristeva articulate them. Here we need to understand the word "articulation" in all its senses— mechanical, phonetic, anatomical, and discursive. For both writers make connections, divide up and reassemble texts, hook them up to the body, hinge their dimensions, and look at their production through the organs of speech. What emerges from this analysis is the immense productivity of their readings and the inexhaustibility of the tiniest fragment of text—a consonant cluster—as they work with it. If I focus on detail (as they do) in part of this chapter, it is because what they are able to do with a syllable from Mallarmé, for example, can tell us a great deal about the premises of their reading practices more generally.

Tracing the connections and disconnections between Derrida's and Kristeva's work on literature also allows us to discover something about the range of practices embraced by the term "post-structuralism" and some of the concerns that pull them together. These concerns have enabled readers from all sorts of fields to ask questions about their own disciplinary practices. Part IV (Chapter 8, co-authored with Peter Cowley) is an open-ended survey of some of these questions. Here we see the diversity of ways in which the proper names "Derrida" and "Kristeva" signify when countersigned by various readers. We look at the strategic uses to which their work is put, whether separately or together, and we ask what is at stake in each of these interventions.

Throughout the book, I have struggled against pretending that I stand objectively outside the texts I study. Instead of trying to find a position independent of any debate between disciplines and theories, instead of trying to treat the texts of my corpus from a point of impartiality midway between the two writers, I have constantly sought to situate myself in and in relation to texts and debates. What may appear from time to time to be narcissistic gestures are not intended to imply that this book is some sort of private reading but rather to highlight the fact that all readings are circumstantial. Neither philosopher nor psychoanalyst, I ask questions shaped by the disciplines of literary studies, "theory," and semiotics. A white Australian woman, living in France at the outset of this project, I turned to books by Kristeva and Derrida for answers to my questions about difference—and found instead more questions.

My copies of Derrida's and Kristeva's texts share shelves in the same bookcase. English translations have now joined the French editions. Where possible I have quoted from published translations, but I have often modified these, usually to highlight an aspect of the original French, sometimes to clarify the sense or avoid a gallicism, and occasionally to correct a misinterpretation. However, where published translations were not available—and this is particularly the case for the latter half of *La Révolution du langage poétique* and for certain articles in *Sèméiotiké* and *Polylogue*—the translations are my own. At one stage, the books were arranged alphabetically by author. Gradually they adopted an order of height and colour. Now they seem to congregate in more random ways, and I encourage this, placing them back haphazardly, musing over the juxtapositions that occur and the readings they could give rise to. For the space of negotiation opened up by the articulation of Derrida's and Kristeva's texts enables questions to be raised in ways that are not available when the texts are studied singly — questions about reading, about otherness, about the dividing lines we draw.

NOTES

1. I use the word theory for convenience, and use it loosely. In no way do I wish to distinguish theory and practice, for example.

2. Here I should distinguish my project from Michael Payne's *Reading Theory: An Introduction to Lacan, Derrida, and Kristeva*. Payne's study shares some of the aims of this book in seeking "to provide a reading of major texts by Lacan, Derrida, and Kristeva and to trace the outlines of the reading theories they propose" (vii). However, in its introductory chapter, it sets up a framework for reading the relations between the writings of these theorists in terms of influence and appropriation, referring to "an intricate network of influences that links these writers" (1) and "Kristeva's critically selective but generous appropriation of [Derrida's and Lacan's] work" (2). Predictably, Kristeva's work is situated with respect to Derrida's but not vice versa. In fact, Payne's book is much more concerned with presenting a profile of each theory than with investigating the complexities of possible relations between them. Payne analyzes three texts by each writer: an introductory essay, a major volume, and an essay on a painting. In each case, the texts are read separately. In my work, on the other hand, I do not hold the texts at arm's (or chapter's) length from one another. They intervene and meddle with each other to produce debates and connections that are not available when they are read apart.

The texts of Payne's corpus include Derrida's "Structure, Sign and Play in the Discourse of the Human Sciences" and Kristeva's *Revolution in Poetic Language*, which I also study closely in Chapter 2. Payne examines their rhetorical strategies as I do. The particularity of my reading of these texts is the focus on a certain practice of division in each case. The hinging together of two sorts of dividing lines that do not coincide and are themselves divided enables me to pursue a question that is distinct from Payne's concerns: how to negotiate between two theories of difference.

3 Cf. Derrida, "The Time of a Thesis" 37, and "This Strange Institution Called Literature."

PART I

Otherwise

CHAPTER 1

Grasp-hoppers

It may seem a little rash, a little like wanting to do the impossible, to propose to investigate the unnameable/the unthinkable in the first chapter. But then, there is always a risk involved in writing on the subject of Jacques Derrida or Julia Kristeva. Any attempt to grasp their ideas and pin them down gives rise to images of an entomologist from another era, haplessly waving his butterfly net, pouncing on air only to see his prey hop away or flit on by. Or finally pinning a specimen in the display case, only to be confronted by its lifelessness, and wondering whether what gave him the buzz in the first place wasn't in fact the buzzing. To study the thought of Derrida or Kristeva in its movement and liveliness, to capture it without trying to hold it captive, is an inherently risky enterprise.

In a sense, this risk is not unlike that which Derrida and Kristeva themselves take in working away at the limits of language, of philosophy, of meaning, at the ungraspable other of thought. They are aware that any clear statement of what it is that lies beyond language has always-already brought the unnameable back from beyond and placed it squarely within the bounds of language. If they regularly describe their objects of study as unthinkable or unnameable, they are also the first to recognize the perils and paradoxes of their project. They make no claims to seize and squeeze the incomprehensible but find provisional ways of stalking what hops beyond their grasp, of indicating the questions that have continued to bug them. Similarly, my aim in this chapter is not to name the unnameable or define its essence but rather to trace carefully the ways in which Kristeva and Derrida indicate limits, the steps they take in trying to find access to the horizons of thought and rationality. For there are striking parallels between their attempts to do this that are sometimes masked by the disciplinary divide between philosophy and psychoanalysis. On the other hand, their efforts to think the unthinkable have never coincided. The divergences between them, however, go beyond questions of discipline and involve conceptions of the limit between same and other. And it is the question of the other and of a relation to the other that is at stake here.

Otherness—whether the other of language and philosophy, the irreducible otherness of others, or the foreignness of what we call ourselves—has never ceased to be a major preoccupation, if not *the* major preoccupation of their work.[1] Leon Roudiez sees Kristeva's work over twenty-five years as insisting on the notion of otherness, strangeness.[2] Kelly Oliver states that "Alterity, otherness, and the stranger are always at the center of her texts."[3] Toril Moi writes: "To think the unthinkable: from the outset this has been Julia Kristeva's project."[4] Derrida himself has described his work as addressing this question. In "Tympan," the preface to *Margins of Philosophy* (articles originally published 1968-1972), Derrida notes that the constant question of the book is that of the limit, in particular the limit between philosophy and its other (x-xi). Similarly, the article "Psyche: Inventions of the other" is said to have been chosen to give its title to a later collection of articles (1978-1987) for the way it reflects the concerns of the texts written both before and after it.[5] It explores the notion of invention and the extent to which the other might escape being our invention, might escape being a projection of the same and of what is already possible. Referring to the general thrust of his project, Derrida states that "The interest of deconstruction, of such force and desire as it may have, is a certain experience of the impossible: that is, [. . .] of the other."[6]

This focus on the other has enormous potential pay-offs, and philosophy and psychoanalysis are not the only disciplines interested. Crucial among issues of race and ethnicity are questions of speaking to/of/for the ultimately unknowable other. High on the gender agenda is exposing what a supposedly universal discourse whittles away from otherness in order to squeeze it into pre-existing categories. Studies of indigenous cultures, of foreign languages and cultures, of race relations, women's studies and post-colonial studies, anthropology, translation theory: all have a stake in finding ways of thinking about the other without reducing it to what we already know and of recognizing an unlived and unnameable experience without sweeping it aside as *simply unthinkable.*

In turning to the texts by Kristeva and Derrida, we need not hope to find a ready-to-think, one-size-fits-all, packaged version of the unthinkable, part of a *prêt-à-penser* collection. But what we might look for is an indication of a path to follow. Clearly the butterfly net and display case are inappropriate metaphors for pursuing the other: the pinning down is punitive. If the hand that grasps only ever captures what was within reach, what it already had a grip on, then perhaps what is needed is a more appropriate gesture.

THRESHOLDS

"Save that if we have said what it is, it is not what we have said." [7]

At the threshold of this study, then, lies a juxtaposition of two early articles that at first glance appear to have little in common, for they share neither decade nor discipline. Derrida's "Violence and Metaphysics: An Essay on the Thought of Emmanuel Levinas" is unambiguously philosophical, whereas Kristeva's references, in "Place Names," come from the fields of psychoanalysis and, to a lesser extent, linguistics. [8] What they do share is a striving for a relation to an other they neither know nor understand, and for a way of expressing an otherness that they cannot identify by name. The texts intersect on the brink of this unnameable. There is no word to do it justice. There is no name that does not do it the injustice of appropriation from the foreign to the familiar, no explanation that doesn't explain away. But there is still something to say. Faced with what cannot be said, Kristeva and Derrida are not struck dumb. In fact they insist that it is imperative to speak.

For Derrida, the limits of thought may be glimpsed when we ask about the possibility of philosophy itself, when we pose the Question of the Question: how can we ask a question that doesn't already assume the limits of its answer? Thought "imprints its form on all ruptures and on the most radical questions" (WD 142) such that we are unable to talk about what escapes philosophy without using the language of philosophy to do so. But this is no cause for resignation: if Derrida stresses that this chicken-and-egg style closure is inevitable, he is not ready to abandon the egg. Or the chicken for that matter. The circularity of philosophical questioning is worth pushing to the very limit. In

"Violence and Metaphysics," Derrida traces Levinas' attempts in this direction, concentrating on the limit that the experience of the other represents, the "face of the other" (Autrui) being a privileged moment of absolute otherness for Levinas.[9] Alterity, like the question of the question, is inaccessible. We are unable to conceive of otherness without giving it our own form (sameness): "*Why* is an experience which would not be lived as *my own* [. . .] impossible and unthinkable? This unthinkable and impossible are the limits of reason in general" (WD 131). There may be no true relation to the other, but paradoxically, Levinas' ethics tend toward this "unthinkable." He seeks to gain access where there is none, to speak of the ineffable. His attempt is naturally hampered by the necessity of thinking and describing the opening towards otherness in the language of reason: "One already foresees the unease to which a thought rejecting the excellence of theoretical rationality will have to resign itself later" (WD 87). However Derrida is not about to condemn this contradiction. He recognizes that there is no other way for philosophy to question itself and even reproduces the paradox in his own strategy. But it is one thing for Levinas and Derrida to explore the inescapable circularity of their projects, and quite another to pass over the paradoxes with a shrug: "we will be incoherent, but without systematically resigning ourselves to incoherence" (WD 84). The role of language here is not to be underestimated: the problems hindering attempts to break down the closure of our thinking are all "questions of language" (WD 109). The "impossible-unthinkable-unstatable" (WD 132) is an indissociable triad. And for what does not translate into words and signs ("this impossibility of translating my relation to the Other into the rational coherence of language" WD 128) there seems to be nothing but silence. The experience of the other is caught between silence and language.

A difficult dilemma. On the one hand, language, the violence of the recuperating discourse explaining otherness in terms of sameness, "the necessity that the other [. . .] not be respected except in, for, and by the same" (WD 133). On the other hand, silence, a nonrelation that is supposed to avoid recuperation, but that ultimately suppresses the other. And according to Derrida, this second choice is the more insidious: "the worst violence, the violence of the night which precedes or represses discourse" (WD 117). The distinction between violence and nonviolence blurs: "pure nonviolence, the nonrelation of the same to the other [. . .] is pure violence" (WD 146-47), and inversely "the irreducible violence of the relation to the other, is at the same time nonviolence, since it opens the relation to the other" (WD 128-29).[10] The division is unclear; the contraries coexist both in language and in silence. Since they are inseparable, we cannot stay silent claiming that in this way we avoid violating the other: "The philosopher (man) must speak and write within this war of light [. . .] a war which he knows is inescapable, except by denying discourse, that is, by risking the worst violence" (WD 117). Remaining silent, within the closure of philosophy and of our own likeness, hoping in this way to avoid the failure of an attempt to disturb these limits, carries equally grave risks.

If the claim to comprehend the other (from entomology to etymology— *com-prehendere*) is akin to seizing the other for oneself and squeezing its otherness out, then ignoring the other is no less crushing. We still need to put out a hand, but not a grasping hand, to make a gesture towards the unnameable, but not a gesture of dismissal. Violence cannot be totally eliminated but can be minimized. To save the threshold from becoming a thrash-hold, the appropriate gesture still needs to be found.

Kristeva articulates similar concerns in a different domain. We find the French text of "Place Names" at the end of a section of *Polylogue* called "Frontiers of Repression," where Kristeva looks towards an outer space of reason: to think where no (wo)man has thought before. Like Levinas/Derrida, Kristeva seeks the limits of the thinkable in the experience of the other, but the other here has a more restricted sense: Kristeva looks for otherness in . . . *babies*. She describes infancy as a sort of borderline case of rationality, a stage in the formation of the future reasoning (reasonable?) subject but not an age of reason. Whereas our (adult) thought processes are largely determined by language, babies are *unthinkable* in the sense that we have no way of understanding what goes on for them without reducing it to what we know: the infant, not yet having acquired linguistic structures, seems to be involved in a sort of unthinking thinking. Historically, Kristeva sees the occasional focus on the child by Western thinkers as an attempt to escape the closure of reason: "the real stakes of a discourse on childhood within Western thought involve a confrontation between thought and what it is not, a wandering at the limits of the thinkable" (DL 276). She locates the child who cannot yet speak at the junction of thought and the unthinkable, at the ambiguous point separating the same and the other. The child is the "nexus of life and language (of species and society)," "the boundary between 'nature' and 'culture'" (DL 271).[11]

We who think, how can we unthink? We who think in language, how can we think beyond language? How can we put our discourse, our reason into question? Kristeva's suggestion: at the very threshold of language and of otherness, baby babble might just do the trick. The problem is that in the history of Western discourse, the heterogeneity of the child has never escaped immediate recuperation: baby babble becomes baby talk; the unnameable is named; otherness is reduced to what we can think and say. Children are *conceived* by adults in adult terms: *concipere, com-capere*, gotcha! And whatever resisted naming or grasping is left behind.

Kristeva analyzes examples of the erasure of the child's otherness by the discourses of Christianity, psycholinguistics, and psychoanalysis. It generally happens in one of two ways: *either* the humanity, language, or libido of the adult is taken as the model for the child (by celebrating Man in the child Jesus, by demonstrating the importance of generative grammar in baby talk, by projecting adult desires onto the child), *or* the heterogeneity of the child is referred to— as another sort of logic/language/libido—but then minimized, or even excluded from the analysis. Otherness is recuperated or forgotten. Kristeva brings the question back to language. In each case, what precedes language is passed over: "The presyntactic phases of childhood semiosis remain outside of this investigation; but also excluded are all semantic latencies" (DL 278). The subject tends to be dated from the "mirror stage" and language acquisition: the unutterable aspects of infancy escape analysis. "Thus, the difficulty, the impossibility that beset such an attempt at gaining access to childhood" (DL 276). Again the problem is double and inevitable: there is the reduction to sameness, or silence and exclusion. Is there then no way of skirting this impasse? Of neither waving otherness aside, nor crushing it as a fistful of meaning (as in the German words for grasping the concept—*Griff/Begriff, fassen/auffassen*). Kristeva and Derrida look to Freud and Levinas respectively for a possible answer, and interestingly use what they find in a remarkably parallel way.

RESONANCE—ECHOES OF OTHERNESS

Sceptical of attempts to escape closure, simply to break out of the chicken-and-egg circularity, Derrida examines possible courses of action from within. Ultimately however he advocates not so much action as a balance between activity and passivity, or more precisely *receptivity.* Striving to know the other as such amounts to seeing self-other relations in terms of a philosophical mastery of the other and positions us firmly within philosophy. But following Levinas' lead, Derrida suggests that rather than straining to get out and get to the other, we need to make ourselves accessible, to open our thought to as yet unformulated questions. Not the upper hand, but the open hand: "Philosophy (in general) can only open itself to the question, within it and by it. It can only *let itself be questioned*" (WD 131).[12] Instead of wanting to explain (away) the other, we could perhaps start by allowing our own vulnerability to emerge and aim for reciprocity. Rather than making statements about the other, we could address the other ("the other of which one does not speak, but to whom one speaks" WD 123), sure of neither audience nor answer, but ever hopeful of initiating a dialogue. These indications guide Derrida in the way in which he approaches the other-who-is-Levinas: "reciprocal interrogation" (WD 84) is both the subject and mode of his commentary: "we will attempt to ask several questions [. . .] the questions put to us by Levinas" (WD 84).[13]

For Derrida, Levinas' thought comes close to momentarily dislocating philosophy from its circular questioning. It "can make us tremble" (WD 82), not because it claims to say, describe, or show the other but rather by "designating a space or hollow within naked experience," where what is beyond traditional concepts of philosophy "must resonate" (WD 83). Resonance: getting a buzz from the buzzing. Sound produced here by sound waves coming from . . . where? This is otherness without the *presence* of the other, without direct access. The other is not there to be held but leaves traces in the form of echoes. The other sets off reverberations that strike a chord within us as sympathetic vibrations transmitted from one space or body to another. Resonance is produced within sameness as sympathetic vibrations, but reproduces otherness, doubling it. In doing so, it disturbs what seemed like a simple opposition: same/other, known/unknowable, inside/outside, us/them. Suddenly we can see that the other is also within. The dividing line is no longer a horizon to break through or an uninterrupted boundary. The limit is repeated within its own bounds: outside and inside are inside-out; same and other are not exterior to one another.[14] Not wishing to reduce otherness, we can try to make out the (equally inaccessible) alterity that echoes within the self: "How could there be a 'play of the Same' if alterity itself was not already in the Same" (WD 126-27). Resonance is far from a simple solution: as we lend our ear to it, the other becomes ours, reflects us. But it also calls us into question. And there is a chance that in doing so, otherness may be heard fleetingly, before it is lost as we assimilate it into thought-as-language.

Reading Levinas, Derrida listens for the other of philosophy, for the play of the other in the same. If "the entirety of philosophy is conceived on the basis of its Greek source" (WD 81), he asks, "will the other of the Greek be the non-Greek? Above all, can it be named the non-Greek?" (WD 82). What he finds is that the limit dividing philosophy from its other is mirrored within philosophy, that otherness resonates. For Levinas, Judaism represents an otherness that calls the Greek tradition into question.[15] Derrida problematizes the labelling of the Jew as the other of the Greek: naming and situating the other in the language of philosophy cannot avoid violating its otherness. Derrida never ceases to seek a "non-site [. . .] from which to question philosophy,"[16] but in the absence of a utopian solution (*ou-topos*), he looks at how the relation same/other translates as Greek/Jew. Although the Jewish philosophical tradition cannot remain thoroughly other when translated into the language of the Greeks, yet, in the confrontation that it provokes, something indefinable, unnameable is able to *solicit* philosophy (WD 152; and Derrida makes the etymology resonate — *sollicitare* — to shake). Ultimately this is a confrontation between philosophy and itself, between the Greek tradition and the Greek thinking of the Jewish, indeed more a repetition than a confrontation, and yet the repetition is not quite identical. Certainly, there is a appropriation of the other into the same, but alterity slips into the gap created by repetition, the gap between two moments of the same. There is recuperation, but it may not be total: "Such a site of encounter can only offer *occasional* hospitality to a thought which would remain foreign to it" (WD 152). This site is less radical than a utopian "non-site," and yet it causes otherness to reverberate, "makes us tremble" (WD 82), and calls our identity, Derrida's identity, into question, revealing the horizon of the unnameable dividing us. For if we try to approach the demarcation line between Jewish and Greek, if we try to examine it or situate it in any precise way, it doubles up and disappears in the "reciprocal surpassing of two origins and two historical speeches" (WD 84) that are not simply exterior to each other. It serves to distance "us" (Derrida? Levinas? we in Western philosophy?) from what "we" believed to be "our" identity. The purely Jewish and the purely Greek in philosophy seem as difficult to isolate as outside and inside, as pure non-violence and pure violence. Echoing James Joyce,

Derrida inquires: "Are we Jews? Are we Greeks? We live in the difference between the Jew and the Greek [. . .]. Are we Greeks? Are we Jews? But who, we?" (WD 153). The same and the self appear as uncertain, as foreign, as the other.

Same/other now appears an impractical division: the limit supposed to separate openness from closure, Jew from Greek, the other from the same, divides and multiplies but remains impossible to locate. We suspected that alterity was unapproachable; now it seems that sameness is equally elusive. We are not who we thought we were. Resonance, in opening the way to the unthinkable other, estranges us from ourselves.[17]

Still trembling, we might ask: what gesture then can we make to the other, given that we don't even have a secure grip on ourselves? What is needed is a gesture oriented outwards but that rebounds and shakes us. We could start by cocking an ear. . . . In "Tympan," Derrida examines the limit self/other represented by the membrane of the ear drum. If philosophy has always claimed to have lent its ear to the other, this listening has been mediated by that ear and decoded internally, such that philosophy has listened to *its* other (a very *possessive* "its"). On the other hand, piercing the ear drum for direct access to the other is hardly a way to improve the quality of the listening. And yet the ear is not merely a barrier: the middle ear is able to equalize internal and external pressures creating continuity between outside and inside; the membrane of the ear drum is oblique to avoid head-on confrontation between two sides, to offer a greater surface area for drumming. The tympanum functions as both limit and passage. For Derrida, the question is how to allow the drum to escape from the hands of the philosopher. The gesture required is to offer this surface to the other's hands, to cock one's ear and offer the drum. To make oneself available and vulnerable, and allow oneself to be questioned or called into question. On that drum, the other's hands will make an impression we will not recognize, an unnameable impression that may resonate within us . . . or may fall on deaf ears.[18]

But what of ears and echoes for Kristeva? How does the unthinkable make itself heard in "Place Names"?

In Kristeva's text, too, we find boundaries multiplied to create ambiguity and reciprocity, such that the other, and what lies beyond meaning, is sought in the same. Kristeva starts by outlining Freud's discoveries concerning the child. Like his counterparts in other fields, Freud attempted to find direct access to the other, to explain the alterity of the child. However—and this is what interests Kristeva—unlike the recuperations already mentioned in psychoanalysis and linguistics, Freud's attempt worked in two directions: he sought not only the adult in the child (the habitual "error," the projection of a "paternal vision of childhood" DL 274) but also the child in the adult. He looked for the vestiges of infancy that persist into adulthood. In other words, Freud problematized the frontier adult/child, same/other, through two "telescopings" working in opposite directions (DL 275). It is the second of these, the childishness that remains in the adult, that launches Kristeva's study: she considers the threshold of the unnameable as it is perpetuated well after the acquisition of language.

If Kristeva initially establishes an opposition between same and other, between the known and the unknowable, between rationality and the unthinkable, such that the child is in an ambiguous position but "our" place within Western reason appears incontestable, she soon exposes the uncertainty of the adult's position. For it is not only the child who harbours unfathomable otherness: there is a similar impenetrability where the drives of the speaking subject are concerned, and precisely because s/he is defined as speaking. There is what remains, and will forever remain, unspoken, unutterable, irreducible — the remains of infancy. Thus the adult's position with regard to the opposition thought/unthinkable is no less ambiguous than that of the infant: there are parts of ourselves that we cannot comprehend. Kristeva directs her attention to this heterogeneous element inhabiting the adult, advocating the questioning "not of he who does not speak (in-fans) but of what within the speaker is not yet spoken, or will always remain unsaid, unnameable within the gaps of speech" (DL 272). Basing her work on her reading of Freud, Kristeva elaborates a distinction between "childhood language" and "infantile language." Childhood language is the language 'spoken' by the infant, and insofar as it is considered as language, is necessarily a projection of maturity: the adult interprets in terms of her own linguistic norms and minimizes any heterogeneous component. In contrast, and by analogy with Freud's work on infantile sexuality, infantile language is what remains from infancy in the language of the (adult) speaking subject: not just coochi-coo style fragments of adult "baby talk" but the rhythm and musicality of language, the physical pleasure of producing vowels and consonants, rhyme, repetition, onomatopoeia. It is by listening to infantile language that Kristeva tries to gain access to the conditions of production of meaning, the passage from the unnameable to the nameable. Accessing infantility is far from being a simple penetration of the world of infancy; infantility is more likely to be mobilized in the mother in response to the child's "question" (DL 281). A dialogue is initiated in which infantile language can be heard as a sort of *echo*. Kristeva speaks of

> the attentiveness that the adult, through her still infantile sexuality, is
> able to perceive in the discourse of a child (boy or girl) while it refers
> her to that level where her 'own' language is never totally
> rationalized or normalized according to Cartesian linguistics, but
> where it always remains an 'infantile language.' (DL 278)[19]

The attentiveness (*écoute* or listening in the original) is not simply that of the adult (and Kristeva refers in particular to the mother) but that which the mother identifies in her baby's babbling. This double tuning in between adult and child is then reflected back, resonating at a point of otherness within the adult, at "that level where her 'own' language is never totally rationalized." The alterity of the infant remains unapproachable but can provoke an echo in the mother, causing a vibration in that tenuous thread that links the subject to the unknowable regions of her being—regression: "this precocious presymbolic organization is grasped by the adult only as regression—*jouissance* or schizophrenic psychosis" (DL 276). Thus the dialogue between mother and child takes place not only in language but also in the body:

> Faced with these anaclises, the adult—essentially the mother—offers
> a disturbed reception, a mobile receptacle, which fashions itself on
> the invocation, follows its winding course and eventually accents it
> with a surge of anguish that the new born analyzer's body produces in
> the analysand. (DL 282)[20]

The mother listens to and responds to the baby's cries, but these distress calls summon forth more than words. They call for physical and emotional reflexes on the mother's part: she answers with what escapes language and rationality in herself, with a surge of anguish, with the other in the self.

Yet even the words of her seemingly rational language are not emptied of their otherness but retain an element of infantility. The unnameable escapes language but—paradoxically—without ceasing to be a part of it. Kristeva traces this other side of language back to a moment in the child's development between non-language and language, between the prelinguistic child and the speaking subject. Before the amorphous world around the baby becomes properly organized into distinguishable parts, before space becomes organized into places, early points of stability provoke laughter in the child (DL 283). The mother's face becomes a privileged focus for this laughter and a prototype of the object for the future subject. Gradually the child's vocalizations develop towards naming as space is structured. Kristeva's hypothesis is that naming (and even the use of nouns) is always linked to this space-becoming-place. As such it carries the memory of the relation with the mother and the memory of the struggle to constitute self and other. And that struggle is never quite over (DL 289-291). These memories can be activated as regression: the reciprocal relation with the child has the capacity to send the mother back to prelinguistic infantility, to the otherness that has never ceased to haunt her and her language, since the beginnings of her own relation with the (m)other. It can send her back to what she has necessarily had to exclude or repress in order to maintain her position as a speaking and social subject. The limit between thought and the unthinkable may divide adult from child but it also splits the adult, who at first seemed to be situated unambiguously on the side of reason.[21]

For Kristeva then, thinking the unthinkably other is not so much a question of reaching out as reaching in and back and down, to the depths of the self and the past. We are no longer grasping at the other to find otherness but putting the self into question. And where Derrida offers the surface of the ear drum, Kristeva offers an *écoute*, a receptiveness, that lets otherness echo through the body.

Two invitations to listen, but neither of them easy to accept or to carry out. The other may ring through but we cannot ring for the other. The tenuous thread of regression, the umbilical link, is not a cord to pull for service. It is an exhausting risking of the self that cannot simply be repeated at will: as soon as it becomes mechanical, it ceases to be effective. Neither could Derridean listening become a foolproof mechanical gesture. It needs constant vigilance and it needs to be continually renewed, or we slip back to claiming to know the unknowable: the other? been there, done that. And Derrida would be the first to warn us that listening is not inherently peaceable. When the corridors of power become an auditory labyrinth, bugs abound. Set a bug to catch a bug—and what is bugging but a form of grasping?

And then there is the seduction by the sirens. . . . Lest we imagine that listening could be some sort of absolute and universally valid gesture, other texts by Derrida and Kristeva point to its pitfalls. In his work on Nietzsche in "Otobiographies," Derrida indicates the danger of opening the ear too wide, allowing it to become the other's. If we become all ears in an indiscriminatory way, we lose the possibility of fine tuning, of finesse and discernment. The cautionary image is not that of the faithful HMV dog, but rather the oversized ear trumpet of the gramophone beside him, not of course listening at all, despite appearances, merely an instrument of hi-fidelity reproduction.[22] Kristeva also evokes the danger of over-attentiveness. *Black Sun* explores the descent into melancholy and depression that occurs if we allow ourselves to be engulfed by the unnameable. If the nostalgic search—through regression—to recover the lost archaic maternal "thing" takes over, there is the danger of a complete loss of self and a loss of language with which to master the world, to get a grip on things. This is the silence, not of exclusion but of asymbolic existence.[23]

Two invitations to listen, then . . . to listen *carefully* . . . but are they the same?

BEYOND REASON

Parallels can be drawn between Derrida and Kristeva's work on otherness. Neither of them claim that it is directly accessible, and indeed both avoid trying to master it as such. Instead they propose—as a kind of otherness—a new relation to the same. New on the condition that it is constantly renewed. In each case the limit same/other is doubled, giving rise to resonance, reciprocity, and alterity within identity. However the echoes do not have an identical timbre: the very notion of what might constitute the other of rationality distinguishes the premisses of the two texts. While Derrida seeks what lies beyond reason at the limit between philosophy *and itself*, for Kristeva, the other of rationality is radically heterogenous to it. In "Place Names," the unthinkable is designated in terms of regression, infantility, the body. By contrast, in "Violence and Metaphysics," what is beyond reason cannot be glimpsed by looking for it *elsewhere*: the limit between reason and its other is not locatable except as "the difference between the question in general and 'philosophy' as a determined—finite and mortal—moment or mode of the question itself" (WD 81). In other words, the limit is between philosophy and itself: the other hovers elusively in the impossible space between reason and its shadow, between two moments of identity. As Derrida explains in "Ellipse" (WD 294-300):

> The beyond of the closure of the book is neither to be awaited nor to be refound. It is *there*, but out there, *beyond*, within repetition, but eluding us there. It is there like the shadow of the book, [. . .] the distance between the book and the book [. . .]. (WD 300)

The other, impossible as such, may be sought in the doubling of the same, in the echo of resonance, the fleeting space of difference created by the time of repetition, time becoming space, space eclipsed by time.

According to "Violence and Metaphysics," in order to conceive the difference between philosophy and itself, "the tradition's origin will have to be summoned forth and adhered to as rigorously as possible" (WD 81). In other words, it is by remaining as close as possible—"*au plus proche*"—to reason and the history of reason that, paradoxically, we may best escape it. Derrida continues: "Which is not to stammer and huddle lazily in the depths of childhood" (WD 81). Next to Kristeva's work, the sentence shocks: we may teeter on the brink of the unnameable but we do not stutter; childishness is laziness. In Derrida's view, a childish stammer could never put the language of philosophy into question; infancy could never confront reason with its other, for this would be regression, and regression is the return to the irrational. For Derrida, what exceeds rationality is far from being irrational: as he explains elsewhere, it is useless to "counter" reason "with some obscurantist irrationalism," for "irrationalism [. . .] is a posture that is completely symmetrical to, thus dependent upon, the principle of reason."[24] Derrida explicitly excludes the irrational: referring to the inability to translate the relation to the other into "the rational coherence of language," he states that "this contradiction and this impossibility are not the signs of 'irrationality'"; they are "*rien moins qu''irrationnel*'"—"anything but 'irrational'" (WD 128, tr. mod.).[25] Rational and irrational are opposites and, as such, complicitous: the irrational is not *other* than reason but simply the negation of reason. What disconcerts reason cannot, therefore, be its opposite but perhaps its shadow, its double.

In Kristeva's view however, we can hardly seek to escape rationality by clinging closely to it. Rather, the dissolution of the subject—through regression—into irrationality is what rational thinking cannot comprehend, can neither know nor contain, a dark shadow not governed by the intellect. It is no longer a question of perceiving through one's intelligence but of assimilating through listening and responding physically and emotionally. The common sense of rationality is overtaken by the senses; reason gives way to resonance. But for Derrida, the glide of the tongue—if there is one—from *raisonner* (to reason) to *résonner* (to resonate) is minimal.[26]

Lurking behind reason, in each case, is a shadow, but the doubles in Kristeva's and Derrida's work do not coincide. In caricature, the range of doubles extends from out-of-step identical twins (philosophy and itself) to Jekyll and Hyde (the rational and the irrational). And whereas the shadow of rationality eludes us in Derrida's text, it surges into Kristeva's in the form of regression and collides with reason. For Derrida, a hiatus is created and conjured away through the articulation of space and time: the delicate membrane of the tympanum is both limit and passage (MP xi). For Kristeva the limit does not appear and disappear. It is a resistant boundary of repression and not overcome without a struggle: we are not before the breach but before the barricades, where conflict is rife. In Kristeva's work, tuning in to the other involves listening across a relatively stable boundary that must remain more or less in place if we are not to lose the possibility of identity.

Cocking one's ear is turning it in a particular direction, "qu'il résonne ou se taise," "whether it resonates or remains still" (MP xxv, tr. mod.). Derrida and Kristeva indicate where the other resonates for them . . . and where it doesn't. However, the differences in resonance go beyond questions of the role of the unconscious or the importance credited to psychoanalysis. An otherness that is not simply exterior implies a problematizing of identity: we are not simply present and accessible to ourselves. Abandoning any notion of a unified self, identical to itself over time, both theories undermine essentialist claims. However, the divisions disturbing identity are represented in terms of contradiction, on the one hand, and discrepancy or mismatch, on the other. Thus beyond the immediate consequences of these theories for work on the other (on difference) are the ramifications for work on the self (on identity) and the necessary crossover between these two categories. Ultimately the force of Derridean deconstruction and of Kristevan analysis lies in their accounts of the production of difference, the creation of an identity or an effect of identity that is not a fixed essence. These are the mechanisms for renewal, and therefore the instruments of possible change. These underpin, to a large extent, the political interest of the work of the two theorists. And these are the subject of the next chapter.

But before going further in this direction, let us pause and listen. If the conditions are right and a sound is strong, it can echo and re-echo. I would like to take a brief look at a couple of specific instances where this work on unthinkable otherness resonates through other texts by Derrida and Kristeva.

One area where it echoes clearly is around questions of race and national identity. Kristeva's *Strangers to Ourselves* explores the condition of and our relation to the foreigner. In it she suggests that we need to recognize the foreignness in ourselves, across an internal boundary, in order to be able to accept the foreigner, neither rejecting nor absorbing (and thus erasing) otherness. Derrida's "Interpretations at War: Kant, the Jew, the German" analyzes texts discussing Germanity and Judaism, which turn out to be far from external to one another. Rather Derrida finds in the texts the Jewishness of the German, the Germanness of the Jew, the one inhabiting the other. However it is not only the foreigner who is within rather than outside . . . but also the racist. In 1986, Derrida became involved in a debate about apartheid in *Critical Inquiry*, when his text "The Last Word in Racism" was attacked by Anne McClintock and Rob Nixon. In his reply, "But, beyond . . . ," Derrida suggests that apartheid is not simply a policy of another regime, outside, over there in South Africa. Rather, the desire to separate us and them, to cordon off the other into a distinct "homeland," gnaws away inside the university (inside us), and shows itself (for example) whenever academics try to protect their disciplinary territory from encroachers.

Another set of questions where the other reverberates through the same concerns sexual difference. Both Kristeva and Derrida rewrite the masculine/feminine opposition in such a way that the feminine is not The Other but an otherness within. Throughout her writings from the early seventies onwards, Kristeva uses *le féminin* to describe the ungraspable as it inhabits *all* speaking subjects, that is to say, the irrepresentable aspects of psychical life. The feminine refers to the vestiges of the maternal body, remnants of the unnameable from the time before self and other, before language, before anything could be named. As the child struggles to separate from the immediacy of mother-child fusion, the mother is abjected: the child tries unsuccessfully to expel the mother from its borders in order to establish a distinct "self" and "other."[27] As we shall see in the next chapter, finally, through identification with a third party, the mother is recuperated as an object (an other) in the symbolic order. However the maternal body cannot be incorporated entirely into signs. The unsymbolizable remainder—the feminine—remains within the subject, accessible through psychosis, analysis, esthetic experience, religion or, as we have seen, motherhood. Thus Kristeva refers to sexual difference *within* the work of Joyce, to the feminine as it pervades the work of Artaud, to the maternal as it is available to all subjects. And when Kristeva writes of women (and of men for that matter), these are not seen in terms of an immutable biological given. Rather "woman" and "man" as sexual identities are constructed through a set of imaginary formations and identifications arising from the various possible relations between on the one hand the language system, social constraints, the family, and on the other hand the sites of sexual pleasure and *jouissance*, the sensuality of mother-child fusion.[28] Rather than simply other to each other, "woman" and "man" are thus other to themselves, each shaped and reshaped by the masculine and the feminine, the paternal and the maternal, the "symbolic" and the "semiotic." If I can see myself in this way, then

> the other is neither an evil being foreign to me nor a scapegoat from the outside, that is, of another, sex, class, race, or nation. I am *at once the attacker and the victim*, the same *and* the other, identical *and* foreign. I simply have to analyze incessantly the fundamental separation of my own untenable identity. (NMS 223, cf. KR 210)

In Derrida's texts, too, the feminine resonates within the masculine. Derrida refers to *Spurs*, "Le Facteur de la vérité" (PC 411-496), "Pas," "Geschlecht," "Choreographies," "Restitutions" (TP 255-382), "Right of Inspection," *Cinders*, "At This Very Moment in This Work Here I Am," and *Memoirs of the Blind* as texts where feminine voices have traversed him.[29] Indeed the last five mentioned are written as the interplay between multiple voices. In these texts, Derrida listens to the call of the other as it speaks within his voice, and it speaks in a woman's voice:

> Each time that a multiplicity of voices has imposed itself on me [. . .] there were always women's voices or a woman's voice. For me, the first way to turn speech over, in a situation that is first of all mine,

consists of recognizing by giving passage to a woman's voice or to women's voices that are *already there* in a certain way at the origin of speech or of my speech. [. . .] I never write about them. In a certain way, I try to let them take over—and keep—speech through me, without me, beyond the control that I could have over them. (*Points . . .* 394).

And in an oft-quoted passage from "Choreographies," Derrida refers to these other voices within, dividing and multiplying us, as part of the dream of a sexuality that exceeds binary oppositions like same/other, masculine/feminine, straight/gay:

The relation [to the other] would not be a-sexual, far from it, but would be sexual otherwise: beyond the binary difference that governs the decorum of all codes, beyond the opposition feminine/masculine, beyond bisexuality as well, beyond homosexuality and heterosexuality which come to the same thing. As I dream of saving the chance that this question offers I would like to believe in the multiplicity of sexually marked voices. I would like to believe in the masses, this indeterminable number of blended voices, this mobile of non-identified sexual marks whose choreography can carry, divide, multiply the body of each "individual," whether he be classified as "man" or as "woman" according to the criteria of usage.[30]

For Derrida, as for Kristeva, sexual difference is not a given. Although there can be "no speech or word or saying" that does not establish or translate "something like sexual difference" ("Fourmis" 73), such a difference is not there to see but to interpret (75). It "does not exist as such, present and real, beyond any reading" (86). It must be constantly reinvented (95) but not from outside, for we are always-already marked by it. Sexual difference determines our reading of sexual difference. Not just the other but the relation to the other is always-already within, dividing us from ourselves.

In separate articles, Elizabeth Grosz reads Kristeva and Derrida to further explore another (perhaps *the*) chicken-and-egg question: which comes first, difference or sexual difference?[31] Or in its more sophisticated form: "does the subject's sexuality become subordinated to the neutrality and sexual indifference of the 'I'?"[32] Now, this is a question Derrida asks of Levinas and also raises in relation to Heidegger.[33] It is a question that needs to be asked and pushed as far as possible but one that can never receive a categorical answer. With regard to both Kristeva's and Derrida's work, the jury is still out. For Kristeva, sexual identity is constructed from difference, but this difference is already marked in gendered terms. In Derrida's view, we should ask how sexual difference becomes opposition, and we should try to think difference before the division in two and to conceive of a multiplicity of sexual markings, but we can do none of these things from outside sexual difference, just as we cannot question philosophy from an outside.

These echoes of the unthinkable other are already venturing onto the terrain of the next chapter which looks at theories of difference and how dividing lines are drawn. Sexual difference, racial or cultural difference, linguistic difference: any of these could have been the basis for an entire book on Derrida and Kristeva. If I have chosen to work on theories of difference in a more general sense, this is not because difference as such precedes gender or ethnic or phonetic difference in either a temporal or logical sense, but because it speaks through them all.

And the uptake of the question of the unthinkable other in this book? The *chora* and *différance* are provisional names given respectively by Kristeva and Derrida to the unnameable. Their non-coincidence will be explored in Chapter 2. The analysis of Derrida's and Kristeva's work on otherness suggests ways in which they could be set up as others-to-each-other but never quite other (*of course it's a set-up, they're being framed*, all through Chapters 3 to 5 in fact). Chapters 6 and 7 focus on the literary text as the shadowy other of philosophy, and Chapter 8 gives an idea of the vast range of ways in which Kristeva's and Derrida's writings resonate in the hands of others and bounce back with new energy.

Neither psychoanalyst nor philosopher, coming from literature and semiotics, I remain deaf to certain frequencies and amplify others: the texts I study are inflected accordingly. But then this is also a lesson of resonance, and indeed of post-structuralism, that resonators modify the timbre, that each reading of a text carries the traces of its re-production . . . me at my open window, bee in the bonnet, listening to grasshoppers munching through hibiscus leaves. . . .

NOTES

1. Indeed Vincent Descombes, in his influential analysis *Modern French Philosophy*, sees the attempt to theorize same/other relations as characteristic of French philosophy since the thirties.

2. Leon Roudiez, Introduction to Kristeva, *Nations Without Nationalism*.

3. Kelly Oliver, *Reading Kristeva* 12.

4. Toril Moi, Preface to *The Kristeva Reader* vi.

5. Derrida, introduction to *Psyché: Inventions de l'autre* 10. In this chapter, "Tympan" (MP ix-xxix) and the article "Psyche: Inventions of the Other" will be regularly invoked to echo "Violence and Metaphysics."

6. "Psyche: Inventions of the Other" 36.

7. John Llewelyn, "A Point of Almost Absolute Proximity to Hegel" 94.

8. Derrida, "Violence and Metaphysics" (WD 79-153), first published 1964. Kristeva, "Place Names" (DL 271-294), first published 1976. The following reading is in no way an exhaustive one but picks up and follows a few parallel moves in the two articles.

9. Simon Critchley is one of several writers who discuss the relation between Levinas' and Derrida's work. In "The Chiasmus," he argues that deconstruction shares "thematic and strategic resonances" with the ethics of Levinas (91), and we shall see that resonance is, in fact, at issue in this text. Similarly Susan Handelman claims that "Levinas is one of the thinkers who made Derrida and deconstruction possible, and Derrida, in turn, has made possible a renewed appreciation of Levinas" ("Parodic Play and Prophetic Reason" 398). Despite the division of "Violence and Metaphysics" into a faithful reading followed by a questioning of Levinas (WD 84), Derridean and Levinasian ideas are not always clearly distinguishable. However the exemplarity of the moves Derrida makes in this text—in the paradoxical Derridean sense of being one of several but also a model to be cited—can be seen in the "resonances" over the decades between "Violence and Metaphysics" (1964), "Tympan" (1972), "Psyche: Inventions of the Other" (1983-84), "Passions" (1992) and *The Gift of Death* (1992) among others (dates as of the first publication or presentation).

10. Handelman sees the question of violence, and "whether there is an ultimate possibility—even utopian—of peace and non-violence in language or philosophy" as an important point of difference between Levinas and Derrida ("Parodic Play and Prophetic Reason" 416).

11. Kristeva has continued to focus on the child as a limiting case of otherness, for instance: "This cross-road Being, the child, between the biological and the symbolic, between the maternal receptacle and a narcissistic

identity, between the absurd and the attribution of meaning [. . .]" ("Événement et révélation" 3). See also "Stabat mater" in *Tales of Love* and "A New Type of Intellectual: The Dissident" (KR 297).

12. This need to open oneself, to prepare oneself for the advent of the other, is emphasized in "Psyche." But "letting the other come" does not imply inertia or resigned passivity: "Preparing for the coming of the other is what could be called deconstruction." It would be a question of "'know[ing]' how to say 'come' and to answer the 'come' of the other" ("Psyche: Inventions of the Other" 55-56, tr. mod.).

13. In "Deconstruction and the Possibility of Ethics," Robert Bernasconi suggests that the problematic relation between Derrida and Levinas in "Violence and Metaphysics" is in fact the space of (im)possibility of the ethical relation for deconstruction.

14. Cf. Derrida's insistence that he has "always attempted to show that the limit or end of metaphysics is not linear or circular in any indivisible sense" (Derrida and Kearney, "Deconstruction and the Other" 111).

15. Cf. "For Levinas, Judaism and philosophy are the pair that put each other in question" (Handelman 420).

16. Derrida and Kearney, "Deconstruction and the Other" 108.

17. From reflection of sound to reflection of light: *psyché* in French can indicate both a large pivoting mirror and the human soul. The reflection of the other in the *psyché* is typically an appropriation: "the invention of the same through which the other amounts to the same when its event is again reflected in the fable of a *psyche*" ("Psyche: Inventions of the Other" 60). And yet "The very movement of this fabulous repetition can [. . .] produce the new of an event" (59). Repetition and reflection can open a gap for otherness: "an invention of the other that would come, through the economy of the same, indeed while miming or repeating it [. . .], to offer a place for the other, would let the other come" (60).

18. Cf. MP xxv.

19. Translation modified: French possessive pronouns do not indicate the gender of the possessor, and Kristeva's focus here is on the mother.

20. This "receptacle," the *chora*, is discussed in Chapter 2. The child is described here as "analyzer" and the mother as "analysand." This is because the mother-child relation puts the mother in touch with her drives, with the non-rational side of her existence. Kaja Silverman is troubled by this trading of places. She sees it as part of a "refusal to assign the female subject a viable place within the symbolic" and seeks to "reclaim the position of analyst" for the mother (*The Acoustic Mirror* 105, 107). However Kristeva does not simply dislodge the mother from her "tutelary role" and position of power (*ibid.* 105)

but rather shows her flexibility in moving between positions. This flexibility marks, not her displacement from the symbolic, but her enhanced capacity for an ethical relation. For the mother-child relation is not only crucial to the child in the formation of what will become self and other; it is also a means for the mother of (re-)establishing a relation to the other. (Elizabeth Grosz makes a similar point, *Sexual Subversions* 80).

21. Kristeva's other texts about maternity similarly take up the notion of interior heterogeneity: during pregnancy the mother is confronted by a "simultaneously dual and alien space" (DL 237) calling her into question (cf. "Stabat mater" in *Tales of Love*, esp. 254-256). And the birth of the child does not put an end to this: the primary narcissism enveloping mother and child blurs self/other boundaries, and brings into play the mother's own lost relation with her mother, with the maternal *chora*. In fact, in Kristeva's work, the psychical vestiges of the relation to the mother's body are always involved in the encounter with otherness. The mother's body that we must lose in order to master language but that we never quite lose (cf. *Black Sun*) is the basis of the otherness we harbour within. In an article that draws on both Kristeva's and Levinas' writings, Ewa Ziarek identifies this maternal alterity as a place to start in elaborating an ethics of otherness ("Kristeva and Levinas: Mourning, Ethics, and the Feminine").

22. *The Ear of the Other* 34-35, 50. Interestingly, in the same text, Derrida/Nietzsche make(s) the connection between hearing and the umbilical cord, between the "obscure circumvolutions" of the ear and the navel, through which waves are transmitted (36). Regression is, however, not the issue for Derrida.

23. Already in *Revolution in Poetic Language*, Kristeva wrote of the possibility of "foundering in an 'unsayable' without limits" (65).

24. Derrida, "The Principle of Reason: The University in the Eyes of its Pupils" 14-15.

25. Cf. "The radical illegibility of which we are speaking is not irrationality [. . .]" (WD 77). Similarly excluded is the unconscious with which "an entirely other [. . .] can no longer be confused" ("Psyche: Inventions of the Other" 61). In "Tympan," Derrida complains of "the confused equivalence" often made today between "the unthought, the suppressed [and] the repressed of philosophy" (MP xxviii).

26. Throughout "Tympan," Derrida plays on this resemblance and its "repercussions."

27. The abject, explored in *Powers of Horror*, is a form of otherness that never quite constitutes a definable Other. It never accedes to the status of object, in that—although heterogeneous—it can never been completely

expelled from the subject. It disrupts the neat organization into inside and outside, self and other, as an inaccessible otherness within.

28. *Sens et non-sens de la révolte* provides the fullest writing out of this construction of sexual difference (197-223).

29. Derrida, "Fourmis" 102n.

30. Derrida and McDonald, "Choreographies" 76. Cf. Derrida, "Geschlecht" 401.

31. Elizabeth Grosz, "The Body of Signification" and "Ontology and Equivocation: Derrida's Politics of Sexual Difference."

32. Grosz, "The Body of Signification" 101.

33. Derrida, "At This Very Moment in This Work Here I Am" and "Geschlecht."

CHAPTER 2

Telling the Difference

THE DIVIDING LINE

> *"The motif of the limit, of the frontier, of the parting line will furrow the whole sequence."* (Glas 189)

> *"'/'—a mark of separation and of unity, of incompletion and arrest, of what cuts and connects, of the leap over the incision"* (Σ 333)

Not all lines are linear. There are loops and zigzags, detours and circuits, and there are dotted lines. The dividing line—whether in Derrida's work, or Kristeva's, or between the two—is unlikely to be of the continuous linear sort, neatly bisecting two discrete halves. And it may connect as much as it divides. Chapter 1 sketched some broad lines of similarity and divergence between Kristeva's and Derrida's work on otherness as a first step in the articulation of their work. But those broad lines need to be brought into focus if we are to trace any sort of dividing line. For that is the purpose of this chapter, to indicate very precisely, in the work first of Kristeva and then of Derrida, the nature of the divisions producing pairs of terms like same and other. Divisions into two take many forms, spawning doubles, dualisms, dichotomies, differences and dialectics. What types of twoness link the pairs of terms in Derrida's and in Kristeva's work? If, as we have seen, they both find the other dividing the same from itself, how is that division produced and reproduced in each case, and what sort of limit or boundary is constituted in the process? And if the other inhabits the same, what relation, what kind of cohabitation is implied? In attempting to answer these questions, it might be possible to see what is at stake in extrapolating a dividing line between the work of Derrida and Kristeva and to assess the chances of their cohabitation of a theoretical space.

If we wish to 'pick a pair, any pair,' the task is easy with Kristeva. We can hardly go past her elaboration of the semiotic and the symbolic, the two modalities that confront each other in her account of the signifying process. And Derrida? No single pair dominates. The choice is seemingly endless: speech and writing, presence and absence, inside and outside, signified and signifier, original and copy, nature and culture, space and time, same and other. No single pair . . . as if any one of those pairs were independent of the series. We may choose at random . . . but in studying Derrida, we will also need to reflect on the notion of choosing at random.

The relation between the two terms of the couples invoked by each writer, the way otherness divides the same, for example, is theorized by Kristeva in terms of a "process of *signifiance*" and by Derrida as — amongst other appellations — a "movement of *différance*." Both "process" and "movement" emphasize the dynamic nature of what they are attempting to describe. I propose to follow this process and this movement by focusing on a pair of terms in Kristeva's and then in Derrida's writing. The aim is to trace the "dividing line" as it occurs in each case, not in the expectation of uncovering some sort of permanently engraved and neatly ruled line making clear-cut distinctions but in order to find a way of marking, a recurring stroke of the pen.

Useful, relatively compact definitions already exist of Derridean *différance* and of the Kristevan dialectical "process" and can be gleaned from a good glossary. In doing a detailed reading of *différance* and of the semiotic at work (at play?), it is not my purpose to duplicate these efforts but to explore what is necessarily reduced in the crystallization to a definition—the *gait* of the text, its functioning as a double practice, the moves made, the strategies and tactics brought into play. Highlighting the manoeuvres, tracking the itinerary from the itinerancy of the text will reveal parallels and cross-purposes and will lay the groundwork for a comparison and for the cross-readings of Part II, the Derridean reading of the semiotic/symbolic and the Kristevan understanding of *différance*. In each case, these are the aspects that will either lend themselves to interpretation by the other . . . or resist it.

There, I've admitted it: this chapter rests on a necessary lie—the claim to be analyzing Derridean *différance* and the Kristevan "process" one at a time, independently of each other. In order to set up the juxtapositions and cross-readings, I intend to concentrate on the way each functions on its own terms, taking the line of least resistance to the texts. But this, of course, involves a certain pretense, in that the orientation of the analysis will always be determined by the articulation to follow: possible points of intersection will be accentuated. A fiction of separation then . . . One upon a time. . . .

SENSE AND SENSIBILITY: KRISTEVA'S SYMBOLIC AND SEMIOTIC

Detailing the process whereby sense is constituted and dislodged is the task Kristeva sets herself in *Revolution in Poetic Language* (RPL).[1] To do so, she develops an idiosyncratic terminology. She uses the term *signifiance*, rather than the more general *signification*, to designate this process in order to emphasize that it is not only a linguistic and social phenomenon but also biological and instinctual.[2] The complex relation between these two aspects is accounted for in the dialectic Kristeva describes between two "modalities": *le symbolique* and *le sémiotique*. In designating the domain of structure, social organization, and linguistic communication as the symbolic, Kristeva takes up Lacan's term in a recognizable way.[3] However, her choice of *le sémiotique* as a provisional name for the unnameable—indicating an instinctual and disruptive force coming from unconscious drives, the body, and the symbiotic relation with the mother and expressed through movement, rhythm, and pre-verbal utterances—is an interesting adaptation of the term *la sémiotique*. *La sémiotique* is the discipline of semiotics, the study of sign systems, the discipline in which Kristeva has situated much of her own work, particularly her early texts. The change of gender from *la sémiotique* to *le sémiotique* can perhaps be seen as an attempt to resignify a science that neglects the body by bringing the body into semiotics.[4]

Symbolic good sense and semiotic sensibility work together dialectically to produce a range of signifying practices. As in the Jane Austen version of the dialectic, we are treated to a goodly dose of passion plus some old-fashioned repression, under the auspices of paternal law as mediated through the maternal body. If sense and sensibility are presented by Austen as opposites yet related, as sisters to each other, Kristeva's symbolic and semiotic are, we shall see, also attached to and divided from each other in a rather elusive way. Like Austen, Kristeva cautions against the dangers that threaten a retreat into either domain exclusively. The refusal of the rule of reason—clinging to semiotic sensibility—is invariably accompanied by a descent into psychosis. But barricading oneself in a fortress of symbolic sense is equally unwise: Austen illustrates the return of the repressed that avenges the denial of desires; Kristeva demonstrates the sterility and redundancy of metalinguistic and purely contemplative discourses. However there are a few obvious differences between the two accounts of the dialectic. For a start, Kristeva's nineteenth-century protagonists (Mallarmé and Lautréamont) are both male. Secondly, there is no happy ending to her text, indeed no ending as such: RPL is a tale of ongoing revolution and of struggle without end. Whilst Austen concludes optimistically with two double syntheses—Elinor and Marianne each achieve an internal union of reason and passion in addition to their matrimonial mergers—no harmonious synthesis seems possible in RPL. Indeed Kristeva's characters experience difficulty in attaining even the most precarious equilibrium between the violent forces that buffet their existence. Finally, in all fairness it should be added that Kristeva's prose is somewhat denser than Austen's. . . .

From the outset of her treatise, Kristeva introduces a division into two. In a parallel move to what we saw in "Place Names," she starts by situating her work in relation to other attempts (semiotic, linguistic and psychoanalytical) to account for the production of meaning. These tend to fall into two camps according to the way they deal with the "extra-linguistic" aspects of the process. One tendency, under the influence of Freud and of Melanie Klein, does not at all neglect pre-linguistic formations and the instinctual and bodily dimensions of discourse but still never manages to integrate them into the "syntactico-semantic functioning" of language (22). They remain external to language, left behind in the transition to the speaking subject. The second tendency, in which Kristeva sees influences as diverse as those of Benvéniste, Husserl, Searle, and Chomsky, recognizes an underlying "'layer' of semiosis" (22), but insists on a subject of enunciation. This subject turns out to be a transcendental *ego* for whom language is primarily a semantic and communicational system. The supposedly extra-linguistic layer—the 'deep structure' for example—is a site of logical and intersubjective connections, that is to say, of relations modeled on those of language and not extra-linguistic at all.

Kristeva's reaction to these two trends is to note what they share and to question the divide that exists between them. In each case, she notes that one aspect of the signifying process is studied at the expense of the other. The first tendency sets its sights on the semiotic, the mode logically prior to language and to the advent of the speaking subject, that heeds only the rhythm of instinctual drives and sensations. The second sees only the symbolic, the more knowable mode that appears with the relation to the other and is a condition of social organization, reason, and communication. The weakness she identifies in both trends is their treatment of one of these aspects to the exclusion of the other. In contrast, Kristeva's project is to bring the two to confront each other by establishing the semiotic and the symbolic as the inseparable constituent elements of "the same signifying process" (24). In her theory, linguistic signification does not evolve in isolation from what precedes or what disturbs it. And vice-versa: the pre-linguistic is not outside the influence of social organization, which is mediated through the mother. And although some signifying practices may lean on one mode to the seeming exclusion of the other, "this exclusivity is relative, precisely because of the necessary dialectic between the two modalities" (24). Never one without the other.

Kristeva thus questions the semiotic/symbolic divide in the first few paragraphs of *Revolution in Poetic Language* yet manages to maintain it, through over six hundred pages in the French edition, as providing the impetus for almost all that the subject does and all that befalls him.[5] If '/' is a mark both of separation and of unity as the epigraph to this chapter suggests, then the nature of the '/' denoting the semiotic/symbolic distinction-and-relation is interesting indeed as an example of a dividing line. For it does not fall like an axe between the two terms, so much as zipper them together: they are inextricably dovetailed and compromised at every stage of their constitution.

A Sense of Rhythm: The Semiotic

If it were possible to isolate one of the two modes to study it closely, it would have to be the semiotic (and this is where Kristeva starts as she elaborates her dialectic), for in the development of the subject, there is a stage before language acquisition, before the advent of the symbolic, before the existence of the subject as such, a stage during which we might imagine the semiotic to function independently of the symbolic. This, however, is not the case.

To explain the pre-linguistic functioning of the semiotic, Kristeva adopts the idea of the *chora* from Plato's *Timaeus*. The *chora* is a nourishing, maternal receptacle or space that, not having form, can only be described approximately and metaphorically. For Kristeva, this is the space that receives pre-cognitive input from the senses and absorbs impulses from (primarily anal and oral) instinctual drives. It is other than language and thought, and yet we shall see that it is ultimately from this otherness that the thinking and speaking subject is generated.

Because it precedes language, it cannot be approached directly using tools of analysis determined by language. Thus the only access to the (semiotic) *chora* is through studying its effect on (symbolic) signification. Or, to put it in terms we have already seen, the only access to the unnameable/unthinkable is through its continuing echo in language and thought. In fact Kristeva is only able to hypothesize the work of the *chora*: she posits a pre-linguistic functioning of the semiotic from its echo: "the semiotic that 'precedes' symbolization is only a *theoretical supposition* [. . .]. It exists in practice only within the symbolic" (68). She is only able to situate it diachronically in the formation of the subject because of the way it functions "synchronically within the signifying process of the subject" (29).[6]

The semiotic *chora* cannot be isolated: not only does analyzing the semiotic bring it into the realm of the symbolic, but even the hypothesis of an independent semiotic *chora* is dependent on its acting upon the symbolic. And the dependence of the semiotic on the symbolic goes even further than this. The semiotic *chora*, although logically and chronologically prior to the symbolic (41), is always-already oriented towards the reign of meaning to come. The *chora* is not yet a sign nor a signifier but is nonetheless "generated with a view to this signifying position" (26, tr. mod.). The semiotic functions "with an eye to the subject" who is not yet formed (41). Language and communication may still be a way off but are already in the process of being constituted. Turned toward the symbolic, the *chora* can only approximate a purely semiotic configuration.

Semiotic and symbolic are further entangled in the "fundamental ambiguity" that has marked the *chora* right from its elaboration by Plato (239 n13): on the one hand it is "mobile, amorphous" (49), unstable and uncertain; on the other hand it is not entirely chaotic but "already regulated" (49), rhythmic in its movement. Although it precedes and opposes social organization, the family and language, "the *chora* is nevertheless subjected to a regulating process, which [. . .] effects discontinuities by temporarily articulating them and then starting over, again and again" (26, tr. mod.). The mobility of the senses is not totally chaotic; it has a sense to it, a sense of rhythm. The repeated description of the *chora* as rhythm (26-30) points to both its mobility and its regularity. The semiotic/symbolic distinction may be radical but is not hermetic: the *chora* foreshadows the symbolic even as it resists it.

The regulating rhythm of the *chora* seems to derive from the indirect influence of the symbolic. Kristeva posits that "social organization, always already symbolic, imprints its constraint in a mediated form" on this semiotic space (27). The symbolic influence passes through an intermediary: negotiating the divide between symbolic law and the ordering of the *chora* is the mother's body. The mother's body is already ambiguous itself: it is subject to family/social organization but is also analogous to the *chora,* described by Plato as a maternal, nourishing space (240 n14). It respects symbolic law but maintains strong ties to the semiotic. Marked by both modes of functioning, it mediates between them and repeats the semiotic/symbolic divide at another level.

The anticipation of symbolic organization is hypothesized even in what would seem the most unsymbolic and instinctual of forces: the drives in the *chora*. These are described as "'energy' charges as well as 'psychical' marks," and they "articulate" the *chora* which is "formed by the drives and their stases in a motility that is as full of movement as it is regulated" (25). Drives are presented paradoxically as not only fluid and agitated, even agitating (energy, charges, motility, movement) but also as vaguely structuring (articulating, forming, and regulating) the *chora* through inscription (marks) and momentary pauses (stases). They are "simultaneously assimilating and destructive; this dualism [. . .] makes the semiotized body a place of permanent scission" (27). The ambivalence does not however establish a balance between opposing forces, for although drives may be "simultaneously 'positive' and 'negative'" (28) and may "produce and/or destroy" (33), the incessant fission is ultimately destructive, dissolving and reversing any temporary structuring. The negative carries the day in "waves of attack against stases" (28). Moreover, the positive moments of stasis turn out to be determined by the negative: their ordering is merely the regular rhythm of pauses separating the repeated destructive charges, the rhythm of a pounding surf, pulverizing without any permanent form.

The overridingly negative impact of drives means that articulation in the semiotic mode remains "essentially mobile and extremely provisional" (25), incapable of supporting any identity: "the semiotic *chora* is no more than the place where the subject is both generated and negated, the place where his unity succumbs before the process of charges and stases that produce him" (28), a process that becomes Kristeva's definition of negativity, in a psychoanalytical/materialist rewriting of the Hegelian notion.[7]

The semiotic *chora* thus precedes but does not escape the symbolic. Inaccessible without it, inseparable from it, the *chora* assimilates the influence of the symbolic through the mother's body in the form of a transient ordering of positive moments articulating destructive waves. The dual nature of the *chora* rules out any possibility of conceiving of it as a homogeneous unity, as an indivisible term of a semiotic/symbolic opposition that at first seemed to split so clearly into two. Nevertheless, despite the ambivalence in the division, the semiotic/symbolic opposition remains effective: powerfully negative, the semiotic processes remain "foreign" to the subject and the signification they help to produce (36); although necessary to language acquisition, they are not to be confused with language (29). But in Kristeva's work, the interaction between the semiotic and the symbolic—between unthinkable otherness and the thinking subject— has always-already begun. There can be no absolute and intact semiotic before the symbolic: a step ahead, the *chora* anticipates what is to come. The dividing line—splitting semiotic from symbolic and tying them together—is mirrored in the very functioning of the *chora*.

A Meeting of Sense and the Senses: The Thetic Phase

Marking the "threshold of language" (45), the thetic phase is the dividing line between the semiotic and the symbolic. But from the very subtitle of Kristeva's section on the thetic—"Rupture and/or Boundary"—it is clear that the nature of this division is problematic: the question arises three times before the chapter begins—"rupture," "and/or," "boundary." Is it then a splitting or a borderline, and are the two necessarily mutually exclusive? On the one hand, the thetic is the limit between the semiotic and the symbolic (48) and thus a boundary, but on the other it cuts into, interrupts the movement of the semiotic as a rupture.

Let us first consider the thetic as rupture. Or ruptures. If the *chora* is a "place of permanent scission" (27), an "infinitely repeatable separability" (239 n13), a rhythm of "rupture and articulations" (26), the thetic phase is equally characterized by divisions. It is defined as "a break in the signifying process" (43) and produces separations, in particular between the subject and his image and between subject and object. But what divides the divisions? Both the thetic and the semiotic are described in terms of rupture, but these two types of rupture have very different consequences, that of the *chora* amounting to an articulation whilst the thetic launches a dialectic.

Apparently, not all ruptures are de-structive. Whereas semiotic scission, though fleetingly ordered, above all dissolves structure, the thetic "is *structured* as a break" (43, my emphasis). Whereas the *chora* generates destructive waves that "lead to no identity" (28), the thetic break establishes rather than destroys and indeed "establish[es] the *identification* of the subject and its object" (43) in "a positing of identity or difference" (43). The thetic break seems able to establish and posit because it is itself structured: it occurs as a binary division. Organized and organizing, it enables oppositions like same/different, subject/object, I/you to appear. These divisions are very different from the semiotic scission which "fragments" (46) and "pulverises" (51) into an indeterminate and possibly infinite number in its waves of destruction. They are also comparatively durable. Once established in the thetic phase, these oppositions are able to bring order to the child's universe and therefore do not simply disappear under the impact of the next instinctual wave. Thetic separations are "set in place" (46) in a way that semiotic stases —mere pauses—are not. Kristeva writes of "a positing [*une position*] of identity or difference," "the positing [*la position*] of signification" (43), where *position* is both a positing or postulation and a positioning. It is interesting that posit, position, and positive are all etymologically related to the Latin *ponere* —to place, for this is what makes the thetic break more "positive" than semiotic scission, structuring rather than destructive in its ruptures, establishing rather than destabilizing. The semiotic and the thetic may both be represented as rupture, but the force of negativity does not determine this rupture to the same extent.

The binary oppositions of the thetic phase therefore rupture with the semiotic mode because this type of split constitutes a qualitative transformation. The positing/positioning gives it some permanence such that it becomes a limit, a "permeable" one (63), "a traversable boundary" that is not "imposed once and for all" (51), but which nevertheless does not simply dissolve once it is created. Kristeva writes that the subject must be "firmly posited" (50). Nothing is less durable on the other hand that the "infinitely repeatable separability" of the *chora* (239 n13), where splits are reversible in the rhythm of "flow and marks" (40). The thetic rupture therefore constitutes a boundary: once these organizing binary splits are set in place, there is structure. It is in this sense that the thetic is the "threshold of language" (45). Oppositions like same/different, subject/object, I/you give access to the realm of thought, of language, of communication and social relations, of the family and law. It is not easy to return to the sensual mobility of the *chora*. In fact, such a return would require us to unthink, to unspeak, to cease to recognize ourselves. To return to the instinctual domain of sensations, we would paradoxically need to take leave of our senses. The thetic break is a resistant frontier that requires a massive struggle to be demolished completely. However, as we shall see, it is far from being invulnerable and is constantly transformed under the "attack" of semiotic drives (49).

A crucial moment in the thetic phase is the mirror stage: Kristeva rewrites Lacan's narrative of identification in terms of the transition from the semiotic mode to the symbolic.[8] Creating the conditions necessary for identification, there is the thetic separation into subject and object which detach themselves from the continuity of the *chora* (46-47). The toddler in front of the mirror is able to recognize himself as self (as subject) when he sees himself as other (as object, as image). Paradoxically this unifying moment occurs as a rupture: the subject is required to "separate from and through his image, from and through his objects" (43). In order to assume the mirror image as his own, he needs to see it as distinct from himself. His identity is therefore alienating: what gives him a sense of wholeness (of oneness, of identity) is the fact of being split into two (identical) parts.[9] For Lacan, there can be no unity, no identity, without such a division. In Kristeva's work, it is for this same reason that the *chora* "cannot be unified" (36). Although it is ordered, there is no binary division (no thetic break) across which unification could occur.

Kristeva follows Lacan further: by virtue of the fact that the subject is henceforth confronted by himself as other, the mirror stage prepares both socialization and signification. The *imago* in the mirror establishes a position for the object/other in general. Up until this point, the mother has always fulfilled the role of other, the provider of all satisfaction, but during the "discovery of castration," the mother loses this all-powerful position which is subsequently available to be occupied by a range of objects/others (46-47). The possibility of these relations is the ticket of entry to the social sphere. Parallel with the position/positing of subject identification is the position/positing of signification which also occurs as a split, as a gap between signified and signifier. As the subject becomes separable from himself in the mirror, he becomes signifiable, i.e. conceivable in terms of signified (the "facing *imago*" 46, the "imaged ego" 48) and signifier (projected by the "agitated body" 46, the "semiotic process" 47, "drive motility" 48). Although the semiotic body and its drives are not directly translated into language, this positioning of the split prepares the possibility of linguistic signification, communication. Despite the unity of each pair of terms, a gap between them in each case defines and continues to separate signifier and signified, subject and image, drives and ego, the "demands made on the mother" (48) and the mother. It is across this productive gap that all desires and acts will be realized.

The concepts of "divided" unity and "always split unification" (49), which progressively loosen their link with Lacanian theory, remain capital in RPL, not only to designate the moment of the subject's identification and the relation of signified to signifier but also to describe the relation between the semiotic and the symbolic in general.[10]

Making Sense: The Symbolic

The divided unity established through the thetic break signals the emergence of a new order, the symbolic.[11] The thetic and the symbolic are not always clearly distinguishable, indeed sometimes the two terms coincide ("symbolic, thetic unity [is] divided" 49), and they are each as paradoxical as they are ambiguous. But the thetic is a transitional *phase* of rupture, a phase that represents the enabling condition for the symbolic. Simplifying, we could say that if the thetic phase is a splitting, then the symbolic is always-already split; if the thetic is structuring, the symbolic is structured. And if the thetic is above all a rupture (a paradoxically constructive rupture), the symbolic is primarily defined by unity (an albeit divided unity).

"The thetic phase marks a threshold between two heterogeneous realms: the semiotic and the symbolic" (48). It is what separates the fluid, fleetingly ordered semiotic from the organized symbolic world of social structure, paternal law, censorship and communicative language. It is the most crucial divide in Kristeva's theory, but what sort of dividing line is it? To what extent is the symbolic divided from the semiotic? Having examined her representation of the semiotic, we should hardly be surprised that the nature of the symbolic is ambiguous, that—despite thetic separation—semiotic and symbolic cannot really be referred to as *separate* at all. Kristeva writes of their "scission" (48), but at each step in the elaboration of the dialectic, the dovetailing of the two modes becomes more complicated, for the symbolic "includes part of the [semiotic]" (49) in an identity split of its own; the subject "transfers semiotic motility onto the symbolic order" (47); there is "a resumption of the functioning characteristic of the semiotic *chora* within the signifying device of language" (50). This is the other dividing the same, inaccessible otherness as it appears within the domain of the thinkable. But how does it occur? The explanation will take us via rupture and disruption to Kristeva's understanding of *signifiance*.

The binary oppositions established during the thetic phase, the "two faces" of the thetic break (55)—oppositions between what is posited and the positing of it, between denotation and enunciation, between imaged ego and semiotic process—give rise to syntactic oppositions like subject/predicate, modified/modifier or even noun/verb. These oppositions stem from the thetic rupture and are its translation into language: "Syntax displaces and represents, within the homogeneous element of language, the thetic break separating the signifier from what was heterogeneous to it" (55). Within language, however, the terms of these oppositions are "permutable" (54, 55) and "reversible" (54).

Reversible?—but this is reminiscent of the scissions of the semiotic *chora*. In the domain of the symbolic we are confronted with another set of reversible divisions. This time, however, they are binary oppositions, oppositions that appeared to have some permanence when we examined the thetic. Kristeva makes the distinction between the thetic and the symbolic explicit: "The *transformation* [from drive to signifier] produced by the thetic is registered only as an intersyntactical *division*" (55). The thetic is a rupture in more than one sense: it operates by binary splits but more importantly operates a transforming rupture between the semiotic and the symbolic, between multiple scission (fragmentation) and the realm of binary oppositions. In fact, the force of its rupture is the fact that it is a rupture between two types of rupture. This is what qualifies it as transformation, a genuine alteration in the scheme of things. Syntactic (symbolic) divisions, on the other hand, can be substituted for one another within language whilst continuing to make sense. Whilst both semiotic scission and symbolic division are reversible within their own sphere, the qualitative leap from semiotic to symbolic, from provisional stases to identificatory splits, from sensory information and "non-sense" to making sense, is not permutable or reversible.

This division between two kinds of rupture can be seen in terms of a difference between two oppositions we could call same/different and same/other, where same/different is difference against a background of identity (subject/predicate or noun/verb within language, charges/stases in the *chora*) and where same/other indicates a radical otherness. Otherness here does not mean another person, an *other* within the *same* social sphere, but *alterity* or what Kristeva terms "heterogeneity." Heterogeneity is linked to unconscious drives and therefore comes from the other realm, the inaccessible and unutterable semiotic. For Kristeva, only the opposition between the same and the heterogeneous constitutes a dialectical relation, one that is not simply reversible. There can be no real transformation, no alteration without alterity.

If ruptures in the symbolic mode are merely reversible oppositions, then this is because drive heterogeneity is absent from the symbolic in the first instance. This absence of heterogeneity within the symbolic can be explained by the fact that the subject is not fully accounted for by the symbolic mode. Although the symbolic heralds the possibility of the speaking subject, the subject of drives is not assimilated into the symbolic. The subject as agitated body and semiotic process remains foreign to it and connected to the semiotic. When the thetic posits signification, the semiotic motility of the subject projects a signified and signifier but is excluded from them: the enunciation is that of "a displaced subject, absent from the signified and signifying position" (54). Unnameable, unsignifiable, it cannot be simply absorbed into language, so although we can speak of the existence of a subject after the thetic phase, this subject is not present as such in its linguistic propositions: "This [thetic] transformation, which produced the speaking subject, comes about only if it leaves that subject out, within the heterogeneous. Indeed, although he is the bearer of syntax, the speaking subject is absent from it" (55). However, without the semiotic otherness of the subject, the grammatical sequence is incomplete. The permutations and combinations available within symbolic language lose their potency, are locked into a sterile redundancy. No renewal is possible without a resurgence of alterity in the form of "a heterogeneous division, an irruption of the semiotic *chora*" (56). Drive heterogeneity thus invades the symbolic. The subject of drives reemerges, disturbing the established positions; otherness erupts and interrupts; the sensors challenge the censors.

The resurgence occurs as a dialectical confrontation, as a violent struggle between two contradictory movements, "an acute and dramatic confrontation" (47) where the semiotic takes the offensive against the symbolic order. The semiotic onslaught is represented as "the corruption of Meaning" (37), "the attack of drives" (49), "an influx of the death drive" (50), "transgression" (62, 65, 68, 69), "breach" ["*effraction* "] (62, 69), "irruption" (49, 63), "explosion" (69). It "disturbs" (55), "breaks up the thetic, splits it, fills it with empty spaces" (69), "constantly tears it open" (62), "breaks through the symbolic border" (79) to "dissolve the logical order" (79). Signification is "shaken" (58). "Shattering" (56) and "pulverizing" (69), dissolving and exploding, the semiotic fragments the thetic, multiplies the divisions to operate an "infinitization" (56) of meaning.

For all its "violence" (79), however, the semiotic does not necessarily succeed in destroying the symbolic, for the thetic boundary has a certain solidity to it. We hope not to lose communication entirely, although it may be transformed. In fact, losing our grip on language and social relations would point to a serious failure of the thetic phase to properly establish a signifying position. The consequences for the subject would be a slide into psychosis together with an inability to signify the experience: "failing to bring off this affirmative moment amounts to missing out on the possibility of meaning" (PL 108). If symbolic language without the explosive return of the semiotic subject is sterile and redundant, the situation of the semiotized subject who has lost access to the social sphere is even less desirable. Just as sense needs to become sentient, sensibility needs to be brought to its senses. If, however, signification and social relations have been "firmly posited" during the thetic phase, the semiotic/symbolic confrontation will give rise to a "second-degree thetic" (50), a dialectical transformation of symbolic language by semiotic drives. For Kristeva, this transformation of language under the influence of drives is best realized in the signifying practice she calls *text*, of which the privileged example is the nineteenth-century avant-garde text. The *text* can be contrasted with communicative language, theoretical or metalinguistic discourse, traditional narratives and esoteric intellectual word play in that these all privilege the symbolic and the transmission of meaning over the semiotic and the sensual side of language.

The specificity of the *text* is to situate its practice at the very edge of meaning, in the thick of semiotic/symbolic confrontation, at the thetic boundary ("the thetic [. . .] is the very place textual experience aims toward [*vise*]" 67) in order to stretch this limit to the limit, to strain it as far as possible without demolishing it completely. The thetic is threatened by the semiotic disturbance favoured by textual practice, but the text also needs to support this limit. Otherwise it deprives itself of meaning, of the possibility of communicating anything through the words on the page, and also of an object for its dislocating movement: "it involves both shattering and maintaining *position* within the heterogeneous *process*" (56); the boundary is simultaneously both "maintained, inevitably, whenever signification is maintained, and shaken irremediably" (58).[12] In other words, unlike "ordinary discourse," the *text* collaborates with symbolic signification only so far as it is necessary to be able to signify the semiotic shattering of that signification. Communicative language is thus maintained but transformed: under semiotic attack, the signifying order is redistributed (55) rather than relinquished, and "the denoted object proliferates in a series of connoted objects" (55). The violence is channeled by language, which affords a certain protection from the attack.

Here the full ambiguity of language (of the symbolic) manifests itself. Language "protects the body from the attack of drives by making it a place—the place of the signifier—in which the body can signify itself through positions" (49). In other words, language redirects the semiotic attack by incorporating it into the symbolic. Semiotic and symbolic are not however synthesized: the semiotic continues to function as a pocket of alterity, a locus of foreignness in the symbolic, attaching itself to elements of language and bubbling up into utterances. This "pocket of narcissism" (49), of the semiotic within the symbolic, serves the symbolic by protecting it from attack, but simultaneously serves semiotic drives, directing them to where they can disrupt productively: the place of the signifier. The heterogeneity of unconscious drives is then able to act on the signifier by insisting on sound, rhythm, prosody, phonation, by introducing gaps in logic and meaning, ellipses in syntax. The overall result is a pluralization of signification: *signifiance*. But although semiotic alterity is accorded a "place" in language, it remains other than language.

If the semiotic, the *chora*, turned out to be indissociable from its opposite, the symbolic is even more so. If a pre-symbolic stage was at least conceivable, a post-semiotic stage is not. The symbolic, far from being separable from the semiotic, is incomplete, doomed to redundancy without it. Not only does the symbolic therefore provide the place and the opportunity for symbolic/semiotic confrontation but it manages to incorporate semiotic heterogeneity without recuperating it. The semiotic functions within language without being reduced to language. It is integrated as a permanent disturbance, as irreducible otherness within identity, renewing it.

Unlike the theories she describes at the outset of her book, Kristeva's theory does not represent the semiotic as an "extra-linguistic" mode, that would only function outside language. On the contrary, although it is logically prior to language, it is never exterior to it. Rather it constitutes "an 'outside' that is in fact internal" (14), working "within and against the social order" (81), "inherent in the symbolic—but also going beyond it and threatening its position" (81). Deeply complicitous at every stage of their elaboration, semiotic and symbolic participate in a dialectic that has always-already begun. And that does not cease, for the thetic continues to reimpose itself after each buffeting in an ongoing generation of *significance*, a "permanent struggle" (81) advancing endlessly without any possibility of synthesis. The two modalities may be inseparable, but they remain irreconcilably opposed: "two opposing terms that alternate in an endless rhythm" (99). If they are interdependent, they are dependent above all on their mutual opposition. On the one hand, law loses its force when it ceases to be threatened by transgression. On the other hand, Kristeva insists that in order to attack the symbolic order, it is necessary to participate in it. Any practice seeking to define itself as subversion without law is destined to "insignificance," for the lack of a language in which to express itself. For Kristeva, the dialectic between law and its transgression by a heterogeneous other is an endless combat where lasting victory for either side could only represent failure.

There is thus a cohabitation of the symbolic by both semiotic and symbolic modes. This far from peaceful cohabitation is what constitutes the divided unity characteristic of the symbolic.[13] Kristeva compares the symbolic to eyelids: a continuous although slit tissue, constituted by a fissure yet bringing together its edges. The unity is that of "a contract—one that either follows hostilities or presupposes them"; it is a site of exchange but "including an exchange of hostility" (49). Eyelids create a dividing line that is both linear and elliptical, that unites and splits, that changes its contours as it blinks and winks. A dividing line that comes as a pair of pairs, a permeable boundary that lets tears flow through, and whose fluttering line follows the rhythm of our dreams. This is the line that claims to separate sleep from our waking hours yet doesn't quite manage to keep them apart. The metaphor highlights the interdependence—even continuity—of the two sides. What it doesn't succeed in showing is their heterogeneity, their asymmetry and the clash of their confrontation, so Kristeva needs to evoke the ideas of contract and exchange. Could it be that eyelids, like symbolic communication and social structure, conceal a certain underlying violence? Does a struggle go on unseen when the lids meet to close our eyes?

The nature of Kristeva's semiotic/symbolic divide is perhaps better represented by another metaphoric topos in her writing. The destructive waves of the semiotic, ready to engulf and submerge the subject at sea, also unleash their power on the shore, here crumbling a coastline before ebbing to allow it to reassert its now altered outline, here depositing material. The shore's contours have only relative stability and the waves leave pools and sandbanks, carve channels and islands, such that the coastline is never simply an unbroken line. The shore is both a front line of endless combat and an ecology, an economy dependent on ebb and flood for the flushing out of stagnant waters.

Like this line, the thetic boundary dividing semiotic and symbolic is paradoxically a site of both destruction and renewal, of violence and dependence, of conflict and contract. And whilst the occasional semiotic tidal wave may wipe out the social structuring that positions us, a resistant thetic frontier is usually able to withstand semiotic attacks. Drives can then be channeled into our symbolic practices in a way that limits their destructive capacity without eliminating their otherness. And so the other inhabiting us, dividing us from our rational, conscious selves, leaves its tidemark on our propositions, its mark of difference.

Revisiting the Boundary: Kristeva's Imaginary

As the tide washes in and out, landmarks are gradually altered, and new formations appear. Kristeva's work, too, carries its tidemarks and in the years since the writing of *Revolution in Poetic Language*, it has continued to evolve. Her insistence on the strength and importance of semiotic currents and on the necessity for relatively stable symbolic positioning never wavers. However, in her later work, from *Tales of Love* onwards, Kristeva focuses less on the thetic phase itself, although she continues to refer to it, and more on what precedes and prepares it: the imaginary.

Kristeva's use of the term *imaginaire*, more and more frequent in her work since 1980, is rather slippery. It is not simply Lacanian, nor does it simply correspond to the semiotic, nor is it to be confused with the idea of fiction in the lay sense.[14] Roudiez, in *Tales of Love* and *Black Sun*, translates it sometimes by "the imaginary" and sometimes by "imagination." Kristeva's imaginary includes, without being restricted to, esthetic creation. Although the term frequently appears in apposition to "literature," "fiction," "writing" and "art," imaginary experience also encompasses various forms of love as well as religion and revolt.

The suffixes *-aire* in French and *-ary* in English (from the Latin *-arius*, *-arium*) sometimes refer to a collection of items: *bestiaire*, *bréviaire*, *dictionnaire*, *glossaire*, *questionnaire*, *vocabulaire*. This seems to me to provide a helpful way of understanding Kristeva's *imaginaire*: as an assortment of images. One of the clearest explanations of Kristeva's imaginary can be found in a short 1988 text, "The Inexpressible Child" (NMS 103-112), in which Kristeva describes it as "a kaleidoscope of ego images that build the foundation for the subject of enunciation" (104). The collection of images is created through a series of identifications: "The imaginary offers the developing subject an image of himself by using the myriad representations of the child's world to mobilize a whole array of identifications" (103).[15] These identifications include fusion with the mother, identification with the imaginary father and secondary, oedipal identifications. But the image of the self is not yet the specular image that will come with the mirror stage. For Kristeva, the grasping of the mirror image by the child is the result of a whole imaginary process that "passes through voice, taste, skin and so on, all the senses yet doesn't necessarily mobilise sight."[16]

In the development of the child, the imaginary is thus a space of drive-related meaning (*sens*) that prepares for linguistic signification by preparing the advent of the speaking subject. It is "between biology and language" (NMS 103), both semiotic (NMS 104) and a sort of "archaic occurrence of the symbolic."[17] After language acquisition it continues to support the unceasing process of identifications that mark any life. However it also represents a space of heterogeneous subjectivity and of psychical transformation where language can be "musicalized," where the signifier can be either pulverized or filled with meaning. It is a space allowing for a transformation of non-sense into sense and for a transfer of meaning (often through artistic creation) into the place where it has been lost (BS 100-103). Both before and after language acquisition, the imaginary thus negotiates the frontier between the semiotic and the symbolic, between the maternal body and paternal law. However, this negotiation appears less violently confrontational than that described in RPL and in Kristeva's work in the sixties and seventies more generally.

How, then, is the imaginary situated in relation to the semiotic/symbolic divide? Although Kristeva's imaginary is described as a space, it is not a space *separate* from the semiotic and the symbolic. Nor is it a space of synthesis. Rather, it is a "divided space" or *espace dédoublé* (BS 200). The imaginary is a space of sublimation where the semiotic is mirrored in(to) the symbolic. The semiotic is confronted with its image and is transferred via this imaginary construct into symbolic representation or, rather, into the modulated *signifiance*. The imaginary is thus a semiotic space that doubles as the entry point for the symbolic.

Like the thetic phase, imaginary identification is a way of accounting for rupture. And if the thetic as "Rupture and/or Boundary" was ambiguous, the imaginary is equally so, for it is used to explain how separation occurs through identification. The coming-apart is a result of a coming-together.

The separation in question is particularly the separation from the maternal body, from the fusion with the mother that risks engulfing the child and hindering access to language and subjecthood if it is allowed to continue indefinitely. At first, separation seems impossible. The child can only partly distinguish the mother's body from its own: her body disturbs the borders that are forming. No longer one with the child but not yet separate, the mother is "abjected": halfway between same and other, unnameable, she seems repulsive, something to be expelled like excrement, like unwanted food.[18] To make the break from the mother-child dyad, a third party is necessary, an Other, a pole of identification. Kristeva calls this third party the "imaginary father." She takes up Freud's "father of individual prehistory" in order to describe a form of loving identification that effects a first separation between a not-yet-ego and a not-yet-object. This form of separation will function as a pre-condition for Lacan's mirror stage.

The imaginary father is not necessarily male but rather has the sexual attributes of both parents. If Kristeva nonetheless refers to this figure as a father, it is because he guides the child away from maternal fusion and towards participation in symbolic (paternal) structures (TL 33-34). In Kristeva's view, rather than gender, what distinguishes the imaginary father is the fact that he represents the object of the mother's love.[19] In aspiring to become the object of maternal love, the child reduplicates this object, identifies with the imaginary father to the extent that he takes himself for this object—an object who is a subject.[20] Now, recognizing oneself as an object ("I" resemble the object of love) is a step on the way from the semiotic body towards a subject position and the development of an ego. And from the position of subject, the child will be able to recover the mother (who is no longer accessible in mother-child fusion, who is lost in any immediate form) as an imaginary object, an object of love and ultimately a nameable object.[21]

The third term is thus involved in a complex relation to the mother-child double. Rather than a term of synthesis, it provides a way out of fusion. The imaginary father is the mother's other, whom I wish to be and whom I therefore reduplicate (and in so doing become my own other) so that the mother eventually becomes my other. He is the means by which I start to separate from the mother and recover her as an imaginary object. He is the pivot around which the beginnings of self and other are constituted. Through him the semiotic flows into the symbolic . . . and this is where the book of love rewrites the revolutionary conflict.

Kristeva's imaginary identifications show another way of negotiating the semiotic/symbolic divide. Indeed each of her books since RPL has explored a further aspect of the articulation of what remain two heterogeneous modalities of psychical functioning. Like revolution, like poetry, parallel to transference in the analytic relation, love is a means of renewing the psyche. It brings desire into language. If the psyche is "one open system connected to another" (TL 15), then love allows libidinal forces to destabilize this system and introduces "the semiotic flow within symbolicity" (16). Renewal occurs as the "memory-consciousness system" of the psyche abandons its routine patterns to "adapt to the new risks of destabilized-stabilizable auto-organization" (*ibid.*). Like revolution, love operates across the permeable boundary between the semiotic and the symbolic. The division must be maintained or the subject founders in an inexpressible fusion love: same and other, language and structure are lost when there is no life-line back to the system of the psyche. The same risk is therefore involved in the semiotic/symbolic encounter of love as that described in RPL: loss of ability to symbolize experience in language. And the same risk is involved in non-encounter: stagnation and moribundity, "the death-dealing stabilization of love's absence" (15). In both RPL and *Tales of Love*, Kristeva argues that psychical renewal requires destabilization followed by stabilizing moments.

A noticeable shift has nonetheless occurred since RPL. The aggressive assault of the semiotic against the symbolic has been absorbed into the "amorous dynamics" (TL 16) of a psyche open to others. Destruction is only one aspect of the destabilizing work of libidinal charges; defence has become openness; irruption has become flow; collision has become encounter. All this through the paradise-and-hell of love. There is thus a shift from violent clash to (no less dramatic) amorous exchange as the waves sweep in rather than crashing on the coast. What remains constant is the irreducible otherness of the semiotic and the symbolic, the importance of the shoreline between them, and the rhythm of the tide.[22]

The temptation to synthesize Kristeva's work into a single coherent theory is difficult to resist. But this would be to close off a system that remains open and adapts. It will not sit still for me to link it to Derrida's work. But then that movement accounts for both the excitement and frustration of reading Kristeva. The chapters that follow do not assume that any once-and-for-all articulation of Kristeva and Derrida is possible, nor that the most recent Kristeva is the definitive one, eclipsing its predecessors. Rather the chapters focus on various textual moments where the theories can be articulated productively But the shifts in Kristeva's and Derrida's work will keep bobbing up throughout the chapters, complicating otherwise neat joins and separations.

DERRIDA— *DIFFERANT* DIVISIONS

"it knots the interlace of the either/or" (TP 236)

Any search for a counterweight to *La révolution du langage poétique*, for a tome among Derrida's publications that elaborates a theory of signification from first principles, is quickly found to be futile. Although "*Différance*" can be read as approaching an exposition—by definition impossible—of the "general system of this economy [of *différance*]" (MP 3), its twenty-seven pages are dwarfed by Kristeva's

634.[23] *Of Grammatology* perhaps? A respectably lengthy and certainly influential text, but one that presents itself as a set of readings, a text constructed from others rather than a manifesto. Similarly, whilst the nature of the binary opposition is a constant preoccupation of deconstruction, there is no overwhelmingly important opposition in Derrida's writing to match the semiotic/symbolic in Kristeva's. Speech/writing, original/simulacrum are moments giving pause to a shifting focus of attention.

Seeking balance, looking for an equal and opposite text to study, is of course counterproductive. The quest pre-empts the question—that of the relation between Derrida and Kristeva—and presupposes the symmetry of their work. So abandoning the search, I propose to trace Derridean division as it operates through a short text, and then to circulate from text to text, marking the variations that constitute its recurrence.

That First Fine Careless Rupture

> *"There is nowhere to begin to trace the sheaf or the graphics of différance."* (MP 6)

> *"Therefore I am starting, strategically, from the place and the time in which 'we' are [. . .]."* (MP 7)

> *"Let us start, since we are already there, from [. . .]."* (MP 9)

> *"We must begin wherever we are and the thought of the trace [. . .] has already taught us that it was impossible to justify a point of departure absolutely."* (OG 162)

To start from where we already are in this study is to double back to the question of rupture, and in doing so to give the lie to any idea of absolute rupture between the two halves of the chapter. But if the aim of this section is to study Derrida's work on its own terms, then a doubtful divide is not out of line. I have chosen "Structure, Sign and Play in the Discourse of the Human Sciences" as a starting point, not because it is a central text that holds the key to Derrida's work but as an example of rupture.[24] Even, perhaps, as an example of an example.

"Structure, Sign and Play" opens with the hypothesis of an "event" whose "exterior form would be that of a *rupture* and a *redoubling*"

(WD 278, original emphasis). Derrida leaves aside the redoubling (the doubling back or repetition) for a moment in order to situate the rupture. The event separates a before and an after. Before, there is "classical thought concerning structure" (279), whereby a structure is organized around a governing center, a fixed origin or reference point, a reassuring moment of presence guaranteeing its coherence and limiting the play of substitutions of the elements surrounding it. After, on the other side of the dividing line, comes a decentering, where instead of a focus on structure, there is a thinking of "the structurality of structure" (280), an understanding of the center as effect, as a function of the structure itself and not its organizing principle. The center then also becomes susceptible to substitution and a locus of unlimited play. The rethinking of language as discourse constitutes such a rupture: signs are no longer anchored absolutely to some external reality that escapes discourse; the supposedly central transcendental signified—Being as presence—ceases to be immutable and becomes permutable, not an essence but an element within a system of differences.

This first, fine, careless rupture is, however, never complete; it is always recaptured. The fact that the decentering occurs as a rethinking of structurality, as a revisiting of the existing system, is already evidence that "disruption [is] repetition" (280): "all these destructive discourses and all their analogues are trapped in a kind of circle" (280) such that "we can pronounce not a single destructive proposition which has not already had to slip into the form, the logic and the implicit postulations of precisely what it seeks to contest" (280-281). This is a recasting of the problem addressed in "Violence and Metaphysics." However, Derrida is not merely repeating himself, or rather, if we accept that no rupture is absolute, then repetition is as good a way as any—indeed the only way—of starting afresh. And if I revisit the problem here, it is precisely to pose the question in another way. Here it will be my purpose to focus on the bifurcations operating through the text, the status of the binary opposition, and the notions of rupture and choice.

Derrida "choose[s] several 'names'" (280) to associate with the "event" of the attempt to break away from metaphysics: Nietzsche, Freud, Heidegger—none central, but all exemplary. He selects "one example from many" (281) in citing the concept of the sign and the attempt to erase the radical difference between signifier and signified in the work of Lévi-Strauss. And to explain it, he rehearses the event, repeats the rupture, when he signals a parting of the ways:

> For there are two heterogeneous ways of erasing the difference
> between the signifier and the signified: one, the classic way, consists
> in reducing or deriving the signifier, that is to say, ultimately in
> *submitting* the sign to thought; the other, the one we are using here
> against the first one, consists in putting into question the system in
> which the preceding reduction functioned [. . .]. (281)

At first, these two paths lead in opposite directions. The "classic way" remains naively within the centered system governed by Being: the opposition signifier and signified is collapsed such that the signifier is the natural expression of an unchanging signified, and language is a transparent window on experience, a direct translation of thought. Lévi-Strauss goes the "other way": signifieds become signifiers indicating other signifieds which in turn signify, extending a chain of substitutions that produces meaning endlessly. The problem is that this erasure of the opposition—signifiers and signifieds are no longer regarded as essentially different from one another—still depends on the distinction signifier/signified. The opposition is both indispensable and indefensible.[25] If Lévi-Strauss questions the opposition sensible/intelligible that is the premiss for this distinction, the paradox Derrida signals is that in order to critique the concept of sign, we cannot simply do without the opposition that determines it: "the metaphysical reduction of the sign needed the opposition it was reducing" (281). The "other way"—which remains otherwise unnamed—joins up with the classic way: one questions, one doesn't, but neither lead outside the metaphysical labyrinth.

Derrida identifies himself with this "other way"—"the one we are using here"—for he too is questioning a structure, reflecting not only on the structurality of structure but going one step further, focusing on the formation in which the thinking of structurality occurs: we could call it the eventuality of the event. The paradoxes of his own project start to become clear. Derrida revisits the opposition before/after, metaphysics/destruction of metaphysics, in order to undo it, in order to show how one term doubles back on the other. However Derrida's "redoubling" or revisiting depends on the rupture it undermines. It depends on the possibility of identifying the "event" of breaking away from metaphysics.

"But there are several ways of being caught in this circle" (281) writes Derrida towards the end of the introduction, and it is these ways within ways that occupy his attention for the rest of the text. We have seen that the first bifurcation is no definitive split: the "other way" intersects with the classic at a crossroads of compromise. But Derrida follows this other way, mindful of its treacherous tendency to snake back upon itself, and identifies further forks along the way. More choices need to be made, for although they are all ultimately circular, the ways of travelling the "other way" are not all "of equal pertinence" (282); they may be "more or less naive" (281), more or less able to formulate the paradox of their predicament.

To mark his way among these ways, Derrida linearizes the labyrinth. But when there is no door (exit or origin) on which to fasten your line, when you have no option but to start from where you are within the metaphysical maze, the choice is great indeed. Before him he finds a number of threads—trails left by the trail-blazers, by those who came to slay metaphysics and whose names he cites. If Derrida chooses Lévi-Strauss "as an example" (282), he is in fact choosing to examine "a certain choice" (282) in the work of the ethnographer, a way of dealing with forks and binary divisions that is elaborated in a *"more or less explicit manner"* (282, original emphasis). But which is it—more or less? Derrida decides to "follow this movement" by choosing "one guiding thread among others" (282), the nature/culture opposition. Very quickly, however, the thread combs out into two strands. . . .

The prohibition of incest—apparently cultural *and* universal—puts the opposition in doubt, and with it, "the whole of philosophical conceptualization, which is systematic with the nature/culture opposition" (283-284). Derrida arrives at another bifurcation: the critique necessitated by such an example ("only one among others" 284) "may be undertaken along two paths, in two 'manners'" (284). On the one hand (the one strand), there is the "daring" way—"systematically and rigorously" questioning the concepts and the history of the opposition (284). This is "the beginnings of a step outside of philosophy" (284). But as we saw in the previous chapter, to question a structure with structured thought is to perpetuate the structure. Woe betide those who claim to take this step, to slay metaphysics and escape from the labyrinth. The Thesean model is deceptive, for the first words uttered by would-be heroes dispel the illusion of salvation and plunge them back into metaphysics: they are "swallowed up" (284)[26] in true mythological style, disappearing into the "body" (284)—the bowels?—of a discourse that is not easily killed off. The daring has a tendency towards the reckless. This is the path of the engineer, who claims to construct an entirely new edifice, to build a new language "out of nothing," to "break" the thread of classic discourse, but who has no choice but to construct from the materials already available (285). The engineer doesn't so much escape the labyrinth as rebuild it. What appears to be outside is always-already inside. What seems new and other is revealed to be more of the same.

Then there is the "other choice" (284), Lévi-Strauss', which consists in "conserving" concepts such as the nature/culture opposition whilst "denouncing" them, "treating them as tools which can still be used" (284), which can even be used against themselves. "Lévi-Strauss simultaneously has experienced the necessity of utilizing this opposition and the impossibility of accepting it" (283). This is not mere self-contradiction, an error of judgment or of logic but rather a calculated tactic. This is the path of the *bricoleur*, the handyperson who tinkers with the existing structure using "the means at hand" (285), recycling and adapting it, transforming it from within, and maybe weakening the structure of the labyrinth in the process.[27] For the metaphysical maze perhaps conceals the means of its own subversion: classic concepts "are employed to destroy the old machinery to which they belong and of which they themselves are pieces" (284). The reuse of the same old concepts is revealed as potentially and paradoxically new. What appears to be inside and part of the maze may simultaneously escape it.

This bifurcation (engineer/*bricoleur*) has parallels with the first one we saw: "daring" and "other" is not unlike "classic" and "other." The classic way—the sacrificial route—naively accepted metaphysical structures as unquestionable absolutes, whilst the other way attempted to destroy them. This second path has now split into "daring" and "other," but the daring, heroic route seems naively so, unquestioning of its own powers and caught in a circle that links up with the classic *en route*. Apparent opposites thus blur. Radical and classical are wound together into a double-stranded thread: blithely attacking (classically radical) and blithely accepting the philosophical *status quo* (radically classical) are both ways that provide sustenance for the metaphysical minotaur. Food for thought. The "other choice," on the other hand, is not a choice of one way over another. Neither is it "on the other hand," but rather a case of using both hands to hold on to both strands, of choosing not to choose. *Bricolage* recognizes and assumes the ambivalence of its way(s). Also double-stranded, the "other choice" twists apart, pulls in different directions simultaneously. Not naively but "in a *more or less explicit manner*" (but is it explicit or not? or both at once?). And at least one of those directions is spun in with the classic way, partially rehearsing it. Lévi-Strauss' discourse, for instance, conserves the notion of rupture — by defining the *bricoleur* in opposition to the engineer — while denouncing the same notion in the engineer's claims. For the *bricoleur* at first appears to be distinct from the engineer, but then we find that the latter is a myth, merely a *bricoleur* in all but name. More seriously, the engineer seems to be "a myth produced by the *bricoleur*" (285), that is to say, *bricolage* is dependent on the dubious notion of the engineer in order to define its practice. The idea of *bricolage* is itself a *bricolage*.[28] There is always a redoubling; the opposition is never clear-cut. The "other choice," then, does not lead in a different direction: it doubles the "daring" path, but wittingly so, more or less explicitly so. It reflects upon it. And reflects it.

Derrida's "guiding thread" thus turns out to be a twist of several strands, leading him nonetheless to "the second thread which might guide us in what is being contrived [woven — *ce qui se trame*] here" (285). The second thread is the double status of *bricolage* as both an intellectual and a mythopoetical activity. Lévi-Strauss' ethnographical discourse is also mythopoetical in that it reflects its object — myth. Derrida remarks on "a few key points" (286). Of course there are two. The first concerns the decentering of the reference myth. Lévi-Strauss is quoted: "'I could, therefore, have legitimately taken as my starting point any one representative myth of the group.'" (286). We hear the echo of Derrida's statements concerning his choice of corpus, whereby the work of Lévi-Strauss and the particular aspects of interest are merely examples among others, chosen at random and not privileged examples. They do not constitute a fixed origin or reference point, and are open to the play of substitutions. The second point concerns the discourse on myth: if there is not only no central myth but no center to myth — no unity or absolute source — then the discourse on myth must also renounce those principles by which it seeks to ground, center and unify myth. Summarizing Lévi-Strauss, Derrida writes: "[. . .] structural discourse on myths — *mythological* discourse — must itself be *mythomorphic*. It must have the form of that of which it speaks" (286). As if by chance, these two key points are found at the very half-way point of Derrida's text. But rather than a central source, they function as a mirror, an axis of reflection and a point of infinite regress, for "Structure, Sign and Play" too, as a discourse on the discourse on myth, is mythomorphic. And as an analysis of rupture and redoubling in binary oppositions, it repeatedly both mimes and undermines (undermimes?) the oppositional structure. More or less explicitly. Derrida treats the reader to a lengthy quotation of Lévi-Strauss including the following:

> There is no real end to methodological analysis, no hidden unity to be grasped once the breaking-down process has been completed. Themes can be split up *ad infinitum* [*se dédoublent à l'infini*]. Just when you think you have disentangled and separated them, you realize that they are knitting together again in response to the operation of unexpected affinities. (287)

"Structure, Sign and Play" can be read as a writing out of the untwining and twining. It has the form of that of which it speaks. This mythopoetical style of discourse, which Derrida adopts to some extent, is *opposed* to a philosophical/epistemological discourse which reaches for a center, a source, unity, for illusory/elusive absolutes and answers. The "second thread" splits, but once again, privileging one strand over another, claiming to break cleanly from philosophical discourse to embrace the mythopoetical, is less easy than it may appear, is indeed naive. The "necessity" of breaking with philosophical discourse is accompanied by "risks" (287). The risk of mythomorphic discourse is that—because it cannot cease to use metaphysical concepts—it may be taken for poor philosophy, for philosophical naivety, for a lesser fellow traveller on the classic rather than the "other way." As the fibres twist together, the philosophical and the mythopoetical become difficult to tell apart. But then again, trying to separate them out, wanting to choose between them, gambling on one rather than the other is a losing game. Should we abandon the idea? Can we? If there is no central, privileged discourse, and if no discourse escapes metaphysics, then, Derrida asks, "are all discourses on myths equivalent?" (287). He admits that the question of choice is a "classic" one—seeking a yardstick, an epistemological standard by which to measure discourse—"a classic, but inevitable question" (288). For in order to compare classic and other, daring and other, engineer and *bricoleur*, the philosophical and the mythopoetical, he has had to assume that the ways of being caught, of being trapped into accepting what we denounce, are not all "of equal pertinence" (282).[29] *More or less explicitly*, Derrida suggests that an awareness and a critique of the paradoxes of one's own practice mean that one can be caught without being caught out.

Back to the labyrinth. Not that we ever left it. The ways are all more or less circular. No passage leads to an exit. Derrida: "What I want to emphasize is simply that the passage beyond philosophy does not consist in turning the page of philosophy [. . .], but in continuing to read philosophers *in a certain way*" (288). Another way? A way that is perhaps "certain" this time? Unlikely. Not which way (thread, path) to follow (all lead to each other) but which way (manner) to follow a thread (any one of many). To show us the way, Derrida takes a detour. Having looked at the sign, the prohibition of incest, the *bricoleur*, the discourse on myth, he substitutes yet another "example": the idea of totalization, the attempt to make an exhaustive inventory of myths. There are of course "two ways of conceiving the limit of totalization," both of which "coexist implicitly in Lévi-Strauss' discourse" (289). Totalization can be defined classically as empirically "impossible": there are just too many myths, or they are too difficult to collect. Or — "another way" — totalization can be defined as "useless": the search for an integral account of the myths of a living culture is meaningless. Meaningless because the nature of the playing field is such that "instead of being an inexhaustible field, [. . .] instead of being too large, there is something missing from it: a center which arrests and grounds the play of substitutions" (289). The play of shifting myths takes the place of the (missing) stabilizing center, the absolute presence or essence of a culture.

We are circling once again around the rupture/redoubling between centered and decentered thought, but not choosing between (and as we shall see in the following section, the only check on this circling is ultimately an ethical one). Derrida describes the coexistence of the two as "the movement of *supplementarity*" (289), an undecidable, for "supplement" can indicate both a surplus (more myths, extra) and an inadequacy (something added to take the place of what is lacking).[30] And "it is not by chance that [Lévi-Strauss] uses this word twice," using the "two directions of meaning" (289). The undecidable is a way of keeping both choices in play. Or should we say, of choosing to keep both choices in play.

Following the thread of play in Lévi-Strauss' work, we find that it "is always caught up in tension" (290). We might suspect that the tension has something to do with being pulled in two directions — classic and other. But in fact it is slightly more complicated than that because there are two sorts of tension, each tugging from two sides. The dividing line divides again. The tension with history is "a classical problem" (290). Lévi-Strauss treats history as complicitous with metaphysics, with a centered philosophy of Being-as-presence. But in his structuralist attempt to bracket or neutralize history, he falls into the trap of isolating a particular moment of presence and accepting a notion of absolute rupture. A complete break with the past requires the concepts of chance and discontinuity to explain transformations and to "replace" history in determining origins. Which is rather little like choosing examples at random or starting from wherever we find ourselves. The attempt to eliminate an origin, a center and presence, leads to "the necessity of non-necessity" (OG 259), "an essential accident" (OG 200). Chance ceases to be arbitrary. What Derrida shows is the breakdown of any clear opposition between the haphazard and the determined. While appearing to be chosen at random, the example becomes exemplary. And when it is not only one element in a chain of substitutions but describes the chain itself and becomes a *mise en abyme* of the text, then "This object among others is not just any object" (PC 391).[31]

The second tension is that between play and presence. "Play is the disruption of presence" (WD 292): the central and centering notion of essential Being is momentarily dislodged, as signifieds/signifiers shift and substitute for each other. However "play is always play of absence and presence" (292). In other words, it depends on the concept it denounces; the opposition presence/absence is what makes play possible. But there are two ways of conceiving this relation, and this is only one of them, the classic way. The radical way would be to conceive of play as preceding the binary opposition and making it possible: "Being must be conceived as presence or absence on the basis of the possibility of play and not the other way around" (292). Presence and absence would no longer be seen as mutually exclusive absolutes but conceived together as an alternative produced by play.[32] This rethinking of play such that it produces the oppositional structure as an effect would similarly "announce [. . .] the unity of chance and necessity" (MP 7).[33] These ways correspond to "two interpretations of interpretation," one classic, nostalgic, that "dreams of deciphering a truth or an origin which escapes play" (WD 292), the other joyous, not seeing decentering as a *loss* of center but affirming "a world of signs without fault, without truth, and without origin which is offered to an active interpretation" (292).[34] The two may be irreconcilable but are also inseparable. Like the masks of the theatre they can only be distinguished in terms of the two "sides" (292) or faces of play.

Rather than encouraging us towards the joyous "other" interpretation, Derrida cautions against choosing, for reasons that should be clear by now. Selecting one way over another is hardly a momentous decision and only seems to lead back to the path abandoned, so "the category of choice seems particularly trivial" (293).[35] Not that we can escape choice. The other possibility (the *other?*—but we are immediately caught again . . . choosing against choosing is still a choice) is to "try to conceive of the common ground, and the *différance* of this irreducible difference" (293). This is like holding the two strands as one thread, seeing the two contrary terms of a binary opposition as complicitous, produced together, as having something in common, sharing a relation of *différance*.[36]

Naturally this yarn ends with a monster—an "unnameable" "monstrosity" (293)—but a monster unlike the one we came to slay before escaping from the labyrinth. The "other way," which largely escaped naming by hovering between categories and reproducing aspects of opposing terms, is a way of thinking two ways at once. Or— another way—a way of thinking two ways together before they become two. Unthinkable? Monstrous and unnameable because it has no recognized form or name that corresponds to categories we know, rupturing with established questions and not yet recaptured, the provisionally named *différance* appears in the last paragraph of the text, where the risk of recuperation is slight but only because very little will be said.[37] We need not suppose that we will be able to simply do without the structure of the binary opposition that *différance* calls into question. We need not suppose that we will not be obliged to choose.

Seeking to slay the minotaur and escape the labyrinth is akin to the idea of "turning the page of philosophy" (288) to pass beyond it. If Derrida suggests that we need rather to continue to "read philosophers in a certain way" (288), then we also need to reinterpret the labyrinth and indeed its inhabitant. After all, what swallows up the daring hero is less often the minotaur than the maze itself, which has no exit and where each fork—each binary opposition—imposes a choice that turns out to be no choice at all. If we necessarily remain to some extent exiles in the labyrinth, dreaming of an unattainable outside of metaphysics, perhaps we can also use the maze against itself, mount our resistance from within the catacombs, using the tensions that support it such that sections collapse under their own weight. And the model for mastering the maze is perhaps to be found within it: neither beast nor man, both beast and man, the minotaur is the image of the undecidable, of the monstrous nonspecies that precedes the alternative. While we stalk it, we could perhaps adopt its monstrousness. How better to follow two paths at once than as some sort of bicephalous monstrosity? Both/neither philosophy and/nor myth, conserving/denouncing classic concepts. More or less explicitly. Vigilantly.[38] Of course this way is far from certain, but with this double game, although we can never entirely escape metaphysics, there is a chance that in going two ways at once— riding on the horns of the dilemma—we may not be entirely caught.

Doubling Back: Revisiting Undecidability

Rather than a step forward, a quick step back. Another complication to the labyrinth. But then, as Derrida has remarked, "If things were simple, word would have gotten around" (LI 119). It is worth noting a change of emphasis in Derrida's work on the undecidable over the years. Of course, this "change" is a doubling back, a revisiting of the notion such that it acquires another value in Derrida's writings.

In his earlier texts, of which "Structure, Sign and Play" is one, Derrida focuses strategically on the undecidable as that which resists the binary opposition and the dialectic. But choosing not to choose is still a choice, and so by *resisting*, by working *anti*-dialectically, the undecidable remains (at least partially) caught in a dialectical opposition. This leads to a further level of undecidability between *différance* and opposition, between the undecidable and the dialectic: "A certain undecidability of the fetish lets us oscillate between a dialectics (of the undecidable and the dialectical) or an undecidability (between the dialectical and the undecidable)" (*Glas* 207).

However the imperative to choose is not lightly dismissed, and in his later texts (from the mid-1980s onwards), Derrida is more concerned with the ethical responsibility to choose. We must make a decision despite the fact that any "pure" choice is impossible, despite the fact that right and wrong, ethical and unethical are never neatly separable from each other. Derrida's vocabulary shifts from that of choice to that of judgment. He recognizes that his earlier work on undecidability could be considered as a "strategy of reservation with regard to judgment in all its forms."[39] And so he insists that undecidability must not be used as an "alibi for staying out of juridico-political battles" (FL 28). Rather, the undecidable "calls for decision in the order of ethical-political responsibility. It is even its necessary condition. [. . .] There can be no moral or political responsibility without this trial and this passage by way of the undecidable."[40] This ordeal, although it must "give itself up to the impossible decision," is not however surmounted or resolved by the decision: it "is never past or passed" (FL 24).[41]

We can see that there is no radical discontinuity between "Structure, Sign and Play" and the argument for decision in the face of undecidability. The decision that is urged is not a solution. It does not tie up the loose threads and indicates no exit from the maze. For every choice has strings attached. Throughout Derrida's texts, decision has always been shown to be both necessary and necessarily inconclusive, both imperative and impossible. In other words, a double bind. In the revisiting of undecidability, however, the emphasis has shifted from one constraint to the other.

Différance

> *"It divides the dividing-line and its unity at once."* (LI 70)

The Derridean dividing line is thus not a demarcation line: it splits and splits again; the strands are spun apart and then together, and weave in with other threads.[42] What is the relation between the strands? Each time that Derrida starts to pull apart an opposition, be it same/other, classic/radical, engineer/*bricoleur*, inside/outside, nostalgia/affirmation, he finds that one term cannot exist without the other, that the radical is supplemented by the classic, that even the classic is not absolute but carries the possibility of its own destruction. As Derrida writes elsewhere, "the word *supplement* seems to account for the strange unity of these two gestures" (OG 144). United opposites: this is a way of rethinking the whole structure of the binary opposition, seeing the terms as generated simultaneously as a product or an effect of the same imperative. But supplementarity, play, and *différance* are just a few of a series of possible names that runs through his texts.[43] They substitute for each other. And as they are not quite synonymous, no one term is central and governs the chain.

In trying to describe the nature of *différance*, Derrida finds it considerably easier to state what it is not than what it is: "neither a word nor a concept" (MP 3), it "*is not*, does not exist, [. . .] has neither existence nor essence" (6); it is "neither simply active nor simply passive" (9), and "is no more an effect than it has a cause" (12). He indicates it as "unthinkable" (19), "unnameable" (26), for any words used to describe it already involve concepts like being and presence that it seeks to undermine. But as we saw in Chapter 1, Derrida does not resign himself to silence before the unnameable and attempts "a simple and approximate semantic analysis" (7) of *différance* to indicate what is at stake. In one of his most affirmative (and therefore riskiest) statements, he proposes that in classical terms, *différance* would be seen as a "process of scission and division," whereby "different things or differences" would be constituted as "products" or "effects" (MP 9, tr. mod.). The word "effects" can be understood here not only in the sense of consequences but also of impressions (as in sound effects, special effects) and even illusions.

The binary opposition classic/other is but one example of such an effect: as a product of *différance*, the complicity of the terms is seen to be no accident, no mere ambiguity, but a structural necessity. But Derrida also turns his attention to speech/ writing, inside/outside, nature/culture, presence/absence, space/time, original/simulacrum, signified/signifier, positive/negative, passive/active, oppositions which collaborate in underpinning a certain philosophy—the one that happens to be available to us. In each case, terms that appear to draw apart are shown to lean on one another. The movement of supplementarity (the supplement of the classic way that makes the radical thinkable, the trace of radicality that allows the classic way to renew itself) means that the poles are interdependent and even reversible. "the positive (is) the negative, life (is) death, presence (is) absence" (OG 246).

> Thus one could reconsider all the pairs of opposites on which philosophy is constructed and on which our discourse lives, not in order to see opposition erase itself but to see what indicates that each of the terms must appear as the *différance* of the other, as the other different and deferred in the economy of the same [. . .]. (MP 17)

There is thus a point at which any binary opposition, no matter how "apparently rigorous and irreducible," comes to be seen as a "theoretical fiction" (MP 18).[44] Although there always appear to be two separate paths, ultimately this is an illusion.[45]

It is not simply the binary opposition, however, that becomes unstuck: sameness too can be seen as an effect of the play of *différance*. We habitually think of repetition as more of the same, but repetition in

"Structure, Sign and Play"—whether it be rereading philosophy, rethinking structure, reusing a concept or revisiting the classic path—is regularly shown to make a difference, even if not a radical one. Even the most faithful (classic) repetition never manages to be absolutely identical: "Once the book is repeated, its identification with itself gathers an imperceptible difference [. . .]. This exit from the identical into the same remains very slight" (WD 295). For Derrida it is this slight split made possible by repetition that allows him to prise philosophy open and glimpse what escapes it: "an imperceptible difference which permits us efficaciously, rigorously, that is, discreetly, to exit from closure" (WD 295). This vigilant style of repetition, which he examines and rehearses throughout "Structure, Sign and Play," opens classic concepts and marks them with a double mark: "every concept necessarily receives two similar marks—a repetition without identity—one mark inside and the other outside the deconstructed system" (Dis 4). What appears to be a unified concept is shown to be equivocal, giving rise to a double reading. The relation between these two marks (inside/outside, conserving/denouncing) is, as we have seen, one of supplementarity and *différance*. Difference and repetition, opposition and sameness, therefore no longer constitute separate or separable categories. The very notions of same and different become suspect: "on the basis of this unfolding of the same as *différance*, we see announced the sameness of difference and repetition in the eternal return" (MP 17, tr. mod.). In Derrida's writing, opposition and imitation cease to be opposed to one other: this second degree opposition is necessarily deconstructed. Both are forms of repetition. Both are constituted by the movement of supplementarity, as difference effects.

Repetition can be taken a step further, for since any apparent unity is susceptible to repetition as its condition of possibility, there is no undivided or indivisible unity. Unity?—just an effect, an impression, an illusion, with about the same probability of existence as the unicorn.[46] What appears unique and unified "is not what it is, identical and identical to itself, unique, unless it *adds to itself* the possibility of being *repeated* as such" (Dis 168).[47] *Différance* thus generates not only the binary opposition and the double but also determines oneness—even the supposed unity and identity of the apparently indivisible and self-present individual: "the subject is constituted only in being divided from itself" (Pos 29).

Not only the subject but the present moment is not present to itself. Rather it is always related to a past or future, always carrying the trace of a past or becoming the trace of the past for a future present: "An interval must separate the present from what it is not in order for the present to be itself, but this interval that constitutes it as present must, by the same token, divide the present in and of itself" (MP 13). This interval of *différance* constitutes what we think of as the singular moment of presence. The supposedly singular is always-already divided. And for Derrida, the movement producing apparent unity is the same movement as that which generates binary oppositions.[48]

The same movement, but not a singular or unique one. In order to count as the same, *différance* works (plays?) repeatedly, unceasingly. The repetition allows us to think of *différance* too as receiving a double mark, as "play" does in "Structure, Sign and Play": simultaneously recuperable by metaphysics and partially escaping it. In other words, we cannot account for this process without trying to imagine the *différance* of *différance*, the play of play, the "trace of the trace" (MP 24).

The dividing line we followed through "Structure, Sign and Play," the thread that split into strands, the strands that spun together without fusing, can thus be seen as the trace of a movement that generates a non-oppositional, non-unifying relation. Whereas we might conceive of a labyrinth as paths leading away from each other and separated by walls, Derrida invites us to understand the partitioning in different terms, as a gap that appears to separate . . . and then disappears to join terms together. An effect of a movement. The difference or deferral that, for Derrida, separates two terms or paths while knitting them together, is a sort of "limit between" that is not a clear boundary. Produced by a movement—a change in position that takes time—it tends to be represented as an interval in space and/or time: a distance, a separation, a detour, a delay, a relay, a reserve (cf. MP 8, 18). Constituted between the dimensions of space and time, it is not anchored to either one of them: *différance* is conceived in terms of *spacing* (the becoming-space of time) and *temporization* (the becoming-time of space, cf. MP 8, 13). The interval of repetition—the moment that separates two instances—opens up a space of differentiation (spacing). And as we saw with classic and radical, the apparent distinction between two opposed terms becomes the interval of deferral between two moments, a revisiting of the same (temporization). The interval appears and gives the effect of an opposition and disappears to give the impression of unity. It has no tangible existence: "This barely existing limit, exceeded as soon as it is posited, is already no more what it is yet and does not even give time to think its time" (*Glas* 220). If it takes place ("What takes place is only the between [*entre*], the place, the spacing, which is nothing," Dis 214), it is neither a place nor a moment but hovers between, fleeting, like movement itself, or like Derrida's image of the fan that unfolds and folds up, conjuring up a space that vanishes.[49] The "strange space [. . .] *between*" is inaudible, invisible and inaccessible (MP 5) without however being absent or hidden (which would only mean hidden somewhere, present elsewhere). Indeed the interval is nothing without even being that. Rather it occupies the impossible space of a contradiction: traceable only through its effects, it is both perceptible and imperceptible (MP 24).

Other representations? They are all similarly impalpable. The limit in question is perhaps a gap, but then again, perhaps not: "the crack between the two is nothing" (*Glas* 207); "the nothing which prevents them from coming together" (WD 164). Perhaps a fold, but one that folds and folds again upon itself (cf. Dis 259). Or a blank ("the regular intervention of the blanks, [. . .] the law of spacing" Dis 178), but a blank within a blank (Dis 265). A margin, not around but between — "an interior margin between two supplementary columns that seem detached from one another" (*Glas* 238) — and not unified but itself divided such that a text is "marked in its interior by the multiple furrow of its margin" (MP 24). The *entre* or between is also an *antre*, a cave or grotto, a hollow space (Dis 212), and an abyss [*abîme*] (Dis 265). The list might start to resemble a thematics of emptiness or of absence if Derrida did not insist upon the "abyssal" function of the interval of *différance* (Dis 230-277, esp. 265). *Différance* does not escape *différance*: the limit is repeated, is *mise en abyme*. The abyss of the abyss, the margin within the margin, the refolded fold make it impossible to give the blank a constant value. The interval that produces the interval partly escapes phenomenology.[50]

A slightly more tangible limit between is the membrane (Dis 213), rather fragile and diaphanous but perhaps a barrier nonetheless. "The Double Session," which in its opening paragraphs raises into capitals the question of a "between," is scattered with such partitions: hymen, veil, screen, curtain. But not only delicate, their partitioning is questionable. The hymen, for example (one example from many), with its double meaning, both is and isn't a barrier and is destroyed in its realization. As vaginal membrane, it constitutes a limit and grounds a series of distinctions: outside/inside, virgin/non-virgin, desire/satisfaction. But as marriage, it denies this limit and represents union and fusion.[51] And traditionally this Hymen is consummated by breaking the hymen. Signifying both virginity and marriage, both a boundary and its elimination, the hymen is undecidable: it "*both* sows confusion *between* opposites *and* stands *between* the opposites 'at once'" (Dis 212). Between two betweens, the hymen is both limit and passage. However as such it doesn't constitute a third half-way term of synthesis, a sort of permeable filter, but rather a *mise en abyme* of the between.

Différance, trace, supplement, *pharmakon*: we may choose at random from Derrida's texts and follow any one of a number of threads. In each case, we learn that the partitions of the labyrinth are not solid walls, that the limit between contraries, or between copies, or between contraries and copies, is more like a gap or membrane, and is no sooner established as an effect than abolished as an illusion. Very disorienting of course for a modern-day Theseus. But perhaps also what allows Derrida not to comply unfailingly with the rules of the metaphysical maze and enables him to avoid *simply* submitting to the imperative to choose.

Classic maze management would have us believe that the best way to find a solution—or at least keep one's bearings—is systematically to turn left. The practice has often been favoured in intellectual circles, where the political left was long seen as leading the way. Derrida's refusal to take the left fork as if it could be definitively separated from the right has earned him criticism on many occasions and was indeed the precipitating factor in his break with the *Tel Quel* group. He has regularly been accused of neutrality, by Kristeva among others. Whether his "vigilant practice of textual division" (Pos 36) can be considered neutral is a debate of importance that will be staged in Part II. For the moment, let us envisage a way of following left and right paths as they cross over, become indistinguishable, and separate out again. As each path splinters and regroups, supplemented by its other, in a landscape of interlocking ways, divided not by walls but by time and place, moment and space.

*

JUXTAPOSITIONS

"like the whole of the text, ciphered to the second power" (Dis 240)

Having held the two analyses in this chapter apart until now, the fiction of separation is over. Two tales of rupture and coupling have been told, but the juxtaposition of the two draws attention to questions addressed by both. A dividing line — a way of understanding difference — has been traced in each case, but between these lines, parallels and discontinuities, intersections and divergences are starting to appear.

Time to take stock. Before any attempt to establish a relation between the theories of Derrida and Kristeva, to hinge them together, there is a need to clarify the issues at stake, by explicitly focusing on the points where the tales meet and part. Firstly, it should be clear that neither dividing line is straight, neither is single or continuous, and neither cuts cleanly into two. Through the tangles and pockets they form, both ways of dividing produce pairs that problematize some powerful figures, namely:

1. Unity. There is no unity as such. Any apparent unity is always-already divided. Kristeva shows that the speaking subject—that being we call "I"—is split by the relation between the symbolic and the semiotic modes. Derrida also argues against the idea of indivisible unity. In order for something to be identical to itself, it must be repeatable, and repetition allows a mark of difference to intervene, dividing it from itself.

2. The binary opposition of discrete categories. Although pairs abound, they are never composed of two separate, clearly distinguished terms that could be set up in simple opposition. The classic and the radical in Derrida's analysis each depend on, supplement and incorporate the other. Kristeva's semiotic and symbolic modes are equally inextricable: neither exists in any pure state; each manifests aspects of the functioning of the other. Their opposition does not require a disjunction between them. Kristeva could only endorse Derrida's statement that "the simple alternative of two opposite forces [. . .] within a homogeneous field cannot account for the internal and displaced division of each force" (*Glas* 97).

3. A third term of synthesis. If Kristeva draws on the Hegelian inseparability of contraries in elaborating her dialectic, she rejects their resolution into a third term of synthesis: the struggle and exchange between the semiotic and the symbolic are ceaseless, unresolvable. In

Derrida's texts, any apparently third term is shown to be a *mise en abyme* of the pair, an undecidable—*both/and* and/or *neither/nor*.

Traversing and undermining 1, 2 and 3, the Derridean and Kristevan dividing lines supplant these figures with that of the double. The pair of inseparable terms hovers between the numbers one and two as a divided unity or a double identity. These doubles, however, do not quite coincide: Kristevan ambiguity and Derridean undecidability may be a mismatched pair. If contraries are complicitous in both theories, they do not appear to usurp each other to the same extent. Whereas Derridean poles reverse such that one term is seen to be a deferred moment of its apparent contrary, the Kristevan modalities each hold their ground against invasion or annexation by the other. The semiotic and the symbolic may well be interlinked; they nonetheless constitute "two heterogeneous realms" (RPL 48), radically foreign to one another. Although oppositions within each domain may be reversible (charges and stases in the semiotic, subject and predicate in the symbolic), the mutual alterity of the semiotic and the symbolic is such that the two can never be confused. Although they influence each other, even mimic each other in some respects, they are not interchangeable: the ordering of the *chora* cannot substitute for symbolic law; the work of syntax cannot substitute for that of drives. Or rather, when these confusions occur, the consequences for the subject are serious.[52] The thetic threshold between the semiotic and the symbolic is not crossed with impunity.

Confusion between contraries and the substitution of one term for another are, however, precisely what happen to the Derridean pair: "through a systematic indecision, the parties and the party lines frequently exchange their respective places, imitating the forms and borrowing the paths of the opponent" (Dis 108). Opposition is shown to be structurally indistinguishable from other forms of difference—or indeed of sameness—such as the relation between copies, or between repeated acts, or between two encounters with the same object. Nostalgia and anticipation may be two ways of traveling . . . or two moments of the same trip. Opposition and identity are not poles apart: identity inhabits opposition; alterity makes resemblance possible.

The representations of the divide between terms diverge in an interesting way. Kristeva's thetic threshold is a resistant boundary, a "barrier of meaning" (RPL 104) across which the semiotic attacks the symbolic and the symbolic attempts to impose its law on the semiotic. Although the semiotic "constantly tears it open" (62) or washes through it, this frontier remains functional and makes itself felt. It may be transgressed endlessly but not effortlessly. In the form of syntactic negation, it serves "as the strongest breakwater [*barrage*] for protecting the unity of the subject and offers the most tenacious resistance" to the "shattering" of communicative language under the attack of drives (124-125). Its relative stability is crucial to the dialectical process of *signifiance*, which

> [. . .] is always produced with reference to a moment of stasis, a boundary, a symbolic barrier. Without this temporary resistance, which is viewed as if it were insurmountable, the process would never become a practice and would founder instead [. . .]. (RPL 102)

In her later work, Kristeva describes the way in which the subject can sink into abjection (*Powers of Horror*) or irrepresentable depression (*Black Sun*) without this protective resistance.

The Derridean divide, on the other hand, takes the form of an interval, and all it seems to resist is approach as it shifts without warning from a gap in space to a gap in time or even disappears altogether to give the illusion of identity. It is no barrier but is produced by the "play of limit/passage" (MP xvi), alternating between separation and circulation. And when the limit does appear as a line, it is a far cry from Kristeva's front line of "permanent struggle [*combat*]" (RPL 81). Instead, it is *oblique*, as Derrida demonstrates in "Tympan" (MP) and "The Double Session," yielding to pressure, minimizing friction. Thus if there is encounter—and it is not at all clear that there is—it can hardly take the form of violent confrontation. Derrida proposes the figure of the oblique so as to "avoid frontal and symmetrical protest, opposition in all the forms of *anti-*" (MP xv). The Kristevan dialectic, on the other hand, although it is not symmetrical and is distinguished from opposition in the form of simple negation by the heterogeneity of its terms, is a head-on clash in RPL and a fiery one at that. But if Derrida avoids confrontation, he does not renounce all forms of transgression or indeed of conflict. In fact he insists on "the irreducibly *conflictual* character of *différance*" due to "the *alterity* inscribed within it" (Pos 101 n15, original emphasis). This conflict, however, is no struggle to the death, no face-to-face confrontation as we find in Kristeva's theory but rather the product of a *décalage*—a lag or a gap. It is the mismatch of halves that can never claim to form a whole, the discrepancy between two instances of taking the same path such that it seems to go in different directions, the internal strife occasioned by the supplement of the classic that separates the radical way from itself, an "'active,' moving discord" (MP 18).

The conflict inherent in *différance* is what prevents it from subsiding into unity or synthesis, as the following definition makes clear: *différance* is "a 'productive,' conflictual movement which cannot be preceded by any identity, any unity, or any original simplicity; which cannot be 'relieved' [*relevé*], resolved, or appeased by any philosophical dialectic" (Dis 6-7). The relation between *différance* and a dialectical movement is what is at issue here, not only with regard to the resolution into synthesis but also with respect to the contradiction of contraries. Derrida explicitly distinguishes "the conflictuality of *différance*" from the Hegelian concept of dialectical contradiction (Pos 44) that Kristeva apparently embraces, however we shall see in the following chapter that turning this distinction into a contrast between the theories of Derrida and Kristeva is a contentious step to take.

The conflictual aspect of *différance* is not exhausted in the discord between terms. There are many passages in Derrida's texts—passages in the sense of textual extracts but also in the sense of crossings—where he writes of it as transgression (Pos 12,[53] 66, MP 12), or *renversement* (overturning as well as reversal, Pos 41, 66, Dis 6), dislocation (MP xxvi, 24, 26, Dis 233, 236), disorganization (Pos 42, Dis 7), invasion (Pos 42), disruption and explosion (Pos 45), terms reminiscent of Kristeva's descriptions of the semiotic assault on the symbolic. What is interesting here is that these disturbances can be carried out obliquely, as a shove from the side rather than as a battering across a front line. And what is shaken or dislocated in the process is not one term under attack by its other but opposition itself. This is less the shattering of a boundary to conquer the other side than a questioning of the status of the boundary as such in a "crisis of the alternative, of the binary opposition, of the *versus*" (Dis 283). In Derridean transgression, "the issue indeed is to go beyond the oppositional limit. Not only a given oppositional limit, but the very notion of the limit as a front between two opposed terms, between two identifiable terms" (PC 376).

Transgression is thus important in the work of both Kristeva and Derrida. However, whereas the Kristevan dislocation and pulverization of the thetic boundary by the semiotic leaves the confrontational structure of the opposition intact, Derridean dislocation disturbs the possibility of confrontation itself.

*

Although both the process of *signifiance* and the movement of *différance* involve double figures of always-already-divided unity, there is a difference in their elaboration which may be crucial . . . or then again may indicate no more than a difference of emphasis. In his texts, Derrida invites us to "try to conceive of the common ground" that precedes an alternative and is even the space of its possibility (WD 293). Opposition, repetition, unity and *différance* itself are all shown to function as doubles generated by and subordinated to the movement of *différance*. If two terms, two tendencies, two paths continue to appear, these are but "moments of a detour in the economy of *différance*" (MP 18), two moments of the same movement—a movement that eliminates the heterogeneity of the two.[54]

In Kristeva's texts, however, it is the heterogeneity of the two terms that dominates. The semiotic and the symbolic give rise to a whole range of signifying practices—from the four described RPL 90-106 to those of abjection, love, melancholy and revolt in Kristeva's later work. All these variations are produced by "the different modes of articulation" of the two modalities (RPL 24). The process of *signifiance* is generated through the dialectic between the semiotic and the symbolic; it is dependent on their resistance to one another, whether in the form of the "permanent struggle" (RPL 81) or the "permanent stabilization-destabilization between the *symbolic* [. . .] and the *semiotic*" (TL 16).

A movement dependent upon the opposition that produces it (Kristeva) . . . or opposition in general subordinated to a movement that produces it (Derrida): is this a radical difference or a difference of emphasis? We could ask the same question about the other distinctions made in these last few pages and arising from the juxtaposition of the two analyses:

- a substitution of terms that causes problems / a systematic confusion of contraries;
- a barrier that partially resists attack / an oblique limit that gives way;
- a contradiction between terms / a conflictual, discordant relation;
- the transgression of an opposition / the transgression of opposition as such.

Do these distinctions constitute heterogeneous theories, or two paths that join up, two ways of visiting the same problem, one a deferred moment of the other?

Between One and Two, the double. But between two doubles (here two double practices), between the process of *signifiance* and the movement of *différance*, there is another level of ambiguity/undecidability. How do the practices fit together? Two dividing lines have been traced, but where is the dividing line between them? There is of course no quick and easy answer to the question. Given that both Derrida and Kristeva theorize difference, any attempt to compare the two engages with their principal preoccupations. Which conceptions of difference could provide the basis for such a comparison? Which sort of dividing line could offer a model for the division? How should the relation between the two practices be conceived of? As a face-to-face encounter, a confrontation? Is there indeed encounter as such, or rather a gap, a hiatus? Could it be a dialectic? Or a *différance*? Should it be thought of in terms of Kristeva's work . . . or Derrida's? The articulation of the two is a question not only of subject matter but of methodology.

My work can hardly lay claim to a position outside the polemic, an independent position of impartiality midway between the two. Nor can it try to synthesize them. The positing of a third term—independent or synthetic—would deny both practices. Instead I propose to explore the nature of the 'between' from both sides of the divide, by borrowing from each practice without definitively adopting the strategies of either. Having studied each on its own terms in this chapter, let us go on to examine each of them against the grain.

NOTES

1. The translation comprises the first section of *La Révolution du langage poétique*, the section of interest to us here. Unless otherwise indicated, quotations of Kristeva in this chapter refer to RPL.

2. *Signifiance* does not correspond to the English "significance," and translators and commentators have tended to remain with the French term.

3. See notes 10 and 11 below.

4. Cf. Kelly Oliver's remark that "from her earliest writings, Kristeva has attempted to bring the semiotic body, replete with drives, back into structuralism" (*Reading Kristeva* 3).

5. Although French pronouns indicate grammatical gender rather than sex, I shall follow Kristeva's translators in indicating a masculine subject. In RPL Kristeva does not address the question of sexual difference in referring to the child and the adult subjects she studies—indeed up until the writing of *Black Sun*—are all male.

6. Oliver discusses the ambiguity of this ordering in Kristeva's work, *Reading Kristeva* 105-106.

7. The question of Kristeva's rewriting of the Hegelian dialectic deserves a volume of its own, as indeed does Derrida's, but I leave such tasks to philosophers. Several very useful readings of the relations between Derrida or Kristeva and Hegel exist, including those in Rodolphe Gasché, *The Tain of the Mirror*, John Llewelyn, *Derrida on the Threshold of Sense* and Michael Payne, *Reading Theory*. I will however venture a brief indication of the stakes involved in Kristeva's uptake of the term of negativity. Although she acknowledges her debt to Hegel (RPL 109, 112), Kristeva (like Derrida, Pos 43) explicitly refuses the Hegelian solution of synthesis (RPL 69). And (like Derrida WD 251-277) she uses the work of Bataille to critique the way in which the Hegelian dialectic recuperates negativity-expenditure-*jouissance* ("L'expérience et la pratique" PL 107-136). However, whereas Derrida is worried by the recuperation into the unity of self-presence (WD 246-247, Pos 43), Kristeva is more concerned by the way that negativity is repressed and suppressed in the unity of the concept and absolute knowing (PL 109, RPL 197) such that consciousness dominates and the possibility of the dissolving of the subject is neglected. Kristeva's rewriting of negativity is ultimately enabled by a dialectical materialist reading of Hegel through Freud (RPL 118) that allows her to envisage a force that "remains heterogeneous to logic even while producing it through a movement of separation or rejection." Such a notion of negativity is "possible because of and in spite of Hegel" (RPL 112).

8. Cf. Jacques Lacan, *Ecrits: A Selection* 1-7.

9. The paradox is already manifest in the double definition of identity: the relation between two identical objects and the sense of uniqueness of the self.

10. Although she takes up aspects of Lacanian theory, Kristeva could never be called Lacanian. The relation between her semiotic/symbolic dialectic and Lacan's tripartite structure of Real, Imaginary and Symbolic is a complex one and is analyzed carefully in Gallop, *Feminism and Psychoanalysis* and Oliver, *Reading Kristeva*. Although the two conceptions of the symbolic often seem to meet, the two elaborations of a pre-linguistic mode take rather different directions. Jane Gallop characterizes the distinction as follows: "whereas the imaginary is conservative and comforting, tends towards closure, and is disrupted by the symbolic; the semiotic is revolutionary, breaks closure, and

disrupts the symbolic" (124). It is interesting to note on the one hand the importance for Lacan of the paternal metaphor (the Name of the Father) along with the symbolic power of the signifier, and on the other hand Kristeva's emphasis on the maternal body and on the pre-symbolic forces acting on the signifier.

11. Oliver (*Reading Kristeva* 9-10, 39) argues that it is necessary to distinguish between the "Symbolic order" and a "symbolic element" within it in order to understand the way in which symbolic and semiotic cohabit the symbolic order. She maintains that Kristeva makes the distinction but uses it inconsistently. I shall argue, however, that there is no indivisible symbolic element in Kristeva's theory, only the force of symbolic organization, i.e., the order itself is the force resisting semiotic attack, an order that is constituted as already divided. Where Oliver's distinction is nonetheless helpful is in indicating Kristeva's departure from Lacan's definition of the Symbolic: Kristeva's symbolic is not only a domain but an active force opposing and traversed by the semiotic.

12. Cf. "'Art' [. . .] does not relinquish the thetic even while pulverizing it through the negativity of transgression" (69); literature "maintains both 'delirium' and 'logic'" (82).

13. Cf. note 11 above.

14. Oliver distinguishes Kristeva's imaginary from Lacan's in *Reading Kristeva* 37-39, 72-76.

15. In a more technical definition, Kristeva writes: "by *imaginary*, I mean the representation of identification strategies (introjection and projection) that mobilize the image of the body as well as the ego and the other, and that make use of primary processes (condensation and displacement)" (NMS 103). When comparing the imaginary to the symbolic and the real, Kristeva describes it as "what the Self imagines in order to sustain and expand itself" (TL 7).

16. "Julia Kristeva in Conversation with Rosalind Coward" 22.

17. "Julia Kristeva in Conversation with Rosalind Coward" 23.

18. Cf. Kristeva, *Powers of Horror*. For fuller discussions of abjection, see the relevant chapters of Elizabeth Grosz, *Sexual Subversions*, John Lechte, *Julia Kristeva* and Kelly Oliver, *Reading Kristeva*.

19. In fact, Kristeva even suggests that the pole of identification need not be a person at all—it could be the mother's work for instance. It must, however, represent something that the mother loves other than the child, something else that gives her life meaning. She says, "for me it is not absolutely necessary to call them mother or father—what is necessary is to have three terms, if you prefer call them X and Y, why not? [. . .] What is necessary for what I call the psychic space to accede to language is the existence of this distance" ("Julia

Kristeva in Conversation with Rosalind Coward" 23). Oliver pursues this question of the gendering of the imaginary father, *Reading Kristeva* 77-78.

20. Cf. TL 24-45, SNR 116-122, and Oliver's *Reading Kristeva* 69-90.

21. In a recuperative analysis, Oliver suggests that "Kristeva's imaginary father can be read as a metaphorical or *imaginary* reunion with the maternal body that takes the place of the real union with, dependence on, the maternal body." (*Reading Kristeva* 79). In fact, Oliver's argument throughout the third chapter of her book is that the imaginary father is a screen for the mother.

22. Oliver notes the parallels as she describes the shift from a theory of semiotic rejection to semiotic separation-through-identification:
Like Kristeva's earlier notion of the logic of material rejection (with which she explains how we separate ourselves from others), the logic of reduplication reproduces itself differently on different levels. Patterns are reduplicated on level after level until thresholds are crossed, the semiotic gives way to the Symbolic, biology becomes culture; but like fractals in geometry, the patterns are recognizable. What the logic of reduplication provides, which the logic of rejection did not, is a theory of identification. (*Reading Kristeva* 72-73)

23. "*Différance*," MP 1-27. On the aim of this article and its impossibility, see MP 3.

24. WD 278-293. Lecture given at Johns Hopkins University, 21 October 1966.

25. Cf. Pos 19-20.

26. They are less graphically plunged [*enfoncés*] in the original.

27. In other texts by Derrida, using a concept one denounces is termed writing "under erasure." Gayatri Spivak explains this term in her Translator's Preface to OG.

28. Cf. OG 139.

29. Cf. "all *bricolages* are not equally worthwhile" (OG 139).

30. Cf. OG 144-145 and *passim*.

31. Cf. OG 163. The paradox of the example is explored at length in OG, from the Preface onwards.

32. Cf. OG 244.

33. Cf. Dis 277.

34. The "two interpretations of interpretation" is a recurring motif in Derrida's work. Cf. WD 67.

35. Cf. "We must not hasten to decide" (MP 19).

36. Even the word *différance* is undecided and undecidable. It hesitates between difference and deferral (from the two meanings of the verb *différer*— to differ and to defer), between a more active and a more passive sense (being

different or differing, being deferred or deferring), and between spellings (the change from *e* to *a* is inaudible).

37. In "Some Statements and Truisms," Derrida describes the "monstrosity" of what is initially unrecognizable, although it may later become the norm: "Monsters cannot be announced. One cannot say: 'Here are our monsters,' without turning them into pets" (80). Interestingly, his example is that of the Johns Hopkins colloquium at which "Structure, Sign and Play" was presented, for Derrida's address and the conference in general have been read as precisely the kind of "event" that Derrida analyzes in his paper.

38. If the classic and the critical inhabit all paths, Derrida suggests that "grammatology is less another science, a new discipline charged with a new content or new domain, than the vigilant practice of this textual division" (Pos 36).

39. "Préjugés: devant la loi" 95, from the opening section of the paper presented at the 1982 *Colloque de Cerisy*. This section was not included in the translation, "Devant la loi."

40. LI 116, cf. *The Gift of Death* 67-70.

41. John Llewelyn explores the ethics of the undecidable in "Responsibility with Indecidability."

42. In *Résistances: de la psychanalyse*, Derrida writes of the importance of "*différance* as divisibility" in deconstruction (48) and shows that there are no single, indivisible threads.

43. Cf. the following "chain" of "nonsynonymous substitutions": "*différance*," "reserve," "archi-writing," "archi-trace," "spacing," "supplement," "*pharmakon*," "hymen," "margin-mark-march" (MP 12).

44. Cf. "At the point at which the concept of *différance* [. . .] intervenes, all the conceptual oppositions of metaphysics [. . .] become nonpertinent" (Pos 29).

45. Cf. "our illusion that they are two" (MP 5).

46. Cf. "do not say its unity, the question posed here being one of knowing whether *a* text could be *one* and if such a thing exists any more than a unicorn" (*Glas* 169).

47. Cf. "The unique—that which is not repeated—has no unity since it is not repeated. Only that which can be repeated in its identity can have unity" (Dis 365).

48. Derrida's notion of iterability—of repetition undoing the binary opposition and dividing identity and presence—is discussed at length in "Signature Event Context" (MP 307-330 or LI 1-23) and in "Limited Inc a b c. . ." (LI 29-110).

49. Cf. Dis 251.

50. Jonathan Culler gives a fuller explanation of the way in which the interval exceeds thematic reading in *On Deconstruction* 211-212.

51. Cf. Dis 209-216, Pos 43.

52. Such substitutions and confusions, when they occur, threaten the signifying position of the subject. Kristeva sees in fetishism the substitution of semiotic stases for the thetic break. This leads to a pseudo-dialectic within the semiotic and prevents the process of *signifiance* from being elaborated. Although this substitution saves the subject from "foundering in an 'unsayable' without limits" (RPL 65), the subject is unable to establish with any stability the positions of self and other, of subject and object that are essential to linguistic and social relations. Less damaging but nonetheless undesirable, what Kristeva calls "contemplative discourse" substitutes stylistic variation for drive heterogeneity, resulting in sterility and redundancy (RPL 95-99).

53. Derrida expresses his reservations about certain uses of the term in this passage.

54. Cf. "But it does not follow, by virtue of this hymen of confusion, that there is now only one term, a single one of the differends. [. . .] It is the difference between the two terms that is no longer functional. The confusion or consummation of this hymen eliminates the spatial heterogeneity of the two poles [. . .]" (Dis 209).

PART II

The Politics of Encounter

The texts have thus far been studied largely separately in order to accentuate certain moves as a basis for a conceptual encounter. The contact has been at arm's length, produced by juxtaposing rather than entangling them. But now the theories will be articulated in more treacherous ways. This section proposes reciprocal readings in a parodic staging of texts that confront, toy with, avoid or subsume each other. A reading of Kristeva's work through Derrida's theories will establish one possible relation, then an analysis of some of Derrida's texts using Kristeva's theories will hinge them in another way.

The basis for this second reading is laid out in *Revolution in Poetic Language* (RPL) where Kristeva devotes several pages to a critique of Derrida's work (140-145). This will serve as a starting point for an apocryphal meeting, but the dialogue engaged will not be limited to the points Kristeva raises. By contrast with this lengthy critique, Derrida's texts mention Kristeva's work but provide no extended commentary on it. Nevertheless, a Derridean reading of Kristeva can be extrapolated from his texts on Freud, Hegel and Plato, and from his deconstructions of the subject, of speech and writing, of signifier and signified.

Before extrapolating any unsigned bilateral negotiations, however, I propose to take a careful look at the textual encounters that are signed, at the explicit references each writer makes to the other, sometimes in the form of footnotes, in his or her publications. This preliminary study will focus not only on the substance of their remarks, but above all on the orientation of these remarks, the way Kristeva and Derrida situate their work in relation to that of the other. To what extent did they consider their work to be compatible at various points in time? In anticipation of the cross-readings, then, a detour via reciprocal but asymmetrical references. . . .

CHAPTER 3

Cross-References

The reading of the references made by Derrida and Kristeva to each other intersects with a story, that of a split (one of several) within the *Tel Quel* group—a rupture, an event, and it is no accident that these terms crop up again here. The story is not told in their texts, but their descriptions of the period when they both contributed to the journal are telling and tellingly different. And what they tell us most are not morsels of gossip from the Paris intellectual scene but ways of theorizing difference.

Kristeva and Derrida both collaborated on the journal *Tel Quel* during the sixties and published major works under its auspices.[1] During this period, Kristeva's references to Derrida far outnumber the reverse.[2] Obviously, the reasons for this disparity are primarily historical. The two careers did not evolve in parallel: Derrida is ten years older than Kristeva and had already published several of his most influential books (including *Writing and Difference* and *Of Grammatology*) before 1969, which was when Kristeva's first collection of articles, *Sèméiotikè*, appeared. The 1968 interview of Derrida by Kristeva (*Positions* 15-36)—the only published conversation between the two—reflects this imbalance. The dialogue is not an exchange of ideas or a confrontation of two theories—as we shall see, such a confrontation is rather to be found in Houdebine and Scarpetta's interview of Derrida—but rather an opportunity for Derrida to expound and defend his ideas.

In *Sèméiotikè*, Kristeva's theories are still far from established: her approach is algebraic rather than psychoanalytical. Her references to Derrida's work at this time show support for his projects. On several occasions she uses elements of Derridean terminology—"trace" and *"gramme"* (KR 83, Σ 38, 110), "dissemination" (Σ 292), *"écriture"* (Σ 279)—but without ever adopting them as her own. She subscribes to some of Derrida's aims and arguments, especially where the critique of logocentrism is concerned (Σ 28-29, 37-38, 89, 136; KR 76, 83), sometimes even expressing her support with enthusiasm, speaking of Derrida's "decisive work" (Σ 89), and of his "admirable reading of Husserl" (Σ 211).[3]

Similarly, in *Language: the Unknown*, also first published in French in 1969, Kristeva emphasizes the importance of Derrida's work. In this introduction to linguistics, Derrida is cited not only with reference to his critique of Husserl's metaphysical project (222), but also in an introductory chapter on the sign, where he is said to have laid the foundation for "a new theoretical science," (17) and in the conclusion to the book (326). As Kristeva remarked around this time, Derrida's work "seems to me to be of capital interest for semiology."[4] Indeed it was an essential reference for the *Tel Quel* group as a whole.[5]

Derrida's sole reference to Kristeva's work during this period is similarly appreciative. It occurs in "The Double Session," which he first gave as a paper in 1969 in front of an audience including most of the *Tel Quel* team. In a footnote, Derrida refers the reader to Kristeva's "Poésie et négativité" for "an interpretation of the entirety of Mallarmé's writing" (Dis 235). There is recognition and approbation, then, of the work of each by the other.

1971-72, however, marked a rupture within the *Tel Quel* group, which was equally a rupture between Derrida and Kristeva. The event was a very public one, but is never mentioned in their texts. In June of that year, a movement within *Tel Quel*—the *Mouvement de juin 71*— announced its break with the French Communist Party, declaring itself "against opportunism, dogmatism, empiricism, revisionism" and "for the thought of Mao Tse-Tung."[6] *Tel Quel* purged its editorial committee of those unsympathetic to this new orientation and the *Groupe d'études théoriques* was temporarily suspended. The journal had long been involved in a series of disputes during which the editors had defended both Derrida and Kristeva against attacks.[7] But the stance taken in 1971 required a clear commitment to *Tel Quel*'s politics. Kristeva stayed. Derrida didn't.[8]

In the years since, Derrida has remained silent on the *Tel Quel* split and has avoided referring to Kristeva's work at all, even when it might have seemed an obvious thing to do.[9] Meanwhile, Kristeva has repeatedly dissociated her work from Derrida's.

In 1983, invited to contribute to the first issue of *L'Infini*, the journal that took over from *Tel Quel*, Kristeva wrote "Mémoire," translated as "My Memory's Hyperbole." She looks back, and with the benefit of 15 years' hindsight, she notes the existence of a clear division at the heart of *Tel Quel* which was perhaps less evident at the time. Let us say that it was less *pronounced*, in the double sense of "distinct" and "declared." She points to a divergence between her work and Derrida's that separated them down to their aims:

> For some, the important task was to 'deconstruct' phenomenology and structuralism as a minor form of a hidden metaphysics. Among these was Jacques Derrida, whose "Introduction" to Husserl's *Origins of Geometry* had been discovered by Sollers [. . .]. For others, among whom I place myself, it was essential to "dynamize" the structure by taking into consideration the speaking subject and its unconscious experience on the one hand, and on the other, the pressures of other social structures.[10]

A couple of pages further on, when mentioning all those who worked on the *Tel Quel* team, Kristeva proposes a "common denominator" that she describes as a "post-phenomenological or post-analytical vigilance" (227). However, she opens this paragraph by referring to "each person who has worked, or who does work with, for, or against *Tel Quel*" (227). For or against: even as she points out what they had in common, she allows tension and conflict to show through. Apparently, what she wishes to emphasize in this essay are the differences: "I would rather re-establish differences" (228). Difference and distance: "In holding to these views, we necessarily felt far removed from both the anti-oedipals and the 'de-constructionists'" (228).[11]

Whereas Kristeva stresses divisions in *Tel Quel*, Derrida has insisted on solidarity, both at the height of the drama and much later. The interview of Derrida by Jean-Louis Houdebine and Guy Scarpetta (Pos 37-96) took place on 17 June 1971. Now the manifesto heralding the *Tel Quel* split was called "Positions du mouvement de juin 71." And Houdebine and Scarpetta, unlike Derrida, remained closely allied to *Tel Quel*.[12] At this critical moment, Derrida assures us that he has "always subscribed" to Kristeva's project (90) and takes the evocation of *Tel Quel* as "an occasion for me to recall a solidarity and support regularly kept up, as you know, for five or six years" (78). Twenty years later, the word "solidarity" is again used, together with "proximity," to describe his participation in the *Tel Quel* group. Bennington, in his at least semi-authorized text, notes the following:

> 1972 [. . .] Definitive rupture with Sollers and *Tel Quel* (in spite of the proximity and a certain solidarity, especially from 65 to 69, J.D. had never been part of the journal's editorial board and had never ceased to mark his independence—not appreciated [*mal supporté*] by his partners, particularly regarding the theoretico-political orientation of the group [. . .]).[13]

Apparently, unlike Kristeva, Derrida did not feel "far removed" from others on the team, although he did not align himself with their politics. His participation in the group was marked by *both* solidarity *and* independence—hardly surprising when we consider Derrida's work on rupture and redoubling in "Structure, Sign and Play."[14]

What is at stake in these readings of the *Tel Quel* period? Is there merely a difference of emphasis in the interpretation of the facts? Or can we read here a tension between different ways of conceiving of rupture? Why does Derrida stress solidarity and Kristeva division, and what does it matter? For evidently it matters very much to Kristeva: following the *Tel Quel* split, more particularly from the publication of *La Révolution du langage poétique* in 1974 onwards, Kristeva repeatedly distances her work from Derrida's, both in careful critiques and in scarcely disguised attacks.[15] Once she has consolidated her theory in RPL, she is obviously at pains to distinguish it from Derrida's and to express her disagreement, whilst Derrida persists in minimizing the contention.

What I would like to suggest is that this is more than the tale of two people falling out, or a story about the competitive stakes in the Parisian intellectual scene. It seems to me that there is strategic value for each theory in either marking distance or insisting on proximity and that the status and the practice of contradiction as difference are at issue here. And to show this, I would like to take a detailed look at a couple of places where Derrida and Kristeva deal explicitly with "contradiction" as they enact their theories of difference with respect to the other theorist: firstly the interview in *Positions* where Derrida refers to Kristeva's work, and secondly the passages in *Revolution in Poetic Language* and in *Polylogue* where Kristeva critiques deconstruction.

A REGULAR SUBSCRIBER

In response to the first question of the "Positions" interview, Derrida describes the relation between on the one hand the movement of *différance* and on the other the Hegelian dialectic with its resolution of contradiction into a third term (*Aufhebung*). In a statement that anticipates Bennington's note and can help us, I believe, to interpret both the arguments and the argumentation of this interview, we read that "*Différance* (at a point of almost absolute proximity to Hegel [. . .]) must sign the point at which one breaks [*point de rupture*] with the system of the *Aufhebung* and with speculative dialectics" (Pos 44). The point of rupture is a point of proximity. For Derrida rupture is not a consequence of distance but appears as a result of the closeness, the *approximation* of *différance* and dialectics. And *différance* signs — leaves its mark, its signature — at the point of rupture. The relation between *différance* and dialectics can only be one of rupture *and* contiguity, a relation of *différance*. It is a "conflictual" relation, in that it can never be resolved — "appease[d] or reconcile[d]" (44) — into a third term of synthesis, but Derrida remarks that this "conflictuality" can only be termed contradiction if it is carefully demarcated from Hegelian contradiction, in other words, if it breaks away at a point of "almost absolute proximity." Derrida's answer takes on the aspect of a *mise en abyme*: the relation between *différance* and the Hegelian dialectic is one of conflictuality (*différance*); the relation between this conflictuality and Hegelian contradiction is again one of *différance*, etc.

True to the description Derrida gives here, the relation between *différance* and dialectics, between conflictuality and contradiction, remains unresolved and unresolvable: the question returns with some insistence half-way through the interview, reappears in the final exchange, and motivates the correspondence that followed the interview and was published with it. And we shall see that both in Houdebine's questions and in Derrida's responses, the arguments advanced are reproduced in the enunciation.

Having sketched a relation (of *différance*) between *différance* and Hegelian contradiction, Derrida is asked by Jean-Louis Houdebine (closely associated with Kristeva), to return to this question and to specify the relation between *différance* and contradiction as it is understood in dialectical materialism (71-74). Houdebine refers to Kristeva's work, in which, as we saw in Chapter 2, contradiction is not resolved into a third term. Derrida is suspicious of the idea of a Marxist "break [*rupture*] with metaphysics" implied in the question (74)—as indeed he is careful not to claim radical rupture by deconstruction (51)—but he goes on to answer: "Now, wherever and insofar as the motif of contradiction functions effectively, in a textual work, outside speculative dialectics, and taking into account a new problematic of meaning [. . .], I agree [*j'y souscris*]" (74, tr. mod.).

But Houdebine doesn't accept Derrida's expression of agreement at face value, and well might he be wary. *J'y souscris*: I agree, I subscribe . . . I countersign, place my signature below another . . . and in the gap between the two signatures alterity slips in. I endorse, leave my mark on the document, re-mark . . . rendering it slightly other.[16] What is agreement but a *différance*, a relation of "almost absolute proximity" producing a necessary rupture that cannot be recuperated into a binary opposition? The contradiction to which Derrida subscribes has been reinscribed in a logic of *différance*.

Houdebine tries to separate out agreements ("I feel that I am entirely in agreement with you on this point, [that there is no unified Marxist view of contradiction]" 75) and possible disagreements ("I was only wondering whether one could consider that in every materialist stand [. . .] one finds the double motif of 'matter' and 'contradiction'" 75). The division into two moments is both what Houdebine argues from this point on in the interview (the distinction between matter and contradiction, and later between spacing and alterity) and his mode of arguing (distinguishing disagreement from agreement). But while Houdebine seeks to disentangle points of rupture from points of proximity, Derrida suggests that they give rise to one another.

Amplifying his question of the relation between "matter/contradiction" and *différance*, Houdebine explains that the question is necessary insofar as "the two kinds of logic [. . .] do not completely overlap [*ne se recouvrent pas exactement*]" (76). This expression is interesting as an objection to Derrida's agreement, for it so clearly echoes the idea of an "almost absolute proximity" that is *simultaneously* a point of rupture. For Derrida, this is answer enough: the non-coincidence, the *écart* (gap or interval 76) already describes the relation as one of *différance*. He replies "what I have written seems to me entirely explicit" (76). For his interlocutors, however, it is not sufficient. They reiterate their concerns in the context of Derrida's analysis of Artaud's relation to metaphysics:

> Scarpetta: Does not this practice of shaking, of excess, of destruction seem to you to derive from a logic of contradiction, released from its speculative investments?
>
> Derrida: Yes, why not? Provided that one determines the concept of contradiction with the necessary critical precautions [. . .]. (76)

It is as if Houdebine and Scarpetta are trying to force Derrida into making a clear yes-or-no, for-or-against statement on contradiction. [17] It is as if they want him to contradict their (dialectical materialist) theory of contradiction. But Derrida is not interested in taking up the position of adversary and avoids the oppositional turn of the interview: he accepts the use of the term "contradiction" (this is the redoubling) whilst pointing to the limits of its use (his rupture with it). He refuses to contradict contradiction (which would after all paradoxically involve affirming it by practising it) and instead performs the conflictuality of which he spoke earlier, the slight mismatch between usages that creates friction and resists resolution.

It is very soon after this point in the interview that, in between references to Marx, Engels and Lenin, Derrida manages to slip in his remark about the solidarity and support he has encountered in the *Tel Quel* group. In other words, it is at the point of contention that he notes the proximity. [18]

Houdebine does not let go. In his next question, he argues that heterogeneity cannot be reduced to the spacing Derrida describes as *différance* but implies two contradictory moments: spacing or difference and the positing [*la position*] of alterity (80). In other words, according to Houdebine (and we can see the parallels with Kristevan theory) heterogeneity must not be confused with other forms of difference, for it is radically—contradictorily—other. When Derrida objects that he doesn't see any incompatibility between their arguments, Houdebine again tackles him on the non-coincidence, the imperfect overlap of the two theories: "is the motif of heterogeneity entirely covered [*recouvert*] by the notion of spacing? Do not *alterity* and *spacing* present us with two moments not identical to each other?" (81). Derrida replies: "In effect, these two concepts *do not signify exactly* the same thing" (81). Once again, what for Houdebine is a question, is for Derrida already an answer. According to the logic of *différance*, alterity and spacing are not identical to each other, indeed they are hardly absolutely identical to themselves, repetition always introducing difference. Derrida stresses, however, that they are "indissociable" (81). Houdebine agrees ("Entirely so [*tout à fait d'accord*]"), but only so as to reiterate his argument: they are indissociable because they are "dialectically, that is contradictorily linked" (81). Despite the expression of agreement, "indissociable" is not being used in the same way by Houdebine and by Derrida. For Houdebine two distinct and contradictory moments are bound together (like Kristeva's inseparable modalities, dialectically bound together in a "permanent struggle"); for Derrida there is no clear limit between them.

The discussion moves on until the very last question, in which Houdebine asks Derrida to speak of the relation between his project and "the Marxist concept of practice, and singularly of signifying practice [. . .] in a semiotics and a semanalysis based on a dialectical materialist logic, which is equally determined on the basis of an intervention of psychoanalysis" (89), and it is in this context that Derrida remarks "I suppose that you are referring to the works of Julia Kristeva" (90). And there can be no doubt: Houdebine uses her vocabulary ("signifying practice," "semanalysis") and her references. In fact in this formulation of his question, Houdebine underlines the maximum number of elements in Kristeva's approach that are likely to distinguish it from Derrida's: dialectical materialism, Marxism, psychoanalysis. He does everything he can to mark a division between the two practices. You might think he was looking for an argument in affirming that it is "very difficult to think of [the signifying process], other than in the form of a contradictory, dialectical process" (89), for this hardly resembles Derrida's descriptions of *différance*. Houdebine seems to want to push Derrida towards taking a position that contradicts Kristeva's.

Derrida doesn't take the bait. On the contrary, he affirms his support; he has "always subscribed" to Kristeva's project:

> I have always insisted on this value of *practice*. Consequently, everywhere, from this point of view, that a general theory, a general theoretical-practice of the "signifying practice" is elaborated, I have always subscribed to the task thus defined. I suppose that you are referring to the works of Julia Kristeva [. . .]. (89-90, tr. mod.)

Whereas Houdebine (as elsewhere Kristeva) attempts to distinguish clearly between the two practices by highlighting their dissimilarities, Derrida minimizes them to accentuate the affinity/proximity between the theories. He "subscribes" to Kristeva's work, countersigns, writes in parallel. There is no confrontation between the two . . . but perhaps a conflictual lack of symmetry, an imperfect overlap creating a rupture that does not constitute a contradiction in the way Houdebine and Kristeva understand the word. Rather than a disagreement (*désaccord*) it is more like a discrepancy (*décalage*), a non-correspondence that may be more or less apparent at various moments . . . an interval that appears . . . and disappears.

Derrida continues with this strategy of approximation and assent throughout the exchange of letters following the discussion. When Houdebine, unconvinced by the agreement, reiterates his difference of opinion over the kind of indissociability between spacing and alterity ("moments whose indissociability is that of a dialectical (materialist) contradiction" 91), Derrida refuses to see any disagreement on this point, or rather he sees no foundation to the disagreement Houdebine claims. The fragment begins with the words: "We agree, then, about the *overturning/displacement*" (93) and this phrase sets the tone for what follows: "but here I suppose that we agree [. . .]. Are we agreed also that [. . .]?" (94); "*Spacing/alterity*: on their indissociability, then, there is no disagreement between us" (94). Derrida insists on this latter point and repeats it just one paragraph further: "the system of *spacing/alterity*, on which we agree" (94). In fact there isn't a single page in this letter where the agreement is not underlined and signed again: "I agree as concerns Bataille" (95).[19] This last phrase is followed by the clearest denial of any possible dissension whatsoever concerning the question of contradiction or spacing:

> *Position* (of alterity): taking into account point 2 (above in my letter), there is no disagreement between us, and, as I said in the interview, I cannot receive your insistence on this point as an addition or an objection to what I have written. (95)

But there is a false note to this accord, a misunderstanding about their understanding, because Houdebine does not agree that they agree. Or rather, every time he expresses some sort of agreement or a compatibility on a point, it is in order to establish a basis from which he can clarify his disagreements:

> I agree with you that the problems you indicate can always reemerge on the basis of this other-position: this is why the moment of spacing [. . .] is essential. But no less essential is the *other* moment, the

moment of alterity (*position* of alterity), whose logic I very cursorily
attempted to define [. . .]. (92, tr. mod.)

Houdebine insists that the two moments need to be distinguished
because spacing "negates" any form of presence whilst alterity
indicates the "positivity" of a heterogeneity that is not simply present
(92). In other words, he distinguishes between positive and negative
moments which, although indissociable, remain distinct in their
dialectic. But for Derrida, for whom poles can be seen as reversible, for
whom a logic of both/and-neither/nor interrupts that of binary
oppositions, Houdebine's moments melt into, even occasion one
another, like the radical and the classic, like rupture and redoubling.

In his letter, Houdebine indicates what is at stake in contradiction:
"the underlying question of this exchange is [. . .] the question of taking
a materialist position [*la prise de position matérialiste*], [. . .] the
question of taking a stand [*une prise de parti*] in philosophy" (91 tr.
mod.). Here Houdebine shows his hand: the interview has been an
attempt to get Derrida to take sides, to come out for or against. But as
we saw in "Structure, Sign and Play," taking a stand—coming out
against a traditional discourse and claiming to rupture with it—is not
Derrida's way. He proposes a rupture not defined by grand gestures but
by minute ones: "there is no *effective* and *efficient* position, no veritable
force of rupture, without a minute, rigorous, extended analysis, an
analysis that is as differentiated and as scientific as possible" (94). Not
a global for-or-against, not a claim to overthrow the *Aufhebung* in one
blow, but subtle, carefully defined points of rupture at points of
proximity.

Derrida writes of "the necessity of reinscription rather than denial"
(94) and practices it throughout the exchange. Reinscribing resignifies
without contradicting: like "subscribing," it does not negate but affirms (*firmare* —to sign). Derrida concludes his reply to Houdebine's
letter with a discussion of the word *position* (taking a position,
positing). His misgivings about this word concern its Hegelian use
(*Setzung*) whereby the other is posited in terms of the same, as object of
the subject. *Différance*, on the other hand, would be a relation in which
the other inscribes its alterity, i.e., inscribes that which cannot be
posited or positivized without losing its otherness (95-96). But Derrida
does not reject the term "position" for it can be reinscribed: "one can
always redefine, beneath the same word (extraction, graft, extension),
the concept of *position*" (96). And he continues not to oppose

Houdebine: "But perhaps the debate between us, on this point, rests on a 'verbal,' 'nominal' misunderstanding" (96). Rather than confronting, convincing and concluding, he suggests "leav[ing] *open* the discussion of this question of the position, of the *positions*" (96). And rather than taking a stand, he "take[s his] leave" (96).

By agreeing to—whilst reinscribing—the notions of the dialectic, contradiction, heterogeneity, practice and position, Derrida is able to embrace Houdebine's arguments and indeed Kristeva's theory along the way. Yet in this embrace, Houdebine's/ Kristeva's dialectical stand is swept up into the movement of *différance*. It disappears into *différance*, deemed to be hardly distinguishable from it.[20] This is one kind of relation between the two theories, a non-conflictual but nonetheless strategic one. It is, however, not the only possible relation between them.

THE REVOLUTION OF *DIFFÉRANCE*

This inconclusive ending to a debate that wasn't may well have seemed unsatisfying to Houdebine and Scarpetta and, indeed, to Kristeva. In any case, she is not content to leave the "positions" question open, and is keen to "take a stand." She does so in both *Revolution in Poetic Language* and in an article first published in *Tel Quel*.[21] After some appreciative references to Derrida in the opening section of RPL regarding his critiques of phenomenology and of the ontological reading of the *chora* (40-41, 239n, cf. PL 57), Kristeva takes up some of the arguments made by Houdebine and supports them with all the force of her elaborate theory of signification in a full critique of deconstruction. Its title makes her accusations clear: "Non-Contradiction: Neutral Peace" (140-146). A year later, in "From One Identity to an Other," her criticisms are aired again: she expresses serious reservations about a certain reading of Husserl, without however naming either the text or its author, mentioning only "the attempts to criticize or 'deconstruct' phenomenology" (DL 131). Her theoretical position has evolved considerably in the eight years since she wrote of Derrida's "admirable reading of Husserl" (Σ 211) and her appraisal in this text is even peppered with a modicum of animosity.[22]

During those eight years, the major development in Kristeva's theory has been the elaboration of the dialectic between the semiotic and the symbolic modalities, and it is to this dynamic organization that we need to look to discover what is at stake in her objections to deconstruction and why her earlier enthusiasm has waned. Kristeva's evaluation and criticisms of deconstruction will be examined in detail in the second of the cross-readings that follow this chapter. To conclude this reading of the cross-references, I shall highlight some of the rhetorical moves she makes to position her work in relation to Derrida's and the strategic work they do in defending her theory.

If Kristeva accuses Derrida of neutrality, she certainly never leaves herself open to such an accusation, plainly supporting certain elements of deconstruction and attacking others. Positive and negative aspects are identified and separated out. She starts by noting its radicality and its usefulness in trying "to push dialectical negativity further and elsewhere" (RPL 140) but then goes on to mark her difference from Derrida, which consists precisely in the importance given to a dialectical contradiction between positive and negative moments. Like Derrida's and Houdebine's arguments in *Positions*, Kristeva's arguments are reflected in her presentation of them, which is confrontational and polarizing. The problem with *différance*, from her point of view, is that it is neither positive nor negative and lacks the force and productivity of either pole. On the one hand, its negativity has been positivized, such that it is unable to produce genuine rupture (141). On the other hand, this positivity is insufficient to guarantee any stability: it stops short of the thetic where it could assure a position for the subject and engage with symbolic structures (141-142). It is as if grammatology were permanently lodged at the point where the symbolic function is in formation but not yet formed (143). Kristeva places deconstruction just before the mirror stage: at the moment when a proto-subject and proto-objects are taking form but are not yet assumed as such or differentiated. Their positioning as opposites — vital to symbolic functioning — has been deferred indefinitely. Deconstruction remains "Neutral in the face of all positions" (142).

This neutral peace, however, is not seen by Kristeva in terms of "support" and "solidarity" such as Derrida mentioned. This is the peace of an abdication of responsibility and an inability to offer support where necessary: "retreat[ing] before the thetic" (RPL 141) (and thus retreating from the positing of a subject) obliges deconstruction to remain "ignorant" both of the subject's social practice and of the possibility of its disintegration, "disinterested" in the first instance,[23] "silent" in the second (142). In Kristeva's opinion, deconstruction "gives up on the subject" (142) and can have nothing to say about social structure or its collapse.

To label Derrida's philosophy as one of "neutral peace" is to situate it in direct contrast to Kristeva's own theory of revolution, and revolution seems to be what is at stake in this confrontation of theories: if Kristeva criticizes deconstruction for denying limits and ignoring constraints (DL 131), it is perhaps because revolution depends on the existence of such conservative forces for its *raison d'être*. It is hard to conceive of a revolution that does not struggle against a constraining power,[24] and the disruptive force of poetic language is no exception, acting against social and linguistic limits posited as relatively stable. And in this revolution there is no place for a non-committal movement that blurs the contrast between opposing forces.

Having no stake in neutrality herself, Kristeva does not balk at contradicting Derrida, and she does so by showing what "*enters into contradiction with différance*" (RPL 144, Kristeva's emphasis) and similarly a page later what "enters into contradiction with what has been traced" (145), which is "heterogeneity." If Derrida interpreted the relation between *différance* and dialectical contradiction as a relation of *différance*, Kristeva retaliates by doing the reverse: *différance* enters into a relation of contradiction with an opposing (heterogeneous) force. And if Derrida managed to subordinate contradiction to *différance*, interpreting contradiction as an unrecognized *différance*, Kristeva turns the tables on him: it is only by "forget[ting]" heterogeneity (143) that contradiction dissolves into differences. *Différance* is thus just one element of an unrecognized process of contradiction in which it needs to "find its place" (145). And deconstruction is made to join the revolution, for "the return of the heterogeneous element [. . .] brings about the revolution of *différance*" (144).

Neutral *différance*, however, does not necessarily survive the revolution. Two scenarios are envisaged, by which *différance* is well and truly neutralized—in the military sense of the word. When the instinctual heterogeneity of drives—the full force of negativity —breaks in and "cuts [it] short" (RPL 144), *différance* risks massive and terminal rupture. Having neglected the thetic function and refused the anchor of symbolic positioning, *différance* is likely to be swept away entirely: the urgent irruption of drives "could pierce and abolish it, and then all symbolic becoming would cease, thus opening the way to 'madness'" (145). The other possibility is that heterogeneity may be deferred indefinitely such that "*différance* would be confined within a nonrenewable, nonproductive redundancy, a mere precious variant within the symbolic enclosure: contemplation adrift" (145). In other words, *différance* would be superfluous, sterile, vain. Obliteration or stagnation: these are the dangers of maintaining *différance* as neither positive nor negative.

Unlike Derridean rupture, the rupture that threatens to annihilate *différance* has little to do with proximity. Kristeva invests a great deal in a form of rupture that is not a subtle delineation, an incomplete overlap or a mismatch that requires minute analysis. When she writes of rupture, she writes in terms of death and rapture: "being put to death" (RPL 142), "leaps, abrupt changes" (144), "revolution [. . .], erotic excess, social protest" (144), "destruction, self-destruction" (144), "mortal jouissance" (145), "flashes, ruptures and sudden displacements" (145). She also invests heavily in renewal (which we can compare to the idea of redoubling), in the continuity of social functioning, family and social structures and communication, all of which are affected by the ruptures. But for Kristeva, rupture and renewal are two consecutive moments, dependent on each other and on their mutual opposition. Were they to merge into the same movement, they would both be neutralized, each losing its force. And indeed, if the distinction between rupture and renewal, between revolution and consolidation, between destabilization and stabilization, were to become blurred, then the dialectical opposition between the semiotic and the symbolic would lose its effectiveness. This is the threat that deconstruction represents for Kristevan theory, as we shall see in the first of the cross-readings (Chapter 4).

Kristeva reproaches deconstruction with its inability either to "produc[e] breaks" (RPL 141) or to account for them (142). In Kristevan terms, deconstruction has a problem with rupture. Her reading of Derrida's project, on the other hand, both breaks with it and shows what "cuts short" *différance* (144). Whereas Derrida could subscribe to Kristeva's work, subtly rupturing with it at a point of "almost absolute proximity," Kristeva's rupture with deconstruction — in the image of rupture in her theory—takes the form of a forceful opposition to some of its tenets.

This chapter has analyzed two conceptions of the relation between Derrida's and Kristeva's theories. Ironically, one argues that they agree whilst the other vehemently puts forward disagreements. Both Derrida and Kristeva manage to interpret the other's theory in terms of their own work. The difference is that Kristeva needs to disagree with and counter Derrida's theory to do so. A deconstructive reading of Kristeva need never argue against Kristeva in order to reinscribe her work. It can resignify it as it embraces it. In contrast with these engulfing, assimilating moves, the Kristevan strategy is one of attack and defence. She confronts Derrida's work and contradicts elements of it.[25]

This reading of the rhetorical moves performed by each of the two theorists in referring to the other indicates ways of doing a Derridean reading of Kristeva's work and vice versa and forms the basis for the cross-readings that follow. These cross-readings, like the "cross-references" that have been the material for this chapter, are perhaps not cross in the same way. Kristeva's crossness certainly has an air of the impatient spirit of the barricades, aiming for direct hits at an adversary, but Derrida's is cross in the sense of a crosswise or oblique movement or of a crosswind blowing the debate off course. These two forms of crossness already tell us a great deal:

—that Derrida and Kristeva each situate their work in relation to the other's in ways that enact their respective theories;

—that there are at least two ways of interpreting the relation between their work;

—and that to claim to be Derridean *and* Kristevan in one's approach, to cite them together unproblematically, is already to choose one of those ways, the Derridean way, just as to position them as opposites is to choose the Kristevan way. And to take either of these ways is to involve oneself in the politics of this encounter, to take sides.

NOTES

1. Both published regularly in *Tel Quel* — Derrida, 1965-70, and Kristeva, 1967-82. It was in the *Collection "Tel Quel"* directed by Philippe Sollers at Editions du Seuil that Derrida first published *Writing and Difference* and *Dissemination*, and that Kristeva's *Sèméiotikè*, *La Révolution du language poétique*, *Polylogue* and *Powers of Horror* first appeared.

2. There are more than a dozen scattered through *Sèméiotikè* — 18, 28-29 (KR 76), 37-38 (KR 83), 89, 97-98, 110, 141 (DL 63),159 (DL 77), 191, 205, 211, 279, 292—and several more in *Language: The Unknown* (17, 222, 326, 332-333). Later references can be found in the following: RPL 40, 140-145, 239; the untranslated latter half of *La Révolution du langage poétique* 450, 602-603; *Polylogue* 57, 156-157 (DL 131), 256, 483 (DL 293); *Sens et non-sens de la révolte* 179, 190, 425. Throughout this chapter, translations other than those indicated here are my own. By contrast, there appear to be only two references to Kristeva (Dis 235, Pos 90) in Derrida's publications.

3. In "Lecture(s) d'une refonte," Jean-Louis Houdebine stresses the contribution of Derrida's work to *Sèméiotikè* (322-324). Philip E. Lewis also writes of intersections in *Sèméiotikè*, pointing out where Kristeva's work draws on Derrida's and where it forks away from it ("Revolutionary Semiotics" 28-30).

4. *Essays in Semiotics : Essais de Sémiotique* 11. This is a reprint of the original introduction to Kristeva's interview of Derrida as it appeared in *Information sur les sciences sociales* VII, 1968.

5. Leon S. Roudiez describes the importance of Derrida's work on language for the whole *Tel Quel* group ("Twelve Points from *Tel Quel*"). Philippe Forest insists on the role of Derrida's work in the synthesis of theoretical positions that became *Théorie d'ensemble* (*Histoire de Tel Quel* 298-321).

6. "Positions du mouvement de juin 71" 133.

7. Cf. the "Tel Quel" pages of the journal from 1969 to 1972, especially in *Tel Quel* 39 (1969) and 43 (1970). Cf. also Mary Ann Caws, "*Tel Quel*: Text and Revolution."

8. Forest gives a detailed account of events during this period and of the strategic value of *Tel Quel*'s maneuvers (*Histoire de Tel Quel* 322-441). He also points to the carnevalesque aspect of some of the more provocative proclamations made by the *Mouvement de juin 71*.

9. In *Khôra*, there is a notable absence of any reference to Kristeva's development of Plato's concept. For Derrida, it is engulfed in "the immense history of interpretations and reappropriations that bustle about *khôra* through the centuries" (35).

10. "My Memory's Hyperbole" 224-225. In addition to the distancing taking place here, there seems to be some point-scoring: while Derrida worries about "minor" problems, Kristeva takes on language, the unconscious and society, and Derrida was after all discovered by her erstwhile colleague and husband Sollers.

11. "Deconstruction" has become "de-construction" and worse is to come . . . (see Note 15 below). One last little quotation on distance, if you'll forgive my narcissism, from a report by Kristeva on the thesis from which this book has evolved. She wrote that she was "not convinced that one can compare two sets of texts so different from one another," although she could "easily understand the temptation to do so, inspired by American and Canadian teaching" ("Rapport après soutenance," Université de Paris VII, October 1990).

12. Forest discusses the circumstances of this interview and the motives giving rise to it (*Histoire de Tel Quel* 366-370).

13. Geoffrey Bennington and Jacques Derrida, *Jacques Derrida* 305. Geoffrey Bennington goes on to write that he has often heard Derrida on the one hand invite people to "read the texts" (and in particular *Tel Quel* from 1965 to 1972) and on the other hand not to place any faith in the "public interpretations/reconstructions" by certain members of the group (305-306), casting doubt on their reliability.

14. And in the light of "Structure, Sign and Play," we can only wonder about what the "definitive rupture with Sollers" might mean in practice— presumably not a complete philosophical break.

15. Under the guise of fiction, and on someone else's lips at that, one can allow oneself to go that much further in criticizing one's contemporaries. An irreverent reference: in *The Samurai*, Saïda is the inventor of "condestruction," an inaccessible pseudo-profound cult theory (109). (In French, the displaced syllables make the expression highly insulting.) Sinteuil, a rather provocative character bearing some resemblance to Sollers, describes Saïda as "Adulterated goods for export" (264) that France sends overseas. It seems that Kristeva particularly resents the very dogmatic way in which some of Derrida's anglophone disciples have embraced deconstruction. See Edith Kurtzweil, "An interview with Julia Kristeva," 217-218.

16. Cf. Pos 65-66 on the transgressive "operation of the double mark." Cf. also "Signature Event Context" on the signature (MP 307-330).

17. In fact Forest's research shows that this was precisely their aim, insofar as a certain theory of contradiction was inseparable from *Tel Quel*'s marxist line (*Histoire de Tel Quel* 367-368).

18. We might note in passing that Derrida has also "always subscribed" to Sollers' concept of history (Pos 58).

19. The underlining of agreement as a way of avoiding participation in oppositional structures is a strategy Derrida uses more than once. It is interesting to note that even in such a polemical text as Derrida's reply to Searle in *Limited Inc* this strategy is put to work, albeit rather aggressively. Searle's refutation of Derrida's "Signature Event Context" (*Sec*, MP 307-330, LI 1-23) was called "Reiterating the Differences," but in his reply, Derrida regularly demonstrates that most of Searle's objections are not objections at all, nor even differences of opinion, but are in fact the same arguments that Derrida makes in *Sec* (LI 47, 105 and *passim*). He adds in the final paragraphs, however, that he is "far from subscribing to all the statements made" in Searle's text "despite all its borrowing from *Sec*" (LI 106), no doubt because the repetition of arguments has—as always—involved reinscription: "a certain practice of citation, and also of iteration [. . .] is at work, constantly *altering* [. . .] whatever it seems to reproduce" (40). In a note to the "Afterword" to the exchange (111-160),

Derrida affirms that he frequently stresses agreements: "I insist on scrupulously citing this phrase in order never to miss an opportunity of underscoring to what point I might agree with Searle. It is a rule that I try to follow in all discussion" (155).

20. Nicholas Royle's amusing anecdote (*After Derrida* 139-140) provides a further example of reinscription by Derrida of Kristeva's work.

21. "D'une identité l'autre," *Tel Quel* 62 (Summer 1975), also *Polylogue* 149-172, translated as "From One Identity to an Other" (DL 124-147).

22. After claiming that the anonymous deconstructions of Husserl become "lodged in a negative theology" denying constraints (DL 131), Kristeva writes later in the article of "what is happening to the discourse of contemporary philosophers, in France particularly" where "the philosopher begins performing literary tricks, thus arrogating to himself a power over imaginations: a power which, though minor in appearance, is more fetching than that of the transcendental consciousness" (DL 138-139). This article appeared just after the publication of Derrida's *Glas*. Derrida's name is never mentioned in these passages, nor at any moment in the article, but the direction of the references seems clear.

23. The original reads: "en se désintéressant de la structure" (*Révolution* 130). Deconstruction appears to show not merely a lack of involvement but a lack of interest.

24. In fact, Kristeva devotes an entire book to this very difficulty (SNR).

25. The recently published *Sens et non-sens de la révolte* provides a perplexing counter-example to this strategy and a postscript to this chapter. In it, Kristeva at one stage seems to appropriate Derridean theory, indicating "an unconscious psychoanalytical implication, the violence of rejection underlying *différance*" (179). Here she supplies the irruption of heterogeneity that grammatology was earlier said to "forget" (RPL 143) and "efface" (145). Could this rather heavy-handed assimilation of Derrida's work mark a shift in Kristeva's tactics (see the end of the following chapter for an exploration of the ambiguities of this text)? Later in her book, however, Kristeva differentiates between Barthes' work (with which she aligns her own) and Derrida's (again insisting on the latter's articulation of the unconscious) (SNR 425). It appears that the psychoanalytical reinscription of *différance* was a preliminary to the distancing. Interestingly, Kristeva's contrast between Barthes' and Derrida's work hinges on the notion of "practice": in order to mark a distinction, Kristeva italicizes the same word Derrida did in *Positions* in order to erase one (Pos 89, italicized in the original 124).

CHAPTER 4

Cross-Readings (1)

KRISTEVAN THEORY THROUGH DERRIDEAN I'S

What follows is not a reading that Derrida has ever undertaken, and it is predictable that were he to embark upon such a reading he would do so in unpredictable ways. Although a simulacrum would be perfectly appropriate here, I intend to eschew impersonation and overt imitation, at least for the moment—although echoes of some well-known texts will be heard throughout the chapter.[1] Rather I wish to investigate the extent to which Kristevan theory can be read in Derridean terms by studying it through the refracting lenses of a few Derridean i's, to wit:

- that capital *I*, pronoun or noun, the subject, the self, but split from itself, not self-present. Does the Kristevan speaking subject enjoy any form of self-presence or unity?

- *I*, the letter of the alphabet, that line, grapheme, mark, stroke of the pen. What of the trace in Kristeva's theory? Is the urgent irruption of the semiotic seen as the unmediated expression of instinctual forces, or is it shown to be waylaid by deferral and difference?

- that *eye* that looks for writing, that does not accept the notion of the primacy and presence of speech but reads the mark in the remark, the citation in the recitation. Does Kristeva privilege the voice with its rhyme, rhythm, prosody as a more immediate form of language?

- from eye to ear: *aie!*, the French ouch!, that exclamation of pain, that cry from the body yet always-already marked by and in language. Does Kristeva's analysis of preverbal utterances connect them to "the myth of the unarticulated cry" (OG 166)?

- *(i)*, that first of Roman numerals, a beginning, an origin, but an origin that is never absolute; that letter of number, the number of unity, but a unity always-already divided. Is there a wholeness at the origin of the process of *signifiance*? What kind of origin is represented by the *chora*?

- *i*, no longer One, but a Latin plural inflexion giving *foci*, *radii*: the apparently singular is doubled, split, repeated. Does Kristevan theory point to defining moments that occur once and for all, that claim a unique status?

- from suffix to prefix: *i*, that common element of prefixes of opposition (il-, im-, in-), denoting binary oppositions. Is the semiotic/symbolic relation a classic binary opposition inviting deconstruction?

- and from opposition to agreement: that *aye* of affirmation that adds without adding to the exchange, often *aye aye*, the supplement of repetition multiplying the openings for difference. What allows Derrida to subscribe to Kristeva's work? How might a Derridean affirmation of its value reinscribe it?

Of course, all these i's provide camouflage for another, or rather, they constitute another I, equally dispersed—the Derridean I who writes these pages. Seduced by both theories, but not wishing to synthesize them, I am drawn irresistibly to a schizophrenic reading strategy to articulate Derridean and Kristevan ways of understanding, here seeing through Derridean eyes, later giving expression to a Kristevan voice.

The dissemination of i's brings pressure to bear on Kristeva's theory. Is there any sense in which this reading can be called a faithful one? And faithful to whom? Certainly less to Kristeva than to Derrida: it is far from certain that Kristeva would fully recognize her theories in this interpretation of them, but then the possibility of "misinterpretation" is implied in the very maneuver. Perhaps it can be seen as faithful to deconstruction in a sense similar to that of Derrida's "subscribing": never quite true to its model, the inevitable gap will show . . . and will be productive.

As suggested by the previous chapter, this reading will tend to embrace Kristeva's work, keeping to the letter of its exposition whilst marking the texts, dotting the i's, punctuating and inflecting the work, reinscribing it in a logic of *différance*. If there are distortions of her theory, these will result not from misrepresentation so much as from a shift of emphasis: certain details may be promoted for analysis whilst major concerns may fade into the background. In a strategic change of focus, importance will be given to those aspects of Kristeva's work that intersect with Derrida's preoccupations.

Because the i's proliferate in various directions, this reading cannot be centered in the way some of the earlier ones have been. It cannot be held together by a single metaphor—whether of insect or of classical myth. There are multiple points of access for a Derridean reading of Kristeva's work, which have for convenience been grouped around the semiotic, the symbolic, and the relation between them. In each of these three settings, an almost perfect fit is achieved between the two theories. I am tempted to say that the reading fits like a glove—in the sense that it engulfs, contains and shapes Kristeva's theory in several directions at once. It fits like tight clothing—with a prod and a push here and there to squeeze in the body. However, at each point of contact, Kristeva's writing rubs, prompting the Derridean I to keep up the pressure to the very limit where a seam starts to split. This chapter aims to show rupture-at-a-point-of-almost-absolute-proximity. The hint of what resists accommodation thus remains visible—if only barely so—and marks the necessity for a Kristevan reply.

To launch the reading and to indicate what is at stake in it, at least in the first instance, I should like to focus on a question articulating deconstruction and psychoanalysis more generally. Towards the end of "Freud and the Scene of Writing," Derrida writes:

> The concept of a (conscious or unconscious) subject necessarily refers to the concept of substance—and thus of presence—out of which it is born.
>
> Thus, the Freudian concept of trace must be radicalized and extracted from the metaphysics of presence which still retains it (particularly in the concepts of consciousness, the unconscious, perception, memory, reality, and several others). (WD 229)

Is it possible to see Kristeva's work as approaching this aim (which is not necessarily her own)? Does she manage to radicalize certain psychoanalytical concepts in the direction towards which Derrida gestures?

*

WRITING IN THE WAVES: PRELINGUISTIC PUNCTUATION

Il commence par se répéter.[2]

Let us start from a point of proximity: the *chora*. In elaborating her theory of the *chora*, Kristeva recognizes the need to extract it from ontologizing representations (RPL 26) and acknowledges Derrida's efforts in this direction (239).[3] She explicitly refers to the "functioning of writing, the trace and the gramme" in Derrida's work which "points to an essential aspect of the semiotic" (40), but an aspect only. Indeed Kristeva leads the way to a Derridean reading of the semiotic *chora*. If Derrida regularly deconstructs the notion of an absolute and simple origin, in Kristeva's theory of signification the work has to a large extent already been done.

At the "threshold" of language, the founding moment that "establishes signification" appears to be the thetic phase (RPL 45), which however is neither a simple origin nor an absolute one. To start with, it is double, being found "at two points: the mirror stage and the 'discovery' of castration" (46). It then never ceases to recur as a "second-degree thetic" (50) in the dialectical process of *signifiance*. Furthermore, Kristeva refuses to accept the thetic as foundational and, following on from Freud's work, investigates "the process of its production" (44). The *chora*, in that it "logically and chronologically precedes" the thetic (41), might constitute a more likely origin, were it not for the fact that, like the thetic phase, it is always "starting over, again and again" (26). Rather than a single, simple, founding moment, the *chora* reveals itself to be a very complex origin indeed.

Kristeva describes the *chora* as semiotic, and in doing so insists on the importance of the etymological signification ("σημειον = distinctive mark, trace, index, precursory sign, proof, engraved or written sign, imprint, trace, figuration") and in particular the idea of "distinctiveness" (RPL 25). Thus her very first mention of the *chora* is already in terms of difference and of the representation to come. The *chora* may be pre-linguistic, but the becoming of the sign system is always-already in progress. Language does not arrive on virgin territory, for the hypothesized origin of the subject, of language and of the signifying process does not precede or escape the work of the *trace*.

The *chora* is said to be semiotic because it is already characterized by distinctions, even divisions. It is "formed by drives and their stases": "discrete quantities of energy" are "arranged according to the various constraints" that check them, and the drives—arranged in this way into waves of destruction and moments of stasis—"articulate" the *chora*. The *chora* is thus formed by the "marks" of drives, by their regulation, that is to say, by the rhythmic alternation of their movement and their arrest (RPL 25). It is always-already punctuated, even constituted, by full stops. The *chora* is therefore not a subsistent entity; it is not simply composed of drives, or of energy as such, any more than language is composed of sound. Just as language is a system of differences, a set of relations between and among signifiers/signifieds, the *chora* is a rhythm of articulations, formed by the difference between charges and stases, by the repeated interruption of drives, its only identity a differential one. [4]

Clearly the *chora* is not an instance of oneness between the self and the world, a mythical origin of pure unmediated natural experience before the division represented by the sign. [5] Although pre-linguistic, the *chora* is neither pre-sense, nor a period of self-presence. The infant does not have direct access to drives and body energy before a split into nature and culture, into the body and thought or language. Instead, drives—not present as such—are apprehended through their traces, the traces of their discontinuity. At this, the most primitive stage in the development of the subject, there is already differentiation (spacing) and repetition (temporization). Unlike the mythical source, the *chora* is neither an absolute origin (it is formed by traces) nor simple (it is already divided into charges and stases) nor present (the traces point to a relation between presence and absence). Kristeva insists upon the graphemic metaphors (social organization "imprints its constraint" on the *chora*, RPL 27). She amplifies the work of the trace and continues to elaborate the process of *signifiance* on this basis: the *chora* itself is not present to the speaking subject but a putative stage, only accessible through its traces—the traces of traces (cf. RPL 68). [6]

If Derrida insists on the trace and the mark and on writing as the model for semiotic systems in general, it is because writing does not give the impression of immediate communication. On the contrary, there is a gap between writing and reading; the moment of reading is deferred, and may be deferred indefinitely. Writing is interpretable in the absence of its author, and may be intercepted by various readers, whether addressed to them or not. The written word is interpretable even when severed from the time, place and context of its production. [7] That is to say, the signifier functions in the radical absence of any permanent link to an immutable signified. Derrida argues that writing functions because of—and not in spite of—this non-presence, delay or interval, and that this gap of interpretability dissociating a signifier from its "origin" is the condition of functioning of any sign. The trace and the interval mark the very possibility of language. Thus the feeling of presence and immediacy in speech is an illusion: the minimal interval between the mouth and ear makes signification possible. Even in the interiority of the mind, it is the interval between thought and itself, between thinking and thought as we perceive it, that enables thought to be understood as such.[8]

Although she devotes a great deal of attention to written texts, Kristeva frequently seems to privilege the voice. When the semiotic irrupts into the symbolic, it acts on the signifier by working on syntactical ellipses and gaps in logic, but above all on sound, rhythm, prosody and phonation. In studying Mallarmé, Kristeva focuses on phonemic patterns.[9] And in an article entitled "Contraintes rythmiques et langage poétique" (PL 437-466), which I should like to dwell on for a moment, she analyzes not only the first sounds the infant makes but also the carry-over of aspects of these sounds into adult speech, studying recordings of Joyce and Artaud reading their texts aloud. At first glance this concentration on speech and the voice could appear to be at the expense of writing and the trace. Closer attention however reveals that Kristeva's findings are far from incompatible with Derrida's. The title of the article, for example, already gives some indication of this: "constraints" and "rhythm" suggest that the baby's earliest utterances are not unformed, unmarked. And indeed this proves to be the case. Although we might suppose the baby's cries to be as far removed as possible from written language, Kristeva demonstrates (a) that they are marks, (b) that they are marked, and (c) that they, in turn, mark. In other words they are triply conceived on the basis of the trace.

The baby's vocalizations may not have linguistic signification, but they are "*marks* of bio-physiological states or of the action of the environment" (PL 440),[10] traces of the infant's circumstances and surroundings. Once again they do not indicate an entity but rather a relation of difference: "All the emissions of sound seemed to be triggered initially by a deprival or a *loss of balance*" (PL 441). The sounds are an exclamation mark, the reaction to an imbalance, a "not enough" or a "too much," whether of milk, sleep, attention or some other requirement (441): they are not the mark of a presence or an absence but of a relation. The idea of imbalance, of course, should not lead us to suppose that there is some prior state of perfect equilibrium and wholeness to be overturned. What gets interrupted is a "continuum between the body and the environment that is maintained through the agency of the mother" (441-442), that is to say, not unity, but a between (the relation body/environment) that is itself maintained by a between (an intermediary), a discontinuous continuum that functions only by virtue of a structure of supplementarity (the mother is both additional and essential to the relation).

The cry is thus the trace of difference (of imbalance) and, given that it constitutes a "response" (PL 442) to the baby's situation, is deferred in relation to it. The interval appears: the sound is not the live transmission of a bodily state, the pure expression of hunger, for example. And the sound is structured: "These marks are subjected to an organizing process of increasing complexity: this is precisely what I term the *semiotic*" (440). Kristeva insists on this ordering process: "right from the prephonological stages, processes occur that structure the flow of sound, which is semiotic although it does not yet signify" (449n). Well before the development of syntactic and phonemic constraints, rhythmic and intonational patterns shape and leave their mark on vocal utterances. These organizing patterns are created through repetition, but this is not to suppose that there is a first time that precedes repetition.[11] There is never an unpunctuated pure flow of sound, if only because the child must breathe and start again (cf. PL 444). In her article, Kristeva represents the baby's cries on graphs indicating frequency and volume in relation to time. She writes the sounds: they become marks on the page. The curves and leaps in the lines clearly show the rhythm of repetition, the wavelength of the semiotic waves. However even the idea of frequency itself—the rate of recurrence of sound vibrations—already points to periodicity: sound is always-already structured by repetition.

The semiotic structuring of sound through constraints has interesting consequences. Although the cries are marks of imbalance in the baby's environment and are thus accompanied by displeasure, the rhythmic regularity of the vocalizations gives rise to pleasure: "It is *repetition* that takes the sound emission of displeasure and articulates it into a regularity, structure or figure that is the first and only inductor of relaxation, or pleasure, in the one who vocalizes" (PL 443).[12] Through the action of the trace (the repeated mark of the difference in the baby's situation), poles reverse; through repetition of the mark of discontent, displeasure turns to pleasure. The opposition is undone: a supplement of sound—that necessary extra—balances the imbalance.

The pre-phonological utterances are thus not only marks and marked but also marking: they have an effect on the baby's circumstances. But the marking goes further than this: repetition enables the child to organize not only sounds but his body.[13] Through repeated cries that gradually become more and more structured, the infant learns to isolate various parts of the body, and to start with, the vocal chords. This is the first step in the "difficult process of learning bodily differentiation" (PL 442). Sounds become associated with areas and functions of the body:

> The *front* pseudo-vowels and pseudo-consonants are emitted by way of a contraction of the *upper* part of the body and the digestive tract: we shall say that they are the mark of an oral drive. The *back* pseudo-vowels and pseudo-consonants are clearly accompanied by a contraction of the abdomen that goes as far as loosening the uncontrolled anal sphincter, as well as by agitation of the lower limbs: we shall say that these are the mark of an anal drive. (PL 445)

Although linked to drives—even attributable to them—these sounds are deferred in relation to them. Kristeva insists that they are the "audible mark" (442) of drives. As infant drives become associated with particular frequencies in the vocalizations, repetition and rhythm work to structure the body and sound, such that the articulated and co-ordinated body develops together with language (456). Even after language acquisition, these semiotic processes continue to leave their mark, becoming "fundamental discourse structuring operations" (465).

Kristeva thus avoids interpreting the infant's early cries as direct expressions of sensations. Neither the vocalizations nor the apprehension of the environment or the body are ever unarticulated or immediate. From the beginning, utterances are structured by the marks and intervals of rhythmic repetition—by the trace. The voice has no primacy with regard to writing; the vocalizations can be seen to be modeled on writing. "All these differences in the production of the trace may be reinterpreted as moments of deferring [*différance*]" writes Derrida apropos of Freud's concept of *Bahnung* (WD 202), and it seems to me that the repetitions and ruptures in the production of the baby's cries and in the functioning of the *chora* can similarly be reinterpreted: marked and marking, deferred and deferring, they are inscribed in a movement of *différance*.[14]

And yet, in this analysis of pre-linguistic processes, whereby Kristeva's work lends itself so readily to a Derridean interpretation, the two theories do not coincide exactly. The Derridean I can but subscribe to the analysis of cries as audible marks. However, if the trace supposes an interval, the interval supposes a space of play: there is room for maneuver that makes it possible for marks to be detached from the circumstances of their production. And here we can see that the point of proximity is simultaneously a point of rupture. Once there is a gap or interval, the mark (the sound) becomes interpretable. No one interpretation dominates or excludes all others, no particular drive for example, no transcendental signified. The certainty of a link—such as the bond between sound and drive—becomes doubtful. But Kristeva does not seem to doubt the link. Not only audible marks, certain sounds appear to have all the earmarks of particular instinctual functions. And as we shall see in Chapter 7, when we examine Kristeva's work on the literary text, even in symbolic language, the semiotic insistence on certain phonemes reveals the action of a particular underlying drive force. Although for Kristeva this drive is not a signified, it does provide sound with a sense that is apparently not detachable but anchors the floating signifier in the body.

Kristeva's work thus leaves a remainder (*un reste*) that resists absorption into the Derridean reading; the overlap of theories is not perfect. Derrida can subscribe to Kristeva's elaboration of the semiotic. Such endorsement, however, necessarily marks her theory, underlining its signs of deferral and repetition whilst bracketing the anal and the oral, the importance of drive involvement.

PRESENCE OF MIND

Let us shift from the infant state (*infans*) to the speaking subject and from a focus on periods and exclamation marks to quotation and question marks. Kristeva explains the transition to speech in terms of the intervention of the thetic break and access to the symbolic realm. The question I wish to pursue, as a Derridean I, is the extent to which Kristeva's speaking subject can be interpreted as a product of *différance*, or whether it stems from a conception of experience as presence.[15]

Kristeva asserts that "the symbolic [. . .] is a social effect of the relation to the other" (RPL 29): the interval linking and separating same and other is at the basis of the symbolic mode. Clearly the symbolic modality—even more than the semiotic—is constituted through differences: its condition of possibility is the thetic break introducing divisions (such as I/me, self/other, I/you, subject/object, signifier/signified) that make signification possible (43-49). These differences appear to be products of *différance*: as we saw in Chapter 2, the binary divisions are reversible and permutable, substituting for one another within language. The relation between terms is one of both identity and difference, whereby the object can be seen as a deferred moment of the subject. Moreover, like *différance*, the movement producing permutable oppositions is apparently inexhaustible: negativity "prevents the immobilization of the thetic" (113), destabilizes it and thus continually gives rise to a "second-degree thetic" (50). The thetic phase is never accomplished once and for all but needs to be repeated over and over again, and in its recurrence, it is transformed: there is of course difference in repetition. In the destruction and regeneration of the thetic position, it is transposed (59-60), thus altering the conditions for signification: "If one grants that every signifying practice is a field of transpositions of various signifying systems (an inter-textuality), one then understands that its 'place' of enunciation and its denoted 'object' are never single, complete, and identical to themselves, but always plural, shattered, capable of being tabulated" (60). Signification is therefore not established once and for all in the thetic phase—it has no permanence or presence in the symbolic—but is continually recreated in the "shattering and maintaining" of the position (56). This is the concept of "practice" to which Derrida subscribes in *Positions*.

What then of the subject of this signifying practice? Presumably the speaking subject has no permanent symbolic presence either and, rather than being planted firmly in the domain of signification, is buffeted at its threshold, at the site of thetic confrontation. Derrida, however, writes that "[t]he concept of a (conscious or unconscious) subject necessarily refers to the concept of substance—and thus of presence—out of which it is born" (WD 229). To what extent is this true in Kristeva's work? Does the link to the body through instinctual drives anchor the subject to a metaphysics of presence? Is the *sujet en procès*—the subject in process/on trial—present in the body, self-present? There is a question mark over the Kristevan conception of the subject.

As we have seen, the Kristevan subject is constituted through a dialectic: as subjects, we are split between the symbolic and the semiotic, neither of which we control since they are determined on the one hand by social and linguistic constraints, and on the other hand by instinctual forces. The symbolic, however, does allow the subject to exercise a certain power, the power of judgment for example: "Negation in judgment, like strictly linguistic [. . .] negation, puts the subject in a position of *mastery* over the statement as a structured whole" (RPL 124).[16] But how masterful is this mastery? It seems that the sense of ascendancy belongs to the Kantian judging subject who feels unified and self-present (118). This subject, however, only corresponds to half the story: the impression of control is only made possible by ignoring the force of negativity acting through, against and in spite of judgment. Generated by negativity but blind to it, the symbolic function is only one moment in the process of *signifiance*: both the unitary subject and his mastery over verbal communication are constantly threatened by semiotic attack, which may be resisted but not controlled. And when negativity unleashes its force against the symbolic, negation ceases to represent triumph and becomes a line of defence, a "breakwater for protecting the unity of the subject" (124-125). The judging subject is incapable of mastering the unfathomable forces of the semiotic and the "heterogeneous economy" that governs them: they remain enigmatic.

Thus the self-presence of the subject who manipulates symbolic structures is illusory: a product of the repression of the semiotic, such presence (or 'presence') can only be partial and precarious. Against the idea of a transcendental, knowing, cogitating and self-present subject, Kristeva proposes her theory of the "subject in process/on trial" (RPL 111), an "impossible unity" (118), a "splitting subject in conflict who risks being shattered and is on the brink of a heterogeneous contradiction" (187). The subject of this process does not dominate it but is created and sometimes swept away by it: "no subject, even a split one, can understand it" (101).

Using the Hegelian concept of negativity—but acknowledging that it still carries the trace of the Kantian subject—Kristeva reworks the idea of presence: "Though marked by the indelible trace of the judging subject's presence, the concept of *negativity* leads this trace and presence elsewhere—to a place where they are produced by a struggle of heterogeneous antitheses" (RPL 118). Rather than the subject and presence *being there*, always-already posited, Kristeva investigates the *production* of the subject's presence in the symbolic mode. In fact, she investigates not only the production of presence, but the production of the very subject through the work of semiotic drives: "the place where a subject—who is always absent from this place—is produced" (167, tr. mod.). Kristeva explicitly states that she is more interested in "what produces the 'I' [*ce qui produit le 'je'*] rather than the operations of that 'I'" (36, tr. mod.). Presence producible and produced, the subject producible and produced: the Derridean I would say that they are but effects, effects of presence and effects of subjectivity created by and through the movement of negativity and/or *différance*. But Kristeva doesn't say 'effects'; she continues to write of presence and the subject and does not feel the need to put quotation marks around them. Kristeva goes on to explore "the movement that produces negation and of which negation is only an oblique mark in the presence of consciousness" (118). She shows how "the text shatters and rebinds experience in the process—the term *experience* implying *the subject* and *presence* as its key moments" (187). It is true that she writes of the presence of the conscious and linguistic subject in order to explode it: any presence is pulverized so as to be reformed and relaunched by the process. Nonetheless, although this presence is partial and pulverized, it is interesting that Kristeva embraces the term, something that the Derridean I would hesitate to do. Kristeva italicizes the very words that Derrida finds so problematic, so clearly linked to a metaphysics of full presence—experience, the subject, presence. Is she summoning this metaphysics or reinscribing its key words? In other words, are the italics to stress her commitment to the terms, or are they the equivalent of quotation marks, indicating a distance from a metaphysics of presence?

Derrida in *Speech and Phenomena* argues strenuously against the idea that the consciousness of the thinking subject is ever self-present. For between mastery and the feeling of mastery, something escapes us. *Différance* intervenes. Because consciousness is never prior to language, is never simply "silent and intuitive" (MP 16), thought is always-already deferred in thought itself. There is only an effect—an illusion—of presence. How are we to read Kristeva's work? When she writes of presence in the symbolic, she is clearly not referring to this kind of self-present consciousness prior to language. Instead, the presence of the subject and the very subject are formed at the same time and by the same means as language. "Life must be thought of as trace before Being may be determined as presence" (WD 203), writes Derrida. Kristeva does this, it would seem, establishing a subject, each phase of whose development is a consequence of traces or marks of difference: producible presence is a network of marks and divisions, generated by negativity. It seems that having argued for the production of the subject's presence, Kristeva uses the term "presence" as a convenient shorthand for a complicated process. She has acknowledged and worked through the metaphysical assumptions usually associated with the word and reinscribed it in her own theoretical framework.[17] As an element of Kristevan vocabulary, there is perhaps no longer any need for quotation marks.

"Constituting and dislocating it at the same time, writing is other than the subject, in whatever sense the latter is understood" (OG 68). For Derrida, the subject always refers "to the substantiality of a presence unperturbed by accidents or to the identity of the selfsame in the presence of self-relationship" (OG 69). But the Kristevan subject seems to answer Derrida's objections and fit in with his concerns. Constantly disturbed, it is always-already being dislocated and reconstituted in an infinite process. Its self-relation is split and interrupted, defined by a between. Its identity is a function of its signifying practice—the "practice" to which Derrida subscribes.

Kristeva hangs on to the term "subject," although in the best of cases the subject will be a "subject in process." Derrida prefers to write of "effects of subjectivity": "I have never said that *there is not* a 'subject of writing.' Neither have I said that there is no subject. [. . .] It's just necessary to reconsider the problem of the effect of subjectivity such as it is produced by the structure of the text" (Pos 88, tr. mod.).[18] Perhaps the question mark that remains over the use of "presence" and "the subject" in Kristeva's work signals a question of emphasis: is she focusing on "*producing* the subject" or "producing the *subject*"? Should we speak of "*effects* of presence" or "effects of *presence*"? A Derridean reply might be: "There is no disagreement between us. Wherever and to the extent to which the motif of presence functions effectively, in a textual work, as a trace or a producible effect, and taking into account a new problematic of meaning, I agree. Yes, Why not? Provided that one determines the concept of presence with the necessary critical precautions."[19] Kristeva and Derrida agree that the subject (or subject effect) is produced (in the movement of *différance*) or generated (through negativity). Derrida declares that "The 'subject' of writing does not exist if we mean by that some sovereign solitude of the author. The subject of writing is a system of relations between strata: the Mystic Pad, the psyche, society, the world" (WD 227).

Similarly, Kristeva's subject is created by the articulation of psychical and social orders and only exists between them.

However, although produced, the Kristevan subject is seen as other than a "system" or an "effect." The site of a process that creates upheaval in the body and pulverizes thought, the Kristeva subject risks madness and death and is at the mercy of conflicting instinctual and social forces. Again the overlap between theories is less than exact, leaving remainders on the fitting room floor, reminders of Kristeva's potential resistance to this process. In sewing Derrida's and Kristeva's work together, this reading is far from seamless. Here we can see the tell-tale signs of a splitting at the seam, a line of tension that may well lead to rupture. . . .

THE DIALECTIC AS DETOUR

Having followed the work of the trace — magnifying glass in hand — in each of Kristeva's modes, I would now like to look in detail at the relation between them: to what extent can the semiotic/symbolic dialectic be reinterpreted in terms of Derridean *différance*? Certainly the split unity of the subject produced in the dialectic is marked by the trace. Nevertheless there are aspects of the system that at first glance sit uneasily with a theory of *différance* and notably its apparent binarism. Let us zoom in, then, on yet another punctuation mark — the /, the stroke between the two modalities of Kristeva's theory. Is this stroke of the caressing kind or more like a blow? Can it — and if it can, should it — be seen along the line(s) of the Derridean oblique between "limit/passage" (MP xi) or "appear/disappear" (MP 23) or indeed between the terms of any opposition that Derrida examines? What would it mean to deconstruct Kristeva's opposition? Would it conflict with her work, or do her texts already anticipate, even initiate, a deconstruction of the semiotic/symbolic opposition?

To explain her theory, Kristeva insists that semiotic functioning is the precondition for the symbolic, that it "logically and chronologically precedes" the thetic phase (RPL 41). Now the firstness of the semiotic and the secondness of the symbolic are troubling for the Derridean I: like the myths of the original that precedes the copy, and of the full presence of speech that precedes writing, this ordering appears to claim to have solved the chicken-and-egg question. However, Kristeva is playing a double game here: on the one hand she puts forward the *chora* as the most primitive mode of the future subject, in order to describe an origin of difference and deferral. On the other hand, she is clearly aware that the primariness of the *chora* is ultimately an untenable argument, "a *theoretical supposition* justified by the need for description" (68). The *chora* is "already put in place by a biological setup and is always already social and therefore historical" (68). In other words symbolic constraints are as much the precondition for the *chora* as the *chora* is the precondition for the symbolic (50). The structure of supplementarity is at work: the symbolic comes after, is additional but is also a necessary pre-requisite. The firstness of the *chora* is a concept already under erasure in Kristeva's writing. But the supplementarity of the Kristevan dialectic does not stop there.

The semiotic/symbolic division seems to invite a deconstructive reading: as in a classic binary opposition, there is complicity between two terms that are nonetheless engaged in a hierarchical struggle. But in a sense, the work of deconstruction is already initiated by Kristeva herself, although she doesn't present it as such, in that she recognizes and emphasizes the ambiguity of the division. Semiotic and symbolic are never presented as two clearly separate terms. On the contrary, there is a clear relation of supplementarity. Derrida explains supplementarity by considering in particular the pairs open/closed, writing/speech.[20] Just as Derrida demonstrates in the latter case that, historically, writing—"interior to speech and essential to it"—has been "contained outside of speech" (WD 197), repressed and ignored, Kristeva demonstrates that extra-linguistic (semiotic) elements have always been excluded from and subordinated to symbolic language. She therefore strives to describe the relation differently, as an interdependent articulation of the two domains. The instinctual semiotic is not dismissed from linguistic functioning. On the contrary: "It exists in practice only within the symbolic" (RPL 68), and far from being subjugated by the symbolic, transgresses it constantly and even dislocates it. And conversely the symbolic plays an indirect role in the semiotic, ordering it through the mediation of the mother. Kristeva works against the repression or exclusion of either term, and if she describes their hierarchical struggle, it is not to valorize one at the expense of the other. The semiotic has no meaning without the symbolic and the latter, if it does not incorporate semiotic functioning, becomes a sterile exercise ready to dissolve under the onslaught of the return of the repressed. Chapter 2 studied the ambiguity of the semiotic/symbolic relation in detail, this "dialectic of two heterogeneous operations that are, reciprocally and inseparably, preconditions for each other" (RPL 66). A Derridean reading of this ambiguity would note that neither mode can exist in a pure state: something is missing from each and can only be supplied by the supplement of its other. The structure of supplementarity is perhaps most obvious in the way that the symbolic protects itself against instinctual (semiotic) attacks: it redirects them into a pocket of semiotic activity within the symbolic, where they can act upon the signifier. Language provides "a pocket of narcissism toward which this drive may be directed" (49). In other words, the symbolic vaccinates itself against the semiotic by incorporating an element of it.

It is perhaps not surprising to find supplementarity between the semiotic and the symbolic when we consider that they are both ultimately generated by a force that in many respects resembles the movement of *différance*: negativity. In the second section of RPL (107-164), Kristeva reworks the Hegelian concept of negativity in terms of her own theory, such that this movement (which she also terms "expenditure" and "rejection") is the force producing both the semiotic ("the movement of material contradictions that generate the semiotic function" 119) and the symbolic ("this semiotic movement, which moves through the symbolic, produces it, and continues to work on it from within" 117), together with their dialectical relation. Like *différance*, negativity is radically heterogeneous to traditional constraints and yet generates their possibility. Like *différance*, negativity is only accessible through its traces: it is "discernible through the *positions* that absorb and camouflage it" (123) and can be registered by language "only as a series of differences" (124).[21]

Thus in both Kristeva's and Derrida's work, two opposing terms supplement each other because they are generated by the same movement. However, when Derrida points to this complicity in Freud's work, it is to go further: "This is why every apparently rigorous and irreducible opposition (for example the opposition of the secondary to the primary) comes to be qualified, at one moment or another, as a 'theoretical fiction'" (MP 18). Following this line of thought, not only would firstness/secondness be a theoretical fiction, as Kristeva herself is happy to admit, but any pair of opposing terms, including the semiotic and the symbolic. Kristeva may recognize the structure of supplementarity on which they are based, but would she go so far as to "renounce any radical distinction" between them (OG 69, tr. mod.)? Kristeva describes negativity as producing discontinuity and deferral, as generating the semiotic and the symbolic, but it is difficult to imagine her subordinating her famous dichotomy to this force.

For Derrida, the play of oppositions is but a "difference effect" produced by *différance*: "What is written as *différance*, then, will be the playing movement that 'produces' [. . .] these differences, these effects of difference" (MP 11). Seen in this way, the semiotic/symbolic confrontation loses much of its force: the division is merely an effect of a movement that exceeds it. For Derrida, the problem is not the relative importance of this or that opposition but the validity of the oppositional structure as such, determined as it is by the history of philosophy. In looking beyond particular oppositions to the more general movement of *différance* that produces them, Derrida indicates the scope of his project: "we will designate as *différance* the movement according to which language, or any code, any system of referral in general, is constituted 'historically' as a weave of differences" (MP 12). Kristeva's dialectical system is easily encompassed in this operation: the repeated action of negativity in the charges and stases of drives gradually structures the subject as a web of differences (the articulation of the *chora*, the thetic break, and symbolic oppositions). But from this perspective, the division semiotic/symbolic has no privileged status. It is simply a particular case, an example among others:

> Thus one could reconsider all the pairs of opposites on which philosophy is constructed and on which our discourse lives, not in order to see opposition erase itself but to see what indicates that each of the terms must appear as the *différance* of the other, as the other different and deferred in the economy of the same (the intelligible as differing-deferring the sensible, as the sensible different and deferred; the concept as different and deferred, differing-deferring intuition; culture as nature different and deferred, differing-deferring; all the others of *physis—tekhnè, nomos, thesis*, society, freedom, history, mind, etc.—as *physis* different and deferred, or as *physis* differing and deferring). (MP 17)

The oppositions are literally mentioned parenthetically, as examples incidental to the demonstration of the relation that determines them all. And if we slipped another example into this list—"the symbolic as the semiotic different and deferred, differing-deferring"—it could almost pass unnoticed. In spite of appearances, this interpretation of Kristeva's system doesn't *contradict* it. There is merely a difference of emphasis,

an underlining of a deconstructive tendency in Kristeva's theory. For
Kristeva is perfectly in agreement that the opposition and the dialectical
movement are produced, that "these oppositions have never constituted
a *given* system" (Dis 5) but are generated and traversed by unstoppable
forces. However, rather than reducing semiotic and symbolic functions
to the status of effects of negativity, Kristeva promotes negativity as
important precisely for producing the semiotic and the symbolic. The
two modalities are not eclipsed by their production; they are not mere
examples of consequences of a quasi-universal movement but dynamics
of capital importance in the functioning of the subject. More
determining than determined, the mainspring of any signifying practice,
Kristeva does not allow the semiotic/symbolic pair to be subsumed by
their common denominator.

Speculating on Freud,[22] Derrida interprets the Freudian dichotomy
between the pleasure and reality principles as a product of *différance*,
its effectiveness stemming from the interval or detour between the two.
Without claiming any equivalence between the Freudian and Kristevan
dichotomies other than a structural one, we could transfer this argument
to Kristeva's theory. It would read as follows:

"Pure pleasure and pure reality
are ideal limits, which is as much
as to say fictions. [. . .] Between
the two the *différant* detour
therefore forms the very actuality
of the process, [. . .]. The detour
thereby 'would be' the common,
which is as much as to say the
différant, root of the two
principles, the root uprooted from
itself, necessarily impure, and
structurally given over to
compromise [. . .]. The three
terms—two principles plus or
minus *différance*—are but one,
the same divided, since the
second (reality) principle and
différance are only the 'effects'
of the modifiable pleasure
principle." (PC 284-285)

The pure semiotic and the pure
symbolic are ideal limits, which
is as much as to say fictions.
[. . .] Between the two the
différant detour therefore forms
the very actuality of the process
[. . .]. The detour thereby 'would
be' the common, which is as
much as to say the *différant*, root
of the two modalities, the root
uprooted from itself, necessarily
impure, and structurally given
over to compromise [. . .]. The
three terms—two modalities plus
or minus *différance*—are but one,
the same divided, since the
second (symbolic) modality and
différance are only the 'effects'
of the modifiable semiotic.

We have already seen that neither the semiotic nor the symbolic exist in a "pure state." Indeed in Kristeva's work they seem to be "ideal limits," even "fictions." And Kristeva herself shows that it is the relation between the two that "forms the very actuality of the process." Although Kristeva could well affirm that "the three terms are but one," a single process of *signifiance*, it is difficult to imagine her agreeing that "the symbolic and the dialectic are only 'effects' of the modifiable semiotic," for she describes the symbolic as "qualitatively different" (cf. RPL 172) from a heterogeneous semiotic. However, it is possible to read differ*a*ntly.

The symbolic can be interpreted as a deferred moment of the semiotic in that it is constituted on the basis of a break modifying the semiotic. This break represents a transformation of material that was previously merely provisionally ordered by semiotic articulation. It is transformed by being structured and positioned, but it is not new material. Objects become detached from the fluid motility of the *chora* and positioned in ways that resist reversal (RPL 46-47). Sounds hitherto organized by rhythms become structured into the language of signification and governed by the split into signifier and signified. Space becomes places. The body marked by drive stases becomes differentiated and organized into parts and localized functions and is ultimately structured by an image of its wholeness in the mirror stage. And this symbolic body is a deferred moment of the semiotic body, as each of these symbolic instances is a deferral of the semiotic instance, separated from it by a break — an interval.

Yet once the symbolic function has been established by the thetic break/interval, the semiotic is not cut off from language and the rule of law. The thetic boundary and the barrage of syntax merely necessitate a detour. Henceforth, the semiotic works *through* the symbolic, which incorporates a part of it. And as the semiotic takes its detour through the symbolic, it also re-routes the latter, diverting language, social constraints and institutions to its own purposes, using them to achieve expression. Social limits provide "not social stability, as economic necessity and naive consciousness would suggest, but *jouissance*"; the paternal instance represses *jouissance*, but "also ensures [its] marking in the symbolic, that is to say [its] formulation and [. . .] existence."[23] The re-routing and appropriation, however, works in both directions: the symbolic uses semiotic contestation for the renewal of language and social practice and diverts the semiotic to where it can act upon the signifier. Thus poetic uses of semiotic stases "not only require the ensured maintenance of this signification but also serve signification, even when they dislocate it" (RPL 65). In fact, contestation and the institutions it contests always, in the final analysis, serve each other, to the extent that it becomes difficult to speak of them as "other" to each other.[24] The semiotic/symbolic opposition loses its orientation. It can be reinscribed as a "difference [. . .] without any decidable poles, without any independent, irreversible terms" (Dis 210). The stroke between the modalities is already a very ambiguous division in Kristeva's elaboration of it. The Derridean I need only lean on it slightly for it to take the form of a revolving door. And the relation can be deconstructed even further, for the semiotic and the symbolic mimic each other and even substitute for one another entirely in certain signifying practices.

According to Kristeva, mimesis and poetic language participate minimally in the symbolic — just enough to signify, to have meaning (RPL 57-58). Modern poetic language especially, with its elements of "instinctual glossolalia" (58), comes very close to avoiding the symbolic function completely but usually ends up reproducing a modicum of grammaticality. The thetic position in mimesis and in poetic language is, however, problematic and seems to be largely taken over by the semiotic: these practices "must posit an object, but this 'object' is merely a result of the drive economy of enunciation" (57). Thus the "constitution of the symbolic as *meaning*" (57) is only imitated. There is a "telescoping" together of the symbolic and the semiotic such that the two functions are brought together, superimposed (60).

Fetishism avoids the symbolic even more dramatically than poetic language. The "denial" of the thetic position leads to its displacement onto drives and objects linked to the body by drives. "Fetishism is a stasis that acts as a thesis" (RPL 64). Again, there is a "telescoping" together of the two modes, but this time the semiotic mimics the symbolic to the point where it substitutes for it.

Kristeva admits the difficulty in differentiating between fetishism and certain artistic/poetic practices, between a mock symbolic and a minimal symbolic. Nevertheless, she argues that they are distinct because art and poetic language, unlike fetishism, maintain signification, even if only to signify the unsignifiable. "The text is completely different from a fetish because it *signifies*; in other words, it is not a *substitute* but a *sign* (signifier/signified)" (RPL 65).

It is not inconceivable, however, that the drive economy and its semiotic stases should mimic the thetic position so well as to blur this distinction, that fetishes should be textualized and texts fetishized. After all, the play of substitutions and the play of signs are all part of the same game, as we saw in "Structure, Sign and Play": signifiers substitute for one another in unending succession. And in fact, Kristeva's very analysis shows that the fetish *is* interpretable, and *does* signify, through a thetic "compromise": "although erased from the symbolic and displaced onto the drives, a 'thesis' is nevertheless maintained so that signifying practice can take place" (RPL 64). The fetish seems indistinguishable from the avant-garde text: between the diminished symbolic and the mimicked symbolic there is only the detour between two interpretations, one a deferred moment of the other.

Not only does the semiotic take on the role of the symbolic in these ways, but, in contemplative discourse (RPL 95-99), the symbolic produces a pseudo-semiotic function. Contemplative discourse is described as a sterile, affected signifying practice without any involvement of drive forces. Negativity is sublimated and excluded from it such that "this *Aufhebung* of the instinctual *chora* is always already inevitably and inseparably symbolic" (96). Contemplative discourse (of which, incidentally, a prime example is "the deconstruction of philosophy" 95) "will mime the dissolution of all positions" (97). In other words, it mimics the semiotic attack on the thetic: "the flow of drives is merely mimed within a simulacrum" (98). Drives are replaced by "strictly linguistic materiality" (98). The result is that "Contemplative discourse is strewn with shifts in style: plays on phonic similarities, obsolete turns of phrase, ellipses, parables" (99). Now, interestingly, the play of phonemes and syntactical and semantic ellipses are precisely what Kristeva examines in Mallarmé's texts, examples *par excellence* of poetic language. How are we to be sure that our poets are not charlatans like "the singer-poets, the manipulators of language" who produce contemplative discourse? It is not just that the latter cleverly mimic the processes of poetic language but that what are supposed to be extreme ends of the scale seem to come together. The miming of the semiotic by the symbolic (contemplation) and the miming of the symbolic by the semiotic (fetishism) are both practically indistinguishable from the dialectic of semiotic and symbolic (poetic language) and quite possibly from each other, unless we have access to some form of inside information on the channeling of drives.

To push the point a little further (and to push the Derridean reading of Kristeva's work to the point where rupture appears): if the semiotic and the symbolic are the pre-conditions for each other, incorporate each other, depend on and use each other; if they mimic each other sufficiently to cause difficulties in distinguishing them; if the symbolic is merely a deferred moment of the semiotic; if both functions are effects of negativity, then is it really feasible to maintain a fundamental opposition between the two? Indeed, is there a point to insisting on it? It might be more interesting to accept that the division is doubtful and to look beyond it: "Far from being simply erased, the oppositions deactivated [*déjouées* — thwarted] [. . .] are, in the same stroke, reactivated [*rejouées*], thrown back into play, but this time as effects, not rules, of the game" (Dis 330-331, tr. mod.).

In RPL, Kristeva goes to some lengths to show that the dialectical opposition of semiotic and symbolic is a process whereby law and *jouissance*, authority and contestation not only contradict each other but simultaneously support and even serve one another.[25] Transgression is valorized but recuperated . . . or perhaps valorized because it is predictably recuperable. Once thwarted, how could this opposition be thrown back into play? Without labouring under any illusions of pure unadulterated transgression that would escape law entirely, can we read in Kristeva's work the possibility of a more disorienting form of transgression, one not so predictable, a *jouissance* that confirms the symbolic order a little less? Perhaps one that *pretends* to confirm it? Or one that by pretending to attack it, doesn't allow it to renew its forces? The thetic object is supposed to halt negativity until the latter returns to pulverize and thus revitalize it. But fetishism only pretends to posit such an object. And contemplation only pretends to expend itself in artistic practice. The symbolic order does not appear to be replenished or invariably strengthened by either practice. The mimetic rehearsal of the dialectic in fetishism and in contemplative discourse, which Kristeva interprets as failed — or at least lesser — examples of signifying practices, may well prove to be more effectively disruptive than semiotic attacks on the symbolic.

But why stop there? Is it possible to mime fetishism? Perhaps even to mime it from within contemplative discourse — a mock semiotic positing a mock thesis, a "manipulator of language" going through the motions of displacing the position of signification onto a signifier that is only apparently erotically charged, but actually emptied of drives? In "Restitutions" (TP 255-382), Derrida examines paintings of shoes and feet and recounts the following anecdote:

> Two psychoanalysts—from London, of course, that sort of thing would never get across the English Channel—said to Magritte: "*The Red Model* is *a case of castration.*" The painter then sent them "*a real psycho-analytical drawing*" which inspired the same discourse from them. (314-315)

The difference between the fetish and the representation of the fetish is a space of play. The fetishistic object is "instinctually linked" (RPL 64) to the body. This link (between the mock-thetic object and drives) is a relation between the semiotic and itself (a deferred semiotic), "a structure of alteration without opposition" (PC 285). But links can be unlinked and relinked.[26] In a mimicking of fetishism such as I have proposed, the mimed erotic investment of the object is also a structure of alteration without opposition, this time a relation between the symbolic and itself. And between these two charades, law and contestation cease to be clearly recognizable: there is no confrontation, but a problematizing of the dialectic.

Here we start to see what really resists a Derridean reading: to interpret the symbolic as a deferred moment of the semiotic is to neglect the confrontation at the border that is all-important in constituting and maintaining the subject, language and social ties in RPL. That the semiotic is generated by a negativity reminiscent of *différance*, that the symbolic functions as a "weave of differences" (MP 12) supplemented by the semiotic—these are shifts in emphasis, minimal distortions of Kristeva's theory. However to give the same status to all the distinctions elaborated by this theory (differences in the semiotic, in the symbolic and between the two) such that all the ruptures (stases/charges in the semiotic, the thetic break, syntactical opposition in the symbolic) are equally unstable, such that they lose not only their particularity but their pertinence, is perhaps to overstep the limit. And in Kristeva's theory, overstepping the limit is less a game than a life-threatening experience.

For all distinctions are not equivalent in her work; all strokes are not equal—they range in effect from the caesura to the seizure. The struggle at the front line between the semiotic and the symbolic is the remainder that cannot be made to fit deconstruction and won't simply be swept out of sight.

And yet . . . in Kristeva's latest theoretical book, *Sens et non-sens de la révolte*, even this line of resistance seems to give and to grant passage to the infiltrating reading through Derridean i's. From time to time, SNR almost reads like a deconstruction of RPL's dialectic. Perhaps Derrida and Kristeva can see eye to eye after all. . . .

FROM REVOLUTION TO REVOLT: NON-DIALECTICAL CONTESTATION[27]

Sens et non-sens de la révolte (SNR) is in many ways a revisiting of the question explored in RPL, namely the role and functioning of esthetic experience as contestation, but in it Kristeva sets herself a specific task: rewriting revolt for the 1990s. Full of *fin de siècle* pessimism—*fin de millénaire oblige*—she sees the late twentieth century as characterized by disintegrating subjects in a post-communist power vacuum. The new world order is a "normalizing and falsifiable order" in which the status of power has changed (SNR 15). Power has become diverted into a regulatory administration that normalizes instead of punishing, such that neither crime nor punishment can any longer be clearly identified. Law has dissolved into "measures," into proliferating mechanisms of deferral to other instances, "open to appeals and referrals, interpretations and . . . falsifications" (17). Kristeva also argues that the era of the subject is drawing to a close and that we are entering that of the "patrimonial person" (18), the person as possessor of a collection of saleable organs. The subject has lost its center and is "scattering into organs and images" (57). In other words, the symbolic order is foundering, falling to bits. Law, power and the subject are all dissolving into the fleeting images of TV zapping. We are left with no clear limits, just an unstable pseudo-symbolic.

To the Derridean ear, this sounds remarkably like a deconstructed version of the symbolic—deferred, locatable only as a series of substitutions, not clearly distinguished from either its imitations or its antagonists. Now the Derridean I (and a Foucaldian one too I suspect) would argue that this is not historically specific to the 1990s, indeed that the mechanisms of power have always been diffuse, divertible, deferrable, interpretable and falsifiable, that the subject has always-already been decentered and dispersed, that the symbolic has only ever been a theoretical ideal and has never been other than a pseudo-symbolic in practice. But this line of argument seems to me less productive here than an examination of what happens to the semiotic/symbolic dialectic in this situation. Given that Kristeva seems to be taking the deconstruction of the symbolic on board to some extent—if only within limited historical bounds—what happens to the struggle between the two modalities that was of such importance in RPL? Is it also reshaped to follow the contours of a Derridean reading?

Kristeva investigates the consequences of dissolving and unlocatable power for the subject. From RPL we know that complete failure by the symbolic to provide clear limits heralds disaster for the subject, who may slide into psychosis or become unable to communicate. In SNR the problem is framed in terms of revolt: sliding social constraints mean that there is no clear instance of Law against which to revolt. How do you mount a revolution against a power vacuum? Kristeva reaffirms her belief in the importance of revolt, irrespective of the efficacy of law and the symbolic: she insists that revolt remains absolutely vital, "a continual necessity to keep alive the psyche, thought and the social bond itself" (SNR 302).[28] However revolution as understood in RPL, with its flavour of the 1968 student and general uprising in France, involved a unified instance of power being threatened by largely transgressive forces. If, as Kristeva observes, power has been hoovered out to the extent that this possibility seems to be excluded, then the concept of revolt must be rethought. It needs to be substantially reworked to cope with a situation where there is nothing to confront but an elusive obstacle, an invisible law. This is what Kristeva undertakes in SNR and, in doing so, moves closer to taking a Derridean line.

Drawing on the detours of the etymological itinerary of "revolt," Kristeva manages to encompass nuances of return and diversion as well as transgression into a much broader understanding than that of revolution in RPL. Kristeva determines "three figures of revolt":

1. "transgression of a prohibition";
2. "repetition, perlaboration, elaboration";
3. "displacement, combinative systems, play" (SNR 40).

The first figure embraces revolution as transgression and confrontation but situates it historically—as merely one possible form of revolt, and a "dated, dialectical form" at that, although still possible in certain circumstances (66, cf. 61). What was once radical is now a classic form. The latter figures are attempts to find a new logic of revolt: the second is the anamnesis or remembrance of things past of the psychoanalytical relation, the return to the past to modify it; the third draws on twentieth-century esthetic production. Although the second and third figures do not slip easily into its generally understood definition, Kristeva continues to use the word revolt to describe them. This allows her to maintain the connection with her earlier work and also emphasizes that the non-transgressive forms she identifies have the same (ultimately conservative) function as revolution or killing the father, namely the renewal of law and the reaffirmation of the social bond (cf. 21, 60, 186).

This broadening of the understanding of revolt brings it rather close to definitions of *différance*.[29] Already Kristeva's etymological search works through revolt as movement (SNR 8-11) to the articulation of time and space in the concept of revolt/revolution (change through cyclic repetition 11-14). It brings together notions of "turn" and "return" (8), "detour" (8, 10, "which repeat[s] and transform[s]" 13, 14) and "temporization" (13), as well as "opposition" (11) and "conflict" (12). The grouping together of the three figures of revolt shows even more striking similarities with Derrida's descriptions of the various effects of *différance*: revolt as repetition can be seen as "temporization" or difference through deferral; "displacement, combinative systems, play" sounds remarkably like the difference of Derridean "spacing," the detour and the play of substitutions. Thus opposition (transgression), repetition and detour are not opposed to each other but are all seen as products of the same force, ultimately with the same effect for the subject. Moreover, this effect is one of supplementarity: the movement of revolt is the supplement, the necessary addition to our existence, without which life would not continue to be life but would stagnate (21). Revolt is the *différance* between life and itself.

Despite embracing what could only be called a deconstructive definition of revolt, Kristeva in no way abandons the theory she elaborated in RPL. Far from merely relegating the symbolic/semiotic confrontation to the first category ("transgression of a prohibition") and to the past, Kristeva strives to make it work in a modified way. She continues to emphasize the importance of both modalities and shows that it is the possibility of new relations between them, new configurations of power and contestation that produce the other two figures of revolt.

Evidence of new relations between the symbolic and the semiotic can be seen in Kristeva's work on Freudian models for language in SNR (72-140). Language is shown to be at the intersection of the psychical and the physical, of thought and sexuality, of the symbolic and drive energy. Now Kristeva's insistence on a notion of language as *signifiance*, comprising both linguistic and extra-linguistic dimensions has not wavered since RPL. What is interestingly different however is her tendency to characterize the relation between these two aspects as "co-presence" in SNR and to downplay any hint of the kind of violent confrontation between them described in RPL (the "irruption" and "attack" of the semiotic which "disrupt[s]" and "destroys" the "defensive construction" of the symbolic, RPL 49-50).

The new configurations of the semiotic/symbolic relation are explored at length in Kristeva's development of the third figure of revolt, which occupies the entire second half of SNR. Kristeva offers glimpses of alternative revolt in the work of Louis Aragon, Jean-Paul Sartre and Roland Barthes. All three writers had more or less fatherless childhoods, but Kristeva focuses less on their biography than on their texts to trace patterns of revolt that do not depend on there being a unified instance of paternal law to oppose in an Oedipal configuration. In Kristevan terms, she finds in each case an involvement of the semiotic in a form of contestation that, rather than attacking the symbolic, finds a way around it.

However, these attempts at revolt are fraught with danger and the chances for success are severely threatened. Although there are moments when they have a sense or make sense, at other times they result in an impasse, in failure and absurdity, hence the "non-sense" of revolt. The failures have a rather ambiguous status, for they both open up and close off the possibility of rewriting the semiotic/symbolic dialectic, as Kristeva hovers between reaffirming and revising her position in RPL, unsure whether to accept that non-oppositional contestation can be effective.

Kristeva interprets Aragon's literary enterprise, in particular "La Défense de l'infini," as a confrontation with the impossible, where confrontation does not mean war. Rather than revolting against the father and law, Aragon was involved in trying to represent the irrepresentable or *a*-thought [*l'a-pensée*], to come as close as possible to the unthinkable underside of language, the semiotic: "Neither knowledge nor action, but with them and through them, *a*-thought deploys [*déploie*=deploys, unfurls, displays] in the flesh of language the polyvalencies of metaphors, the semantic resources of sounds and even the throbbing of sensations" (SNR 254). Unlike the oppositional semiotic/symbolic relation Kristeva describes in RPL, the relation here seems to be one of following the semiotic as closely as possible, miming it, moulding language to its fluid shape, such that only a slight gap—a *différance*—separates the irrepresentable and its representation. *A*-thought becomes discernible as Aragon attempts to translate sensorial excess—feminine *jouissance*—into language.[30]

In RPL, Mallarmé and Lautréamont were also seen to be attempting to represent semiotic excess. However, given what Kristeva regards as the impotence of the symbolic in Aragon's work, his writing doesn't seem clearly to fit the RPL description of "poetic language." In fact it comes rather close to her definition of fetishism (semiotic stases substituting for the thetic position).[31] The danger in Aragon's writing is that there is nothing to hang on to but a mirage, nothing to support *a*-thought but the shimmering of sense provided by feminine *jouissance* (SNR 270). Aragon thus runs a double risk: if *a*-thought goes too far in denying the symbolic (for example by retreating from any kind of communicable signification), he risks a complete collapse of identity (psychosis); on the other hand, if he takes the mirage of sense to be sense, he risks setting up feminine *jouissance* as a mock phallic order (fetishism). But its proximity to the borderline seems if anything to make Aragon's practice more valuable as a possible solution to the problem of revolt against a power vacuum. Valuable, but not necessarily viable. The challenge is to maintain a practice "in the crucible of *a*-thought" (255), at its point of becoming.

This is strikingly similar to Kristeva's reading of Artaud's risky, even life-threatening borderline practice in "Le Sujet en procès" (PL 55-106). Artaud too saves himself from collapse into emptiness and saves his work from complete loss of any signifying capacity through an ephemeral identification with the "spasmic asymbolic functioning" of feminine *jouissance* (PL 78). There is, however, a significant difference between "Le Sujet en procès" and SNR. In the analysis of Artaud's work in the former, "the moment of destruction, of annihilation of subjective unity, the moment of mortal anguish or, more simply, 'emotional confusion' thus yields before the affirmation of a *productive unity*; or rather, the moments are indissoluble in the process" (PL 85). This "second moment" of the dialectic, the reassertion of symbolic unity and meaning into which the semiotic will burst forth again "is of capital importance" (PL 104). In SNR, on the other hand, Aragon is seen to avoid the moment of affirmation in his texts. The second moment, which seemed to be Kristeva's point of resistance to a Derridean reading, slides.

However there is no renunciation of the dialectic at this stage, only a questioning of it. For ultimately Aragon is unable to sustain his borderline practice. He suffers a crisis of confidence in the imaginary to the extent of burning his work and attempting suicide and finally opts for the "lifebelt" (SNR 295) of political action with the Communist Party and the stability of coupledom with Elsa. His revolt is cut short. Here Kristeva sees the impasse, the non-sense, the "insanity" (*insensé* 294) of a revolt bypassing the symbolic. The antidote to a loss of (symbolic) identity is to join something, anything (308). Membership of the Communist Party being a more conventional (oppositional) form of revolt, Kristeva sees in it the desire to repair the father and symbolic law, to struggle against the invasion by the feminine and the terrible sinking into *a*-thought, to survive the destabilization caused by the revolt Aragon attempted.

According to Kristeva, Aragon's esthetic revolt offers a glimpse of a new kind of contestation, and yet in failing it seems to confirm the mechanisms of revolution in poetic language as outlined in the seventies and to reassert the inevitability of the dialectic. There is nonetheless an important shift in Kristeva's position. In "Le Sujet en procès," Kristeva declared that "*the absolute rejection of the thetic, subjective and representative phase is the very limit of the avant-garde experience*" (PL 102, original emphasis). In SNR, she is no longer arguing for the necessity of the thetic position but lamenting that it still seems necessary. When the need for symbolic anchoring makes itself felt in a dramatic way, it is cause for regret. Rejection of the symbolic is no longer said to be an absolute limit—she looks at the possibility of pushing back this limit—but it is absolutely risky. Will she find a viable example of her new kind of revolt, a confirmation that the dialectic can be avoided?

Sartre is Kristeva's second example of someone who takes the risk. Not exactly the same risk as Aragon, although his mode of contestation is also intra-semiotic, bypassing the symbolic. The revolt this time is not Oedipal because it is Orestein. Kristeva studies *Les Mouches*, which is not about killing the father or even the substitute father but about killing the mother and cutting all ties with the social group. Kristeva interprets the Orestein configuration thus: given the instability of the symbolic, Oedipal revolt cannot fulfil its dialectical function of elaborating the autonomy of the subject, so the subject is obliged to break more archaic bonds—the attachment to the mother and even to biological survival (SNR 337).[32] Because there is no reliable instance of the symbolic available for attack, the semiotic turns back upon itself. The semiotic substitutes for the symbolic as the object of destruction. Rather than revenge on constraints and law through the putting to death of the other, this is the death of the self as unitary consciousness (348-349), a liberation from the self in the annihilation of self.

Unlike Aragon's attempt to represent the irrepresentable, which almost set it up as a substitute phallic order (fetish), Sartre puts the semiotic to death. He rejects all identity, not just symbolic positioning but even semiotic stasis. Once again, however, this revolt seems to be unsustainable. The ideal of pure non-identity is also an identity of sorts and therefore a trap: Kristeva reads "nausea" in Sartre's writing as the trace of the refusal of identity coupled with the impossibility of this refusal (SNR 352-365). After *Les Mots*, Sartre, like Aragon, is seen by Kristeva to renounce the imaginary, lured by the ideal of political action. The surge of negativity and otherness in language gives way to negativity incorporated in overtly political characters and themes (379-381). Kristeva expresses her disappointment: Sartre's work loses its emotional substratum and participates in a more conventional (oppositional) form of revolt.

Yet again, a revolt avoiding the second moment of the dialectic (the affirmation of a renewed symbolic) is said to fail in the long run. It seems to confirm the view of revolution articulated in RPL as the only viable one—to Kristeva's chagrin in the nineties. Kristeva obviously has her doubts about the necessity of dialectical opposition but cannot quite accept a deconstructed version of her theory, whereby the semiotic and the symbolic substitute for each other, where their opposition gives way to imitation. But third time lucky. . . .

Roland Barthes is Kristeva's third example of an attempt at a new form of revolt. Barthes' revolt does not consist in contradicting paternal authority but in showing up where it is false, faltering or lacking (SNR 389). Rather than a transgressive revolt against the established order, it engages in a form of play that shows the instability of meaning and sense, the power vacuum in language. This "discreet," "invisible" revolt is neither more nor less than the practice of interpretation, endlessly deciphering and displacing (391), a "practice that destabilizes even the elementary support of signification constituted by the unities and rules of language" (444) and thus threatens the very possibility of unified symbolic meaning. Barthes shows that "natural" meaning and the subject said to possess it are nothing but fictions. His writing allows us to "decipher the decentering of the subject and of history" (425). Kristeva sees his revolt in the fact that he continues to interpret at the very moment at which sense dissolves (394), thus exposing the symbolic as merely a pseudo-symbolic.

Now in case we should be tempted to connect this displacement and deferral of meaning with the Derridean concept of writing [*écriture*], Kristeva explicitly—although not altogether convincingly—distinguishes them, on the grounds that the Derridean notion merely refers to an "intrapsychical functioning" rather than a socio-historical one (SNR 425).[33] However the representation of Barthes' strategy as endless interpretation (402) ruling out the possibility of a transcendental signified seems to give the lie to this denial.

This is one of several indicators of a tension at work in Kristeva's chapters on Roland Barthes, a tension that jeopardizes her project at the moment of its achievement and undermines her stated desire to find a form of revolt that can function when the symbolic is effectively sidelined. Of course, a great deal is at stake: if Kristeva *can* locate such a revolt in Barthes' work, her investment in the dialectic of RPL is under threat. Barthes' revolt does not end in impasse like those of Aragon and Sartre. It is clearly seen as successful. What is not always clear is the extent to which it is dialectical and the meaning of "dialectical" when the term is applied to Barthes. Is his revolt of the non-oppositional kind, necessitated by a foundering symbolic, or does it slip back into the pattern of transgression? At the very moment when Kristeva claims to identify a successful, non-transgressive revolt, it seems to be recuperated by the semiotic/symbolic dialectic.

Kristeva's argument is that Barthes' alternative form of revolt is successful because he manages to turn the shortcomings of the sign into signs, gives a sense to the non-sense or to the loss of symbolic sense and replaces the threat of existence without symbolic law by the pleasure of *écriture* with its sensuous substrata (SNR 444-445). Barthes appears to use the (pseudo-)symbolic against itself. He thus avoids Sartrian nihilism and gives voice to semiotic *jouissance* without apparently elevating it to mock symbolic status. By making sense of the loss of sense, he manages to remain between thought and *a*-thought. He neither seeks to preserve the symbolic from dissolution nor stabilizes *jouissance* in a lingering representation. It seems that this was what

Aragon and Sartre were able to do fleetingly but not to sustain: to maintain that loss of sense as meaningful, to walk the tightrope without needing to call for a symbolic safety net.

Here the semiotic/symbolic relation is far from oppositional: the symbolic shifts and dissolves virtually of its own accord, whilst Barthes strives to speak the unutterable semiotic (SNR 392) and translates the less representable, sensuous "body" of meaning into language (394). A deconstructive reading would point to each modality as the other deferred. At the very least, the relation can be seen as a peaceful coexistence of the two.

Kristeva nevertheless insists that Barthes' practice of *écriture* is dialectical (SNR 404-405, 412). However the dialectic is unlike the conflictual one of RPL and even unlike the "dated, dialectical form" (SNR 66), the "old, dialectical model" (61) of the transgression of a prohibition described earlier in the book. The word seems to have been emptied of any hint of opposition. Barthes' "dialectic" is represented in terms of translation (394, 407), transformation (401), transmutation (400) and translanguage (401), in fact, any "trans-" *except* transgression. It seems to be a dialectic of displacement without opposition. The violent confrontation of RPL has vanished. *L'écriture* has become an "intermediary" (400) for the semiotic and the symbolic rather than a battleground.

But I speak too soon: in the final pages of the analysis, co-presence gives way to collision and the old two-beat symbolic/semiotic dialectic of the transgression and re-establishment of law seems to take over again: negativity pulverizing unity (SNR 439), symbolic constraints blocking negativity (440). A change of heart on Kristeva's part? If we check with her earlier text on Barthes—"Comment parler à la littérature," first published in 1971—we find that, apart from a few stylistic changes, these pages (SNR 439-443) are directly lifted from it.[34] How can we interpret this recycling of material that seems to run counter to the project of the book? A short-cut to the end? A tension in Barthes' work? Or a fundamental ambiguity about the aims of the project?

It is true that Barthes' relation to the revolt led by the *Tel Quel* group in the sixties and seventies could be a source of ambivalence. And when Kristeva writes of Barthes' semiological (ad)venture, we cannot forget that she herself was a fellow traveller. It is difficult to imagine *Tel Quel*'s revolt fitting into a paradigm of non-transgressive confrontation: they declared "war" on symbolic unity—social, linguistic and subjective (SNR 397).[35] Unlike Barthes', *Tel Quel*'s revolt was hardly "subtle" (425), "discreet" or "invisible" (391). And yet this distinction is not always clear: the two tend to be assimilated at certain moments of the analysis (235-237, 394-398). Reading the recycled pages from *Polylogue* towards the end of the section on Barthes, one gets the impression that he too was waging the *Tel Quel* war or that they had muscled in on his revolt. Perhaps the ambiguity in Kristeva's reading of Barthes' work results from an attempt to identify her own revolt with that of Barthes.

However, I suspect that it is yet another sign of a hesitation with regard to the revisiting of her theory. If Kristeva has modified her analysis of Barthes' work slightly between the seventies and the nineties, the real re-reading going on in these chapters of SNR concerns the symbolic/semiotic relation—less struggle, contradiction and conflict and more co-presence, deferral and displacement. But Kristeva still seems to be hovering between these two possibilities, not quite ready to relinquish the contradiction, not quite ready to affirm the deferral.

And the hesitation is warranted. For if we were to argue (in a Derridean sort of way) that instability of meaning—the slipping and sliding that Barthes exposes—has always-already been at work, undermining our efforts at transparent communication and abetting the avant-garde in its use of poetic language, then we would have to go back to RPL and the analyses of Mallarmé and Lautréamont to question the dialectic there. To what extent was it really conflictual? Was Kristeva's insistence on the palpable hostility between the semiotic and the symbolic really crucial? Were the symbolic order and the unity of meaning and of the subject necessarily reaffirmed in the text between waves of semiotic destruction? Or were they effects of an ever-shifting play of meaning? Is it possible that esthetic production in the nineteenth century also made sense of the loss of sense without relying on a strong symbolic instance against which to struggle? Despite Kristeva's insistence to the contrary, it could be that the dialectic was never essential to her theory. The shift identified in SNR confirms a reading of the semiotic/symbolic dialectic as detour.

Once again, however, the Derridean reading is overstepping Kristevan limits, for the power vacuum is situated historically in SNR: the difficulty of mounting a revolt against an unstable pseudo-symbolic is a clearly delimited historical necessity, a late twentieth century substitute for more conventional forms of revolt under less than ideal circumstances. If we read the text on these terms (on Kristeva's terms), SNR builds upon RPL rather than undermining it. It shows the extreme difficulty of social functioning when the symbolic is unreliable.

But are Kristeva's limits enforceable? Not just historical limits are in question here, but limits more generally. Throughout SNR, Kristeva is looking for new configurations of the semiotic and the symbolic, whereby they no longer oppose each other, *but nonetheless remain distinct*. Despite the instability of the symbolic, the limit between the two somehow remains in force. The ambiguity of her analysis in fact stems from trying to keep certain oppositions decidable, whether they be semiotic/symbolic, new revolt/old revolt, success/failure, sense/non-sense. Her analyses of Aragon, of Sartre and even of Barthes, on the other hand, show that sense and non-sense are never far apart, that success and failure accompany each other, that "one loses and wins on every turn" (MP 20), that the new and the old (the radical and the classic), the non-oppositional and the oppositional are inseparable, undecidable, even indistinguishable at times.

Seen through Derridean eyes, the powerful divide that Kristeva maintains between the semiotic and the symbolic, even when the latter is failing, stops her from going a step further in her enquiry and identifying what may be a more subtle form of revolt. For in her opening chapter she already describes an interesting configuration: the pseudo-symbolic—the "falsifiable order"—is not a simple transgression of Law but a mimicking of it that may already constitute an invisible form of rebellion. With its mechanisms of deferral that substitute endlessly for unified power and Law, it seems very like Barthes' endless deciphering and displacing of meaning. Add a little reflexivity and the pseudo-symbolic becomes ironic, potentially undoing the system. Rather than a case of unlocatable power, perhaps it amounts to irrecuperable revolt; rather than a problem for contestation, it could already constitute a form of revolt.

As Kristeva's argument unfolds, it touches several times on the question of the simulacrum. She locates the miming of revolt at the heart of the matter. Esthetic practice finds its *raison d'être* in mimesis, in "the need to mime the revolt" of the primitive horde against the father in the form of religion and later art (SNR 33). However, as far as Kristeva is concerned, there is miming and miming, and only *true* mimesis, involving *genuine* revolt, will have the desired effect of reaffirmation and renewal of the social bond. Here again, Kristeva draws the line, and here again, the Derridean I is tempted to push beyond the given limit, not by breaking through it but by rereading Kristeva's theory and making the line disappear.

Constant in Kristeva's work, from RPL to SNR, is the insistence on a particular kind of truth: the authenticity of esthetic experience as it pulverizes the subject, pushing him to the edge of insanity. Indeed in SNR the possibility of falsification is repudiated on several occasions: Aragon is described as "an authentic alchemist of language, a true player who played to the limit" (SNR 309), in whose work "the stylistic fragmentation reflects the hurricane shaking the writer" (293). Similarly, when Sartre writes of play-acting, Kristeva insists that this is not some "artificial flippancy that wouldn't truly involve the subject" (347-348). The experiences of these writers stand out from an all-too-common "charlatanism" (29). The truth of esthetic experience marks the limits of revolt—and of play. But what is to stop a writer (the Derridean I for example) from faking esthetic experience . . . even *jouissance* . . . in such a way as to produce a subtle revolt? A certain ironic distance, not just from the symbolic but from one's own esthetic practice—pretending to risk body and soul, or identity, pretending to represent sensual experience at its least representable—may not count as revolt or even as poetic language for Kristeva, but perhaps, as a form of play, it has its place as contestation ("displacement, combinative systems, play" 40).

This Derridean celebration of mimicry as play and of a diffuse and deferred law undoing itself is, however, somewhat alien to Kristeva's project. If she describes a situation resembling a deconstruction of the symbolic, it is cause not for affirmation but for anguish. The failure of the second and positive moment of the dialectic to reassert unity is not merely a problem for her theory but a social problem of some urgency, a threat to the social fabric and the consolidation of the subject within it. Revolt as play is thus not to be confused with a game and certainly not a game of hide-and-seek with Law, trivializing the danger.

The Derridean reading of the dialectic as detour has been not merely invasive but abrasive. The reading of the semiotic and the symbolic as interchangeable has smoothed off points where Kristeva's theory doesn't quite fit, rubbing out her limits of play. The Derridean I subscribes to Kristeva's theory by turning struggle and defense into free circulation, by turning her front line into a dotted line and then signing on it. But throughout each stage of the reading, pockets of resistance have accumulated, causing it to bulge at the edges. So far, the only splits have been Derridean ones—here and there a point of rupture at a point of absolute proximity. However, the pressure is mounting, and there are signs of an imminent Kristevan rupture—a bursting in the form of an outburst, an "irruption," an exclamation.

Against this reading then, against the engulfing of the dialectic by the movement of *différance*, it is the turn of Kristevan theory to strike back.

NOTES

1. A frequent echo will be that of "Freud and the Scene of Writing" (WD 196-231). Derrida's analysis of Freud's work has particular relevance for the articulation of Derrida's and Kristeva's theories.

2. "It begins by being repeated" (*L'Ecriture et la différence* 366, omitted in translation WD 249).

3. Kristeva refers to Derrida's earlier texts: Dis 159-160 and Pos 75, 106. His *Khôra* did not appear until 1993.

4. Presumably, the very idea of energy itself as present and subsistent is misleading, as a closer examination of the concept would reveal it too to be defined in differential terms, as a capacity to produce difference, to produce an effect.

5. This reading challenges Judith Butler's claim that Kristeva neglects the cultural work of representation and elaborates a view of drives and of the *chora* as simply pre-cultural, pre-symbolic (*Gender Trouble* 88). It also questions David Fisher's claim that because the *chora* is other than language; it therefore contests Derrida's argument that there is nothing outside the text ("Kristeva's *chora* and the Subject of Postmodern Ethics" 97). (A Derridean reading of) Kristeva's description of the marking of the *chora* indicates that it may be textual without being linguistic.

6. My supposedly Derridean reading of the *chora* in Kristeva's work bears little resemblance to Derrida's *Khôra*, which focuses on an aporia in the Platonic text and the *mise en abyme* of Plato's discourse on *khôra* (Derrida uses the term without the article). This is because Kristeva, far from engaging in a detailed reading of Plato, borrows his term and makes it serve a particular purpose in her theory. Intersections of *chora* and *khôra* are however possible and pertinent. Derrida demonstrates that *khôra* is not a stable support for marks, which can only be ephemeral (cf. Kristeva's provisional articulation and reversible ruptures). He shows that *khôra* precedes binary logic (just as the semiotic *chora* "logically and chronologically" precedes the binary opposition associated with the symbolic) and exceeds it: *khôra*'s logic is rather one of

either neither/nor *or* both/and (cf. the "fundamental ambiguity" of the *chora* described in Chapter 2 above).

7. Derrida elaborates the argument fully in OG Part I.

8. Cf. "The unheard difference between the appearing and the appearance (between the 'world' and 'lived experience') is the condition of all other differences, of all other traces, and *it is already a trace*" (OG 65). For a full exposition of Derrida's argument, see *Speech and Phenomena*.

9. *Révolution* 220-263.

10. In this and subsequent quotations, the emphasis is Kristeva's unless otherwise indicated.

11. Cf. Derrida: "For repetition does not *happen to* an initial impression; its possibility is already there [. . .]. It is the very idea of a *first time* which becomes enigmatic" (WD 202).

12. Cf. "[. . .] it is only when he manages to organize his sound flow into a sort of non expressive regularity, and through repetition, that the resulting saving in instinctual energy induces in him a drop in muscular and nervous tension" (PL 443).

13. Cf. "[. . .] the constitution of a sound and body structure [*une structure sonore et corporelle*]" (PL 444).

14. Tilottama Rajan also remarks on the way in which voice and writing inhabit each other in Kristeva's work. She, however, sees this as a critique of Derrida, arguing that Kristeva thus "rewrites Derrida, by deliberately failing to coincide with the latter's opposition between writing and voice" ("Trans-Positions of Difference" 221). After all his efforts to undermine this opposition, I fail to see how Derrida can be held responsible for maintaining it.

15. Cf. "'Experience' has always designated the relationship with a presence, whether that relationship had the form of consciousness or not" (OG 60).

16. Negation in judgment (the "not" of logical opposition) and linguistic negation (saying "no," producing negative utterances) are symbolic operations and not to be confused with negativity, the heterogeneous force linked to the destructive waves of the semiotic. Cf. RPL 117-118 where Kristeva contrasts the two in terms of Kantian and Hegelian philosophies.

17. This is not unlike Lévi-Strauss' *bricolage* or Derrida's writing "under erasure" (writing a word and striking it out but allowing us to read both the word and the lines through it). I suspect that this kind of shorthand in Kristeva's writing is what has led to the many contradictory classifications of her work. After reinscribing a term within her theoretical framework—"feminine" for example—Kristeva tends to go on using it without regularly reminding the

reader of the limitations of its use, without a discursive form of quotation marks.

18. Cf. Pos 84 and Derrida and Kearney, "Deconstruction and the other" 125. Derrida discusses the deconstruction of the subject at length in an interview with Jean-Luc Nancy entitled "'Eating Well,' or the Calculation of the Subject" (*Points* . . . 255-287).

19. Cf. Pos 74, 76, 95 for the sources of the pastiche.

20. Cf. OG Part II.

21. Although it is useful to highlight parallels between *différance* and negativity, the two movements do not coincide—for either theory. *Différance* neutralizes negativity according to Kristeva, whilst for Derrida, Hegelian negativity is closely linked to a dialectic that *différance* explicitly works to undo.

22. "To Speculate—on 'Freud,'" PC 257-409.

23. *La Traversée des signes* 20.

24. In "The Principle of Reason: The University in the Eyes of Its Pupils," in an argument parallel to the one I am making here, Derrida analyzes the way in which research (literary studies, for example) and institutions (the military, for example) serve each other: "It is impossible to distinguish between these two sets of aims" (12). Cf. also "Some Statements and Truisms" in which Derrida shows that the destabilizing and stabilizing functions of any theoretical movement (including deconstruction) are ultimately inseparable.

25. The argument is continued in Kristeva's *Sens et non-sens de la révolte*.

26. In "Restitutions," Derrida examines the logic of attachment/detachment that determines the notion of fetishization.

27. An earlier version of this section was published as part of "From Revolution to Revolt: Kristevan Contestation for the Nineties," *Southern Review*, 30.2 (1997) 146-158.

28. Cf. "the necessity of revolt-culture in a society that lives, develops and doesn't stagnate" (SNR 21). Leaning on Freud's *Totem and Taboo*, she argues that one of the lessons of psychoanalysis is that "happiness only exists at the price of a revolt" and that we need to measure ourselves against a prohibition or an authority in order to experience *jouissance* (20).

29. Cf. Derrida's reference to "permutations, substitutions, displacements" (*Khôra* 65).

30. Kristeva's definition of "the feminine" has remained constant through her texts: "it is not a question of a particular woman or of women as social individuals [. . .] but a part of the psychic life of every subject, as that which is enormously difficult for either sex to represent" (SNR 253). Similarly, feminine *jouissance* is only about female sexual experience insofar as the latter is a

"fantasmatic representation" (294) or "example" of "sensorial experience at its most excessive" (292).

31. Indeed Kristeva uses the term fetishism to describe surrealism in general SNR 303.

32. Kristeva gave a rather different interpretation of Orestes in "Le Sujet en procès" whereby the subject took refuge in sterile symbolic metalanguage (PL 76).

33. In fact, her psychoanalytical reinscription of Derrida's theory makes it difficult to recognize: "the architrace, underlying any trace in the graphemic sense of the term because it articulates the level of the unconscious" (425, cf. 179).

34. "Comment parler à la littérature" (PL 23-54), translated as "How Does One Speak to Literature?" (DL 92-123). The passage in question can be found PL 39-42, DL 107-109.

35. In her semi-autobiographical novel, *The Samurai*, Kristeva describes herself and her *Tel Quel* colleagues as samurai, as warriors (cf. SNR 237, 397).

CHAPTER 5

Cross-Readings (2)

KRISTEVA STRIKES BACK

These two cross-readings are far from symmetrical. In the last chapter we saw an assimilation of Kristevan theory by Derridean in an engulfing interpretation. A different set of tactics, however, is required in order to negotiate Derrida's work from within the framework of Kristeva's. This chapter will be characterized by distancing and opposition, attack and defence. Clearly, it will not merely constitute a reply to the previous one but will allow Kristeva to take the offensive. It is not exactly easy, however, to mark one's distance from a moving object, from a philosophy that claims neither to propose theses nor to defend positions but which instead resembles a set of strategies, receding before any advance.

Much of the chapter will be in dialogue form, as a debate allowing a frank exchange of views to take place. Dialogic and dialectical, this is my Kristevan fantasy, the contest of theories, the face-to-face encounter between the semiotic/symbolic dialectic and *différance*, where the texts talk directly to one another. It is difficult to imagine Derrida being drawn into such a contest. He certainly managed to sidestep this sort of confrontation in his exchange with Gadamer.[1] It is in this sense that the chapter is a Kristevan reading, not so much because Kristeva gets to put her case for the subject on trial but because Derrida is also summonsed, required to answer Kristeva's accusations and to defend his non-thesis as a thesis rather than perform it. This adversarial encounter would not necessarily be appropriate in a Derridean context; it is not usually a deconstructive strategy. Precedents do exist, however. Derrida has been known to respond to accusations and even to attack in response.[2] And so we shall start with some accusations.

But before doing so, let us examine for a moment the nature of the fantasy dialogue. Is this fantasy a "supposition resting on no solid grounds" (O.E.D.)? In fact, there are several fantasies involved here if we take the word not only in the sense of a representation of desire but in its archaic sense of phantom, for the "Kristeva" and "Derrida" invoked are but illusive likenesses, ghosts or counterfeit versions of those who sign their texts thus. What do these phantoms represent? Are the Kristevan and Derridean voices hallucinations or imposters? Do they obey a dream logic or the logic of the simulacrum? Certainly there is the condensation of dream logic, as thirty odd years of texts are synthesized into relatively coherent voices. And I am haunted by the logic of the simulacrum: Is my phantom Derrida faithful to the original? . . . but in which of his texts do I find the original? There is also the logic of repetition as passages are quoted and inevitably transformed in the quoting—sometimes turning into sound bites during the synthesizing process. The synthesis to which I am referring is, of course, more of the electronic than of the Hegelian sort. As the synthesizer produces speech or music by combining syllables or sounds in multiple ways, so these voices are produced from combinations of bits of text and extrapolations from these. And just as the synthesizer is able to produce phrases it has not produced before, so these voices do not represent the sum total of Kristevan or Derridean discourse but one realization of their potential. The illusion of presence —the phantom — is thus created by textual productivity; the speech is based on writing.

This fantasy then indeed rests "on no solid grounds," on no reality, on no person, on no authorization. At best it leans on shifting terrain: the only justifications I offer are textual references. And it raises certain problems. Firstly there is that of a certain streamlining of the voices, particularly of Kristeva's. The odd frequencies are dropped to produce a recognizable timbre; atypical statements are neglected. The fantasy dialogue makes it difficult to do what, for example, Kelly Oliver does in *Reading Kristeva* when she highlights the perplexing contradictions in some of Kristeva's positions. The following "Kristeva" is inevitably a fairly coherent version of Kristevan theory. In order to highlight points of dissension between the two theorists, it centers around the Kristeva who engages with Derrida and argues against aspects of his theory, the Kristeva of the seventies, and indications of shifts in her position are relegated to the footnotes. Invoking an earlier Kristeva as the basis for the dialogue would allow the disputes to be merely hinted at. With the later Kristeva, on the other hand, analogous points could be made and similar tensions could be found, however, the positions would be less clear-cut and the tone would perhaps be more conciliatory as Kristeva's vocabulary moves from thesis-and-rejection to stabilization-and-destabilization. The following, then, does not present an immutable "Kristeva" but the most productive one for the purposes of this cross-reading.

Plurivocity is, however, not entirely lost: the Kristevan voice does modulate from time to time to her later work, and Derridean texts from several decades are (re)cited together, creating a polyphonic overlay. This very polyphony, on the other hand, creates a second hazard, that of dehistoricizing the writings. The synchronic presentation of Derrida's texts in particular means that the development of his work is obscured. Time is largely erased and with it the emphasis on this or that feature of their practice over the years. What emerges from this, on the other hand, is an appreciation of the general consistency of Derrida's philosophical project.

Closely related to this danger is a third, that of decontextualization. The strategic and contextual import of any given text, of any statement, is lost in the patchwork of citations that follows. I would nonetheless argue that in any use or application of Kristeva's or Derrida's texts (indeed, according to Derrida, in any reading of them), they are de- and re-contextualized. Their use in the dialogue may be a more sweeping recontextualization, but I consider it to be consistent with the theories in question, whilst furthering the strategic aim of this chapter, which is to maximize the import of possible points of contention between the two theories.

In short, there are several good reasons *not* to stage this debate. If I proceed nonetheless to do so, it is not through sheer foolhardiness, but because I believe that a useful articulation of the theories can be achieved. Kristeva's accusations against deconstruction demand a response and an engagement over certain points, and the opportunity for these is here provided. The dialogue, however, fulfils not only this purpose but also cross-purposes, as it periodically highlights misunderstandings between two voices that do not always speak the same language.

And yet at times one has the impression that the two voices are one, that they are one split voice—mine. And this is also true. For the bits of text are synthesized into *my* fantasy, which is less pastiche than

projection and identification. The dialogue is also my inner dialogue-
monologue, in which the Derridean I and the Kristevan I confront each
other, and the theories jostle, not for position, but around the notion of
position. Voice or voices? Neither two nor one, both two and one, the
voices of this chapter are the voices I hear whenever I read or write.
They are not disembodied but inhabit my voice. They haunt me. They
are the reason for this book.

*

A last bit of voice-over to clarify the starting point for the
discussion. As I mentioned in Chapter 3, Kristeva's accusations are
made in her six-page critique of deconstruction in *Revolution in Poetic
Language*, where she indicates what "enters into contradiction with
différance" (RPL 144), what collides with it and disrupts it, producing
breaks. She points to what *différance* cannot assimilate or "gather up
[. . .] without leaving any remainders" (144), what resists being swept
along by its movement. She calls it *heterogeneity*. Kristeva claims not
only that deconstruction neglects this heterogeneity, which determines
the semiotic, but that it also refuses the thesis, the thetic position giving
access to the symbolic. In other words, according to Kristeva, Derrida
is blind to what is essential in each of the two fundamental modalities
of the signifying process, ignoring the positive moments and
misinterpreting the heterogeneity of negativity. This makes *différance*,
on the one hand, unable to account for social structure (communication,
law, the family) and the social functioning of the subject and, on the
other hand, oblivious to the renewal of this structure through rejection
(negativity).[3]

But let us look at these shortcomings one at a time. Like Kristeva,
let us separate (problems with) negativity and (problems with)
positivity into two moments.

DRIVE OR DRIFT

Kristeva approaches Derrida's work by comparing *différance* to
negativity: "[Grammatology] is, in our view, the most radical of all the
various procedures that have tried, after Hegel, to push dialectical
negativity further and elsewhere" (RPL 140). Like negativity,
différance is defined as a movement, a "process of scission and
division" (MP 9) bringing contraries together as it produces their
difference, and only perceptible through its traces. Moreover, the two

ways of conceptualizing such a movement both claim to link the known and the unknown, the knowable and the unknowable, the "inside" and the "outside" of thought. For her part, Kristeva writes of the way in which negativity generates (and renews itself in) the dialectic between the symbolic and the heterogeneous semiotic, where "heterogeneity" is described as the radical other of language, thought and the sign, "nonsymbolized and nonsymbolizable" (145),[4] a corporeal excitation or drive force that is "left out" [*reste en dehors* —remains outside] of symbolic structures (180).[5] Similarly, Derrida writes of *différance* as an economy that "brings the radical otherness or the absolute exteriority of the outside into relation with the closed, agonistic, hierarchical field of philosophical oppositions, of 'differends' or 'difference'" (Dis 5).

KRISTEVA[6]—But Derrida's initial positing of radical alterity only enables him to exclude it more easily from his analysis, for the "exteriority" on which he focuses in his work is hardly exterior to thought processes at all: Derrida's work remains at the level of contemplation, of metalanguage, theory and philosophy, divorced from the unleashing of drive forces. The gap of *différance* separating language and its other, deferring otherness in relation to thought, remains irreducible, even constant, such that they never meet. It is almost as if heterogeneity is being kept at bay by *différance*. Drives are only available as traces to be interpreted; their force—the surge and impact interrupting thought and language—is never felt as such. In fact we could say that drive energy is the repressed underside of *différance* . . . a repressed that, of course, returns.

> Although it begins by positing the heterogeneity in which *différance* operates, doesn't grammatology forget this heterogeneous element [. . .]? Doesn't it infinitely delay this heterogeneous element, thus following its own systematic and philosophical movement of metalanguage or theory? Indeed grammatology seems to brush aside the drive "residues" that are not included in the *différance* toward the sign, and which return, heterogeneous, to interrupt its contemplative retention [. . .]. (RPL 143)

If instinctual energy is able to be deferred, it must also have the opportunity to reassert itself, to swell and burst through *différance*, disturbing not only the processes of language and thought that remain foreign to it but the very mechanism of deferral as it does so. Without this participation by drives leading to the renewal of the system, the role of *différance* would be severely curtailed: "*différance* would be confined within a nonrenewable, nonproductive redundancy, a mere precious variant within the symbolic enclosure" (RPL 145). If this does not eventuate, if there is indeed production and transformation where *différance* operates, it is only possible because negativity returns as "the irruption of the nondeferred and impatient drive charge in *différance*" (144-145). There is confrontation and contradiction between the in(de)finite delaying of heterogeneity on the one hand and the force of rejection on the other. Instinctuality works within and against *différance*, but its work is unseen or ignored by Derrida.

[Conjured forth in the Kristevan fantasy, a Derridean voice ventures a direct reply.]

DERRIDA — Nondeferred? Impatient? When I read your work, it is clear to me that vocal emissions are deferred in relation to drives and that drives are only accessible through their traces, always-already deferred.

KRISTEVA — I am speaking of the immediacy of the heterogeneous element itself, before it leaves any trace. As readers/analysts we can infer the work of drives through the way they mark a text, a phrase, a sound; however, as subjects traversed by corporeal forces, we cannot ignore the nondeferrable action of drives. The marks of drives are not traces of traces without origin or end; they point directly to the materiality of the body and its energy. "This instinctual heterogeneity — neither deferred nor delayed, not yet understood as a becoming-sign — is precisely that which *enters into contradiction with différance* and brings about leaps, intervals, abrupt changes, and breaks in its spacing" (RPL 144).

DERRIDA — If we are speaking of radical alterity, there is no question of bringing it back into the closed and hierarchical structure of the binary opposition, which would totally erase its alterity and make it symmetrical to the same. "In order to be something completely other, it must not oppose, must not enter into a dialectical relation" with thought and language for example (PC 318, tr. mod.). The terms are heterogeneous but not contradictory.[7] The relation is of another kind. Ultimately it is this dynamic *relation* that I call *différance*. It "designates *nothing*, nothing that *is*, no presence at a distance" (Pos 81, tr. mod.).

KRISTEVA — Heterogeneity or radical alterity does not exclude contradiction or confrontation. Certainly, contraries will not be equal and opposite; there will not be a simple, symmetrical contrast between two mutually exclusive terms, but the relation is nevertheless one of "heterogeneous contradiction between two irreconcilable elements" with "asymmetrical functions" (RPL 82), "a struggle of heterogeneous antitheses," "a *conflictual state* which stresses the heterogeneity of the semiotic function" (RPL 118).[8] Without the sudden surge of heterogeneity erupting into *différance*, there can be no real rupture, and this is where deconstruction has a problem: *différance* dissolves into mere differences or nondynamic distinctions (cf. 144). Radical and classical cannot clearly be told apart because the so-called radical is merely novel; there is no recognition of the drive investment of, say, the avant-garde, engaged in a genuine revolt. A simple change of perspective will show pleasure and displeasure merging if the orgasmic energy associated with *jouissance* is disregarded. Without interruption by heterogeneity, *différance* can only be a regular delay, a predictable time-lag between the unsymbolized and the symbolized. *Différance* can be seen as merely the process of becoming-trace or becoming-sign. Meanwhile, the irrecuperable remainder of drive energy that cannot be incorporated into communicable (symbolic) signification is forgotten.

DERRIDA —But *différance* is, by definition, unnameable, nonsymbolizable. It is heterogeneous to thought.

KRISTEVA —"materialism and Freudian practice [. . .] show that it is impossible to gather up the heterogeneous element into *différance* without leaving any remainders" (RPL 144).[9] You focus on the traces of heterogeneity—delayed, ordered—showing that they indicate the economy of *différance*. But these traces don't tell the whole story: instinctuality remains excluded, nonsymbolizable; a part of the drives escapes the becoming-trace of *différance*. This remainder acts without deferral: it consists of

> drives [. . .] whose arrangement in and through the body of the subject constitutes the topography of his fragmentation and of his investment without delay or deferral [*différance*] in biological and social matter that is nonsymbolized, but always already organized. (PL 56-57)

DERRIDA —This "disposition," "topography" and "organization" indicate a spacing in the drives that cannot be distinguished from temporization or delay. *Différance* is at work here, not only as deferral but as differences.

KRISTEVA — I do not accept that spacing (difference) and temporization (deferral) presuppose each other, and it is the temporization of *différance* that I particularly take issue with, the becoming-trace, the becoming-sign ("the *différance* toward the sign" RPL 143). It functions as a movement of "symbolic retention, delayed becoming-sign-subject-Being" (144). By infinitely deferring immediacy and the present, your concept of writing attempts to repress the heterogeneous element. There is "an unconscious and psychoanalytical implication, the violence of rejection underlying *différance*," which, although it remains unrecognized, aids deconstruction.[10] But this heterogeneity cannot be included into the becoming-sign of *différance*. What cannot be symbolized can never be accounted for within an economy of *différance*. It can however be signified as rhythm or prosody in the process of *signifiance*.

DERRIDA — But it is precisely this (non)relation between the unnameable and the nameable that I focus on; it is precisely this relation of unknown/known, absence/presence, escaping/becoming-trace that *différance* indicates, whilst trying to radicalize the notions of absence and presence, of unknown and known, of openness and closure. There is no disagreement between us.

KRISTEVA — But the Derridean nonsymbolizable is always-already trace, or is always-already in the process of becoming a trace, of being symbolized. You gesture towards the unthinkable, the unnameable, but from the very moment when it is recognized as nonsymbolizable, you cease to credit it with having any effect. It is pushed aside, forgotten. I propose that we consider a dynamic heterogeneous element, active in its silence, shaking the subject to the core before we can apprehend it in the form of traces.

DERRIDA — Even if we take the drive without regard to its relation to the linguistic sign, it does not escape *différance*, or rather, it escapes as *différance*. What you call the "nonsymbolized and nonsymbolizable" drive cannot avoid "the drive's *relation to itself*" (PC 403), its "auto-heterology" (404-405) or "the driveness of the drive" (403), a *différance* that is, as you say, dynamic. Furthermore, as far as heterogeneity is concerned, there can be no direct access; it can only be approached through its traces. If heterogeneity shakes the subject, there is necessarily an interval between the shaking and the all-shook-up, between the action of the drive and our perception of it. We can only contemplate heterogeneity or alterity insofar as we interpret its traces within sameness.

KRISTEVA —Contemplate, contemplate . . . we have to try to feel, to get away from metalanguage, to put ourselves on trial/in process in order to listen to the rhythm of the body. The avant-garde textual experience, for example, makes use of symbolic, communicative language but "inscribes within it a whole translinguistic, semiotic, instinctual continent, that grasps the subject at levels irreducible to the position of language."[11] That is what is involved in discovering alterity within sameness. Let's leave aside the study of traces that are only available to our intelligence in order to try to experience heterogeneity in its immediacy. In particular I am referring to the heterogeneous element underlying the text, informing its production.

> We need to leave the confines of language in order to understand that which operates in a developmental and logical stage prior to the constitution of the symbolic function [. . .]. We must *leave the verbal function* and move toward what produces it, so as to understand the process of rejection which pulsates through the drives in a body that is caught within the network of nature and society. (RPL 122, tr. mod.)

DERRIDA —Leave language? Leave signs and traces behind? Firstly, I find it difficult to accept a clear distinction between the symbolizable and the signifiable for they seem structurally indistinguishable. The concept of the trace does not only refer to linguistic signs. Rhythm and gesture are traces just as much as words are. (Indeed, I take the trace much further, as the principle by which everything is marked or divided from itself, as the mark of a discrepancy that allows us to see something as the same as itself while it is being repeated.) All these traces function textually: they refer to other traces in a chain of signification without ever reaching a referent that is fully present and that has no need of interpretation. Which brings me to my second point: "*Il n'y a pas de hors-texte*"; "there is no outside-text" (OG 158).[12] "There is nothing outside context" (LI 136), nothing that is not textual in its functioning. Let us take your avant-garde textual experience for example. "there are only traces here, traces of traces without tracing, or, if you wish, tracings that only track and retrace other texts" (*Glas* 79). We do not simply take leave of our intelligence, of language and textuality in order to read or to write such a text; we do not make an exit or reach an outside. Signifiers refer to other signifiers; they function metalinguistically. Each text positions itself among other texts, each sign among signs, each trace among traces. There is no text whose "origin" is not other texts, no language that is not always-already metalanguage, no experience that is accessible other than through language.[13] And we do not leave language when we write.

KRISTEVA —This kind of approach seems to see the signifying process "only as a *text* (in the sense of a coded or deviant distribution of marks), without perceiving the drive rejection that produces it" (RPL 155). But "there is more than a language object in the heterogeneous process of *signifiance*" (DL xi), and the avant-garde text "obliges the reader not so much to combine significations as to shatter his own judging consciousness in order to grant passage through it to this rhythmic drive" (DL 142). The libidinal forces underlying the text are ungraspable. But we should not use their inaccessibility as a pretext simply to leave aside the production of the text and focus only on its linguistic aspects, the "concatenation of signifiers" (*Glas* 157).

DERRIDA —The production of the text is textual too: "the production, if it attempts to make the not-seen accessible to sight, does not leave the text" (OG 163).[14] But

> the concept of text I propose is limited neither to the graphic, nor to the book, nor even to discourse, and even less to the semantic, representational, symbolic, ideal, or ideological sphere. What I call "text" implies all the structures called "real," "economic," "historical," socio-institutional, in short: all possible referents. (LI 148)

This of course includes drives. This is what I mean when I say that "there is nothing outside the text" or outside context.

> That does not mean that all referents are suspended, denied, or enclosed in a book [. . .]. But it does mean that every referent, all reality has the structure of a differential trace, and that one cannot refer to this "real" except in an interpretive experience. (LI 148)[15]

KRISTEVA —The production of the text may be textual in the sense of the "geno-text"—the generation of *signifiance* at the level of the semiotic mode—but it is *extra-linguistic*, and we need to escape the confines of language and the referential to experience it.[16] In my writing, there is

an invasion of positivist theoretical neutrality by the very experience
of the subject of theory, by her capacity to put herself in process/on
trial, to go beyond the confines of her unity — be it split — and to then
return to the fragile site of metal anguage in order to formulate the
logic of this process that she has glimpsed if not undergone. (PL 55)

Let me clarify this: I don't underestimate the importance of
philosophical method and metalanguage. On the contrary, my texts
often involve an "intra-theoretical endeavor" (*ibid.*). But this type of
exercise on its own is far from being able to "'account for' [the] strange
signifying functioning" we call art (*ibid.*) or for "semantico-syntactic
anomaly" (RPL 144). It seems to me that the only way for the subject
of theoretical writing to appreciate the force of Artaud's glossolalia, for
example, lies in a conjunction between theory and the dissolution of
signs (asymbolia). That is to say, we need to "try to intervene in
conceptual systems [. . .] using the experience that the subject of theory
herself could have of this strangeness" (PL 55); we need to take leave
of our senses, as it were, and to go as far as dissolving our own speech,
without, however, losing it definitively. And then we must be able to
recover our metalinguistic capacity and integrate our experience into
our texts, as "an 'I' that has undergone this process in order to return to
his former position and give voice to its poly-logic" (DL 184). We need
to be able to leave and return.

DERRIDA — What you say about giving voice to the process merely
confirms my point: you can only refer to this process through
interpreting it. There is a gap of difference between your experience
and your interpretation of it. As far as dissolving language is concerned
(and it is not to be confused with "leaving" language), you need only
look as far as *Dissemination, Glas, The Truth in Painting, Ulysses
Gramophone*, to see that this is precisely what happens in my texts:
syntax and semantic unity are shattered to open up the field of
possibilities, to allow fragments of language to circulate freely, to
realize at least partly the "chain of virtualities" (Dis 277) they open up.
The sign is constituted and deconstituted: "It has its breaking in itself"
(*Glas* 150).

KRISTEVA — Your puns, word-play, and play on the signifier in
general "bypass [. . .] the subject" (RPL 98). The "process" — the
reforging of the subject that can be seen in the work of Artaud,
Mallarmé, and Lautréamont for example — is only imitated by
grammatology. For the latter operates without the participation of

heterogeneity, without drive investment, without the disintegration and scattering of the subject. It's a play of mirrors, of copies multiplying like a series of paper dolls—the "unfolding" of the simulacrum (*ibid.*)—indicating perhaps the limit of heterogeneity, but never crossing that limit, instead infinitely deferring it.

DERRIDA —I would certainly agree with you that deconstruction unfolds the simulacrum,[17] but I would go still further by saying that there is nothing but simulacrum, in which the "real" or the "original" cannot be distinguished. Thus the fact of "returning" to metalanguage (if we were to suppose that we had ever been able to leave it) "in order to formulate the logic of this process" in a theoretical text (PL 55) also constitutes a kind of simulacrum, a repetition seeking to reproduce— dare I say imitate—the process. But even if we were to accept that this rehearsal of the process somehow required a genuine involvement of drives, how is it to be distinguished from a text that would only imitate the witnessing of the process? How am I to tell the difference between, for example, a theorist dissolving her own speech and a theorist employing what we might come to see as the stylistic conventions of this dissolving of speech? Drive or drift? How do you distinguish, on the printed page, between word play and sound patterns originating from "genuine" subconscious drives on the one hand and, on the other hand, those coming from mere craftsmanship, or from what you see as the intellectual manipulation of language?

KRISTEVA —To quote you: "I simulate unceasingly and take my pleasure nowhere" (*Glas* 65). The distinction between drive involvement and its imitation is abundantly clear in your case. More generally, however, because you remain within metalanguage, you cannot account for "expenditure, semantico-syntactic anomaly, erotic excess, social protest, *jouissance*." *Différance*, as a movement of "symbolic retention, delayed becoming-sign-subject-Being," necessarily represses the heterogeneity underlying such expenditure. However, the repressed element returns, and erotic excess and social and linguistic disturbances bear witness to "the revolution of *différance*" (RPL 144).

DERRIDA —We need to remember that the movement of *différance* is inseparable from that of dissemination, a movement that involves the notions of expenditure and excess far more than that of retention— symbolic or other—and whose very name evokes and plays with the metaphors of orgasm and "erotic excess" as you put it. To disseminate is to scatter the seed, to disperse semen instead of inseminating. Not only does the trace retain and hold in reserve, it also gets spent or lost, is erased. If there is a "becoming-sign," there are also innumerable and inevitable interruptions and discontinuities. There is the ungraspable alterity that escapes the becoming-sign. Furthermore, a theory of *différance* or of dissemination does not distinguish between the functioning or the becoming of the sign and the functioning or becoming of the "semantico-syntactic anomaly," or even the disintegration of the sign through the scattering of the signifier. These are all forms of dispersal of traces. As for social protest, like all forms of head-on opposition, it can be read as yet another manifestation of the effects of *différance*. These "excesses" do not contradict *différance*; they are entailed by it, swept along in its movement. They do not point to "the revolution of *différance*" (RPL 144) so much as its endless, non-dialectical motion.

KRISTEVA —In what you say, everything happens at the level of thought. You write as one of the "manipulators of language" (RPL 97). There is no engagement of drives. All unconscious mechanisms are repressed. Your dissemination is only an intellectual game, that doesn't involve the dissolution of the subject.

DERRIDA —And yet all the work of cryptonymy, of play on the proper name, including my name ("Derrière le rideau," "Der," "Da," "Déjà," "Ja"), is a dissemination of identity, of an identity that was never unified or whole to begin with. [18]

KRISTEVA —You pull words to pieces without tearing yourself apart. And the sign itself is never pulverized but floats in empty space, making itself available for other connections. This is merely "contemplation adrift" (RPL 145). "The deconstruction of philosophy (which is aided by psychoanalysis)" fits clearly into what I call the discourse of contemplation, in which "instinctual dyads"—or pairs of terms that receive their momentum from often unrecognized drives— "are knotted in nonsynthetic combination in which 'plus' and 'minus' interpenetrate like the ends of a magnetized chain." Like the opposite poles of a flexible magnet they join together to "close up a ring that has no outside but can be endlessly dissected, split, deeper and deeper, ever boundless and without origin, eternally returning, perpetually trapped" (95). In deconstruction, plus and minus, positivity and negativity, yes and no, redoubling and rupture, the classical and the radical are made continuous through a ceaseless splitting of the terms. This continuity is only possible because negativity—the movement of contradiction and rupture—is shut off from the drives that generate it. It becomes a pale imitation of itself, confined within the symbolic, closed off from the outside, from an extra-linguistic outside-of-thought. To compensate for this, "contemplative discourse is strewn with shifts in style: plays on phonic similarities, obsolete turns of phrase, ellipses, parables" (99). These are only esoteric "devices of the signifier's drifting" (99). Locked within the symbolic, the subject creates an illusion of drive investment. We are given the impression that the "core" of the signifying process is "unmasked" (98).

> But this is an illusion, for, emptied of its heterogeneous contradiction, withdrawn from material discontinuity and social imbrication, the flow of drives is merely mimed within a simulacrum and its unfolding, a sidestepping. The enunciation of this hollowing out of drives constitutes a drifting [*dérive*] of the signifier within the boundaries of the symbolic. (RPL 98)

If I use the term "drifting" (98, 99, "contemplation adrift" 145), it is because such a practice denies the symbolic anchoring of the subject whilst doing nothing to decenter it (which would require the unleashing of drives). It "disavows the subjective" (98).

DERRIDA — By insisting on the anchoring of the subject, it seems to me that you try to limit play: "The desire to restrict play is, moreover, irresistible" (OG 59). The word "drifting" or *dérive* often appears in my texts and precisely in order to refuse any definitive anchoring, whether subjective or other. But in fact "I have abused this word, it hardly satisfies me." It seems to suggest a loss of some previous anchoring and a uniform movement away. "*Drifting* designates too continuous a movement: or rather too undifferentiated, too homogeneous a movement that appears to travel away without any jerkiness from a supposed origin." But the movement is more random and unpredictable than this, even resembling the "irruptions" of which you speak, and any moorings are far too tenuous to serve as anchor. Rather, there are "effects of anchoring" but also "collapses of the coastline, strategies of approach and overflow" (PC 261, tr. mod.).

KRISTEVA — A simulacrum of irruption! Such examples of collapsing are trivial, anodyne. They involve no investment of drive energy. If the anchoring of the subject is only considered as an effect or an impression, its crumbling is of no consequence. The subject remains intact. You say it yourself: "I 'play at coming'" [*je 'joue à jouir'*] (*Glas* 65).[19] Deprived of the heterogeneity needed to confront them, your entire strategy attempts to avoid the constraints of law and institutions; indeed it hardly recognizes their existence, let alone their importance to the survival of the subject. And the subject remains hidden rather than allow his anchoring to become obvious. As you say: "If I write two texts at once, you will not be able to castrate me" (*ibid.*). There is a kind of fear of recuperation that amounts to a fear of recognizing the necessity and inevitability of the symbolic order. The result is a form of metalinguistic writing without any investment of the subject, thus without process, force, or meaning. In pretending to take leave of symbolic constraints, the subject of such writing denies his own power, even claims impotence. In your words: "I castrate myself" (*Glas* 65). Meanwhile he consolidates his influence.

> This subject of enunciation either says nothing or else dissects his speech for the sole purpose of becoming the focal point where all the other signifying systems converge. One could say that his discourse becomes hysteric only to position itself better within the place of impregnable transference—dominating, capturing, and monopolizing everything within the discourse's obsessive retreat, which is haunted by power/impotence. There is nothing that does not refer to it (because) it is never there. (RPL 97)

You only fragment words and syntax in order to realize the "chain of virtualities," the capacity of your text to link up with and capture any other text, whether it be real or virtual.

DERRIDA —But my text is not central, is not a "focal point" where texts converge. There is as much (if not more) dispersal as convergence, expenditure as retention. I do not try to realize the totality of the chain or contain it; my texts merely provide possible links for an infinite number of chains. My texts are captured as much as they capture. They are cited and harnessed to other texts, where they continue to proliferate, far from their point of production. If power games are inevitable, my texts are not clear winners and can be taken up in any number of unpredictable ways in contexts that I could never even hope to control. Dissemination is "nonmasterable" (MP 248), "a play in which whoever loses wins, and in which one loses and wins on every turn" (MP 20).

KRISTEVA —As I said, "haunted by power/impotence". You are like the subject of contemplative discourse who "sets himself up with even more power inasmuch as he will mime the dissolution of all positions" (RPL 97). You "write[] in a style similar to that of an outmoded avant-garde" and "disavow[] the law" (KR 300). Your wordplay and generally playful style seek to deny your position of authority . . . all the better to exploit it: "the philosopher begins performing literary tricks, thus arrogating to himself a power over imaginations: a power which, though minor in appearance, is more fetching than that of the transcendental consciousness" (DL 139). Frankly this is unethical, an abuse of power.[20] Faking *jouissance*, you pretend to risk your status as subject in order to mask the symbolic sway you hold.

SPLITTING *LA DIFFÉRANCE*: TWO MOMENTS

Without genuine drive input, without the involvement of a heterogeneity that is extralinguistic and outside thought, the subject's functioning is confined to a stale symbolic. The semiotic is repressed and negativity is positivized such that it cannot revitalize the system. However, not even the symbolic functions effectively in deconstruction: its positioning of the subject is denied by a form of drifting that attempts to avoid all attachments and pretends to dissolve all positions. Kristeva's argument against deconstruction is thus twofold: deconstruction is said to deny the heterogeneity essential to the functioning of the semiotic and to side-step the positioning crucial to the symbolic. Ultimately, however, these two objections come down to the same sticking point: Derrida does not distinguish between two moments (positive and negative, position and pulverization, identification and destabilization) and thus does not recognize the relation of contradiction that underpins Kristeva's theory. Unlike Kristeva, he does not see heterogeneity as opposed to or invading thought/language but as partially escaping it in a non-oppositional way. And it is this same difference in logic (contradiction versus(?) *différance*) that gives rise to Kristeva's disagreement with Derrida over the "thesis" or "position" on which the symbolic is said to depend.

For there to be contradiction, two movements or moments are necessary; a more or less solid position needs to exist, against which heterogeneity can launch its assault. That at least is Kristeva's thesis. Without such a position, the heterogeneous disperses into indifference, poetic language—indeed language in general—is silenced.[21] The thetic position has to be affirmed in order to be negated, in order for the movement of rejection to have meaning. Even the avant-garde texts that approach the limit between signification and its nullification must take up a provisional position: they appropriate language before dissolving it (and themselves) in their signifying practice. [22] And then, having shaken signification, they posit a "thesis"—if not of a particular meaning, at least of a "signifying apparatus" [*dispositif signifiant*]—so that the process of the text is produced between sense and non-sense, between the symbolic and the semiotic, and is not cut off from communicable language (DL 134-135).

Derrida, however, avoids position in favor of movement and, in particular, in favor of detour. [23] Detour is a form of movement that avoids any set direction. It never stops: rather than establishing positions or positing theses, it "unceasingly dislocates itself in a chain of differing and deferring substitutions" (MP 26). [DERRIDA—"but in order that you have no fixed point where you could rest" (*Glas* 248)]. In this way, *différance* avoids the engagement of the position in opposition, for that is what position and positing are said to entail: "*in positing itself*, that is, in opening itself to negativity and in becoming opposition" (*Glas* 168).

Let us look closely at Derrida's undoing of positions, most pertinently in relation to drives. The most explicit presentation of his "hypothesis"—a nonthesis—is to be found in his reading of Freud's *Beyond the Pleasure Principle*. [24] Derrida sets himself the following task: "I would like to make legible the non-positional structure of *Beyond* . . . , its *a-thetic* functioning" (PC 261). Attentive to the *démarche*—the movement, step or gait—of the text, Derrida seeks to demonstrate "the essential impossibility of holding on to any thesis within it, any posited conclusion [. . .] of the theoretical type in general" (*ibid.*).

On the very first page of "To Speculate," Derrida writes of proposing "another logic" (PC 259) but not without immediately putting the words "proposition" and "logic" under erasure. He connects together the notions of position, opposition and juxtaposition, theme and thesis, to examine other ways of linking or connecting, announcing "a 'logic' of the *beyond*" beyond the logic of the position: "without substituting itself for this logic, and above all without being opposed to it, opening another relation, a relation without relation, or without a basis of comparison" (260). Derrida's reading of Freud is above all concerned with the ways in which the pleasure principle (PP) and the reality principle (PR), life and death drives can be linked by means of this "other" relation, which could also be called *différance*.

The relation between the PP and the PR is in the image of Freud's text which doesn't proceed by position and opposition, by a thesis that defends itself against others but "advances without advancing, without advancing itself, without ever advancing anything that it does not immediately take back, for the time of a detour, without ever positing anything which remains in its position" (PC 293). It does not seek to demonstrate in the traditional philosophical manner, but "constructs-deconstructs itself according to an interminable detour" (269). What drives Freud's writing "is not dialectical, does not proceed by oppositions in the final analysis. If it necessarily produces dialectical *effects*, [. . .] it doesn't go through negativity, lack, opposition" (401, tr. mod.). It is nonetheless "subject to a rhythm" (269), the rhythm of a lop-sided gait, forever in movement because unbalanced.[25]

In parallel with the movement of the text, the pairs of drives are asymmetrical. The PP and the PR do not oppose each other as thesis and antithesis (and avoid synthesis at all cost). Derrida writes of the "abyssal 'overlapping' [. . .] of what Freud is supposedly writing, describing [. . .] and, on the other hand, the system of his writing gestures" (PC 320). And the relation is even doubled in Derrida's textual performance, where the strategies reflect those he discovers in Freud's text, bypassing theses, making a detour around positions, "without ever advancing anything that it does not immediately take back."

As we might expect, according to Derrida, the PP/PR relation is not an opposition: the one principle is not "posited" in such a way that the other could oppose or attack it. The relation is rather "an alterity that is even more irreducible than the alterity attributed to opposition" (PC 283), "a structure of alteration without opposition" (285). The reality principle is not the renunciation of pleasure but its postponement. The obstacles to immediate enjoyment do not put into question the general tendency toward pleasure: the reality principle merely imposes "a detour in order to defer enjoyment" (282). The PR thus serves the interests of the PP (282); it is not other than the PP but a deferred moment of the PP, its *différance* (286). Not only is pleasure *deferred* by the PR; it is also *displaced* by the mechanisms of repression. Repression is pleasure experienced as displeasure. The location of pleasure has shifted: "what is pleasure *here* is displeasure *there*" (290, tr. mod.). And yet it was only our *experience* of pleasure and displeasure that ever distinguished them in the first instance (288). Without even going into the question of masochism, it seems that nothing can be reliably opposed to pleasure: what seems to be its contrary (the reality principle or displeasure) inevitably turns out to be merely pleasure deferred or displaced. "Perhaps it is that the PP cannot be contradicted. What is done without it, if anything is, will not *contradict*: firstly because it will not oppose the PP" (293, tr. mod.). Freud works through the notion of a death drive that would be *beyond* the PP, and yet in the game with the spool (*fort/da*) the notion of beyond (*fort*) seems to be already inscribed in the PP, a product of the PP that can be brought back within the realm of pleasure (*da*). "The death drive is *there*, in the PP, which is a question of a *fort:da*" (323). It cannot be opposed to pleasure any more than the PR can. Rather than opposition, there is a relation of *différance*. The only instance that really seems to contradict pleasure is the PP itself, in a sort of auto-hostility: in a move obviating any need for the PR, the PP itself limits pleasure in order to achieve mastery over it (399-400).

The notion of pleasure becomes more and more enigmatic. The PP is divided from itself, different and deferred in relation to itself. Its functioning can only be understood as *différance*. It produces its own other, an other not opposed to it: "The PP remains the author of everything that appears to escape it or oppose it" (348, tr. mod.); "the pleasure principle [. . .] enters into a contract only with itself," it "encounters no opposition" but "*unleashes* in itself the *absolute* other" (283). It is the relation to the self that constitutes the relation to the other (403).

KRISTEVA — In refusing to recognize the dichotomy of drives that Freud presents, you have chosen to ignore Freud's dualism, a point on which he is quite categorical in *Beyond the Pleasure Principle*. He writes:

> Our views have from the very first been *dualistic*, and today they are even more definitely dualistic than before—now that we describe the opposition as being, not between ego drives and sexual drives but between life drives and death drives. Jung's libido theory is on the contrary *monistic* [. . .].[26]

"But Freudian theory is more than a theory of dualism, it is a theory of contradiction and of struggle" (RPL 170). For Freud goes on to write of the struggle from the very first between the life and death drives (*ibid.*).

DERRIDA — We cannot simply take these statements at face value. "The decisive firmness with which Freud reaffirms dualism within this oppositional framework, the dogmatic tone, the inability to do anything other than to assert" (PC 366) all point to stakes beyond the scientific ones, and in particular to the duel with Jung over the succession of the psychoanalytic movement. The debate between the idea of two drives and that of a single drive is largely a false one, for if we follow the PP and the PR in Freud's text, this opposition makes no sense: the "two" drives are entailed in one another and the "single" drive divides into two. The so-called dualism is characterized not by contradiction and struggle but by complicity and reversibility: "there is no more opposition between pleasure and displeasure, life and death, within and beyond" (PC 401, tr. mod.).

KRISTEVA —You say that the pleasure principle "*unleashes* in itself the *absolute* other" (PC 283), and this is your case against Freud's dualism. Certainly, the other is within the same, the other even stems from the same; it is nonetheless the case that the other is opposed to the same. It is an *opposition*—within sameness—that creates alterity. Similarly, in my own work, I have never denied the common origin of the charges and stases of drives within the semiotic, nor indeed of the symbolic and the semiotic. On the contrary, I have drawn attention to it. But proving that one term produces its other or serves the ends of its other says nothing to refute its functioning as an opposite. And proving that one is dependent on the other hardly negates the dialectical contradiction of the two terms.

Negativity in general is fundamentally ambiguous in the way that you describe. Rejection is characterized by both a movement of separation and the momentary arrest of this movement. "Repeated drives or the shocks from energy discharges create a state of excitation. Because it remains unsatisfied, this excitation produces, through a qualitative leap, a repercussion that delays, momentarily absorbs, and posits that excitation" (RPL 171). At this stage the positing can be called "stasis" (or "mark" or "engram") but this stasis will go on to provide the basis for the thetic position, the sign and the ego. Negativity thus produces positivity. Rejection creates its own brake, checking itself in order to relaunch the scission that defines it. In other words, the ambiguity of rejection constitutes an opposition within sameness: "Although repeated rejection is separation, doubling, scission, and shattering, it is at the same time and afterward accumulation, stoppage, mark, and stasis" (171). This is what needs to be read in Freud's *Beyond the Pleasure Principle*. To start with, this opposition is not dialectical, but the repetition of the confrontation between drive charges and stases eventually manages to create "thetic heterogeneity" (171) giving access to a new, heterogeneous space, a domain that is radically other—the symbolic.[27] And between negativity and the other arising from it, a relation of contradiction is established, with all the conflict and struggle that such a relation implies.

DERRIDA —But the "charge" and the "stasis" are both traces of rejection; they both stem from it, so one "is not opposable, does not differ" from the other. This is "a structure of alteration without opposition" (PC 285).

KRISTEVA —There is no reason for alterity-stemming-from-the-same not to take the form of opposition and even of contradiction. Stases and charges work together, but against each other as a pair of contrary and contradictory terms. We can more easily understand the mechanism of negativity creating its own opposite by studying the separation into subject and object, the positing of the object. Rejection creates a rejected element, an outside, an other, that is to say it "posits an object as separate from the body proper" (RPL 123), an object that thus becomes signifiable. From that moment on, "the outside, which has become a signifiable object, and the predicate function operate as checks on negativity" (123). These checks are "*positions* that absorb and camouflage it" (123). Although they are constituted by the passage of rejection, they "bear the brunt of its attacks" (124). Rejection thus both posits and opposes its other, producing an opposition between radical others.

DERRIDA —The position is only rejection deferred; it cannot be opposed to it.

KRISTEVA —Although established by rejection, the thesis, the position and the thetic phase giving access to the symbolic function are indeed opposed to rejection in that they are qualitatively new. "The quantitative accumulation of rejections upsets the mark's stability" such that it "ends up being rejected into a *qualitatively* new space, that of the *representamen* or the sign" (RPL 172).

DERRIDA —I don't really see that the sign is qualitatively new or essentially different from the mark. Both are a form of trace. Both function in the same way.

KRISTEVA —Inscribed in linguistic signs is a powerful system of constraints, comparable to law and social systems. Whereas marks are fluid, unstable.

DERRIDA —I have always found signs also to be fluid and unstable. . . .

KRISTEVA —In refusing—or repressing—the thesis, you only recognize in the gramme the unstable stases that precede signification. The trace and writing in your work "can be thought of as metaphors for a movement that retreats before the thetic but, sheltered by it, unfolds only within the stases of the semiotic *chora*" (RPL 141-142). However, "[r]ejection destroys the stasis of the mark" and, to continue its trajectory, requires "a new unifying stoppage" before it can renew its attack, its process of division. In this moment of unity, "something more than a mere mark—a *representamen* and an ego—will finally crystallize." Thus, in the wake of the mark, rejection "sets up a qualitatively different thetic phase: the sign" (172, cf. 66-67).

We must distinguish here between the "dichotomy" and the "heteronomy" of drives (RPL 167).[28] In order to produce the subject and the sign, the dichotomy of drives (their existence as pairs of contradictory forces, their simple articulation into charges and stases at work in the *chora*) doesn't suffice: it is "not enough to ensure our bodily survival because it cannot check the drives' endless facilitations" (67). A decisive "alteration" (67) is required, in order to produce a dialectical relation from this unstable and reversible articulation. This transformation must introduce heterogeneity into an opposition previously composed simply of non-dialectical contraries (charges/stases), by creating a new space and, at the same time, a heteronomy between "the biological foundation of signifying functioning and its determination by the family and society" (167). It is a "quantitative accumulation" (172) which becomes a "qualitative leap" (66). The opposition thus produced is one of irreducible heterogeneity between the semiotic and the symbolic. It allows for a renewal of the process whereas the articulation of the *chora* only introduced variation.

But when I speak of "alteration," I am not referring to your "structure of alteration without opposition." In fact, there is opposition at both levels—both in the dichotomy of drives and in the semiotic/symbolic heterogeneity. Indeed, it is the opposition (between drive charges and stases) that *produces* alterity (the qualitative difference of the sign), a symbolic other against which rejection redoubles its attacks.

DERRIDA —If one stems from the other, if the two work together, the thesis and its rejection "are but one, the same divided" (PC 284). They compose the rhythm of the same jerky but incessant movement.

KRISTEVA —But in this "same movement" we need to distinguish two moments or else the movement stops. The positive moment of marking or stasis "is rejection's self-defense, its relative immobilization, which, in turn, allows the reactivation of drives" (RPL 171). Without it, "rejection could not produce something *new* and displace boundaries; it would be merely mechanical repetition of an undifferentiated 'identity'" (171). This lack of difference, this "nonrenewable, nonproductive redundancy" (145) is precisely the risk you run. For in order to give rise to "a new becoming of *différance*" (145), there have to be positive moments against which drive heterogeneity can expend itself in a dialectical struggle. Unfortunately, the "mark" of "trace" in your theory gives way under the slightest pressure. Even the sign is only ever hesitatingly proffered and never firmly fastened to meaning or the social sphere. It offers no resistance to the movement, so *différance* becomes its own object. With nothing to get its teeth into, it ends up chasing its tail.

DERRIDA —I do not see the mark or the trace as pauses in the movement of *différance*. And certainly I do not see the sign as a solid wall for *différance* to bounce against. Rather than halting *différance*, signs/marks are merely effects of the movement, indicators that it has been at work, traces of its passage. For there are no moments of respite for *différance*. It is always at work, always moving.

KRISTEVA —And yet, as you yourself say, it moves without advancing (cf. PC 269). Without "the mark thwart[ing] rejection in order to reactivate it" (RPL 171-172), *différance* can only be tautological, repetitive, sterile. Repetition is not in itself renewal. There needs to be a qualitative change if we are to avoid "nonproductive redundancy" (RPL 145). "The prefix 're' [in rejection] indicates not the repetition of a constant identity but rather a renewal of division through a new unifying stoppage" (172). The thetic moment "crystallize[s]" this unity that will be "re-jected" again, and in doing so "founds the *logic of renewal*—as opposed to the logic of repetition—within the signifying process: rejection$_1$—stasis$_1$—rejection$_2$—stasis$_2$—(etc.)— *Thesis*— rejection$_n$—stasis$_n$" (172).

DERRIDA —If there is a lack of understanding between us on this point, it extends as far as the notion of what constitutes newness. Advancing certainly gives an impression of novelty and yet so often is also a continuation of the same old path. The radical is always-already compromised. In repetition, however, there is difference through deferral: redundancy is simultaneously renewal. The movement of *différance* "in the irreducible novelty of its repetition" (PC 304-305) does not take refuge in undifferentiated identity but produces difference within identity.

KRISTEVA —Difference in identity is more than mechanical repetition. From the work of Lacan, we know that subject identity, for instance, is constituted on the basis of a split. However the two aspects of this "split identity" do not simply coincide. In the mirror stage, the positing of the imaged ego is no mere copy of the drive motility of the subject.

DERRIDA —And yet it is a mirror image.

*

[For Kristeva, there always seem to be two moments, two movements forming one: position and opposition making for dialectical progress. For Derrida, there is another kind of relation, whereby one is divided without ever quite becoming two in a series of repetitions that doesn't advance but is nonetheless ever new. But this characterization of the Kristeva/Derrida relation is reminiscent of Freud's comparison between his dualism and Jung's monism. Is the dualism/monism distinction sustainable when "two" and "one" are both disturbed by the double? And does it matter whether *différance* splits into two moments or whether the symbolic and the semiotic are one?]

KRISTEVA —What is really at stake in this debate over the position is its consequences for the subject. It is symbolic positioning that establishes subject identity and anchors the subject to the social sphere, where constraints are not lightly broken. The transformations prepared by imaginary identifications and established by the thetic break are not fleeting and do not dissolve easily. It is for this reason that distinctions like subject/object and same/other have a sense and give access to Meaning. Without this disjunction—a real discontinuity—without the position of the other, the subject has no points of reference. His identity can hardly be constituted and is condemned to remain fluid. The constant movement of *différance*, without halts or accumulation, forever slipping away before any position or taking a detour around it, thus has serious consequences with regard to the subject's development and social practice. By avoiding conflict at every turn, by avoiding the theses, positions and oppositions that mark the access to and participation in social and linguistic structures, *différance* remains in a sort of pre-thetic from which social stakes are excluded.

"[T]he grammatological deluge of meaning gives up on the subject and must remain ignorant not only of his functioning as social practice, but also of his chances for experiencing *jouissance* or being put to death" (RPL 142). In seeking to erase the distinction between semiotic and symbolic rupture, between the dichotomy of drives and the thetic break, deconstruction neglects the subject's integration into the social sphere, his acceptance of social structures and/or his resistance to them. I would argue, on the other hand, that the complicity between the semiotic and the symbolic does not prevent there being a crucial break between them. Language acquisition, communication and family structures bear witness to the fact that thetic and symbolic distinctions are not ephemeral, that certain limits are not erased as soon as they are posited, that there really are decisive ruptures, bringing undecidability to a halt to make way for symbolic law.

By denying the thesis and the "thetic character of the signifying act" (DL 131), deconstruction seems not only to abandon meaning and the subject but also to refuse the limits making communication and social identity possible:

> [. . .] through discrediting the signified and with it the transcendental ego, such 'deconstructions' balk [*se dérobent*] at what constitutes one function of language though not the only one: to express meaning in a communicable sentence between speakers. (DL 131, tr. mod.)[29]

DERRIDA —I have never denied or shied away from the possibility of communication. All my work depends upon it. Similarly I have never denied the relative stability of a vast set of meanings within relatively stable contexts. For example, to read Rousseau I rely on the conventions of

> the French language (its grammar and vocabulary), the rhetorical uses of this language in the society and in the literary code of the epoch, etc., but also a whole set of assurances that grant a minimum of intelligibility to whatever we can tell ourselves about these things today [. . .]. (LI 144)

Were there no "minimal consensus" within the academic community regarding language usage and literary, philosophical and rhetorical traditions (to mention just a few of the contexts determining my work), there would be no point at all to my reading, writing or lecturing. This stability enables even debates such as this one to take place, by providing contexts where "it should be possible to invoke rules of competence, criteria of discussion and of consensus, good faith, lucidity, rigor, criticism, and pedagogy" (LI 146). However—and this is a condition of possibility of communication—the very idea of stability presupposes the possibility of instability. And the fact that misunderstandings occur (between us, no less) confirms this (LI 144-151). For meanings are not fixed, and contexts and institutions are always in the process of transforming themselves.[30] Meanings can only ever be *relatively* stable—more or less agreed upon. And there can be no rigorous dividing line between the fixed and the flowing. The play of *différance* is everywhere at work, potentially destabilizing meanings: the repetition of the "same" word in the "same" context acquires an imperceptible difference, altering the possibilities of interpretation. Identity—the identical—is inevitably in flux. Deconstruction "is" above all this destabilization (cf. LI 147), a "maximum intensification of a transformation in progress" (FL 9).

KRISTEVA —Whilst the distinction between more and less stable cannot be drawn definitively, it cannot be ignored. I do not wish to argue for the absolute fixedness of divisions in the symbolic or for pure motility without stasis in the semiotic. Nonetheless, I would contend that there is a limit between the steadiness of one and the agitation of the other and that this dividing line carries consequences. We must recognize that certain limits —social and/or linguistic—can be located. Not only are they relatively solid but they do not yield without offering some resistance, and this is important. These limits—self/other, inside/outside for example—are not hermetic and are not fixed for all time. However they allow the subject to assume an identity and thus to function as a speaking subject. Identity is then further elaborated in terms of group identity (gender, family, political, national, etc.). The limits enabling this organization constitute a protective barrier, a breakwater against the pulverization of identity by drive energy. Such identity protection is "a biological and psychical necessity" (SNR 43); it is a question of survival, both for the individual and for the social group (49). In fact, as I explain in *Powers of Horror*, if these limits are not sufficiently stable, if our very identity within the paternal order is seriously threatened, then our reaction can be a violent one of disgust, rejection and hate. The need to establish firm limits guaranteeing identity can then result in repressive nationalistic or fundamentalist movements seeking to exclude the contaminating other in the name of "purity."

On the other hand, these limits must not be immutable. Their renewal—through transgression, revolt or love for example—is also necessary:

> Undoing [*desserrer*] these confines of the "proper" and the "identical," of "true" and "false," of "right" and "wrong," becomes a necessity for survival, because symbolic organizations, like organisms, only endure on condition that they are renewed and experience *jouissance*. (SNR 43)

The Oedipal revolt against the father and movements of social protest are examples of this destabilization, which always involves a risk. We see another form of revolt in esthetic experience, in the "process" of the subject who risks his identity in order to renew it. And the opening of one psyche to another through love is a further way of dissolving and reviving these divisions, provided we do not lose them entirely in merging with the other.

What I wish to emphasize in all these scenarios is that although limits may be displaced and transgressed, they do not slide effortlessly away. There must be a "moment of struggle, one that particularly threatens or dissolves the bond between subject and society, but simultaneously creates the conditions for its renewal" (RPL 208). To see law, the family, language in a state of constant evolution or variation that is not the result of contestation or libidinal investment is to refuse to recognize their very real power at a given historical moment and to repress the struggle and energy involved in displacing them. The speaking subject anchors himself to the limits defined during the mirror stage and the thetic phase but also tears himself loose from this mooring periodically. These two eventualities are to be neither confused nor ignored.

DERRIDA — . . . Perhaps he just slips his mooring. . . .

KRISTEVA —To slip one's mooring is to remain in a kind of pre-thetic phase where shifting is unimpeded by positions. But there is no question of blithely drifting. In *Black Sun* I examine what happens when thetic separations and identifications are not properly set in place: the subject does indeed slip—into psychosis and loss of speech. In order for the subject to be properly positioned in language, the separation from the maternal body must be effective: the maternal "Thing" (for the child as yet has no relation to an object) must become posited, objectified, symbolizable. The maternal body needs to be relinquished as an unnameable "Thing" and found again (although never quite the same) in language, as an object (BS 40-44). The subject who cannot accept this separation between self and (m)other falls into depression and asymbolia. Floating around or away from positions, as you seem to advocate, is catastrophic for the subject, who loses access to the symbolic function.

On a larger scale, in Western countries over the last twenty years we have seen the dangers of the kind of destabilization that you celebrate: power has become more fragile and seems to shift of its own accord; instances of law are deferred to one another such that they become increasingly unlocatable (SNR 15-24, 58). This historically specific phenomenon has serious consequences. The subject *is* able to slip a tenuous mooring rather than engaging in revolt. He is thus unable to be properly integrated into social structures in the way Freud indicates in *Totem and Taboo* and may become excluded. Having no clear instance of symbolic authority available against which to rebel, his choices are vandalism or robotic consumption of the entertainment culture that is dished up to him (SNR 21). These are the consequences of an ineffectual symbolic, of avoiding positions.

But your sidestepping of the thetic limit is indicative of a more general denial:

> any reflection on *signifiance*, by refusing [*se dérobant à*] its thetic character, will continually ignore [*se dérobera à*] its constraining, legislative, and socializing elements: under the impression that it is breaking down the metaphysics of the signified or the transcendental ego, such a reflection will become lodged in a negative theology that denies their limitations. (DL 131, tr. mod.)

DERRIDA —"My response [to this question or objection of a 'negative theology'] has always been brief, elliptical, and dilatory" (HAS 7), but let me tackle it more directly.[31] Certainly all predicates seem inadequate to describe *différance* (or the trace, writing, the hymen, the supplement, etc.). It "'is' neither this nor that, neither sensible nor intelligible, neither positive nor negative, neither inside nor outside, neither superior nor inferior, neither active nor passive, neither present nor absent, not even neutral [. . .]. It 'is' not and does not say what 'is'" (HAS 4). However "negative theology consists of considering that every predicative language is inadequate to the essence, in truth to the hyperessentiality (the being beyond Being) of

God" (4). Now *différance* is not ineffable in this mystical way (11). The fact that it is unnameable is not due to an essence or hyperessence that is not captured by its epithets. It represents no form of being *beyond* Being (cf. 7-8). On the contrary: if it cannot be described adequately, it is because it *falls short of any form of being*: it would be "'before' the concept, the name, the word, 'something' that would be nothing, that no longer arises from Being, from presence or from the presence of the present, nor even from absence, and even less from some hyperessentiality" (9).

KRISTEVA — If I compare deconstruction to a negative theology, it is because it "retreats before the thetic" and sidesteps constraints (RPL 141). Nothing is affirmed. There is no positive moment allowing the subject to position himself and no recognition of the limits represented by law and of the psychical importance of the effort to displace them.

[A THIRD VOICE interrupts. Whose? Mine. But which one?] — In Derrida's work, the sign is placed and displaced. And the placing/displacing of the sign is carried out by virtue of the same movement, creating effects of stability and instability with little to distinguish them from each other: there is thus slippage rather than struggle, and drift rather than dispute. It is not a question of establishing and then contesting limits. Rather there is an endless substitution of limits as they continue shifting, carried by a movement that both radicalizes and recuperates. For Kristeva too, it is indeed the same movement — that of negativity — that produces the dialectic between the positing and the pulverization of the sign. However it never ceases to maintain the tension between them. There is no undecidability between the solidity of the thetic position and provisional semiotic stases, between the nameable and the unnameable, between stability and destabilization. The poles are not reversible.

We can already see this divergence in the descriptions of the trace/mark in the work of each theorist. We have seen that the Derridean trace is always in the process of "appear[ing]/disappear[ing]" (MP 23); it is "simultaneously traced and erased," as "the simulacrum of a presence that dislocates itself, displaces itself, postpones itself, properly has no site" (24, tr. mod.). Presented and conjured away in the same gesture, the limits it draws offer no resistance. Kristeva, however, does not accept a conception of limits whereby instead of constraining the subject, they give way. In her theory, the trace (or more frequently the "mark," "accumulation," "arrest" or "stasis," RPL 171), is considered as a positive moment that doesn't simply fade or float away, even though it may ultimately be destroyed. The mark, like the Derridean trace, is "on the way to becoming the sign," but this is because "it prefigures the sign's constancy and unity" (172). Obviously the mark is not about to disappear by itself. In fact, in order for it to yield, there needs to be another moment, distinct from and yet incorporating it: "Rejection, which integrates the mark, is its destructive moment, and, in this sense, is part of the production and destruction of the sign" (172).

On the one hand, "appear/disappear"; on the other, "production-destruction." For Derrida, a constant shift; for Kristeva, a struggle involving creation and annihilation.[32]

"On the one hand . . . on the other": an apparently even-handed gesture but one that reinforces the idea of opposition between Kristeva and Derrida, opposition between struggle and slippage, opposition between two interdependent movements and one double movement — all oppositions that Derrida could question. And indeed might, were his voice not constrained here by the polemics of this debate, a debate that is — we should recall — my Kristevan fantasy. "On the one hand . . . on the other": this seemingly impartial voice that interrupts the dialogue, weighing up the two theories as if it belonged to a detached observer, is perhaps not as neutral as all that. Although it doesn't take sides, it participates in a structure and a dynamic that has an effect. It intervenes in a way that is not simply benign or uninvolved. But here we have two definitions of neutrality that do not quite coincide and are indeed the object of further discussion.

NEUTRALITY

KRISTEVA — By neglecting heterogeneity, deconstruction "positivize[s]" the negativity of drives (RPL 141) or "neutralizes" it (142). Then, by refusing the thetic moment, it neutralizes positivity as well. Floating and drifting between reversible poles, the undecidable oscillates without producing breaks or accounting for rupture. This is "ideal neutrality where, for lack of contradiction, everything slips away" (RPL 98). Limits fall in succession without any hint of fierce combat. Deconstruction recognizes no clear distinction between social constraints and their contestation, but sees shifts occurring without confrontation.

> Neutral in the face of all positions, theses, and structures,
> grammatology is, as a consequence, equally restrained when they
> break, burst, or rupture: demonstrating disinterestedness toward
> (symbolic and/or social) structure, grammatology remains silent when
> faced with its destruction or renewal. (RPL 142)

Ignoring the restrictive nature of law, deconstruction has nothing to say about the subject's practice of revolt and the kind of revolution that can take place in poetic language for example.

DERRIDA —Deconstruction has often been accused of neutrality and this is one of the most common misconceptions regarding my work. It is true that deconstruction is difficult, even impossible, to situate politically, for it is not a position, but a set of ever-shifting practices, repeatable (and each time slightly different) in an infinite number of circumstances. But "Were there only one [deconstruction], were it homogeneous, it would not be inherently either conservative or revolutionary, or determinable within the code of such oppositions. That is precisely what gets on everyone's nerves" (LI 141). "It is 'inherently' nothing at all" (*ibid.*). It cannot be reduced to an essence outside of the particular instances where it intervenes. "Deconstruction does not exist somewhere, pure, proper, self-identical, outside of its inscriptions in conflictual and differentiated contexts; it 'is' only what it does and what is done with it, there where it takes place" (LI 141). Deconstruction belongs neither to the right nor the left, precisely because it calls the opposition into question. The undecidable, however, does not "cancel out" pairs of opposites but unbalances established configurations and especially hierarchies. Its intervention is one of "strategic dissymmetry" (Dis 207n). For undecidability is not indeterminacy. Rather it "is always a *determinate* oscillation between possibilities [. . .] [that] are themselves highly *determined* in strictly *defined* situations (for example, discursive [. . .] political, ethical, etc.)" (LI 148).

Of course, if deconstruction were really as neutral as its detractors suggest, it wouldn't attract such violent criticism. The fact is that although deconstruction cannot be aligned with a particular politics, it is never apolitical. Although it does not lead an offensive, it is not inoffensive.[33]

KRISTEVA —I am not interested in determining whether deconstruction is "inherently" conservative or transgressive. My own work shares this same ambiguity. I do not take sides with conservative (symbolic) or revolutionary (semiotic) forces to the extent that I would wish to see one crush or annihilate the other. On the contrary, such a victory could only result in stagnation or delirium. If I sometimes seem to privilege one over the other it is in order to redress an imbalance in our culture and our discourse.[34] Similarly I take no interest in pigeonholing your work or mine on the left or the right of the political spectrum. In fact I have always objected to the interpretation of social conflict in terms of homogeneous groups of indivisible subjects, in conflict with each other but not with themselves, whether in Marxist ideology (PL 17, 60, RPL 136) or in feminism (KR 209).[35] But I would level the same sort of criticism at deconstruction: it remains neutral with respect to the subject. "[T]he struggle, the implacable difference, the violence [needs to] be conceived in the very place where it operates with the maximum intransigence, in other words, in personal and sexual identity itself, so as to make it disintegrate in its very nucleus" (KR 209). The subject of deconstruction, however, is never called upon to leave his (unrecognized) position of symbolic unity in a domain of "theoretical neutrality" and "metalanguage" in order to experience the shattering of that position (PL 55).

DERRIDA —Whilst I am happy to recognize my use of metalanguage (for I cannot imagine how my words could function other than metalinguistically, by referring to other signifiers), I do not accept the accusation of theoretical neutrality. Firstly, "deconstruction, as I have often had to insist, is not a discursive or theoretical affair, but a practico-political one, and it is always produced within the structures [. . .] said to be institutional" (PC 508). Secondly, it intervenes precisely against claims of theoretical neutrality, against claims that theoretical discourse can ever be neutral. It exposes the supposed neutrality of a discourse invoking oppositions such as pure/impure, normal/parasitic, genuine/false, serious/nonserious and shows that it depends on a hierarchy of politically charged terms. "For it can hardly be denied that these value-oppositions constitute hierarchies, that they are posed and repeated as such by the very theory which claims to analyze, in all neutrality, their mere possibility" (LI 71). Similarly, deconstruction intervenes in a discourse that claims political neutrality and that dissociates itself from an ethical context. "Geopsychoanalysis" for example analyzes what is at stake in the seemingly neutral statement by the *Association Psychanalytique Internationale* condemning human rights abuses in the most general way, without mentioning the role psychoanalysts have been called on to play in carrying out torture, in particular in Latin America. As far as "personal and sexual identity" are concerned, these concepts have been abundantly problematized and shown to be infinitely divisible in my work.

KRISTEVA —We seem to be speaking at cross-purposes. Here again, your work, although useful in a pragmatic way and laudable in its undoing of metaphysical oppositions, never goes beyond the contemplative plane of metalinguistic discourse. You say nothing of the possibility of transgression and revolt, of practices that involve the subject intimately. Your calculated "intervention" is never a real combat. Yet struggling against authority and prohibitions is how we measure ourselves, our happiness, our *jouissance*, our freedom (SNR 20). Revolt is "an integral part of the pleasure principle" (SNR 20). Freud has shown the social importance of revolt: by integrating the subject into power structures, it cements social ties and renews and transforms the social fabric (SNR 30-36, 53-54). However, as an interiorized conflict—heterogeneous contradiction or the "process" of the subject—revolt revitalizes the psyche and is the means of esthetic production (RPL 195-234). Struggle is "a continual necessity to keep alive the psyche, thought and the social bond itself" (SNR 302).

DERRIDA —If I "avoid frontal and symmetrical protest" (MP xv), this is hardly due to a lack of interest in social structures. But to struggle against the binary opposition is already to be caught by and in its structure. There is a certain absurdity to this struggle: it confirms and even depends on the laws it transgresses.[36] This interdependence of law and contestation is something you freely admit in your work. Now, pragmatically speaking, in order to achieve a change in the status quo, it is often necessary—*as a first step* —to engage in this kind of struggle. This is what I call the "indispensable phase of reversal" (Dis 6). "To deconstruct the opposition is first of all, at a given moment, to overturn the hierarchy. To overlook this phase of overturning is to forget the conflictual and subordinating structure of opposition" (Pos 41, tr. mod.). However this phase never seriously puts the system that produced the hierarchy into question—your "renewal" is merely a reaffirmation of the existing dynamic—and so I stress that it is essential to go further: "To remain content with reversal is of course to operate within the immanence of the system to be destroyed" (Dis 6); "to remain in this phase is still to operate on the terrain of and from within the deconstructed system" (Pos 42). We must "mark the interval between" on the one hand an overturning within a hierarchy of oppositions and on the other hand the disorganization of that hierarchy by "undecidables" (Pos 42-43), between its inversion and its invasion by concepts (for want of a better word) that are "dislodged and dislodging" (Pos 42). Then we can see that what appears to be confrontation or struggle "is *already* the effect of movements of destructuration and of restructuration which are *already* at work" (PC 508). This is how borders are destabilized and redistributed.

KRISTEVA—Concerning the inefficacy of direct attack, I have argued something similar in essays such as "Women's Time" and "A New Type of Intellectual: The Dissident."[37] Certainly, direct attack remains within the discourse it seeks to overturn, and, certainly, we need to go further than this and rethink oppositions (KR 209, 295). Your challenging of metaphysical dichotomies such as man/woman is exemplary in this regard and has contributed toward "the demassification of the problematic of difference" (KR 209). But where deconstruction remains neutral is that, whilst problematizing identity, it does not go as far as putting identity into "process." "This process could be summarized as an *interiorization of the founding separation of the socio-symbolic contract*, as an introduction of its cutting edge into the very interior of every identity whether subjective, sexual, ideological, or so forth" (KR 210). The internal divisions that slice into identity in this way cannot be characterized as gaps or intervals deferring encounter. They give rise to an often violent exchange involving risks for personal and social equilibrium (KR 209).

What is important here is not so much the efficiency of contestation in dissolving limits. We even know that their annihilation is undesirable, that any signifying practice depends on maintaining limits, and on the (at least partial) functioning of the laws of language. No, rather it is transgression as it is played out within and against subject identity that is important, the process/trial and the esthetic practice that may result from it. Deconstruction remains blind to this process pulverizing social/family/linguistic laws. It only sees a futile combat, lost before it is begun, and ignores the textual productivity and the subject's "chances for experiencing *jouissance* or being put to death" (RPL 142).

*

Let us allow the voices to fade away, the Kristevan one having had the last word. Any end to this debate can only really be an interruption at an arbitrary point; the theories of permanent struggle and of infinite deferral are not likely to bring the debate to a definitive close. Has this then been a futile struggle? In terms of its function as a Kristevan reading, the answer is no. It has put pressure on the points of rupture between the theories to the extent that it has torn them apart. It has enabled Kristeva's work to confront and criticize Derrida's, to demarcate itself and to indicate irreconcilable differences from its other.

Is there a winner then in this contest? Not a clear one. In describing his game as one "in which one loses and wins on every turn" (MP 20), there is a sense in which Derrida cannot lose. But then, the Kristevan interpretation is that by investing in neither the position of the subject nor that of meaning, he has nothing to lose. Here we see the stakes of the discussion, indeed the point of the debate. Kristeva's accusations against deconstruction are a way of taking a stand against what she sees as a sort of cave-in of criticism. In an uncontrolled slide, criticism toys with the literary text, treating it as a pretext for a torrent of verbiage that bears witness to no struggle and to no risking of identity. For Kristeva, this kind of technical dexterity in critical writing is merely a poor imitation of the internal upheaval marking the texts of the subject in process/on trial.

However, as we have seen, the collision of texts and theories that Kristeva invites and incites only belongs to a Kristevan articulation of the theories, whilst a Derridean reading is able to incorporate, even swallow up, Kristeva's work. Or graft itself onto it. In the Derridean reading, there is not sufficient incompatibility between the theories to provoke a rejection of the graft.

On the one hand . . . on the other. My text has zigzagged back and forth, studying one practice and then the other, each one first on its own terms and then in terms of the other. This cleft strategy has brought the two together without synthesizing them. Has it done so in a neutral way?

The Derridean I would have to say no. Oscillating between the corpora and between reading strategies, "without ever advancing anything that it does not immediately take back, [. . .] without ever positing anything which remains in its position" (PC 293), this book nonetheless intervenes in Kristeva's and Derrida's work, selecting and emphasizing certain aspects at the expense of others to show proximity and rupture between them. Rather than an even-handed approach claiming not to take sides, this is a lop-sided intervention, swinging from one bias to the other in a "strategic dissymmetry" that "must be constantly readjusted" (Dis 207n). Derrida might call it *boiteux*: it has the rhythmic gait of a limping runner whose best chance of keeping balance is to keep moving.

Could Kristeva accuse me of remaining in a domain of "theoretical neutrality' and "metalanguage"? Quite possibly, and yet the schizoid strategy I adopt is one not of minimal but of two-fold investment: it involves a double identification with Kristeva and with Derrida. Transference and narcissistic investment, pointing toward the part of desire in my work? Or simulacrum, a way of hiding and avoiding taking sides or making judgments?

If judgment there is to be, it cannot be made at this point. The idea of "law" has hardly been discussed. And the (Derridean) passage through undecidability—the trial—has a way to go yet. Or should we say that the (Kristevan) confrontation of theories is far from exhausted. But perhaps these can be moved onto another terrain, one that shows more clearly the purchase these theories have, what can be achieved through their use. The following section of the book (Part III) zooms out from the focus on theorizing difference to look at Derrida's and Kristeva's work on the literary text, a privileged object of their attention. In this way, their work can be articulated around a common corpus, for both have written on texts by Sollers, Mallarmé, Artaud and Joyce. Naturally, these latter will not be read as stationary objects, outside the debate. They will not serve as anchors but as hinges. The swinging movement is not about to stop.

There is just one problem before we start examining the literary text: how to recognize it. . . .

NOTES

1. Hans-Georg Gadamer, "Le Défi herméneutique"; Derrida, "Bonnes volontés de puissance"; Gadamer, "Et pourtant: puissance de la bonne volonté," *Revue internationale de philosophie* 38:151 (333-347). See also PC 506-508 on the nature of confrontation.

2. See, for example, *Limited Inc*, "But, beyond . . . ," "Biodegradables, Seven Diary Fragments." Niall Lucy analyzes the first two of these debates, together with the exchange with Foucault, in his lucid and pedagogical *Debating Derrida*. By concentrating on these encounters, he produces a "Derrida" much closer to the "Derrida" of this chapter than to the one of Chapters 3 and 4.

3. Although the points are made here using the vocabulary and theory of RPL, parallel Kristevan arguments could be put forward in terms of her later

work, whereby deconstruction would be unable to account for and distinguish between, on the one hand, the unifying symbolic identifications maintained through a third term and, on the other hand, their destabilization through libidinal forces.

4. By "nonsymbolizable," Kristeva means that it cannot be incorporated into the symbolic. It is however still signifiable as semiotic rhythm, melody etc., cf. RPL 180.

5. In fact, Kristeva uses "heterogeneity" in RPL to indicate not only the radical alterity of drives but also to describe the relation between the heterogeneous element and the symbolic, e.g. "two heterogeneous realms" (48), "this heterogeneity between the semiotic and the symbolic" (66).

6. The following dialogue is, to say the least, apocryphal. Derrida and Kristeva are hereby formally absolved of any responsibility for words not appearing as referenced quotations.

7. Cf. *Glas* 209.

8. The word "element" is often used in the English translation of RPL to provide a noun where none is necessary in French: "deux inconciliables" becomes "two irreconcilable elements"; "l'hétérogène" becomes "the heterogeneous element." "Element" should not be read here as an indivisible entity but rather as a quality or factor. Cf. Chapter 2, note 11.

9. See preceding note.

10. SNR 179, cf. 425. Cf. also RPL 95.

11. *Révolution* 582.

12. The translation of this sentence as "there is nothing outside the text," although preferable in terms of English syntax has, I suspect, encouraged some of the more uninformed and unwarranted attacks on deconstruction.

13. Cf. Derrida, *Speech and Phenomena*.

14. Cf. Dis 35.

15. Cf. Derrida, "But, beyond . . ." 167-169.

16. Cf. RPL 86-87 and the discussion of the pheno- and geno-text in Chapter 7 below.

17. Cf. "The Double Session" (Dis 173-285).

18. Cf. *inter alia* "Fors," *Glas*, *The Ear of the Other* 76-77, *Points* . . . 26, 51-52, 120. Cf. also John P. Leavey, Jr., "This (then) will not have been a book . . ." 112-122.

19. It would be less easy for "Kristeva" to make this point in relation to Derrida's more recent "Circonfession" with its confessional diary entries, its poignant account of his mother's hospitalization and its vulnerable writing out of circumcision.

20. Cf. Kristeva, Preface to *Desire in Language* ix, and Margaret Waller, Translator's Preface to RPL viii.

21. Although, in her later work, Kristeva writes of a destabilization of identifications rather than of an assault against the thetic, the distinction between two moments (positive and negative, stabilizing and destabilizing) remains crucial. If primary identifications are too fragile to secure secondary (symbolic) identifications positioning the subject, then fusion-love and nostalgia for the lost maternal body threaten to swamp the subject, casting him/her adrift in asymbolia and depression.

22. Cf. *Révolution* 339-340.

23. Cf. "[. . .] forcing the substitution of *discourse*, the detour made obligatory by sites, for the punctuality of the *position*" (WD 194).

24. "To Speculate—on 'Freud'" (PC 257-409).

25. Derrida develops the notion of a lop-sided rhythm or step in *Glas*.

26. *The Standard Edition of the Works of Sigmund Freud*, 18:53. Quoted by Kristeva (RPL 169) and by Derrida (PC 366).

27. Cf. Kristeva's discussion of the qualitative leap from the orality of sucking and chewing to the orality of language (TL 26). Incorporating the speech of the other involves a process firstly of introjection and fusion but then also of restraining libido, displacing and deferring it to another level. Identification, like rejection, creates its own brake. Through repetition, a threshold is crossed, giving access to the qualitatively different (symbolic) domain of language.

28. Cf. PL 64. Cf. also the two kinds of rupture discussed in Chapter 2 above.

29. *Se dérober*—to shirk, evade, sidestep, refuse, balk at, slip or shy away from, hide from (*Robert Collins Dictionnaire*).

30. Cf. Derrida and Attridge, "This Strange Institution Called Literature" 73.

31. Kristeva is far from alone in describing deconstruction as a negative theology. Derrida makes a lengthy reply to such criticisms in "How to Avoid Speaking: Denials" and and further analyzes the issues in "Post-Scriptum." For further discussion of the relation between deconstruction and negative theology, see Harold Coward and Toby Foshay, eds., *Derrida and Negative Theology* and Kevin Hart, *The Trespass of the Sign: Deconstruction, Theology and Philosophy*.

32. And in Kristeva's later writings, when the semiotic/symbolic relation is somewhat less antagonistic, "stabilization-destabilization," a crisis between fixation and flow, entrenchment and disturbance.

33. The question of the neutrality or otherwise of deconstruction has been widely debated in critical texts. See for example Cristopher I. Fynsk, "A Decelebration of Philosophy," Rodolphe Gasché, *The Tain of the Mirror* 136-142, Jonathan Culler, *On Deconstruction* 172-175, Michael Ryan, *Marxism and Deconstruciton.*

34. Cf. John Lechte, "Art, love and melancholy in the work of Julia Kristeva" 39.

35. Kristeva has often made this point in interviews ("Two Interviews with Julia Kristeva" 123, "Julia Kristeva in Conversation with Rosalind Coward" 24, "Talking about *Polylogue*" 114, "Julia Kristeva" (interview with Jardine and Menke) 113-114). Cf. Oliver, *Reading Kristeva* 154.

36. Cf. OG 165.

37. KR 187-213 and KR 292-300.

Literary Connections

INTERVAL

Although the following chapter opens Part III, it can also be read as a kind of Interval, suspended between two parts of this book and participating in both. Straddling the divide between the articulation of theories of difference and the analysis of their purchase on literature, it mobilizes both these questions at once in order to ask another: how do we distinguish between literature and its others? The fine line marking the limit between the literary and the non-literary is a precarious tightrope to tread. This particular interval is therefore not the ice-cream break between two halves of the show(-and-tell) but is itself a performance of the dividing line. In the center ring then, let us follow Kristeva and Derrida as they move along the high wire. Interestingly, we shall find that in both cases the performance brings them before the law.

CHAPTER 6

Encountering Literature

THE EVOLUTION OF POETIC LANGUAGE[1]

Revolution in Poetic Language (RPL) and *Glas* were both published in 1974. The texts share certain preoccupations (the Hegelian dialectic, the signification of phonemic patterns for example), and yet it would be difficult to find two texts more different in style and rhetoric: Kristeva's densely theoretical, a performance of strength; Derrida's textual acrobatics playfully disturbing the norms of critical discourse. Despite a more lyrical and more accessible style in her theoretical texts since the 1980s, Kristeva continues clearly to separate critical and literary practice, a separation which is only emphasized by her ventures into fiction.[2] She makes her position explicit in the preface to *Desire in Language*, where she argues against "identifying theoretical discourse with art—causing theory to be written as literary or para-literary fiction" and writes of "the necessity of adopting a stance involving otherness, distance, even limitation" (DL ix, cf. 145-146). She positions her theoretical work "on the brink of fiction without ever completely toppling over into it" (ix). Perhaps the closest Kristeva comes to toppling in is in "Stabat Mater" in *Tales of Love*, where an analysis of the maternity of the Virgin Mary is juxtaposed with a very personal, fragmented text on the experience of motherhood. But however poetic this and other recent texts may seem, Kristeva considers them to be other than literary. Derrida's texts, on the other hand, do not show this same wariness of toppling into and acknowledging their participation in literary discourse. They seem to tumble in and out of literature at times.

If we think of such texts as *Glas*, *Spurs*, and "Envois" (PC 1-256), any dividing line between philosophy and literature is difficult to discern.[3]

Kristeva obviously considers the lit/crit distinction to be an important one. In fact it is a variation on a division that runs throughout her work and in which she invests heavily. From her earliest publications, Kristeva differentiates between poetic and non-poetic language. Both "Pour une sémiologie des paragrammes" (Σ 174-207) from 1966 and "Poésie et négativité" (Σ 246-277) from 1968 develop this distinction. In these texts, as in RPL, Kristeva turns to Mallarmé and Lautréamont to find a realization of poetic language. However, if we can read RPL as the culmination of this work, it is also true to say that the poetic language Kristeva was referring to by the mid-1970s was not defined in quite the same terms. The notion had evolved considerably along the way. Then, later in the decade, when she was renouncing political engagement in favor of a greater involvement in psychoanalysis and work on a more individual level,[4] her focus moved to artistic work not considered avant-garde.[5] With this shift came a tendency to refer to "esthetic experience," "literature" and their role in the imaginary more often than to "poetic language."

Alice Jardine identifies three Kristevas, she of *Sèméiotikè* in the sixties, she of RPL and *Polylogue* in the seventies, and a Kristeva of the eighties from *Powers of Horror* onwards.[6] It seems to me that for each of these Kristevas there is a poetic language. Nevertheless, throughout the evolution of the concept some things remain constant: the potency of poetic discourse and a certain kind of logic of the boundary in which it participates.

Kristeva's poetic language has never been an object. It does not refer to poetry any more than it does to prose. It is not linked to any features of form. Rather it is a practice or a mode of functioning—even perhaps a performance. The term is derived from Roman Jakobson's "poetic function" of language, and Kristeva's elaboration of the concept was initially part of an attempt to dynamize structuralism, to move beyond its ahistoricism and static analyses. In *Sèméiotikè*, poetic language is thus variously described as a "semiotic functioning," a "signifying practice" (247), an "activity freeing the subject from certain linguistic networks"(178) and a "dynamism shattering the inertia of language habits" (179). Clearly it can be no more confined to a book than Derrida's "text." As Houdebine writes, "definite products (texts) obviously result from this practice, but these are themselves readable only in the dynamic of the signifying operations that produce them."[7]

But what characterizes a performance as out of the ordinary? The essays from *Sèméiotikè* cited above distinguish poetic language from non-poetic language on the basis of the *negativity* at work in the former, but it is only towards the final pages of "Poésie et négativité" that negativity takes on the psychoanalytical association with the rejection drive that we saw in the discussion of RPL.[8] For most of the article and throughout "Pour une sémiologie des paragrammes," Kristeva discusses the types of logical negation at work in poetic language. These are simultaneously forms of transgression and are evidence of *dialogism*.

The concepts of dialogism and monologism are derived from Bakhtin's work, which Kristeva was largely responsible for bringing to the attention of the West. Dialogism or 0-2 logic resists monologism or 0-1 logic. Monologism is the logic of the binary opposition, the up-down, true-false, yes-no, either-or alternative of mutually exclusive terms. It is the logic of law. As such it typifies communication and non-poetic language, practices which submit easily to the laws of signification and grammar, not to mention the law of gravity. In fact, any writing or reading that proceeds "by identification, description, narration, exclusion of contradictions, establishing of truth" (Σ 183) belongs to monological discourse. In poetic language, on the other hand, the relation true/false, positive/negative, real/fictional is realized as a "non-synthetic union" (254), whereby opposites coexist simultaneously and without synthesis to form an "undecidable that does not seek to be resolved" (191). Poetic language participates in 0-2 logic or dialogism, a dream logic (151) which is not disturbed by contradictions. Dialogism bypasses the 1 (202), the "true" of true/false logic, and its 0 no longer corresponds to "false." Neither true nor false (the 0 of 0-2 logic), both true and false (the 2), the poetic signified brings together "even radically opposed semes" (188). Like the acrobat, who doesn't levitate or negate the law of gravity but uses it to defy gravity, poetic language defies law. Law is not simply broken but both negated and affirmed—its very logic is transgressed. Poetic language is neither grammatical nor agrammatical; it is paragrammatical. In *Sèméiotikè*, this kind of logical contradiction not only distinguishes poetic language but constitutes it (190-191). However, although poetic language resists monologism, it does not escape it. Dialogism is not simply opposed to monologism in an exclusive binary structure. It already includes monologism as it denies it (202), presupposing the 0-1 interval without stopping at it. Poetic language is thus not only dialogical; it is ambivalent. Ambivalence, in Kristeva's Bakhtinian vocabulary, represents the "permutation of two spaces," monological space and dialogical space (153). Poetic language thus functions as a dyad of law and the destruction of law (179), as a dialogue of discourses (181), as a dialectic (179).

Although Kristeva scarcely mentions dialogism after *Sèméiotikè*, its logic continues to prevail and it is interesting to note the parallels between this and her work in RPL. The symbolic—coextensive with law, God, syntax and meaning—could be interpreted as a monologism exceeding the space of the text and joining up with psychoanalytical considerations. Similarly, the semiotic, with its ruptures and articulations, embraces contradiction and embodies the ambiguity of dialogism. And between the two, the dialectic resembles Bakhtinian ambivalence: the contradiction between two heterogeneous spaces, between law and transgression. This evolution is already foreshadowed in the final pages of "Poésie et négativité" where Freud's work is evoked: the "incessant to-ing and fro-ing between logic and non-logic" of poetic language (Σ 265) becomes "this constant passage from the sign to the non-sign, from the subject to the non-subject, that is poetic language" (Σ 275). In fact this latter description of poetic language as an oscillation through the void—a kind of trapeze act—never ceases to remain valid in Kristeva's work.

In RPL and *Polylogue*, the question of poetic language moves beyond considerations of various kinds of logical negations and toward negativity or instinctual rejection. The contradictions of dialogism are assimilated into the instinctual, translogical semiotic mode that traverses not only binary logic but all symbolic functioning, dissolving the sign and pulverising meaning. In poetic language, the semiotic modality tends to dominate the symbolic (PL 160/DL 134): "Poetic language emphasizes [. . .] the negativity of the drive that destroys the thetic" (*Révolution* 236).[9] However, just as monologism was not absent from poetic language in *Sèméiotikè*, so the symbolic remains essential, guaranteeing the possibility of signification. From RPL onwards, it is the maximum involvement of the semiotic without the complete loss of the symbolic that identifies a signifying practice as poetic language: "The text remains [. . .] a 'poetic language' in that it is more than ever a discourse introducing drive facilitation and its stases right into symbolic-linguistic proceedings" (*Révolution* 618); "the text brings the signifier as close as possible to the instinctual heterogeneity [of *jouissance*]" (581). In order for drives to be introduced into signification in this way, the subject must undergo a process/trial and dissolve from the position of signification and judgment before later re-engaging with linguistic and social structures. If the Kristeva of the seventies focuses on avant-garde texts (whether of the late nineteenth or the twentieth century), it is because this is where the "process" seems most intense. The subject is liquefied in the passage from the verbal to the pre-verbal and goes as close as possible to losing his capacity for language altogether. It is no longer the acrobatics of logic as such that set a performance apart from the mundane but the personal risk involved. The drive of rejection which tears the subject away from meaning also dislodges him from law and the social order in general, linking the revolution of poetic language to political revolution.

The third Kristeva—the Kristeva of the later texts—is less concerned with political revolution than with individual psychical life and focuses on a much wider range of literary and artistic endeavor than avant-garde texts. Whether she is analyzing abjection, love, melancholy or revolt, in each case esthetic experience is of primary importance. It is still characterized by the process/trial of the subject — the risky passage from language and social identity to the unfathomable regions of existence and back again—but it is now celebrated for what it can achieve for the individual, whether the artist/writer or even to a certain extent the audience/reader. And what it achieves is not insignificant. The irruption in poetic language of the semiotic into the linguistic signifier is seen as the mark of the "true-real" (*le vréel*) of psychical experience.[10] Literature, art, music and dance thus afford the subject a kind of truth. But truth is not all: they offer nothing less than survival.

In *Powers of Horror*, literature is a means of surviving abjection. The experience of abjection arises from an indistinction between self and other, a blurring of the limits between inside and outside. This disturbance of identity stems from the initial confusion between the mother's body and the child's. Abjection is thus bound up with the relation to the unsignifiable body of the mother from which the subject never quite manages to detach himself completely. But literature is a way of naming this unnameable aspect of existence, the otherness within the self. It is an experience of borders and of a region where identity is yet unformed, a "descent into the hell of naming, that is to say of signifiable identity" (207). And it is a means of surviving this experience by transforming it into language and even into beauty: literature is "the ultimate coding of our crises, of our most intimate and most serious apocalypses," "an elaboration, a discharge and a hollowing out of abjection through the Crisis of the Word" (208).

Our inability to relinquish the unsignifiable maternal body is shown in *Black Sun* to be the source of depression. But the imaginary — in the form of esthetic experience—is once again a lifeline: it functions as "a tense link between Thing and Meaning, the unnameable and the proliferation of signs, the silent affect and the ideality that designates and goes beyond it" (100). The link is a bidirectional one: integrating the unnameable into language but also transferring meaning where there is none (103). Art, poetic language are ways of "overcoming [. . .] latent loss" (129). They are "an antidote to depression, a temporary salvation" (170). They accompany the subject down into the depths of depression as far as the eclipse of meaning (147) but through the sublimation of the experience, protect him from collapsing into asymbolia (165).

In *Tales of Love*, too, the sublimation effected by literature offers salvation or at least survival of the experience of love. Both love and literature destabilize the self through narcissistic identification with the other (279). However the imaginary is simultaneously an "antidote" to this crisis (381) for the artist struggles to "name what is closest to the unnameable along that loving curve made up of narcissism" (314). It is through metaphor (the "transporting" of meaning) that the experience of love is introduced into language, for metaphor itself is a dissolving of borders between subject and object (268). Finally and most recently, in *Sens et non-sens de la révolte*, literature again offers "salvation" (281) through sublimation. By making it possible for us to pass between thought and a-thought, it enables an experience of revolt and thus of "psychic survival" (114).

In Chapter 1, we saw the difficulty of lending an ear to the unnameable otherness within, dividing us from ourselves. If poetic language, literature and art have been by far the most frequent objects of Kristeva's analyses, it is because they offer the least dangerous means of gaining a limited access to this alterity. Much less destructive than psychosis, they also allow us to find a way back to identity. As a potential cure for the crises of abjection, depression, love and stagnation, esthetic experience rivals the psychoanalytic cure, which also attempts to accompany the subject/patient from the nameable to the unnameable and back again. However the death-defying oscillation via art or literature, whereby the subject swings through emptiness, boasts something that analysis rarely claims to offer: beauty.

But we have ceased to follow the performance of division between poetic and non-poetic to gape at the breathtaking feats of literature. As indeed Kristeva does. Back to the groundwork.

At the time when she introduces the concept, Kristeva tirelessly insists on the particularity of poetic language (Σ 255, 257, 264, 265, 274, 276), its specificity (Σ 190, 246, 247, 248, 264, 273, 274) and its radical difference (Σ 188) from all other semiotic practices. This is carried through into her later work but tapers off noticeably.[11] The insistence on specificity and particularity whereby Kristeva seeks to mark the bounds of poetic language can be contrasted with Derrida's work, characterized not by containment but by overflow (*débordement*). For each time we claim to identify the grounds for distinguishing, for example, between literature and non-literature, or between citation and original, or between the *mise en abyme* and the enclosing narrative, Derrida contests the validity of the distinction and shows the "contamination" or "parasitizing" that occurs between the terms.[12] Far from seeking to define the specificity of a practice or figure or structure by confining it, Derrida (in general) looks into the possibilities of grafting and citation that make any singular practice generalizable and potentially omnipresent. No practice exists in its pure state, but only because it may be (re)appropriated, quoted, continually marked and disseminated. Any text or element of a text may *a priori* be repeated and reframed or grafted onto others. This, according to Derrida, is the condition of language and of textuality in general: a sign, in order to be a sign, must be repeatable. The most singular phenomenon or event (a signature, a proper name, a date, a literary work in its uniqueness) is singular by virtue of its iterability.[13] And what is poetic here may be prosaic there, transplanted into another discourse, or merely recited until it becomes tired, mundane. Circus acts are a lot less awe-inspiring when practiced on the swings in the park. Conversely, repetition out of context ensures the possibility that any utterance may become poetic. Using these arguments, we may ask to what extent what is said by Kristeva to be specific to poetic language is actually valid for language in general.

In her early work, Kristeva explores the idea that poetic language transgresses the logic of binary oppositions such as "true-false, positive-negative, real-fictional" (Σ 247). However, as we have seen, Derrida shows that such metaphysical oppositions are far from hermetic, that "the positive (is) the negative" (OG 246), that one term supplements the other, and that such supplementarity, far from being the exclusive domain of the poetic, is the general condition of language. In "Poésie et Négativité," Kristeva works through a concrete example of poetic ambivalence which happens to concern the concrete: the transgression of the opposition "concrete vs general." This opposition is supposed to function unproblematically in non-poetic language, which "designates either something particular (concrete and individual), or something general" (Σ 251). A few lines from Baudelaire's "Une Martyre" describing a room serve as an example of a poetic utterance which disorganises this opposition by confronting us with something "concrete and non-individual" (*ibid.*), for "it is neither concrete, nor general" and moreover "the signifieds are both more concrete and more general that in speech" (252). Kristeva goes on to argue that "the poetic signified simultaneously refers and doesn't refer to a referent"; it refers to "precise" but "non-existent" referents, using for example "animate qualifiers for inanimate objects ('voluptuous furniture,' 'dying bouquets')" (253). In contrast, "[t]he bouquets are not dying, the furniture is not voluptuous in non-poetic speech" (*ibid.*).

Referring to Derrida, we would have to contest the legitimacy of Kristeva's distinction. "White Mythology," for example, problematizes the idea of the specificity of metaphor. [14] The "dying bouquets" may well become the dead flowers of everyday language, just as ordinary discourse may lie, or the most banal advertising may fix upon a concrete object and generalize it. As for the laws of logic excluding ambivalence, which are supposed to be valid for non-poetic language but redundant in a poetic text (Σ 258), we can find innumerable counter-examples in the illogicalities, ambiguities, incoherencies and of course the contradictions which abound in our efforts to communicate. Everyday language brings forth more anomalies than we care to admit. And according to Derrida, the undecidability that the Kristeva of *Sèméiotikè* considers specific to poetic language undermines every opposition.

If, in Kristeva's later texts, poetic language is defined by the involvement of drives and the disruption of symbolic law, we saw in the previous chapter that Derrida's arguments concerning citation cast serious doubt on this definition. And on its seriousness. After all, nothing disturbs the law of gravity so much as a bit of levity. Transgression is hardly limited to our more ernest instincts. Or is clowning to be scratched from the poetic program? Mallarmé's "Un coup de dés" may point to drive activity, but does my quotation of it or my mimicking of it automatically follow suit? And will my reading of it tomorrow call forth my body in the same way that it does today? These questions are put to rest to some extent by Kristeva's insistence that poetic language is a signifying *practice* and not a text as such, that it is the instinctual contribution to any performance that marks it as poetic, and yet this practice involving drives does seem to attach itself immutably to some precise textual objects. Mallarmé's "Prose," for example, through its phonemic patterns, remains inseparable from the drive of rejection that engenders it. The possibility of the detachment of such a text from the process of its production is not envisaged. Furthermore, Kristeva claims to be able to distinguish between authentic and fake drive involvement, between the genuine performance and doing it with mirrors, a claim Derrida would have to treat with some suspicion.[15] "There would be no cause for concern if one were rigorously assured of being able to distinguish with rigor between a citation and a non-citation" (LG 58), but of course we are not. As regards the ability of poetic language and of esthetic practice more generally to transfer unnameable otherness into language, Derrida argues that all language carries the mark of the unnameable, the trace of a *différance* that escapes signification whilst making it possible.[16] What Kristeva sees as specific to the poetic, Derrida identifies as widespread, open to all. Literature may well take us down into the abyss and back. But then so does bungee-jumping.

However, on looking more closely at Kristeva's work, we find that this reading—a dissemination of the principles of poetic language—is not inconsistent with Kristeva's project. For if she insists on particularity, it is of rather an unusual kind. The specificity of which she writes is, in fact, not the restricted case but the general one.[17] Thus Kristeva argues that poetic language is where language may be realized in its infinity, whereas ordinary language, in introducing restrictive laws of logic, is the limited case: "Poetic language [. . .] contains the code of linear logic" (Σ 178). Kristeva develops this argument: poetic language "cannot be [. . .] a sub-code. It is the ordered infinite code, a complementary system of codes from which we can isolate [. . .] ordinary language, scientific metalanguage and all artificial sign systems—which are all only subsets of this infinity" (179). Poetic language in its infinity encompasses the lower categories of language, and among them, "ordinary" language. It represents what might have been possible for any form of language were it not for the introduction of restrictive laws.

The idea that any language has the inherent capacity to become poetic is reiterated by Kristeva in her texts from the seventies. Here the laws restricting non-poetic language have become repressive—in the psychoanalytical sense. In *Polylogue* we find that poetic language merely highlights the normally unrealized aspects of language in general: poetic language "awakens our attention to this undecidable character of any so-called natural language, a feature that univocal, rational, scientific discourse tends to hide" (PL 161/DL 135). And in *La Révolution du langage poétique*, we learn that "poetic language in general, and the modern text in particular, restore to language one of its potential but repressed capacities: that of introducing the 'passions' into meaning" (226-227). It is as if communicative language were cut off from its sensual underside, whilst poetic language restitutes what in fact belonged to language all the time. Paradoxically, however, it seems that in order to be the infinite code, poetic language must have quite a specific mechanism, as if, in order to be the general case, it were necessary to be a very special case. The particularity of poetic language is to cross boundaries, rather than be confined by them. Poetic language continually operates across the dividing line, whether it be between the monological and the dialogical or between the symbolic and the semiotic, the nameable and the unnameable. In calling these limits into question, it transgresses logical and social law, whereas non-poetic language remains restricted within the bounds of Law.

The restricted case, however, is again less easy to restrict than we might at first suppose. If we turn to ordinary language, we find that it too overflows. Kristeva argues that in poetic language (unlike ordinary language), the signification of an element alters when it is repeated, and adds a supplement of meaning (Σ 258-259). In a footnote, she is however obliged to admit that her distinction is an "abstract" one: "In fact, a semantic unit repeated in 'ordinary' discourse can receive a new, connotative signification, but in this case 'ordinary' discourse loses its purity and functions 'poetically'" (259, n.17). Derrida would doubtless go even further, arguing that this distinction is always-already blurred, that the opposition is undermined by the constitutive possibility of citation opening the way for the "the possibility in every text of its becoming-literature," (LG 64, tr. mod.) and thus that ordinary discourse—like poetic language—has no purity to lose.

Kristeva, it seems, is not unaware of the mildly arbitrary character of the dividing line she draws between poetic and non-poetic language. Like other dividing lines in her work, it is necessarily ambiguous and permeable, hiding pockets of resistance. The opposition is fundamental to her analyses, but difficult to locate, operative without being absolute. And it depends on a further dividing line—monological/dialogical, symbolic/semiotic—which must also continue to function even as it is challenged. Gradually, from the mid 1970s onwards, Kristeva becomes less intent on demarcating and distinguishing the poetic/esthetic/literary from the ordinary, focusing rather on what it can achieve, on the life and death issues in which it participates as it crosses boundaries. In fact she ceases to insist on its specificity at all, pointing rather to the parallels between religious, artistic and psychoanalytical discourses and practices. Here the proof of the poem is in the patient, in its effect on the individual.

Perhaps then, we should pursue the question in the other direction: if undecidability, metaphor and the mark of the unnameable are constitutive of language in general, if nothing can enable us rigorously to tell the literary from the non-literary, then can no useful distinction be made? Are all performances equal? Must we renounce any attempt to trace a dividing line, to judge?

Of course the generalizing move we have identified in Derrida's work—seemingly specific traits are shown to be the general rule—is not simply that and does not simply operate in the opposite direction to Kristeva's work. In fact, it parallels Kristeva's paradox of the particular (the particularity of the general case) in identifying a constitutive link between the singular and the general. The opposition general/specific, like so many other binary oppositions, cannot separate out its terms definitively. In Derrida's work, it is regularly seen to be complicated by the exemplarity of the example: the example is always a meeting of the specific case and the general rule for its exemplarity makes it generalizable. Similarly, the proper name and the signature are both absolutely singular and necessarily repeatable.[18] Following this logic, let us examine a specific text of Derrida's in which he discusses both the general question of literature . . . and the relation between the specific and the general.

LITERATURE BEFORE THE LAW

In *"Devant la loi"* ("Before the Law"), Derrida studies Kafka's short text also entitled "Before the Law."[19] After drawing attention to the axiomatic consensus by which we accept it as belonging to literature (and having an author and an identity guaranteed by law), Derrida asks the question "Who decides, and according to what criteria, the membership of this narrative in literature?" (131). Now whilst showing that literature cannot be isolated or defined as such may be the predictable thing for Derrida to do, this argument does not engage with the fact that we continue to use the term literature, and with a very wide consensus as to the objects to which it refers. In this essay, Derrida is therefore less interested in the "generality" of the laws of literature than in "the singularity of a process [*procès*] which, in the course of a unique drama, summons them before the irreplaceable body, before this very text, before 'Before the Law'" (131).

The question of who and what decide literature is inseparable from the question of law, for it is a question of judgment. And whilst the law of literature may be general, the relation to this law, and indeed to any law, can only ever be specific, in the singular judgment of an individual case. But in any such trial, in the process of judgment, how close do we come to knowing the law that determines the process, the Law of Literature in this case? Kafka's man from the country, who naively believes that law is universally accessible, waits before the law, waits for the law, waits before the guardian to the first of many doors for admittance to the Law. But he never gets past that first door, a door intended for him alone. The law itself is not available: access to it is continually deferred. The law is not present; there are only acts of judgment. For if the law *were* present, paradoxically there would be no judgment: "At the most there would be knowledge, technique, application of a code [. . .]."[20] There would be no decision. The law "is neutral [. . .] and remains thus indifferent, impassive, little concerned to answer *yes* or *no*" (142). The law does not judge; judges do. Although there is law (or perhaps *because* there is law), we are still obliged to judge. This opens up the very possibility of ethics.

The law of literature is one such law. "The text would be the door" (144) through which we might hope to know it. But we do not get beyond the door and gain access to an essence of literature nor indeed to an answer or referent or immutable signified. We do not confront the law, just the door: "there is no literature without a work, without an absolutely singular performance" (146).[21] So how do we judge this performance as literature? Kafka's text is said to be not only literary but "obviously rich in philosophic content" (133). Derrida's reading is brought to bear "at the point where the difference between philosophy and literature seems both most certain and least clear," (133) for in order to read Kafka, he also refers to Kant's and Freud's writings. And what he finds is that "Kant almost introduced narrativity and fiction into the very core of legal thought" (133) and that Freud cannot account for the origin of law without relating it as a fable, just as Kafka's text itself is not readable without "drawing on some other source of knowledge" (143), for example, the discourses of philosophy, psychoanalysis, science, literary criticism or religion. The circulation of discourses, their mutual implication is not a question of influence: whether Kafka read Freud "is not important here"; the temporal relation between their writings "is of little interest to us" (134, cf. 136). Rather we could say that the discourses of fiction and law, literature and philosophy necessarily parasitize each other, are ultimately inseparable.[22] "What would be a literature that would be only what it is, literature? No longer would it be itself if it were itself" (147). Locked into a pure self-identity, without the performance, citation and diversion of other discourses, what could such a "literature" possibly include?[23]

In another text, "The Law of Genre," in which law and literature are again simultaneously summonsed, and the general and the specific—the genus and the species—are again implicated, Derrida writes of "*la loi de débordement*," "the law of abounding, of excess, the law of participation without membership" (LG 63). A text participates in a genre or in several genres, "yet such participation never amounts to belonging" (65). What he says of genre seems equally to apply to discourses: a text participates in literature (and philosophy and psychoanalysis) without being confined to it.[24]

If we judge Kafka's "Before the Law" to be literary, it is not because it is *separate* from other kinds of discourse but perhaps because of its "movements of framing and referentiality" ("Devant la loi" 146). These conditions are however too general to define literature.[25] Ultimately the text does not appear directly before the law of literature but before its guardians—"author, publisher, critics, academic archivists, librarians, lawyers, and so on" (147)—who, in judging the work to be literary, can always refer and defer to other guardians legitimated by a whole set of laws and social conventions.

*

Is it mere coincidence that Kristeva and Derrida both explain literature as a conjunction between the general and the specific, the universal and the individual, and in terms of *un procès*, a process or trial?

For Kristeva, the particularity of literature/esthetic practice is to realize the potential of language/sign systems in general by involving those aspects of the latter that are usually repressed and minimized. This occurs when the subject in process/on trial passes between the symbolic and the semiotic, engaging both modes in a realization of the infinite. Thus what is specific to literature does not confine it but draws it out from the page, from the object, takes it beyond the bounds of communicative language to galvanize and call into question the subject's bond with the social group, his relation to the body, to the mother and other others.

Similarly, Derrida's analysis of a literary text, at the very moment when he focuses on it as literature, on its literariness, shows its participation in a multiplicity of proliferating discourses, and activates the text's relations with, for example, philosophy, psychoanalysis, law, history and other literary texts. Literature is not confined to literature.

It is in this sense that the work of both Kristeva and of Derrida is seen as post-structuralist and is said to have been instrumental in the move outward from the navel-gazing "self-sufficient text."[26]

However the meeting of an unlimited number of discourses in the reading of a particular literary text is not the principal conjunction of the general and the specific in Derrida's "Devant la loi." Rather, it is the specific appearance of a text before (the guardians of) the general law of literature. Deciding what is literature can never be the mere application of a rule: The presence/absence of a distinctive feature is never sufficient. It is always necessary to appeal to further authorities. Determining literature involves a process like that of law, culminating in a judgment.

For both Derrida and Kristeva, then, literature involves both judgment and a suspension of judgment. And although judgment is not suspended in the same way, in both cases literature is defined by a particular relation to law. For Derrida, there is the process of law, the trial of undecidability that precedes any judgment. This is Derrida's performance of the dividing line. He puts his weight on the fine line strung up between philosophy and literature and slides back and forth, showing the way in which they parasitize each other. Finally, however, he must come down on one side or the other, ending the suspense without eliminating or resolving the undecidability. Kafka's text is judged to be literary.

For Kristeva, literature is determined by the process of the subject, who leaves and then returns to the realm of judgment. However, in this case, it is not the exercise of judgment that determines literature, but the conviction that judgment has been suspended. Here the tightrope walk is not so much the division between literature and criticism/theory/ordinary language but the literary performance itself. Suspended over a void threatening depression, abjection and the disturbance of identity, buffeted by drives, language is the only thread carrying the subject between points of symbolic stability or law. Literature is the product of such a crossing—on condition that you *do* look down.

Curiously, getting a firm grip on law, on the points of stability, doesn't seem to be problematic in Kristeva's earlier work. The symbolic seems clearly identifiable and accessible. It is only those who have never achieved a solid thetic position—those who have plummeted into the unnameable or become caught in the void—who find law and social structures out of reach. Normally it is the instinctual semiotic that is inaccessible. This contrasts markedly with the Derridean reading, where it is law that is ungraspable, always deferred and referred. What holds Kafka's text up as literature, what keeps the tightrope suspended, is no solid pillar of law, no identifiable force, but a network of wires, of tensions balancing and relaying one another, held in place by pegs that can be moved from one performance to the next. Kristeva, however, makes it clear in *Sens et non-sens de la révolte* that when law functions in this way—unlocatable, endlessly deferred—then something has gone horribly wrong. The symbolic is failing to provide us with a law that we can confront and against which we can revolt.

Ultimately, it is the relation between law and its other (whether that other be transgression, madness or the eclipse of law) that distinguishes the two conceptions of literary practice from one another. And predictably, the relation is each case is in the image of the relevant theory of difference. For both theorists, law and its other are inseparable and inevitably pre-suppose each other. Thus Kristeva argues in her early work that "Without prohibition there would be no transgression [. . .] we should rather speak of their inseparable cohabitation" (Σ 183) and, much later, that "the question of revolt defines itself [. . .] in relation to the law" (SNR 197). Thus Derrida writes: "There is not madness [*folie*] without the law; madness cannot be conceived before its relation to law" (LG 81). And if Kristeva maintains that transgression is necessary to the survival and renewal of law, Derrida, too, insists on their constitutive interdependence: "And suppose the condition for the possibility of the law were the *a priori* of

a counter-law [. . .]?" (LG 57); "The law and the counter-law serve
each other citations summoning each other to appear [*se citent à
comparaître*]" (LG 58). However, by locating this mutual dependence
within the framework of her elaboration of language and of the
speaking subject, Kristeva ensures that law and its other can never be
confused. The ambiguity of poetic language as it oscillates between
sense and non-sense in no way signifies an interchangeability of these
terms. Although law changes and is renewed, although what was once
transgression may become law, although meaning may be transferred to
the site of dissolved meaning, the two poles always remain distinct. In
order for esthetic practice to procure *jouissance* for the subject or to
save him from depression and asymbolia, law must survive as law:
"However elided, attacked, or corrupted the symbolic function might be
in poetic language, due to the impact of semiotic processes, the
symbolic function nonetheless maintains its presence. It is for this
reason that it is a language" (DL 134). Only in this way can the subject
preserve his status as a speaking subject. Somersaulting over the abyss,
it is essential to remember which way is up and where safety can be
found.

   In Derrida's work, however, law and non-law cannot be reliably
opposed to one another: if "[t]he foundation of all states occurs in a
situation that we can [. . .] call revolutionary," then law is always
inaugurated in non-law. "That which threatens law already belongs to
it" (FL 35). The law of law—that which legitimates law—can only be a
post-hoc self-legitimation of the foundation of law in non-law. It can
only be an endless referral of responsibility from guardian to guardian
within the jurisdiction and discourse of the law. The law of law is
therefore that part of law that escapes law: "There is something decayed
or rotten in law, which condemns it or ruins it in advance" (FL 39).
This is the folly or madness of the law (cf. LG 80). This is folly-law:
"Madness is law, the law is madness [*C'est la loi, c'est une folie, la
loi*]" (81).[27] The dizzy spinning of Derrida's text leaves us far less
certain than Kristeva's as to which way is up.

   For Derrida, literature functions on the same principles as law (LI
134, TI 12, "Devant la loi" 138) or more precisely as law-folly. It does
not involve an oscillation between law and folly because the interval
between the terms appears and disappears. No workable opposition can
be maintained between them. One is merely a deferred moment of the
other.

One of Derrida's definitions of *la folie* is the instability of the logos, the untameable polysemy of a signifier such that it can never be unified into one meaning (TI 17). In this light it is interesting to consider the range of meanings associated with the French *folie*: anything from an extravagant gesture to hare-brained antics to delirium and insanity. In Kristeva's and Derrida's writings we see *la folie de la folie*, for each has a tendency to privilege some of these associations and neglect others. Derrida's hide-and-seek between law and folly shrugs off the darker side of *la folie*, the speechless, painful worlds of depression and abjection. On the other hand, when Kristeva writes of *la folie*, she is referring to psychosis.[28] Absorbed in the suspense and drama as the subject hovers between life and death, speech and silence, she perhaps overlooks the element of play in the performance and the playfulness of esthetic production in general. In fact, her emphasis on the specificity and truth of poetic language acts to protect it from parody. Meanwhile Derrida plays [*joue*] at/with law: "To stake the law [*jouer la loi*] is to twist or transgress the law, but it can also mean to repeat or mime one's law" (TI 13). The theatrical representation or rehearsal of law, which undermines the Kristevan oscillation between law and the transgression or collapse of law, is excluded from Kristeva's concept of the esthetic. In the literary circus, while Kristeva puts the spotlight on the dangerous balancing required to survive, Derrida brings clowning into the high-wire act, and bounces back up from the safety net. Is it an empty miming of literature, as Kristeva would have it . . . or its carnivalization (in which case it would amount to a carnivalization of a carnivalization)?

It is commonly argued that carnival is complicitous with law, sustaining it whilst providing a temporary suspension of its rule. Kristeva's account of esthetic practice—the suspension of and return to symbolic law—can be read in parallel with this analysis of carnival and of its usefulness: merriment and foolery become euphoria and have a purpose; play, for Kristeva, is primarily therapeutic. Derrida's remarks on law, however, although they too underline the complicity between law and folly, problematize this understanding of carnival. For if Derrida is only too ready to agree that law is suspended in the circus atmosphere, it is not at all clear that the suspension of law is ever over, that we find our way back from folly to law. We always seem to be left dangling. For when the literary performance concludes, do we leave the circus and find law? Or do we exit through the tent-flap into another Big Top, that of the legal or academic or financial circus for example, where law and folly continue to mimic each other disconcertingly. Even away from the sawdust and greasepaint, the law of gravity is not necessarily able to fix up and down in place. It all depends on which side of the globe you're on or on what co-ordinates you plot on the graph.

Waiting for a law that is never present or accessible but always deferred can be Kafkaesque. On that, Derrida and Kristeva agree. Derrida, in "Devant la loi," points directly to Kafka's work and Kristeva, in *Sens et non-sens de la révolte*, underlines the alienating, nightmarish quality of the situation where law is endlessly referred elsewhere. But Derrida hardly lingers on despair in the Kafka text, and amongst other discursive networks, he points to the noses in the text, the hairs in the nostrils, the hairiness of the setting, Fliess' olfactory musings, in short to the comic inseparable from the psychoanalytical, the philosophical, the historical and even perhaps the tragic in the text. Sometimes I suspect that it is not only folly that leads me to want to articulate Kristeva's and Derrida's work and, in particular, their work on the literary text, but *la folie de la folie*, the irreducible polysemy of *la folie* that leads us to and through pain as well as play. I look to Kristeva and Derrida to find ways of reading both the delirium and the delight of the literary performance. Bringing the two together in this way is risky, I admit, but it seems to me that waiting for the law is a little like waiting for Godot. Our sanity may be precariously compromised. There are times when life is unspeakable and unbearable. But while we wait for the law that never presents itself, like Beckett's clowns, we might as well also have some fun.

NOTES

1. An earlier version of this section was published in *In the Place of French. Essays in and around French Studies in Honour of Michael Spencer*, Brisbane, University of Queensland, 1992.

2. Since the publication of her semi-autobiographical novel *The Samurai*, two other novels have appeared: *The Old Man and the Wolves* and *Possessions*.

3. Cf. Derrida's discussion of the classification of his work as philosophical or non-philosophical in *Points . . .* (411-413). Cf. also Derrida and Attridge, "This Strange Institution Called Literature" in which Derrida remarks: "what interests me today is not strictly called either literature or philosophy" (34). Attridge argues that the opposition philosophy versus

literature is "an opposition that Derrida has patiently chipped away at in his readings of both kinds of text" (Introduction, *Acts of Literature* 13).

4. Cf. "Julia Kristeva in Conversation with Rosalind Coward" 25.

5. The general movement of the *Tel Quel* group away from avant-garde literature is detailed by Forest (*Histoire de Tel Quel* 509-511).

6. Alice Jardine, "Opaque Texts and Transparent Contexts" 24. Cf. John Lechte, *Julia Kristeva* 4-6.

7. Houdebine, "Lecture(s) d'une refonte" 327-328.

8. See Chapter 2.

9. Quotations marked *Révolution* rather than RPL are from the latter half of the volume which was not included in the published translation.

10. Cf. "The True-Real" (KR 216-237). Toril Moi glosses the true-real as "a truth that would *be* the *real* in the Lacanian sense of the term (KR 214).

11. See RPL 104-105, 180, DL 124, 134, PL 275, BS 100.

12. Cf. De Nooy, "The Double Scission: Dällenbach, Dolezel and Derrida on Doubles" which shows that whereas Dällenbach seeks to identify the specificity of the *mise en abyme* and Dolezel that of the double, Derrida insists that these figures, far from being special cases, merely highlight the condition of textuality in general.

13. The arguments are spelt out in (among other texts) "Signature Event Context" (for the signature), "Aphorism Countertime" (for the proper name), *Shibboleth* (for the date), "Ulysses Gramophone" (for the literary work).

14. MP 207-271. In this article, Derrida argues that literal meaning has always-already been expropriated, such that all language could be seen as dead, dying or worn-out metaphors. However these metaphors ("dead," "worn out") cannot account for the role of metaphor for they are determined by it. Rather they mark its blind spot. Philosophy depends on its metaphors but cannot dominate them from outside metaphor. A philosophy of metaphor is no more sustainable than a philosophy of literal language: the becoming-metaphor and the becoming-literal of meaning are always at work in language. Cf. "Either everything we say is metaphorical [. . .] or nothing is metaphorical; or neither and both" (John Llewelyn, *Derrida on the Threshold of Sense* 78). Rodolphe Gasché gives a detailed reading of "White Mythology," linking it to the question of the general and the particular (*The Tain of the Mirror* 193-318).

15. See for example RPL 97, SNR 309, 347-348.

16. Cf. *Speech and Phenomena* and *Of Grammatology*. Of course, as we saw in Chapter 1, Derrida's unnameable does not coincide with Kristeva's.

17. Forest also remarks on this paradox (*Histoire de Tel Quel* 256).

18. Cf. Attridge's analysis of the complex interdependence of the singular and the general in Derrida's work (Introduction, *Acts of Literature* 14-21).

19. Derrida's *"Che cos'è la poesia?"* (*Points* . . . 288-299), which focuses on the poetic or the poematic, might have been an obvious text to study in this chapter. With its hearts and its hedgehogs on the road, it could have led us to (or before) literature along a different route.

20. *Préjugés* 94 (from the untranslated introduction to "Devant la loi").

21. Cf. Derrida and Attridge, "This Strange Institution Called Literature" 40-46, 73.

22. Cf. "In the content of literary texts, there are always philosophical theses" ("This Strange Institution Called Literature" 49).

23. Cf. "If there is no essence of literature [. . .] if what is announced or promised as literature never gives itself as such, that means, among other things, that a literature that talked only about literature or a work that was purely self-referential would immediately be annulled" ("This Strange Institution Called Literature" 47).

24. It is to this argument that we need to look if we wish to decide the status of any of Derrida's texts, which each mark their participation in a number of discourses.

25. In "This Strange Institution Called Literature," Derrida again writes of literature having "a *suspended* relation to meaning and reference" and again suggests that this is in fact true of all language (48).

26. Cf. Michael Riffaterre, "The Self-Sufficient Text."

27. Cf. "[. . .] this very reason whose madness they [subversions] demonstrate rather than opposing to it, from the outside, another madness" (TI 22).

28. See, for example, RPL 82, 145, SNR 230, 396.

CHAPTER 7

Articulating the Text

Having identified or judged a text as literary, what do you do with it?
How is the text articulated? What does it articulate? And how do you
articulate that? The premise for what follows is that reading is largely a
matter of making connections, of finding ways of putting the
multifarious parts of a text together, of connecting a text with the other
texts/contexts that form/transform a culture, of personally connecting
oneself to a text as one reads. But the term "articulation" perhaps better
covers the various ways in which connection and disconnection
mutually entail each other. What I wish to do in this chapter is look at
how the theories of Kristeva and Derrida can be articulated around the
way in which they articulate the text—in all the senses of the word:
mechanical, phonetic, anatomical and discursive. For both of them have
ways

- of making connections,
- of dividing the text up to reassemble it flexibly,
- of hinging its dimensions,
- of examining its production through the organs of speech,
- of hooking it up to the body and to other discourses,
- and of formulating these processes in various articles (Lat.
  articulus).

And these ways of articulating the text can, in turn, be articulated
around some of the objects of analysis to which Derrida and Kristeva
have both turned over the years. These, as we shall see, range from the

minute (the syllable *or*, the consonant cluster) to the so-called "infinite text."

The question of scale thus needs to be addressed, for sizeable sections of the chapter are devoted to Derrida's and Kristeva's work on tiny morsels of text. What is the status of this kind of detail, both in their readings and in mine? The importance of detail in their work allows us to investigate the mechanics of reading as they read, the nuts and bolts and machine oil of articulating a text. For what they do with mammoth texts like *Finnegans Wake* or *Remembrance of Things Past* is predicated on what they are able (and enable us) to do with a repeated word, syllable or image. Rather than accepting a text as a finished product ready for the consumer, its closed and varnished casing concealing all moving parts, Derrida and Kristeva go for the do-it-yourself adjustable model and tinker with the text, making it work in ways not advertised by the manufacturer.

Watching them fiddle with words and letters, with syllables and phonemes, with the most basic materials of language and textuality, I wonder at the accusations of abstraction sometimes leveled at "French theory." Would it really be possible to read a text in a more concrete way than this?

The main reason, however, for focusing in detail on the way in which Derrida and Kristeva focus on detail, is the seemingly inexhaustible productivity of this aspect of their work. Derrida draws out about half of the massive *Glas* from one word; Kristeva generates some fifty pages of *La Révolution du langage poétique* from work on repeated phonemic groups. And putting these two together multiplies the possibilities for inventiveness. The profusion of connections, the orgy of interpretations that their readings produce do not drain the texts that Derrida and Kristeva study but lead us, their readers, to contribute further to the surplus of textual output. In this way, the infinite text is extracted, decompressed from the tiniest grain of its matter.

HOOKING UP TO INFINITY: THE LIMITS OF THE INFINITE TEXT

Of the many intersections in the corpora of texts on which Derrida and Kristeva have written, Philippe Sollers' *Nombres* is the clearest coincidence. Hardly a coincidence at all of course. In 1969, both theorists devoted lengthy texts to analyzing the most recent publication of their *Tel Quel* partner: "Dissemination" (Dis 319-407) and

"L'Engendrement de la formule" (Σ 278-371). Forest describes the textual encounter thus:

> Around *Nombres* [. . .] a transition takes place: two systems of theoretical coordinates are superimposed for a moment before the sheer scale of what separates them emerges into the light of day. Not at all by chance, Sollers' novel gives rise to two authoritative and, in retrospect, obviously rival readings: Derrida places his commentary under the sign of an interminable and irreducible "dissemination"; Kristeva shows that *Nombres*, marking within itself the presence of the "geno-text," sees itself as a "return [*remontée*] to the very germ where meaning and its subject dawn." The development of post-structuralism, the future history of *Tel Quel* are to be found in this as yet unnoticed divergence. [1]

What interests me in this commentary is the way in which it identifies the 1969 textual encounter as the site of rupture-at-a-point-of-absolute-proximity. The superimposition of the two articles on Sollers is disturbed by the friction of rivalry, such that the invisible interval appears. It does not however appear-and-disappear as a Derridean reading of the relation between the two might suggest. Instead, and more in keeping with a Kristevan reading, Forest shows the split blowing out into a gulf of separation. Let us examine the texts in question and the marks of superimposition and separation. And since the texts focus on *Nombres*, let us start with a number of sorts — infinity.

Both Kristeva and Derrida describe *Nombres* as an infinite text. But it is not only *Nombres* that is unlimited: for Kristeva, poetic language itself is infinite. And Derrida goes even further in describing textuality in general in this way. Derrida writes of textual constellations and labyrinths where "the references [are] infinite" (Dis 334). Fragments are only readable "within the well-calculated play of [. . .] an innumerable polysemy" (Dis 327), in a "numerous plurivocality, absolutely disseminated" (Dis 344). And his famous line that "There is no outside-text" (OG 158) is explained further in "Dissemination":

> [. . .] the text never in fact begins. [. . .] You find yourself being indefinitely referred to bottomless, endless connections [. . .]. [The text] can be neither maintained nor contained in the clasp of a book. Text as far as the eye can see [. . .]. (Dis 333-334, tr. mod.)

Kristeva similarly insists on what she calls the "infinitization" (Σ 327) of the text with its "infinite engendering" (Σ 330) and "the plurality of the infinite geno-text," (Σ 303). She writes of an "infinitely multiple text—and not multiple with respect to one, but multiple with respect to the multiple" (Σ 353).

The enthusiasm of the two theorists on this subject is not tempered by the fact that the unlimited text seems to be produced by virtue of certain constraints. Thus Derrida describes "the finite/infinite structure of the apparatus" (Dis 299) and Kristeva "the minimal closure that sets the infinite in motion" (Σ 362, cf. 365-367). Kristeva explains the paradox in the following way: "Instead of a combination of units in a whole, the unlimited signifier uses differentials" (Σ 297). These differentials (repeated elements) "restore infinity through a finite system of marks" (Σ 298). Totality, wholeness and fullness are not to be confused with infinity; rather they represent a kind of upper *limit* (*ibid.*). There are parallels between this and Derrida's explanation of the infinite in "Structure, Sign and Play." It is the lack of fullness and closure in the finite case that makes infinite play possible:

> [. . .] a field of infinite substitutions only because it is finite, that is to say, because instead of being an inexhaustible field, as in the classical hypothesis, instead of being too large, there is something missing from it: a center which arrests and grounds the play of substitutions. (WD 289, cf. 280)

Evidently, the text's infinity is not an all-encompassing immensity that would hold everything in its accumulation. Rather it is an unstoppable movement from which nothing can be sure of escaping.

The infinite text thus arises through the articulation of the finite — the words on the page for instance—and the infinite transformations of which it is the locus. From what we have seen in previous chapters we might expect this, in Kristeva's case, to take the form of contradiction (the "dialectic" and "polemic" between the finite and the infinite, between "position and infinitization," PL 195-196). In Derrida's case, we might anticipate that it be called *différance* or supplementarity, as the finite is infinitely replaced, as signified and signifier substitute for each other. And this is so. But there is more than one way of articulating Kristeva's and Derrida's work here.

The production of the infinite through the finite is also called *engendrement* in the one case and *dissémination* in the other: two metaphors of generation and germination, of seed and sperm, of propagation and proliferation. Interestingly, in these seminal texts, the dissemination occurs without seeking to claim paternity, and the engendering does everything but give birth to meaning. In the "haphazard productivity" of dissemination (Dis 48), "the preface, as semen, is just as likely to be left out, to well up and get lost as a seminal *différance*, as it is to be reappropriated into the sublimity of the father" (Dis 44, cf. 304). And Kristeva insists that

> this engendering engenders no "phenomenon [*fait*]" outside itself. It is the engendering process, the accumulation and development of "germs," germination, and has nothing in common with the creation of descendants, of a product that would be external to it [. . .]. [. . .] the germination refrains from becoming a generation, that is to say from "giving birth," from having offspring—Meaning. (Σ 285)

Textual liberation and promiscuity? Whatever meanings may come about from these practices, neither Derrida nor Kristeva nor Sollers, for that matter, is going to adopt or maintain them. Both engendering and dissemination describe a germinating process whereby the text is not fathered or mothered (by a conscious subject, by intention), but continually generates itself in ways that cannot be mastered by either writer or reader. Both describe a process whereby no element or aspect of the text can be recuperated into a single, unified meaning. Now, the impossibility of mastering the meaning of the text does not mean—as both advocates and opponents of criticism as anything-goes free-play have sometimes claimed—simply walking away from meaning. As Rodolphe Gasché points out in relation to Derrida's work, the "search for meaning should not be abandoned but rather intensified, and in such a manner as to account for the ultimate possibility of these texts' meaninglessness."[2] And this is what Derrida and Kristeva each proceed to do. However, the two studies of the infinite proliferation of the text and of meanings seem to focus in different directions. Kristeva looks towards the germ, towards a genesis that is not an origin but a productivity. She "goes back [*remonte*] vertically through the genesis" of signification that she calls *signifiance* (Σ 280) in order to find what the reduction to a communicable meaning obscures (286).[3] Derrida looks away from the germ and towards the scattering of seed that may or may not germinate where it falls. He does not go back but forward, *sans retour*, writing of "the impossible return to the rejoined, readjusted unity of meaning" (268, cf. 351). *Engendrement* thwarts the supposed unity of meaning at an origin; dissemination thwarts unity of meaning at a destination.

This apparent difference in the time of the text is also a difference in its space. Given the shared investment in the proliferation of the infinite text, it may not represent a deep or profound difference, but it does involve a difference of depth.

HINGING DIMENSIONS

Question: When is a text a volume?

Derrida: When the book is closed, when it is a heavy tome. But we can open it up, leaf through its pages, such that its continuous surface appears.

Kristeva: The text is and has a volume when we restore to it the vertical dimension of its infinite productivity. We need to struggle against the reduction of this volume to a flat surface.

Clearly, the two ways of working lead in opposite directions: volume to surface, surface to volume. Throughout Kristeva's work, we find a "transformation of the line into volume" and a stratification beneath the surface (Σ 13). Throughout Derrida's, we witness instead the text's *déploiement* from volume into surface as it unfolds like a fan, unfurls like a sail. Nevertheless, in each case, the writer's insistence on depth or surface is seen as an expansion of the text, an extension of its space. Derrida writes of the "spaciousness" that operates "through folding, flexing back, deploying, expanding" (Dis 236). Kristeva writes of the linguistic units that "open up into volume by getting in touch, through the structured surface of speech, with the infinity of translinguistic practice" (Σ 82).

The unfolding of the text's surface and the stratification of the text to give it depth are both ways of amplifying the text and of metaphorically locating its articulation with infinity. But these are not merely different spatial metaphors for more or less the same idea. They involve differences in the very conceptualization of the text, in the kind of infinity available to it, and in what in means to read a text. And although the most detailed descriptions of the spatial organization of the appear in their early work, neither Derrida nor Kristeva has abandoned these ways of visualizing the opening up of the text to give free rein to its signifying possibilities. Let us then look closely at what is involved in the move from surface to volume or from volume to surface.

The spatial model Kristeva uses to elaborate her theory of the text is explicitly stratified; it has layers and depth. It is intended to replace an image of the text as a purely linguistic structure, a linear chain or flat surface, for such an understanding constitutes a flattening out of the dimensions of the text, an "obliteration of the density [*aplatissement de l'épaisseur*] that constitutes sign, sentence, and syllogism (and consequently, the speaking subject)" (DL 127), a "despatialization" of the text that "reduces volume to a surface, practice to a sound chain, and substitutes intentionality—meaning—for the dimension thus hidden" (Σ 78). Such flattening allows us to see only the horizontal plane of the text, the upper layer, what Kristeva calls the pheno-text and which is none other than the printed text, the text as linguistic phenomenon (Σ 280). There is however another dimension to be considered: "The geno-text adds *volume* to the *surface* of the pheno-text" (Σ 284). The geno-text is the generating process underlying the pheno-text and through which the pheno-text can be interpreted as *signifiance*. It is not to be confused with Chomsky's deep structure, for it is not a structure at all but an abstract level of functioning, through which a signifying subject is engendered. In *Revolution in Poetic Language*, it becomes clear that this occurs through the organization of instinctual energies: the geno-text encompasses both semiotic processes (including "drives, their disposition, and their division of the body, plus the ecological and social system surrounding the body, such as objects and pre-Oedipal relations with parents") and the advent of the symbolic ("the emergence of object and subject, and the constitution of nuclei of meaning involving categories: semantic and categorial fields") (RPL 86).

The reading of the text as text avoids crushing this dimension and instead works at the line where pheno- and geno-text meet, where the geno-text is discernible in the pheno-text (Σ 280-281). The text "explodes the surface of language" (Σ 13) and "sinks a vertical in the surface of speech" (Σ 8-9). The thin Saussurian sign—signifier and signified like two sides of a page—acquires depth and becomes volume (Σ 300).

There is no ambiguity concerning the spatial relation joining the geno-text to the pheno-text. It is not only a question of the verticality of the former and the horizontality of the latter: Kristeva regularly insists that the geno-text is to be found *underneath* the pheno-text, and constantly uses the words *sous-jacent* and *sous-tendre* to describe the way in which the processes of the former underlie the linguistic surface of the latter. The geno-text is a "deep" mechanism of forces (*Révolution* 215) in which "A measured language [is] carried away into rhythm to a point beneath language" (DL 179).[4] The geno-text links the pheno-text to its instinctual basis: the drive investments of rhythm and sound "remain subjacent to the pheno-text but line it [*le doublent*] with a semiotic 'stratum'" (*Révolution* 225). "The geno-text can thus be seen as language's underlying foundation" (RPL 87).

The volume of the text is thus a layered volume, and this layering is apparent in all facets of its functioning: the polylogical text is an "area of heterogeneous strata (drive-sound-language)" (DL 186) with "a multiplied, stratified, and heteronomous subject of enunciation" (DL 173); its time is "stratified, polyphonic time" (DL 201). The stratification of the text means that instinctual "irruption" becomes a veritable eruption, as the vertical engendering axis invades the horizontal linguistic axis. The geno-text manifests itself as a volcano, but also as an abyss—"*cet abîme du géno-texte*" (Σ 308), an unfathomable vertical chasm.

Like Kristeva, Derrida reads against the linearity of a text[5] but not in order to plumb its depths. The detours and networks that form through and around the text extend in all directions but without adding to its thickness. Even the Derridean "abyss" is presented as a surface: "The labyrinth here is an abyss: we plunge into the horizontality of a pure surface" (WD 298). Whilst Kristeva digs down deep to make contact with hidden and buried aspects of infinity, Derrida attempts to demonstrate that what is unfathomable in the text is not profound or deep. Beneath the surface of the words, there are only . . . other pages. What is said to be hidden behind or beneath the text also functions textually, that is to say, as a surface.

Derrida's preferred representations of textuality are those that oscillate between surface and apparent depth or thickness, like the fold, the veil and the sail (*le voile/la voile*) or the fan in *Dissemination* which all seem to hold hidden dimensions but which unfold, open out or simply fall to reveal more surface. Not that the full surface could ever be exposed: there is always the fold within the fold to be unfolded. The spacing of *différance* can never be exhausted. The surface is thus not a horizontal plane opposed to a vertical dimension. The fold moves through various planes as it unfolds: the horizontal becomes vertical in the movement of unfurling. And the volume appears and disappears in the fold.

Similarly, the inside of the text, the notion that a text might have an interior and thus might *contain* a meaning, turns out to be an illusion created by the tucks in the text: "since everything begins in the folds of citation [. . .], the inside of the text will always have been outside it" (Dis 316). The signs that are brought together on the page are also already used conventionally—and unconventionally—in other texts and contexts. The significations made available in a text depend on our familiarity with these repeated uses. In short, a text is only readable because it is a tissue of citations. The meaning it seems to contain only appears by virtue of its relations to other texts. Conversely, of course, what appear to be outside the text (other texts, referents, etc.) are always-already inside by virtue of this same principle of citation. The glove can be turned inside out: interior and exterior are merely surfaces that exchange places. Since outside and inside cannot be reliably opposed to one another, "there is no outside-text" (OG 158), but neither is there any inside-text. Like a sail that suddenly billows out, intertextuality is produced from surfaces sewn together, pieces of canvas that may stay furled or may unfurl, and whose breadth depends on a breath of air, a gust of wind.

As the surface of the text is unfolded, it extends well beyond the book. In "Freud and the Scene of Writing" (WD 196-231), Derrida seeks to demonstrate the "superficial" nature of psychical structure in Freud's writings: according to Freud's analysis, psychical structure does not consist of a surface and hidden depth but of a set of surfaces. Derrida follows the metaphor of the "Mystic Pad" that Freud uses to explain his conception of the psyche,[6] and comments on the spatial aspect of the model:

> Let us note that the *depth* of the Mystic Pad is simultaneously a depth without bottom, an infinite allusion [*renvoi*], and a perfectly superficial exteriority: a stratification of surfaces each of whose relation to itself, each of whose interior, is but the implication of another similarly exposed surface. (WD 224)

On the one hand, the model allows us to imagine "infinite depth in the implication of meaning." However, on the other hand, there is "the pellicular essence of being, the absolute absence of any foundation" (*ibid*.). The volume of the model is only a result of the relation between stratified surfaces. We could speak of a "volume effect." The psyche itself is not deep: its apparent depth is merely an effect of the distance separating the surfaces. Similarly, "The subject of writing is a system of relations between strata: the Mystic Pad, the psyche, society, the world" (WD 227). Echoing this text elsewhere, Derrida writes of a "stratified network" of complex relations between what is traditionally understood as "history," "economics," "psychoanalysis," "politics," etc. in the theater of the mental world, the inside-outside of the mind (Dis 236). The subject has no consistency or solidity. Rather it resembles a network of surfaces with zero density.

Derrida's strata are thus not the same kind of strata as Kristeva's and do not have the same effect. Whilst Kristeva's layers give thickness and depth to the text, Derrida's "stratified network" is more of an intertextual and citational latticework, a net of texts with gaps and spaces creating an effect of depth between the pages. Derrida's strata aerate the text. The layers of writing resemble the adjustable slats of venetian blinds, where there is "neither a permanent contact nor an absolute break [*rupture*] between strata" (WD 226) but rather "the spacing that guarantees both the gap and the contact" (Dis 261), and where the horizontal only becomes vertical to create another surface. These are merely effects of the network that links and separates, spreading out in all directions.

The fold that unfolds thus makes a space and even creates itself in a sort of spacing. *Différance* is glimpsed in the time of citation, in the phrase that opens up another book in the middle of a page. "The *a* of *différance* marks the *movement* of this unfolding" (MP 22). Similarly, the layers and the juxtaposition of surfaces points to spacing, for between the layers we find nothing but the relation, a relation of difference. "What takes place is only the *entre*, the place, the spacing, which is nothing" (Dis 214). Spacing without depth.

For Kristeva, this way of reading seems to flatten out the text, to ignore or crush its dimensions. The text becomes hollow: inflated or deflated, it is without substance. It folds back upon itself rather than allowing access down into the extra-linguistic domain of instinctual energy.[7] According to Derrida, drives only manifest themselves textually, that is to say, as traces, as marks on more surface, but Kristeva affirms clearly that what may be glimpsed of the text's generation and germination in the depths underlying the text is not reducible to a superficial phenomenon. It is not a question of citation but of the very becoming of the speaking subject, a subject with a biological existence prior to language and doubling it and with a social existence, both of which determine the text to a large extent.

Dissemination and engendering. The spatial organization is already readable in these names: a scattering across the surface; a germination in the depths. And clearly, the difference in metaphors is not a decorative difference but a conceptual one. For Kristeva, the links between texts and between the ways in which a text functions (pheno- and geno-text) are not all of the same kind. In fact there is a radical difference, even an opposition between linguistic connections on the one hand and instinctual and inter-subjective connections on the other. Thus the vertical only meets up with the horizontal at the perpendicular. It pierces and traverses it, but there is no rotation of axes that would allow the two to coincide. There is a fixed angle between them: "this verticality that unites [the surface and the germ of signifiance] whilst opposing them" (Σ 346). In order to fulfil its function, the orientation of the geno-text must oppose the orientation of the linguistic text. There must be two textual mechanisms (pheno- and geno-text, language structures and the organization of instinctual energy forming the subject), working together in a dialectical rhythm.

For Derrida, however, the horizontal and the vertical do not represent absolute points of reference and are not even opposed. They can always be seen from another angle. In fact, if we want to see the horizontal become vertical and then those two planes become one, we need merely to fold the page. Along the diagonal, of course. The various kinds of connections that can be made across and between texts—graphic, phonic, metaphorical, instinctual, philosophical—all function in a similar way, as a kind of citation that unfolds a text within a text, a surface across a surface.

In spite of these differences, Derrida and Kristeva have a common purpose with regard to the space of the text, and this concerns the limits of the text, the question that opened this chapter and is perhaps characteristic of post-structuralism. If the infinity of the text does not consist in a simple overflow towards an outside, then that infinity is to be sought in other conceptions of the text, in the folds or depths of the text. Neither Kristeva nor Derrida seek to extend the text from some kind of periphery. They see no limit *around* the text, no boundary to be crossed. Derrida: "*There is* frame, but the frame *does not exist*" (TP 81); the text (of metaphysics for example) "is not surrounded but rather traversed by its limit, marked in its interior by the multiple furrow of its margin" (MP 24). The limits at which they work/play do not run around the edge of the text but appear like folds, seams or stitches. They are points where the outside and the inside merge: "at the seam between the geno-text and the pheno-text" (Σ 298), at "a certain limit which does not bound all the text's powers from the outside but rather, on the contrary, through a certain folding-back or internal angle of the surfaces, conditions their envelopment and development in the finite/infinite structure of the apparatus" (Dis 229). It is thus at the joints of the text that one works (*la jointure* Σ 284), not inside but at the "internal angle," at the threads "*interlacing* the inside and the outside" (TP 243), at the geological joint, the fissure operating through heterogeneous layers of textuality. At the angle between the horizontal and the vertical, whether it be a right-angle (Kristeva), or a variable angle (Derrida) which, like the parallel pleats of an accordion, fans between zero and 180 degrees.

Certainly, Kristeva and Derrida are not looking for the same infinity. But they start at the same place. At the gaps or faultlines between and within fragments of words.

DIVIDING INTO DISTINCT SYLLABLES

For let us be quite clear about this: to articulate the text, the first step is to disarticulate it, to dismantle and divide it. On this point, Kristeva and Derrida agree. From the time of their work on Sollers onwards, both theorists are involved in a dismembering of the text that allows them to articulate it in ways rather different from those of structuralism and thematic criticism. Their work on Mallarmé —in "The Double Session" (Dis 173-285) and in the untranslated second part of *La Révolution du langage poétique* (205-291)—is exemplary in this regard and this is no accident. Mallarmé's *Les Mots anglais*, his attempt to classify words and their meanings according to the letters and sounds they contain, is cited and resonates through these texts.[8] Equally important references for the *Tel Quel* group in general at this time are Saussure's *Anagrammes*, which Starobinski published during the sixties in *Tel Quel* and elsewhere,[9] and also Freud's work on the interpretation of dreams. Each of these investigations points to the possibility of dissolving words and combining bits of them in ways that make both sense and non-sense. Thus in their analyses of Mallarmé especially, but to a certain degree throughout their writings and still in their work today, Derrida and Kristeva take the text to bits.[10]

Derrida, like Mallarmé, is interested in "the dissection of the word" (Dis 255) in order to explore "the formal, phonic, or graphic 'affinities' that do not have the shape of a word, the calm unity of the verbal sign," "the play that takes the word apart, cutting it up and putting the pieces to work" (*ibid.*), all of which are ignored by thematic criticism. The word is "dislocated, dismembered" (285), its "moving parts" are shifted, set out of phase, displaced in the crumbling of the phrase (236); signs "begin to function like signifiers unhooked, dislodged, disengaged from their historic polarization" (*ibid.*).

Similarly, Kristeva writes of the "division of meaning, of the proposition, of the mot," of their "pulverization" (*Révolution* 212) such that "the morpheme or the lexeme [. . .] finds itself dislocated" (222); "every morpheme, every 'word' appears as a foreign, opaque entity to be divided" (227); the word "splinters into a thousand facets" (*ibid.*); "every signified is subdivided" (237) in a "dispersed [*éparpillée*] articulation" (252). Kristeva studies phonemes and "phonic groups" (221): fragments of words, fragments of fragments, morsels of morphemes, products of an un-chaining that unleashes the signifying possibilities of the text.[11]

But the reading does not consist in the mere milling of signs: "this 'pluralization' of the *Bedeutung* [. . .] is not an indefinite drifting: a signifying arrangement [*dispositif sémiotique*] is reconstituted" (*Révolution* 238); "One must reconstitute a chain in motion, the effects of a network and the play of a syntax" (Dis 194). Rereading (*relire*) and rebinding (*relier*) go together.[12]

JOINING IN A FLEXIBLE ARRANGEMENT

The bits and pieces thus communicate. In the texts on Mallarmé (but also more generally in Derrida's and Kristeva's writings) the fragmentation is accompanied by the creation of "networks" (Dis, *Révolution* passim), of "constellations" (*Révolution* 222, 251; Dis 257), of "chains" (Dis 194, 277) and "linkages" (Dis 253, 278), of "relays" (Dis 195), of "combinatory systems" (*Révolution* 217), of "configurations" (Dis 277), of "connections" (*Révolution* 257), of "series" (Dis 253), of "accords" (*Révolution* 222), of "affinities" (Dis 255, 263), of "alloys" (Dis 262, 282)—all open "associations" (Dis 280) without a center. These are mobile communication networks: before they have had time to be fixed in place, the chains are reformed, for as Kristeva remarks, "One does not begin with the part in order to reach the whole" (DL 175). Assembling the pieces does not mean constructing a unity from them, as they are continually, infinitely redispersed and recombined.

The connections are often made by the ear: for Derrida, paragraphs "are consonant" with one another (Dis 280) and sounds are "reflect[ed], repeat[ed]" (282) creating "repercussions" among signifiers (277, 278). Kristeva writes of "[n]etworks of alliteration" setting up "associative chains that criss-cross the text from beginning to end and in every direction" (DL 169). But the eye is equally able to identify networks in "*graphic procedures*: the strokes of a grapheme, the arrangement on the page, the length of the lines, the blanks, etc." (*Révolution* 219). Similarly, Derrida writes that "all 'substances' (phonic and graphic) and all 'forms' can be linked together at any distance and under any rule" (Dis 277). In this way, "[d]isplaced almost at random [. . .] dislocated, dismembered, the 'word' is transformed and reassociated indefinitely" (Dis 285).

The network is thus one of "linkages and rifts" (Dis 253), or, as Derrida puts it in *Glas*, of *coupture* — both cutting (*coupure*) and sewing (*couture*) (249): a piece is detached "in order to restitch it somewhere else" (77). For Derrida, it is the same "play of articulations" involved in "splitting up" a word and "reinscribing" it (Dis 255). But this is part of a more general movement that links up into a chain of signifiers including *différance* and dissemination. We see it in the hinge (*la brisure*) that is both fracture and joint (OG 65-73), in writing ("constituting and dislocating [the subject] at the same time" OG 68), in the game with the spool that "reassembles the reassembling *and* the dispersion" (PC 309). The disintegration is productive: destruction and construction occur simultaneously in deconstruction.

For Kristeva, the network functions in a similarly double way, for it both multiplies and unifies. On the one hand, "[u]nivocal signification finds itself pulverized: the *Bedeutung* is there, but is multiplied and tends to disappear in a network of differences that 'musicalize' meaning" (*Révolution* 238). On the other hand, "in so-called free verse and subsequently, this phonic network remains the only constraint [. . .] that restores a unity to the process" (*Révolution* 221).[13] The alliterative networks and rhythmic patterns of poetic language are "ways of organizing, if not of totalizing, the drives dividing the fragmented body" (*Révolution* 258), and thus allow the subject to regain a signifying position. In this way, they enable the subject both to regain unity and also to signify the dismemberment and dislocation of the "process" he has undergone. Kristeva calls the network a *dispositif sémiotique* and defines it in the following manner:

> a new organization is constituted through the linking of morphophonemic, syntactic, pronominal or logical series. [. . .] new translinguistic "figures" arrange themselves, transversal to the thetic phase, multiplying it into a new network and tending to dissolve it. We shall call this new organization [. . .] a semiotic arrangement [*dispositif sémiotique*]. (*Révolution* 207)

The *dispositif sémiotique* is thus an organization, a linking and a network (*réseau*), but it nevertheless manages to multiply and dissolve. As in Derrida's texts, the *réseau-lution* is simultaneously a *dissolution*; the organization disorganizes and vice versa. However, and this is not the first time that we have come across this kind of contrast, whereas for Derrida the paradoxes of dissemination are produced by the same movement, the ambiguity of the Kristevan network results from the dialectical engagement of two inseparable but opposed forces, from the two moments (pulverization and thetic unity) of the subject.

The unity of which Kristeva writes is not to be confused with univocality or single meanings, for these are "replaced" by ambiguity or polysemy (*Révolution* 219). The "signifying differentials" or repeated phonemes "organize a meaning [*un sens*]" which exists alongside linguistic signification such that there is "a perpetual swinging between signification, meaning [*sens*] and non-sense" (230). Meaning is thus not unique but still constitutes a unity: it is shattered but nevertheless organizes itself, such that the poem is paradoxically a "scattered [*éparpillée*] but nonetheless solid articulation" (252) and "[t]he *truth* that the text signifies is no longer unique but plural and uncertain" (289). Such organization giving rise to unity, albeit plural and fragmented, cannot avoid being seen as problematic for Derrida, who writes of dissemination as "escaping the horizon of the unity of meaning" (MP 322).

POLYSEMY OR DISSEMINATION?

Derrida explicitly seeks to substitute dissemination for the notion of polysemy, arguing that the latter remains tied to a presence of meaning and that it tames the irreducible dispersal of the text down to a manageable number of masterable meanings.[14] In developing his argument, Derrida affirms the strong tie between polysemy and the seme, meaning: "All the moments of polysemy are, as the word implies, moments of meaning" (Dis 350); "polysemy [. . .] is organized within the implicit horizon of a unitary resumption of meaning" (Pos 45, tr. mod.).

The move from polysemy to dissemination is primarily a move against thematic readings such as those undertaken by Jean-Pierre Richard and Paul Ricœur. Derrida maintains that "It is not enough to install plurivocality within thematics" (Dis 350, tr. mod.), a challenge with which Kristeva would certainly agree. However Derrida's argument also cuts across Kristeva's theory:

> If there is thus no thematic unity or overall meaning to reappropriate beyond the textual instances, no total message located in some imaginary order, intentionality, or lived experience, then the text is no longer the expression or representation (felicitous or otherwise) of any *truth* that would come to diffract or assemble itself in the polysemy of literature. (Dis 262)

Although Kristeva's unity in no way stems from an intentionality, it does represent a truth resulting from lived experience—an unmasterable experience dissecting the body and language. Unity restores the minimal mastery over language and the body that is necessary in order to be able to signify oneself. A continuous dissemination without a moment of truth/unity, a dislocation of the text not held together at least minimally by sounds and rhythm could only end up by petering out, losing signification irretrievably.

But whereas Kristeva describes the loss and restitution of unity in the process of *signifiance*, for Derrida, unity has only ever been lost. If, for Kristeva, "the polysemy of the signifying differentials and their instinctual charges comes to replace the loss of meaning" (*Révolution* 236), for Derrida, the "impossible return to the rejoined, readjusted unity of meaning" is impossible precisely because there has never been any pre-existing unity to lose (Dis 268). Now neither Kristeva nor Derrida is referring to a simple or originary unity, or to a meaning lost and restored intact. Both reject the notion of a single unifiable and retrievable meaning. The reconstitution of meaning/unity in Kristeva's readings is never simply a reconstruction but rather amounts to a renegotiation of the possibility of signifying. Thus the restored unity in Kristeva's work functions like the thetic phase, as a moment of resistance against the absolute loss of the subject position and of the communicative function of language. The phonic network is even described as a "substitute for thetic unity" (*Révolution* 219). Derridean dissemination, however, is not concerned with preserving guard-rails for the subject. It scatters the seed "*en pure perte*"—"wastefully" (Dis 149), to be lost (44, 48). It sees itself as more radical than polysemy in that it never pauses to gather meaning. Ultimately the relation between polysemy and dissemination is that between the thetic position and *différance*, between the two moments of Kristeva's theory and the continuous double movement of Derrida's. It seems to me that Derrida's explanation would also be acceptable to Kristeva:

> The difference between discursive polysemy and textual dissemination is precisely *difference* itself, "an implacable difference." This difference is of course indispensable to the production of meaning (and that is why between polysemy and dissemination the difference is very slight). But to the extent that meaning presents itself, gathers itself together, says itself, and is able to stand there, it erases difference and casts it aside. (Dis 351)

For Kristeva insists that meaning must gather and say itself and stand there, resisting the implacable movement of *différance* for the sake of the subject, whilst for Derrida, the shattering and scattering is continuous and only ever creates fleeting associations.

*

The associations—fleeting or otherwise—take the form of a veritable alchemy around the example of *or*. *Or* works as a kind of net-word for polysemy/dissemination. In French its dictionary meanings are grouped around (1) a precious metal (gold) and (2) a logical conjunction ("now then," archaically meaning "now" in time). But both Kristeva and Derrida spend a page or two examining this group of letters/sounds as it appears in Mallarmé's and make it resonate far beyond these sets of significations. It is fascinating to witness the immense productivity of the tiniest particle of text in their hands (ears, eyes, mouths . . .). And the different directions in which they take it. The fact that Derrida's work on *or* is to be found in a footnote should not deter us from giving it our full attention. Is it merely by chance that note 62 intervenes soon after the imperative "And now we must attempt to write the word *dissemination*" (Dis 262)? Let us take this text by one of its margins and juxtapose it with a page from *La Révolution du langage poétique* to see how the o's are join(t)ed together in *or*.

JOINING THE BONES (*LES OS*) TOGETHER

> The signifier OR (O + R) is distributed there, blazing, in disks [*pièces rondes*] of all sizes: "outdoORs" [*dehORs*], "fantasmagORical," "stORe" [*trésOR*], "hORizon," "mORe" [*majORe*], "exteriOR" [*hORs*], not counting the O's, the zeROs, the null opposite of OR, the number of round, regular numerals lined up "toward the improbable." (Dis 262)

> Preponderance of /ʀ/ [. . .]. Furthermore, we notice a dichotomy in the vowel system [. . .] between closed, unrounded front vowels and rounded back vowels: /e/, /i/—/o/, /u/. [. . .] /ɔtɔʀite/ particularly brings out the group /ɔʀ/, repeated in /lɔʀskə/, inverted in /apʀɔfɔdi/, and taken up in the fourth line of the following stanza [. . .]. Moreover, this differential is overdetermined by numerous occurrences [. . .]. (*Révolution* 247-248)

The sound *or*: *le sonore*, a golden vein in the text. As the tongue glides towards the palate and vibrates against it, it sets off other vibrations—corporal, textual—creating unlimited networks of meaning and beyond. Tongue and language, body and corpus intersect through phonetic, syntactic, semantic, graphic, instinctual and theoretical articulations. But these relays are not all important in the same way in each text.

For Derrida, the first connections are above all visual: he starts from the golden *or*, converted into round coins (*pièces*), to find zeros (number and value). At first it is the roundness of the zero, of the graphic O that engages the linkage between syllables—rhyme as usual waiting till the end of the line. The phonic (speech) is not to be privileged with respect to the graphic (writing).

For Kristeva, the roundness is rather that of the lips in the production of the labial back vowels, of which /ɔ/ is one. Although it also circulates in an economy of values, no numerical figure is put on these: the "phonic values" come from "vocal and consequently instinctual investments," and in the case of *or* are above all organized into a dichotomy between the destructive anal instinct and the incorporating oral one, between "the anal drive of the open back vowels" and "the oral drive of the liquids (l'), (r'), (m)" (*Révolution* 225).

The repetition of an element such as *or* allows Derrida to make associations "at any distance and under any rule" (Dis 277) in Mallarmé's text, and beyond. "*Or*, that substantive noun, that adverb of time, that logical conjunction" (263) becomes a conjunction in a wider sense, for through this syllable, Derrida links not only the metal, the color, the hour and the connector, but "once more," "decor," "unicorns," "sonorous," etc. (Dis 263-264). The particle of language circulates in every direction to create connections that are never definitive.

Kristeva similarly exploits these networks by linking words and lexical fragments to each other. In a painstaking reading of Mallarmé's "Prose," she relates the occurrences of the sound group *or* in the fourth stanza of the poem, not only to each other but to the numerous occurrences in other poems by Mallarmé, to "*dort*" [sleep], "*aromates*" [herbs], "*carreaux*" [window panes], "mournful," "encore," "aurora," "horrible," "trophy," etc. (*Révolution* 248). But this great variety of signifiers is filtered in the Kristevan interpretation. For *or* is a "signifying differential," one of those groups of phonemes that through repetition helps to organize the *dispositif sémiotique* and shows the marking of the text by instinctual forces (207). "Through all its occurrences, the signifying differential [*or*] bears the semes of 'negativity,' of 'death' and of the '*jouissance*' inseparable from death" (*Révolution* 248). All the words containing *or* reinforce these semes, "condensing" the signification of the stanza such that it can be distilled into "A violence destroying unity [. . .], the vanishing [*évanouissement*] of meaning that follows, and the pleasure that these two movements induce" (*ibid.*).

This condensation of signification goes hand in hand with the multiplication of meanings, but the apparent paradox can be explained: it results from the multi-level reading that Kristeva undertakes. She not only links fragments to each other on the horizontal linguistic plane (multiplying meanings) but also links them to the underlying instinctual strata (with its more limited range of meanings). Thus the repetition of a linguistic element works in two directions, one horizontally establishing links "between semes belonging to different morphemes and lexemes" to produce "a *strongly ambivalent* if not *polymorphous semantics*," the other connecting the phoneme "to the articulating body:

to the articulatory apparatus initially and then, through drives, to the whole body" (222).[15] This is the multiple unity of Kristevan polysemy.

For Derrida, on the other hand, if a "vanishing of meaning" occurs, this in no way represents the signification of a text. Rather than arriving at such a signification, interpretation must perpetuate the play of sounds and the proliferation of senses away from attempts to unify them, whether via the body's drives or via themes. In "The Double Session," the body that articulates sounds is primarily heard in laughter, as death and orgasm are mimed in the reading of Mallarmé's *Mimique*. Furthermore, whilst Kristeva considers that the phonemes bear semes ("porteur de sèmes" *Révolution* 222, cf 248) and carry drives (231),[16] *or* doesn't hold anything in Derrida's work. On the contrary, "*or* is reduced by this play to the vacant sonority—with its chance decor—of a signifier" (Dis 264); Mallarmé "pours out [*déverse*] all its tunes" (Dis 263, tr. mod.). For Derrida there is no condensation of signification but an emptying out, a dispersal of semes, sense and seed.

*

PRODUCING THROUGH THE MOVEMENTS OF THE ORGANS OF SPEECH

The relation between language and the body/drives in Kristeva's and Derrida's work begs for closer examination, and the obvious point to start is where language is closest to the body—in the mouth. Unlike *or*, the sound group *gl* seems to get stuck somewhere on its way out of the mouth. It is not even a syllable but a kind of gulp or half-strangled burp. Kristeva gives it attention in *La Révolution du langage poétique*, and in "Le Sujet en procès" (PL 55-106), she attempts to explain the mechanism whereby drives are introduced into language and leave their mark on the text through such sounds. Derrida focuses on *gl* in his work on Genet in the right-hand column of *Glas* which, like "The Double Session," insists on the possibility of chaining together and unchaining words and syllables. In *Glas*, however, the body is much more present/absent: it is endlessly referred to, and described in all its elements . . . but not necessarily approached. It remains a sort of impasse; its proximity cannot lead to access.

Tongue-tied

> *"Through the contractions and relaxations, veritable instinctual dramas are played out."* (Révolution 258)

> *"And glas, a profusion of names sleeps in those letters."* (Glas 46)

Derrida himself connects his work on *gl* to the work done on *or* in "The Double Session" : "*Glas* must be read as 'singular plural' (fall of the *or* in the double session). It has its breaking in itself" (*Glas* 150). There is the same disintegration of words and multiple combinations of the fragments. But whereas *or* was ceaselessly linked up into fine golden chains and bright constellations, *gl* is gluey, gluggy and sticks close. No more talk of crystallizations to indicate the assemblies; *gl* forms an "agglomerate" (141), an "agglutination" in the "signifying paste" (149).

gl sticks close to the body that produces it, close to the voice (voice translates as *glas* in certain Slavic languages, 79) but even closer to the gluttonous mouth that gulps (glug-glug) and gurgles and gobbles with its globs of spittle around the glottis. "The text is spat out. [. . .] And since the question here concerns a glottic gesture, the tongue's work on (it)self, saliva is the element that also glues the unities to one another. Association is a sort of gluing contiguity [. . .]" (142, tr. mod.). But *gl* not only glides through the mouth. It lubricates a number of passages:

> [. . .] gl begins to spurt [*gicler*], to trickle [*dégouliner*], to drip [*goutter*]: out of the mouth or the tail of the stilite, of the tube of vaseline, of the nursling's esophagus. Sperm, saliva, glair, curdled drool, tears of milk, gel of vomit—all these heavy and white substances are going to glide into one another, be agglutinated, agglomerated [. . .]. (139)

The network certainly seems to have changed: the diaphanous, impalpable veil/hymen of "The Double Session," has become a mucous membrane and we are called upon to imagine "the spit or plaster on the soft palate [*voile du palais*]" (121). The only aeration seems to come from the bubbles of saliva that burst. The generally heavy glueyness, however, never sets solid. Although less volatile than the quicksilver fragments of "The Double Session" that float in and out of an infinity of possible combinations, *gl* is viscously mobile, ready to stick where it can: "gl remains open, unstopped [*débouché*], ready for all concubinations, all collages" (236). Like *The Blob*, it oozes over other elements, clinging to them in a "rhythm of sucking [*ventouse* = suction pad]" (153), engulfing them in new agglomerations whilst its former prey unglue and free themselves. The "contiguity (contact, suction, aspiration)" occurs "without reducing the unsticking games [*jeux de décollement*] necessary to the sucker [*ventouse*]" (152, tr. mod.). Could it be that these glairy globules are what *gl* signifies? Does *gl* inevitably stick to slimy substances and secretions according to Derrida? Of course not. The corporeal coagulation doesn't hinder other clusters from forming: *gl* also sticks—sometimes protractedly—to gladiolus, to the glinting sword (*glaive*) of the gladiator, to class and classification, and to the bell series: *glas-cloche-Klang-Glocke*-tinkle (*glas* in French sounding the death-knell). In English *gl* could hardly avoid a glistening, glimmering, gleaming glow from time to time or then again a glum, lugubrious gloom (interrupted by glee). It could even take on an ocular slant (glance, glimpse, ogle, goggle). Everything is possible, there are no natural attachments to glue, or to bodily secretions, or to anything at all: *gl* is like the thief or beggar-woman who "appropriates everything, but because she has nothing that is properly hers" (150). The anchoring of *gl* is uncertain, provisional. If Derrida highlights this or that occurrence of *gl*, for example the series of words linking it to the mouth, or to flowers (gladioli), or even to the simultaneous occurrence of these two in Genet's texts, it is not in order to alight on its signification but in order to study the possibilities offered by *gl*: "Now, this double series [flower/spit], which we could track a long way, interests us and makes a text only to the extent of a remain(s) of gl [. . .] that belongs neither to one nor the other, makes them adhere somewhere to one another" (149, 160). What is important is not this or that seme that reappears insistently, but the way in which the words regroup, the way networks are established and re-established around *gl* without ever absorbing it completely, such that there would be no remainder. There is always a bit of *gl* left over that can stick to something else.

Kristeva, meanwhile, argues that there is indeed a natural attachment holding *gl*: *gl* is tongue-tied. It can never detach itself absolutely from its lingual origin but continues to be determined—at least in part—by its point of articulation, by the movement of the tongue from back to front, from the soft to the hard palate. To support this argument, Kristeva cites the work of Fonagy concerning the role of drives in the formation of sounds.[17] Fonagy's research demonstrates a link between sounds and drives in the child's prelinguistic vocalizations, showing that various biological functions are accompanied by particular pre-phonemes. This link is said to diminish in importance, without however disappearing, in the process of language acquisition. According to Fonagy, and in Kristeva's use of this research, the sound/drive link is monovalent. Hence one can identify

> [. . .] the oral drive of the liquids (l'), (r'), (m) and of the closed front vowels; the anal drive of the open back vowels; the urethral drive of the unvoiced fricatives (f), (s), (ʃ) and possibly the tendency to phallicize this drive in the voiced fricatives (v), (z), (ʒ); the aggressive drive, of rejection, in the voiceless plosives (p), (t), (k) or the voiced plosives (b), (d), (g); the phallic-erectile drive of the trilled (r). (*Révolution* 225) [18]

Insofar as it is formed by the passage from a voiced guttural stop to a liquid, *gl* thus designates the oralization of rejection. This association of *gl* with aggressive and oral drives persists after language acquisition but to a lesser degree. In savoring the sounds of *gl*, however, we can still feel the way in which the constipated straining and subsequent release (relief) of the guttural plosive /g/ (/g/ and /k/ being included in so many expressions of disgust and rejection—ugh! yuk! erk! *beurk*!) give way to the more than just palatable, mouth-wateringly luscious, delicious, lickable liquid /l/. Language—the tongue one speaks—cannot be dissociated from the movement of the tongue. *Langue* and *langue* are tied together.

In her analysis of Mallarmé's "Prose," Kristeva deals with this group of phonemes explicitly as they occur in the word *glaïeul* (gladiolus): "In /glajœl/, the general movement is from the back to the front, via a palatization /j/ that transmits the tension of rejection /g/ into an oral sublimation /l/" (*Révolution* 256). Let us note carefully however that *gl* does not simply signify aggressive or oral drives according to Kristeva but, under certain conditions, indicates their activity in a particular text. The drives represent another layer of meaning underlying the symbolic signification established by the lexical and syntactic norms of communication. It is only by studying "the phonic rhythm, its instinctual basis and its semantic overdeterminations" (*ibid*.) together that we could hope to discover the significations of any *gl* in a (con)text.

But this is to speak as if the object of these analyses is unproblematically the same for the two authors. Which brings us to the question to which Derrida returns time and time again: what is *gl* ?

Kristeva replies without ambiguity: *gl* is a "signifying differential" (*Révolution* 251), a group of phonemes that marks the instinctual organization of the text and is thus the point of intersection between the geno- and the pheno-text. In the case of *gl*, the signifying differential is more precisely a "plosive/guttural/liquid group" (*ibid.*), but we should add that "in a text, the *sounds of language are more than phonemes*" (222). According to where they are articulated, the signifying differentials "imply different instinctual investments" (223) and thus afford the possibility of "actualizing the semiotic *chora* within the language system" (226).[19] *gl* thus enables the sublimation of aggressive drives into an oral drive to be realized in the text.

Not just any phonemes can be considered capable of indicating drive activity, for after language acquisition, the sound/drive correlation weakens. In determining which elements may constitute a signifying differential in a particular text, it is necessary to examine the patterns of repetition: "the element that recurs (in the stanza, in the poem, or throughout Mallarmé's texts) plays a differential role. [. . .] The repetition indicates a kernel of resistance" (*Révolution* 259). Drive activity can only be located where phonemes are repeated. The repetition indicates a modification of linguistic functioning produced by the resistance and insistence of certain drives: the signifying differential shows a *"tendency toward autonomy"* (223) — through repetition it takes on a life of its own. Drives however are not the only factor at work here. In language, lexical and syntactical constraints are also crucial in determining utterances. Thus the repeated phonemes constituting signifying differentials are semanticized in two ways: "under the constraint of their instinctual basis on the one hand, and according to the possibility of their belonging to various lexemes on the other" (233).

Kristeva examines the recurrence of *gl* in Mallarmé's "Prose." After having isolated a pattern including *gl* and connoting relief and *jouissance* in the instinctual body, Kristeva takes up the definition of *gl* given by Mallarmé ("desire, as if satisfied by *l*, expresses joy, light, etc. with this liquid"[20]). She declares that "[s]everal occurrences of the same signifying differential indicate these semes," pointing to the contexts where *sanglot* (sob), *gloire* (glory) and *glissant* (sliding) appear (*Révolution* 251). Further on, Kristeva notes that the oral sublimation effected by the movement of /g/ towards /l/ — "this process of sublimation so clearly marked by *gl*" (251) — is reinforced by the semantic overdeterminations of *glaïeul*. Through its etymological link with *glaive* (sword) — the /v/ offering a phallic resurrection — and through its alliterative link to other words in the poem, *glaïeul* connotes "a putting to death that implies a glory and a posthumous symbolic power" (*Révolution* 256). The (phallic) power of (oral) language triumphs over the death drive. The negativity of rejection is incorporated into the symbolic in a sublimated form. *gl* is thus not just any combination of phonemes. It is emblematic of the instinctual movement of the poem as a whole and is even exemplary of the functioning of poetic language in general. The organization of sounds (whether in *glaïeul*, "Prose" or poetic language) "absorbs rejection, deflects it from one's body and orients it towards the symbolic function to renew the latter" (258). The sublimation of the anal into the oral in *gl* is a step towards the sublimation of rejection into language, of the unnameable into the nameable.

The grouping of phonemes or clusters of phonemes into words and morphemes multiplies their signifying possibilities, presumably preventing any univocal interpretation from being established. *gl* is plurivocal in belonging to *sanglot*, *glissant*, *gloire*, *glaive* and *glaïeul*. This plurivocality does not however exist at an instinctual level where the guttural-plosive-to-liquid origin of *gl* indicates anal and oral drives unvaryingly. Paradoxically, it is the lexical plurivocality that indicates the instinctual univocality: it is the recurrence of phonemes in various lexical situations that signals the insistence of this or that drive.[21] The plurivocality of the text is contained by the "phonic and rhythmic coherence, which at the same time limits and permits the free associations inspired by each word or name" (BS 162). The distinction Kristeva makes between lexical semanticization and instinctual semanticization is thus rather uncertain: the former always seems to confirm the latter, as if not only *gl* but also the meanings of the different words to which it may belong were already determined by the very limited range of drives associated with that back to front movement of the tongue.[22] Going one step further, it seems that the meaning of whole poems and even of poetic language in general often comes down to that same movement from the anal to the oral, the struggle to sublimate rejection into language. For when Kristeva examines sound groups elsewhere (*or* for example), she seems to find predominantly the same pattern. And given that virtually any combination comprising /p/, /k/, /b/, /d/, /g/, /o/ or /5/ followed by /l/, /r/, /m/, /i/ or /e/ can indicate an oralization of rejection, it is hardly surprising. Thus in Nerval's "El Desdichado" "the transposition of the speaking body asserts itself through a glottic and oral presence" (BS 161). Thus a Narcissus "will oralize [language], but he will also endow it with the entire secret and intense weight of anal modeling" (TL 126, and Kristeva adds: "There is enough there to establish premises for all of art"). Thus in the Song of Songs the repetition of units of discourse "suggest[s] the importance of the death drive in the amorous invocation" (TL 92-93). Thus Artaud's work in general is divided between rejection and the oralization of rejection according to "Le Sujet en procès" (PL 55-106).

It is worth taking a moment to look at Kristeva's analysis in the latter text, which relies less on Fonagy's narrow interpretation of phonemes than on a more general grouping of sounds. On the one hand, there is the anal drive of destruction invested in Artaud's grunts and eructations (PL 98): "Artaud's interjections and expectorations translate the struggle, against the superego, of a nonsublimated anal drive" (73). There is a coherence to the incoherencies. Ughs and glugs are explained without remainder. On the other hand, in Artaud's more lyrical lines, Kristeva sees the sublimation of the anal drive: "It is as an oralization of returned rejection that we can interpret the melody, harmony, rhythm, 'sweet' and 'pleasant' sounds and poetic musicality that we find in all Artaud's phrases" (73). If Kristeva's interpretation again hovers between the anal and the oral, between destruction and sublimation, it is because she sees her task as "defining the text not with regard to its 'signified' nor its 'signifier' [. . .] but with regard to the way rejection is deployed in it, to the oralization of rejection" (PL 97). In accomplishing this, however, she is destined to find largely the same forces at work in every poetic text as rejection attacks symbolic language and renews it through sublimation.

Thus *gl* can be burped up as a strangled half-syllable, its oralization cut short, or it can glide musically through the mouth. Either way, it remains anchored to its articulatory and instinctual basis.

gl in Derrida's texts, however, resists any such anchoring and even escapes definition as a group of phonemes or of phonetic elements: "I do not say either the signifier GL, or the phoneme GL, or the grapheme GL" (*Glas* 119). In fact, it is not even a fragment, for that would suppose the existence of a whole of which it would be a part: "This is not an element; gl debouches toward what is called the element" (236).

gl cannot be pigeon-holed or classified as belonging to any category of language: "this barely pronounceable writing is not a morpheme, not a word [. . .]. gl does not belong to discourse" (TP 160). This doesn't mean that it doesn't participate in language and certainly doesn't mean that it would oppose language as "the myth of the unarticulated cry" (OG 166): *gl* "is not however an insignificant phoneme, the noise or shout naively opposed, as nature or animality, to speech" (TP 160).

Like *différance*, *gl* has no essence but tends instead to be defined in negative terms: "It is not a word [. . .] even less a name" (*Glas* 236). Unspeakable, *gl* escapes names and naming—even that of *différance*: "Mark would be better, if the word were well understood, or if one's ears were open to it; not even mark then" (119). It escapes any determinacy:

> It is also imprudent to advance or set GL swinging in the masculine or feminine, to write or to articulate it in capital letters. It has no identity, sex, gender, makes no sense, is neither a definite whole nor a part detached from a whole
>
> gl remain(s) gl (119, tr. mod.)

So *gl* is nothing but *gl*, which is to say that it can appropriate anything but nothing definitively.

Between the "gl" (106) and "obal" (109) of "global," interrupting the adjective claiming to be all-inclusive, Derrida terminates a series of negative sentences with an affirmation : "What I am trying to write— gl—is not just any structure whatever, a system of the signifier or the signified, a thesis or a novel, a poem, a law, a desire or a machine, but what passes, more or less well, through the rhythmic strict-ure of an annulus" (109). *gl* seems to be what slips through totalizing structures, what prevents a text from ever being whole, what prevents a reading from accounting for everything. It's the leftover that refuses to be bound to a text, that escapes incorporation into closed systems. If Derrida asks, "What, in sum, is it all about?" (118), the answer has nothing to do with the sum of things. His work on the word *glas* in Mallarmé's "Aumône" shows the impossibility of saturating the context (150-153). His reading of Genet makes no claims to present the "complete text," just glimpses of *gl*. Neither is it an anthology of Genet, a representative selection but just "some morsels of anthology": "Nevertheless, all these morsels cannot, naturally, be bound" (118). *gl* is what confounds structuralist readings by refusing to respect the dictum "tout se lie."

Unlike Kristeva's reading of "Prose," in which fifteen pages of analysis show how the articulatory movements involved in each line of the poem work together to absorb the drive of rejection, unlike her reading of "El Desdichado" in which she shows the "phonic and rhythmic coherence," Derrida's *Glas* shows the impossibility of pulling all the bits together. *gl* is precisely what defies coherence and cannot be absorbed, a remainder, debris, a scrap sometimes carried along and sometimes abandoned in the movement of the text, a bit of recyclable garbage with no value of its own, a bit of . . . well? a bit of what? In *Glas*, the network articulating the bits becomes a net that "only retains remains" (169). It also resembles a dredger: "The toothed matrix [*matrice dentée*] only withdraws what it can, some algae, some stones. Some bits [*morceaux*], since it bites [*mord*]. Detached. But the remain(s) passes between its teeth, between its lips" (205). Caught in the net(work) or left behind, retained or dropped, either way *gl* remains a remainder, a sort of supplement without any identity of its own. For a remainder is a surplus (an extra, more than is necessary) but also not enough (a small quantity); it is both what is left over from something and what cannot be integrated into it.[23] Neither a part nor a whole, neither dependent nor autonomous, *gl* remains *gl*, a remainder—but of what exactly we will never know.

We do however know where it goes. It seems to pass where language and the tongue meet—"between its teeth, between its lips" (205)—or "through the rhythmic strict-ure of an annulus" (109). *gl* is "what passes"; it cannot be fixed but passes between the organs of speech and of mastication, via the tongue, through the glottal stops, into language. Or between the (vocal?) cords of the language net to escape *la langue*. Or is passed through a sphincter. A bit of textual waste, *gl* passes through without being integrated into language but without being independent of it.

In *Glas* Derrida writes constantly of the body . . . but in order to better avoid being fixed by or in a body that would be *un hors-texte*, an outside-of-text. For what is said—about the mouth, the lips, saliva—is said in a particular tongue; it must pass via language. The two kinds of *langue* are contiguous, even continuous. Mobile, elusive, the body that pronounces *gl* floats, carried on a liquid consonant, clings for a while to some signifier or other.

We find another explanation of Derrida's enterprise a little further on in *Glas*:

> The object of the present work, and its style too, is the morsel.
>
> Which is always detached, as its name indicates and so that you don't forget it, by the teeth.
>
> The object of the present piece of work (*ouvrage*) (code of the dressmaker) is what remains of a bite, a sure death [*une morsure*], in the throat [*gorge*]: the bit [*mors*].
>
> Insofar as it cannot, naturally, bind (band) itself (erect).
>
> Graft itself at the very most, that it can still do. (118)

Yet again, *gl* passes via the mouth, by word of mouth, but without ever quite leaving the mouth. Morsels remain between the teeth, at the back of the throat. A part of it passes into language but to be grafted without binding or erecting itself there. *gl*— body or language? Neither one nor the other. And both at once. *gl*: what passes . . . and what remains. What passes—through the rhythmic stricture of the glottis—into language, to glue itself provisionally to morphemes, to words, to meaning. And what remains "at the back of my throat" (195), stuck to the "humid surface" of the tongue (141), stuck to the fluid body, tangible but ungraspable.

Derrida is far from underrating the corporal associations of the bit of *gl*—in fact the body intervenes everywhere—but he hesitates to situate the limits of the body, the limits of its participation in words and phrases sounding (the) *gl*. The body makes itself felt in language, and no border can be fixed between them. Derrida blurs the limit between *la langue* and itself: the surfaces of text and body are continuous; the folds in the page are folds in the skin and vice versa.[24] And *gl* is dispersed over them, giving the slip to any attempt to gather it in one place.

Kristeva similarly emphasizes the inseparability of the body and language, drawing attention to the work of the body in modifying language and the work of language in transforming drive energy. However, in contrast to Derrida, she stresses that the two are heterogeneous, not continuous. A resistant limit between them prevents free circulation in either direction. If the instinctual body nonetheless clears a passage into language, the border crossing produces a double transformation: The drives are sublimated and the linguistic material is modified. Rejection is oralized as it is channeled into *gl*, and *gl* is repeated due to the insistence of the drive.

The link between rejection and *gl*, however, does not entirely convince Derrida.

Highly Motivated?

"The glue of chance makes sense." (Glas 140)

The idea of the motivation of language or of the linguistic sign — whether the determination of /gl/ by aggressive and oral drives or the motivation of an entire text or type of utterance by rejection—is problematic for Derrida. Of course if the motivation of the sign presents difficulties, the arbitrary nature of the sign poses no fewer.

In *Glas*, Derrida deals explicitly with the question of the motivation of the sign and in particular Fonagy's theory of the instinctual basis of language.[25] He contests Fonagy's conclusions, without however taking up a contrary position, for he juxtaposes them with Saussure's on the arbitrary nature of the sign, playing off one against the other, finally casting doubt (yet again) on the binary opposition, this time between motivated and unmotivated, between constraints and freedom.

In Fonagy's research, Derrida notes a couple of passages where the text seems to contradict itself. At one stage, Fonagy concludes that a univocal correlation between sound and drive is impossible (*Glas* 159). Derrida subscribes readily to this idea but remarks that it seems to compromise Fonagy's entire project. At another point, Fonagy declares that because each sound comprises not one but a set of articulatory and acoustic traits, it can represent several drives at once. Derrida remarks that this casts doubt on the correspondences previously established and adds:

> And what would happen if the drives (what are they all about?) were not content to converge, economically, in one same phonic or acoustical "representation," but were divided instead, verily undecided between one another in their internal contradiction? (97, tr. mod.)

Derrida here questions, not the existence or work of drives but the logic by which they would work coherently together to motivate a sound, a word, an utterance. He does not reject out of hand the notion of the role of drive activity in sound production but is dubious about the possibility of isolating a particular drive in a particular sound and, indeed, of even identifying drives that would be unified, distinct and knowable as such. Why should *gl*, open to all collages, ready to glide through the glottis but also stick like glue, to sound the *glas* or hail glory, to gleam or to gurgle, be limited to the anal/oral drive pair? What drive couldn't let out a *gl* ? And how would we distinguish between this pair of complicitous drives, to decide that there was a movement of "oralization" rather than a canalization in the other direction?

Derrida challenges Fonagy on another score: Why do drives supposedly motivate some words and not others? Why don't they determine proper names? (159-160). If we need to hesitate before interpreting "Mallarmé" in terms of maternal milk (which is what Fonagy's work on /l/ and /m/ might suggest to us), perhaps we shouldn't rush to lend univocal instinctual significations to . . . *gl*, for example.

Nevertheless, Derrida does not claim that *gl* (for example) is unmotivated. On the contrary, he demonstrates throughout *Glas* the numerous possibilities of motivation (or rather remotivation), and even (re)demotivation of *gl*, often coming teasingly close to a psychoanalytical interpretation. What is important is that the motivation is never originary nor definitive according to Derrida. Following on from an analysis of Saussure's *Cours de linguistique générale* (*Glas* 90-95), in which he proposes that the theory of the arbitrary nature of the sign goes both too far and not far enough, Derrida seeks to re-elaborate the question of the motivation or otherwise of the sign around *glas*. If Saussure sought to demonstrate the arbitrary nature of the signifier in relation to the signified "with which it has no natural connection in reality" (cited *Glas* 91), Derrida begins by studying the question not from the point of view of motivation but by wondering whether one can speak of any durable connection—natural or not—between the signifier and the signified:

> Constraining for the subject (the "individual"), the signifier [. . .] would be "unmotivated" in relation to the signified (which? where? when?), to the referent (which? where? when?). What is the individual? reality? nature? And, above all, the connection? (91)

Before speaking of the motivation of the signifier in relation to the signified, we need to specify to which signified we are referring. Saussure seems to take this for granted, as if one signified were simply obvious. Given that a signifier can be linked into an unlimited number of semantic and other networks, given that it slips through meanings as contexts change and even in the repetition of the same context, Derrida wonders how a single unified signified could possibly be attached to it. The problem is not simply to decide whether the signifier is motivated, in an onomatopoeic way, for example, but whether there could be *any* kind of tie between a signifier and a signified. In *Glas*, Derrida never ceases to refer back to the example of *gl* and to its way of attaching and detaching itself to and from the "signifying paste" (149) and even examines "what remains of the detachment of the connection [*l'attache*] and always comes to add more on" (91). Any bond, whether it is supposed to be natural or arbitrary, permanent or provisional, seems to pose the same question(s) for Derrida, that is to say, how does it come to be attached/detached?

Saussure, in pursuing his argument against natural attachments, attempts to demonstrate that there is no such thing as pure or authentic onomatopoeia. Firstly, the imitation of the sound or "natural" noise is always "approximate and already more or less conventional" (cited *Glas* 92) in conforming to the phonemic constraints of the language in question. And secondly, once it is accepted into this language, the imitation undergoes the same phonetic evolution as the other elements of the language, which often makes it lose its onomatopoeic character. In other words, it becomes arbitrary. But whereas Saussure wants to support the arbitrary and the becoming-arbitrary as a general rule governing the signifier/signified relation, Derrida analyzes his arguments in order to take them in the opposite direction. If a signifier can become arbitrary, if it can lose its motivation, why wouldn't it be possible for a signifier to retrieve a motivation, for it to become onomatopoeic or, rather, to create "effects of onomatopoeia" (93)? Why wouldn't it be possible for the word *glas* (from the Latin *classicum*, Saussure's example) to become the echo of the sound of a bell, or for *gl* in other contexts to assume the noise of a viscous liquid? "Thus onomatopoeia, the gesture dormant in all classical speech, will be reawakened" (WD 188). Such imitation, according to Derrida, is certainly never perfect, but is always-already underway. For Derrida, if on the one hand there is no onomatopoeia that is not partly arbitrary, then neither is there any pure and authentic arbitrariness on the other; there is no arbitrariness that could not become motivated under certain conditions. The opposition cannot be sustained: motivation and arbitrariness parasitize each other. The unattached signifier attaches itself . . . naturally.

Derrida shows it by playing with *glas*, displaying its uses. For a while *gl* is inseparable from glue and the glairy, glaucous glob; it cleaves to the cloaca. At each occurrence *gl* agglutinates and coagulates. Provisionally. (But already in this gluggy group there are several *gl*). And then, elsewhere, *gl* is de/re-motivated, thanks especially to texts by Poe and Mallarmé (*Glas* 150-159). "There is — always — already — more than one — *glas*" (150). Across the languages, *glas* sounds and resounds in "the clamor and the clangor," "the jingling and the tinkling" of the bells, the *Klingen* and the *cliquetis* of the *cloches*. *gl/kl* becomes a sort of kernel of sound and meaning, "Which does not mean (to say) that there is an absolute kernel and a dominant center" (158). It is first and foremost an effect ("the +L effect," 159), an effect producing effects.

The remotivation (*gl* becoming bell-like in *glas* and *cloche*) is here produced not only between "signifier" and "signified" (an already suspect distinction for Derrida) but in the circulation of *gl* in and between texts, and even in the movement between languages of a text such as Poe's "The Bells":

> *mimesis* recharges itself and operates from one text to the other, from each text to its theme or to its reference, without the words originally resembling things and without them immediately resembling each other. And yet *the resemblance reconstitutes itself* [. . .]. (*Glas* 154, my emphasis)

Too bad if there is no etymological relation between the words to start with, between *dingue* (crazy) and *dinguer* (to fall) for example: "It's really a shame but it can be repaired" (95, tr. mod.). A word can become motivated in relation to another. Even between a flower and spittle (the gladiolus/glob series, 147-149) or then again between the flower and the sword (*glaïeul/glaive*, 49-52) a resemblance can establish itself. But the resemblance is not only semantic and is not anchored in a referent. It is not even tied to the sound of *gl* but arises through the rhythm of *gl* as it recurs in a text: "The semantic element is struck by the rhythm of its other [. . .]. This other [. . .] is unceasingly reemployed according to a mimetics that is not related to a real sound, to a full content, but indeed [. . .] to relational rhythmic structures with no invariant content, no ultimate element" (157-158). The glue-glug-glob series does not constitute a signified of *gl* or even a set of signifiers signifying a *gl* sound or a *gl* seme but represents an effect that is created (motivated) in the relation between the *gl*. And the other of the semantic is not elsewhere than in language, in the multiple relations working through language(s).

The notion of the re- and de-motivation of the signifier is also mentioned in Kristeva's work but is said to occur according to less random principles than in *Glas*. In Kristeva's view, this or that word or phoneme cannot be permanently motivated. The motivation is only produced when the phoneme is repeated in a text and disappears when there is no such insistence. Kristeva and Derrida could thus agree that the motivation of *gl* is an effect created by repetition. They could similarly agree that sounds can be semanticized "according to the possibility of their belonging to various lexemes" (*Révolution* 233). The probability of disagreement only arises apropos of a univocal psychoanalytical interpretation of the ties between sounds and drives. In Kristeva's theory, the alliterative and assonant networks manage to activate a "phonic-instinctual memory" (DL 169) connecting them to precise drives associated with the sounds during the pre-linguistic phase. However Derrida suggests that such drives are difficult to isolate and identify. *gl* might pass from the anal to the oral, as Kristeva argues, but what is to stop it sliding in with the phallic, saliva becoming sperm in the to-ing and fro-ing between the glob of spittle and the gladiolus: "the analogy flower-spit with which what one loves (to see dead) is covered, passage from the flower to spit, from phallus to sperm, from gladiolus (glaive of justice, sword of the virgin) to the seminal drool, and so on" (*Glas* 149).

And yet, a Kristevan reading of *Glas* would show that this is precisely a result of the instinctual motivation of neighbouring phonemes, in this case the phallicizing voiced fricative /v/ erecting *glaive* and *glaviaux* and the oralizing closed front semi-vowel /j/ making *glaïeul* drool. Similarly the differences between the other groups of *gl* exploited by Derrida can be explained in terms of the presence of back vowels (the /u/, /o/ and /ɔ/ of the glue-cloaca-glob-gloom-glaucous series marking a reinforcement of rejection, of the anal drive) or front vowels (the /i/ and /ɪ/ of the gleaming, tinkling *glas*, emphasizing oralization) (cf. *Révolution* 225). In English this distinction can be made even more clearly than in French, for the articulation of /l/ is determined by its phonemic context: the /l/ in glob is a dark /l/, the back of the tongue cleaving to the soft palate, whereas the /l/ in gleam has a forward articulation, the tip of the tongue close behind the teeth. Thus the *gl* of glob doesn't even approach an oral sublimation of its anality, whilst the *gl* of gleam is already more than half-way to the lips.

But this explanation only goes so far: Kristeva herself writes of the intertwining of the various drives: The oral drive, for instance, is *"carried* and [. . .] *determined* by rejection" (PL 74). And we find that those same anal back vowels reappear in glow, glory, glossy and *cloche*, which one would expect to be able to align—in context of course—with the gleam team. No doubt Derrida would enjoy furnishing other counter-examples to Fonagy's correspondences, spitting out the phallic /v/ of *glaviaux* and erecting *glaïeul* around the oral /j/, or taking the piss out of glacial, glassy, glossy and glisten ("the urethral drive of the unvoiced fricatives" *Révolution* 225). For ultimately Derrida is less interested in circumscribing and assigning meanings than in extending them as far as possible. Sarah Kofman suggests that this indeterminacy is the most important contribution that deconstruction could make to psychoanalytical readings:

> "Graphematics" here teaches psychoanalysis that if it wishes to escape metaphysical reduction, it must not halt the indeterminacy of the writing of dreams, of symptoms and of literature, but must continually relaunch it in indefinite play. (*Lectures de Derrida* 90)

To this end, neglecting no opportunity, Derrida extends the play of *gl* into theoretical writings. Without subscribing to the reductive interpretations offered by Fonagy, Derrida uses them—as he uses the *Littré* and *Wartburg* dictionaries, the writings of Mallarmé and Genet and any other texts he happens to come across—so as to multiply the operations of *gl*. The essay that claims to explain words and texts by anchoring them deep in the instinctual body only contributes to the proliferation of lateral connections. *Glas*, far from determining a signification for *gl*, endlessly relaunches its play.

Derrida brushes with psychoanalysis, flirts with it.[26] He plays with the "name of the father," describing a sensation without taking it further: *"Derrière:* every time the word comes first, if written therefore after a period and with a capital letter, something inside me used to start to recognize there my father's name, in golden letters on his tomb, even before he was there" (*Glas* 68).[27] He gives the example of *"Derrière le rideau* [behind the curtain]" for us to enjoy analyzing. His attention is directed to everything related to the body, but he advances no hypothesis relating to "instinctual motivation." Genet's *Le Journal du voleur* doesn't indicate an anal drive but rather is "narrated in the annal style" (163). With regard to a passage from this text, Derrida invites the reader to take note of the fact that "the word *cul* [ass] has not been written. Its hole (*trou*) is only discerned between collar (*col*) and neck (*cou*)" (163). We might similarly note that the word "anal" doesn't appear in Derrida's commentary, which doesn't stop it from resonating. But the anal interest does not determine the sounds for Derrida, and is not at the origin of the words or utterances. It is not an indissoluble bond between the text and its production, but rather one of an infinite number of networks in which the text may be engaged. It is not an answer, a point of arrival, for try as we might, the associations and agglutinations of the text, of any morsel of text, can never be exhausted or halted.

Thus Derrida does not accept a psychoanalytical answer to the question "what does *gl* mean?" Or rather, he accepts an infinite number of these "answers," none of which would be *the* answer. Furthermore he questions the question in that it already anticipates the anchoring of *gl* in an "elsewhere." Derrida considers that the explanations(?) he gives should suffice, repeating in a glottal version of Gertrude Stein's line that *gl* is *gl* is *gl*. Even glued to glue, *gl* is nothing but *gl*, *gl* indicates nothing else, nothing other than *gl*. "If *gl* does not suffice for you, if no enjoyment remains in it for you, if you can't give it a fuck, if you want to render gl, [. . .] one more try" (*Glas* 123, tr. mod.). Those who expect other solutions, who wish to escape from the lexical labyrinths and find an answer will be disappointed:

> For those, however, who would not regard gl as a satisfactory response—since they expected some response in the first place; those for whom gl says nothing—since they believed gl was saying nothing in the first place—[. . .], let us suggest that the theoretical question [. . .] will produce [. . .] the following thesis: every thesis is (bands erect) a prosthesis; what affords reading affords reading by citations [. . .]. (168)

Thus *gl* doesn't refer to a stable signified of some description. It doesn't get out of textuality and into something else, it doesn't move out of texts to attach itself to drives, for example, but circulates from text to text in the widest sense of the word and is repeated and cited without expressing-carrying-signaling-manifesting anything but other *gl*. *g l* circulates between literary and philosophical texts, psychoanalytical writings and dictionaries in phrases that are continuously crushed to bits and recycled.

If Derrida resists the psychoanalytical solution of attachment to a drive, he is, nonetheless, fascinated by its solving-dissolving maneuvers. In *Résistances: de la psychanalyse*, he flaunts-conceals this resistance-attraction, while examining what there could be within psychoanalysis that resists psychoanalysis. In particular, he shows the auto-resistance dividing the concept of analysis, starting with its etymology: the archeological or anagogical movement of *ana* tying back to the simple origin and the elementary solution; the "philolytic" movement of *lysis* marking dissolution and decomposition, an untying (33). Thus the analytical imperative to tie the symptom to a cause or a solution is inevitably undone by the push to continue to analyze:

> Because dissociability is always possible [. . .], because we must always and can always analyze, share, differentiate further, because the philolytic principle of analysis is invincible, we cannot gather anything whatsoever in its indivisibility. The archeological or anagogical principle of analysis is always destined to failure. (48)

And indeed this is what keeps Derrida working away at psychoanalysis, reading and rereading Freud: he cannot stop analyzing. He cannot arrive at an answer, at a single united thread or indivisible chain. A few lines further on, Derrida adds: "The possibility of unlinking [*déliaison*] is also, of course, the sole condition of possibility of linking [*liaison*] in general" (*ibid.*).

Like analysis, the repetition compulsion—*fort*/*da*, pushing the spool away and reeling it in, rejecting and accepting—hovers between untying and tying (*Résistances* 17). Endlessly repeated throughout the work of Mallarmé, Genet, Derrida and so many others, *gl*, too, is said to glide back and forth between the anal and the oral, between the dissolving drive of destruction and the incorporating drive that fuses together. But would this mean more than that *gl* continually glues and unglues itself to and from any form of determinacy?

Kristeva is indeed among those "who would not regard *gl* as a satisfactory response." Certainly there is a remainder, but it is not entirely uninterpretable. The remainder indicates what is heterogeneous to meaning: "A floating signifier? A senseless flow that produces its own signifiance" (DL 190). As it is repeated, passing from word to word, from seme to seme, from sense to nonsense, *gl* generates, not a linguistic signification but a *signifiance* that escapes the mastery of the subject. If *gl* has no meaning, the drift towards nonsense nevertheless has a sense that we can discover via our senses—in the pleasure of wordplay, rhyme and alliteration, a sonorous sensual pleasure. Kristeva writes of an "eroticization of the vocal apparatus" caused by "a return of oral and glottic pleasure" (sucking and expulsion, fusion with and rejection of the maternal breast) which would be at the basis of "the introduction into the order of language of an excess of pleasure that is marked by a redistribution of the phonemic order, the morphological structure and even the syntax" (PL 74). In language we experience "the joys of chewing, swallowing, nourishing oneself . . . with words" (TL 26). Pleasure and death: the struggle against the signifier (against the symbolic systematic face of language) "brings us to the heart of *jouissance* and death" while the semioticization of the signifier — "through subtle differences in rhythm or color, or differences made vocal or semantic in laughter and word-play)—keeps us on the surface of pleasure in a subtle and minute tension" (RPL 179-180, also PL 91).

But where the pleasure of the text is concerned, sometimes it seems that whilst Kristeva is explaining it, Derrida is tasting it (or at the very least miming it): "You could analyze this +*r* effect, like the +*l* effect in *Glas*, analyze it coldly and practically. But you could also orchestrate it [. . .]" (TP 174). For Derrida, the symphonic performance is likely to be not only more pleasurable but also a more effective demonstration of +*l* than an explanation.[28]

To want to explain *gl* definitively comes down to an attempt to master the text, to tame and limit the text, according to Derrida. He on the other hand claims to be far from "procuring [. . .] the rule of production or the generative grammar of all [Genet's] statements" (204). Kristeva's reaction to the unmasterability of the text is rather different. In the face of the temptation to "mime [the] meanderings" of literature "rather than [. . .] positing it as an object of knowledge" (DL 145), Kristeva opts for a theoretical stance, seeking

> not to renounce theoretical reason but to compel it to increase its power by giving it an object beyond its limits. Such a position, it seems to me, provides a possible basis for a theory of signification, which, confronted with poetic language, could not in any way account for it, but would rather use it as an indication of what is

> heterogeneous to meaning (to sign and predication): instinctual economies, always and at the same time open to bio-physiological sociohistorical constraints. (DL 146)

The subject of this theory is, however, no longer the masterful subject of thetic consciousness but a "questionable subject-in-process" (*ibid.*).[29]

If there is pleasure to be had in *gl,* is it to be found in anticipation (the hunting of the *gl* and other snarks) or in satisfaction ("a satisfactory response," the indication of instinctual economies)? Here we can juxtapose two ways of gesturing towards the unnameable, irreducible residue of *gl,* two ways of putting one's own language into question. Whilst appearing to avoid metalinguistic explanation, Derrida's miming of *gl*—the repetition and extension of its play—has a metalinguistic force: it tells us about language. Between the *gl,* between the various manifestations of *la langue* in the hide-and-seek of language and the tongue, we glimpse the functioning of the remainder. Kristeva's analytical theory on the other hand, distinguishes itself as other than literary experience and measures this otherness that never ceases to challenge it. In doing so, it locates the semiotic remainder of *gl* in an instinctual economy and suggests that an experience of it might be available to subjects who can put themselves in "infinite analysis" (DL 146), to subjects-in-process.

*

These ways of articulating the text—of taking it apart and putting bits together—do not constitute an exhaustive list of things to do with literature. Far from it. Rather they amount to a few basic operations already theorized in Kristeva's and Derrida's early work. We have already seen that Derrida also uses literary texts to ask philosophical questions, just as Kristeva uses them to ask questions about horror or revolt. However the splitting and splicing of the corpora of texts-bodies-discourses at the micro and macro level is always involved in the questioning, is always there for the asking.

But let us turn to a couple of later texts, produced at a point where Kristeva's and Derrida's writings intersect very neatly in terms of time and place and object.

FILIATION AND FILAMENTS: *LES FILS DE JOYCE*

Confronted with the prodigious literary production of James Joyce and offered the opportunity to speak, what do you single out for attention? The possibilities seem inexhaustible. Both Derrida and Kristeva were given precisely this opportunity when they were invited to address the Ninth International James Joyce Symposium in Frankfurt, 11-16 June, 1984. The choices each of them made are in many ways emblematic of their work in the eighties and take up questions discussed in their other writings from the period. The links with their analyses of Sollers, Mallarmé, Artaud and Genet from the sixties and seventies similarly remain clear. But somehow their preoccupations had seemed much closer a decade earlier.

In "Joyce 'The Gracehoper' or the Return of Orpheus," Kristeva reads *Ulysses* and points to the role and the mechanics of identification in the creation of fiction. Identification—the way in which we assimilate the other and transfer the self into the other—is what sets the imaginary in motion. It is its "motor" (167), its "genesis" (168), and it occurs through love. The multiple identifications of the artist/author in *Ulysses* confront us repeatedly with the very point where the subject comes into being, the space where an image "coagulates" (180). Kristeva describes love and the identifications it entails not only in literature but in Christianity and in the relations of transference and counter-transference between patient and analyst. Given that "under the Law of the Other, I am never ideally One" (171), identifications are the stuff of which the whole psychical adventure is made.

Two years previously, Derrida had said "Two Words for Joyce," concentrating on "He war" in *Finnegans Wake.* In "Ulysses Gramophone: Hear Say Yes in Joyce," he narrows his selection down to one word from *Ulysses,* one ubiquitous and immensely productive word: *oui.* But this one word is hardly one, unique and unified. It occurs in Joyce's text as "yes," "ay," "I will," etc. as well as "*oui*" (all of which tend to appear in the French translation as *oui*), not to mention phrases like "he nodded." But the yes of assent or of consent is far from the only yes in the text: there is the yes of engagement, the yes of the signature, the yes of obedience, yes as question, the yes on the telephone to confirm that one is listening and calling to the other. Derrida goes further: *yes* is the supplement of affirmation implied in the utterance of any word or statement; words like "I" or "language" are derivative with respect to *yes* (298-299). In "Ulysses Gramophone,"

Derrida looks at the networks of *oui* and discusses the relation between chance encounters and the text that seems to pre-program them all to ask questions about the institutionalization of Joyce studies, the foundations of the James Joyce Foundation.[30]

Between these disparate discourses, however, between the engendering of the imaginary and the dissemination of *yes*, intersections appear. In both texts, what Kristeva and Derrida single out in *Ulysses* is not single. It is both split and repeated. And it involves a relation that is as much a relation to the self as a relation to the other. From Grasp-hoppers to Gracehopers, from the Tympanum to the Gramophone, a web is spun.

Bernard Benstock, in his introduction to the proceedings of the symposium, writes of the "web" that "interweaves itself" between the many papers of the conference, and it is only to be expected that this kind of open-ended association should be associated with Joyce's work.[31] In "Ulysses Gramophone," as in "The Double Session," Derrida too speaks repeatedly of networks, webs and nets, of chance associations, combinations and juxtapositions. Mallarmé's "constellation" has become Joyce's "galaxy of events" (UG 258). *Oui* is linked to any number of websites. The phonic and graphic connections bring together "the *yes for the ears*" (*ouïe*—hearing, *ouï-dire*—hearsay) and "the *yes for the eyes*" (*eyes*) (267-291), resulting in "the gramophony of *yes*" (269). But *les fils*—the threads or wires, and Derrida insists on the metaphor—mesh not just with those of "The Double Session" or even *Glas* but with virtually all of Derrida's writings. The gramophony, like *Of Grammatology*, "records writing in the liveliest voice" (276); the telephone calls (*coups de fil*), letters, postcards, telegrams call up *The Post Card*; the call of the other takes up "Violence and Metaphysics," "Psyche: Inventions of the Other" and *The Ear of the Other*; the multiple yes links up with "A Number of Yes"; the translation of yes into *oui* and of *oui* into *oui* echo "Des Tours de Babel"; the space between *oui* and *oui* is a space of "Différance"; the "yes" of Molly's monologue leads us to the gendered "yes" of "The Law of Genre" and the question of gender in *Spurs*; the foundations of the James Joyce Foundation remind us of "Before the Law" and "Force of Law," and these are merely some of the most obvious references to Derrida's other texts. The list is not intended to be exhaustive. Rather than "Ulysses Gramophone" connecting with virtually all of Derrida's writings, it would be more accurate to say that it connects with all of Derrida's writings virtually.[32] It networks them without centering them and makes them pay off in another direction. "For a very long time, the question of the *yes* has mobilized or traversed everything I have been trying to think, write, teach, or read" (UG 287). But everything Derrida has been trying to think, write, teach, or read is in fact only a modest account of the connections. In "Ulysses Gramophone," we find that Joyce's "yes" also connects randomly with potentially anything that Derrida has seen, touched, smelt or bumped into—towns traveled through, advertisements seen, phone calls and pharmaceutical purchases and, of course, his drives (to and from the airport, and driving his mother). Every aspect of the life and work of Jacques Derrida seems to be already linked into "Ulysses Gramophone," and through it into Joyce's *Ulysses*. For the infinite network of Derrida's text mirrors his description of the Joycean text:

> Everything we can say about *Ulysses*, for example, has already been
> anticipated [. . .]. We are caught in this net. All the gestures made in
> the attempt to take the initiative of a movement are found to be
> already announced in an overpotentialized text that will remind you,
> at a given moment, that you are captive in a network of language,
> writing, knowledge, and *even narration*. [. . .] Yes, everything has
> already happened to us with *Ulysses* and has been signed in advance
> by Joyce. (UG 281)[33]

Derrida's personal odyssey with its detours and adventures is not so much brought to the text as pre-programmed by it, along with all his writings. What appears to be outside the text is always-already incorporated into it and even incorporated into the tiniest fragment of it. For all the threads of *Ulysses* can be picked up from this or that part of the text: "All these telephonic lines can be drawn from one paragraph" (272).[34] Let us just try to draw one(?) thread from Derrida's text, one we have followed before—inside/outside—to see where it leads us this time.

Benstock describes the Frankfurt symposium as a confrontation between on the one hand the Joyce establishment and on the other hand non-specialists in Joyce studies such as Derrida and Kristeva: "Frankfurt staged the meeting between those invited in from the outside to talk to (and with) the insiders; inevitably, of course, the distinctions between 'inside' and 'outside' began to blur [. . .]."[35] Derrida's address, which opened the Symposium, no doubt precipitated as it underlined the necessary collapse of this distinction. Invited as an outsider, how could he be anywhere but inside "a corpus that includes virtually all those bodies of knowledge treated in the university (sciences, technology, religion, philosophy, literature, and, co-extensive with all these, languages)" (UG 283). But if everything (including philosophy, Derrida's writings and his chance encounters) is to be found inside *Ulysses*, if "everything is internal" and "everything can be integrated" (*ibid*.), then where does that leave the Joyceans? On what basis can they define their expertise? What kind of authority, legitimacy or paternity can they claim? The Joycean text undermines the divisions delimiting fields of expertise and with them the marks distinguishing any legitimate heirs. As Joyce writes, "Paternity may be a legal fiction" (cited UG 304).

Although the overwhelming capacity to encompass any aspect of culture is highlighted by *Ulysses* or *Finnegans Wake*, Derrida suggests that this is in fact the general case of literature, of the text. Joyce's work merely makes it explicit (282).[36] Indeed the same could easily be said of Derrida's work, for competence in the matter of the Derridean corpus, like Joycean competence, knows no bounds. The texts demand expertise across a spectrum of fields yet dismantle the partitions between disciplines in which one could claim expertise. And everything we may write about them already seems to be foreseen by them: "Everything we can say after it looks in advance like a minute self-commentary with which this work accompanies itself."[37] All the reader of Joyce or Derrida can do is affirm the text, repeat it, subscribe to and countersign it. All I can do is say *yes* to the text. And yet, the repetition obeys the logic of the double mark, marking the text both within an existing frame and taking it elsewhere: "And yet the new marks carry off, enlarge and project elsewhere—one never knows where in advance—a programme which appeared to constrain them."[38] The echo is simultaneously a response. As I say *yes*, the potentially omnivorous text is made to engage with the irreducible singularity of the circumstances of my reading: "For the countersignature signs by confirming the signature of the other, but also by signing in an absolutely new and inaugural way, both at once, like each time I confirm my own signature by signing once more [. . .]."[39] The only way I can respond and say *yes* to the text of the other is to put my singularity into play. In this way I bring chance elements of my biography to the text . . . and find that the text already has something to say about them, responds to my response.[40] But being able to bring anything to the text does not mean being able to say just anything about the text (as careless critics and even proponents of Derrida's work have sometimes claimed). Signing one's name always contracts an ethical obligation. Countersigning a text makes me accountable for the way in which I affirm the text of the other and the otherness of the text. The ability to respond entails a responsibility.[41]

In chapters 3 and 4 above, we looked at the assimilating moves whereby Derrida is able to subscribe to and reinscribe Kristeva's theory. But for Derrida, this practice is characteristic of reading and writing in general and can be described in terms of grafting, citation, countersigning, or even compared to the blob of *gl* that oozes over all elements with which it comes into contact, gluing and ungluing itself to and from them.[42] In "Ulysses Gramophone," Derrida writes of an "odyssey" of "circular reappropriation" (302), a continuous movement that "holds open the circle that it institutes" (302). Although Derrida mentions it in relation to the positing of the self in the yes (of the I in the Ay), this circle that never closes, this odyssey that never arrives but which nonetheless encompasses all detours and eventualities also seems to describe the general movement of the Joycean text . . . and the Derridean text. For "Ulysses Gramophone" works in parallel with *Ulysses*, quoting and reinscribing it—saying *yes* to it—in such a way that the inclusion is mutual. If *Ulysses* engulfs Derrida's work, "Ulysses Gramophone" is no less engulfing—of *Ulysses*, of all of Derrida's writings, of my readings of them, plus an unlimited number of other texts . . . including perhaps Kristeva's.

Like Derrida, Kristeva describes an odyssey—the odyssey of the speaking subject through the vicissitudes of life—and draws on personal experience: her own as a psychoanalyst and Joyce's (his biography). Life's journey is a process of identifications whereby the subject is constituted and renewed. It is by becoming one with the other that I become One (JG 168, 173). Now identification is not merely a form of mirroring. It is an assimilation of a separate entity, an assimilation that is real, imaginary and symbolic, for it involves bodily processes, images and signs (171-172).[43] It is "a transference of my body and of my psychic apparatus in-process-of-gestation—therefore incomplete, mobile, fluid—to an Other, the fixity of which is, for me, a point of reference and, already, a representation" (168). "Transference," "transfer," "transport," "transfusion," "transubstantiation" and "transcorporality," identification means carrying my semiotic body into the other's and representing it there, bringing it to the threshold of language. But, like the love of the other (love for the other/the other's love) that makes it possible, it works in both directions: simultaneous with this transport towards the other, there is also the oral assimilation of the other; together with the transfusion, there is fusion. Similarly, transference is accompanied by countertransference: as analyst, Kristeva's body becomes the patient's body.[44] Through interpretation and verbalization she replaces his symptom. In this way, not only (symbolic) sublimation into language but also (real) bodily modification occurs through identificatory mechanisms.

Identification is thus a way of taking the unnameable within me to a point where it can be translated symbolically, a way of negotiating between the semiotic and the symbolic. The identifications on which Kristeva focuses precede and enable the Lacanian mirror stage. They belong to neither the semiotic nor the symbolic but rather open up an imaginary space of separation from the mother's body that makes access to the symbolic possible. They are associated with some of the different kinds of love Kristeva details in *Tales of Love*. On the one hand, there is *eros*, a devouring of the other, a destructive assimilation based on the model of the narcissistic, projective identification with the mother. On the other hand, there is *agape*, an unconditional love like that of the Christian God, a love that descends upon me from the other and which is based on an identification with the pre-Oedipal or imaginary father, the supposed object of maternal love, a primitive form with the sexual attributes of both parents. The identification with the imaginary father (*agape*) is a way of separating from the violently symbiotic relation of primary narcissism with the mother (*eros*). Transferring my body into the father's is a step towards the symbolic realm of Meaning, and the possibility of assuming a subject position, but unlike the Oedipal *structure* and the stern father of Lacanian *law*, this form of paternal identification involves a *movement* towards a father of unstinting *love*. There is, however, no simple binary opposition between instinctual, maternal *eros* and symbolic, paternal *agape*. The two are inseparable. The imaginary father is also a mother: His body always carries the memory of the mother's. And union and division occur together, through one another, for my identifications with the imaginary father are always accompanied by my erotic separation from the mother: "It is in order to separate myself from the *amor matris* (subjective and objective genitive) that I enter into the legal fiction that constitutes my identity as subject" (JG 176). For Kristeva, if paternity is a "legal fiction" as Joyce writes, it is because paternal identification is the imaginary mechanism that enables access to the symbolic arena of law.[45]

Kristeva expands on her psychoanalytical theory of identification in her reading of *Ulysses* not so much in order to explain the text as to discover what *Ulysses* can tell us about identification and, in particular, about the identifications that preside over the creative process (the engendering of the text). The "massive presence of identificatory themes or narrative operations" in the text (JG 169)—eating, the obsession with the Eucharist, fatherhood, eros (largely associated with Bloom), *agape* (with Dedalus)—points to Joyce's Catholicism, and the probability and importance of some identity-threatening incident in his life. Not that Kristeva is interested in pinpointing parallels between fictional and biographical events. Rather she seeks to explore the relation between life and text more generally. The author is "dependent upon [*tributaire de*] his biography for the life of his works" (174). There is a "transfusion" (*transvasement*—more literally "decanting") of the artist's psychical life into his characters (178). Life flows into the text like blood. The secrets of a biography can be kept from the work, but not the libidinal push (eros or *agape*) that is "reabsorbed by the ubiquitous identificatory process" of Joyce's writing, "which is both avid and unstoppable" (171). This is identifiable in the text: We identify with it as we read.

Kristeva sees Joyce's writing as an odyssey of fluid identifications and constant metamorphoses. But the capacity for renewal through further identifications is characteristic of both artistic experience more generally (which includes not only writing but our experiences as readers) and also love. Love and art are both ways in which we "preserv[e] our psychic space as a 'living system,' one that is open to the Other, capable of adaptation and change" (JG 169), the difference being that art manages to *speak* these identifications. If Joyce, for example, tends not only to remain open to multiple identifications but to give voice to them, Kristeva hypothesizes that this is because the artist/author in general clings more than most of us to the imaginary father (174). Like the subject-in-process of Kristeva's earlier work, he remains as close as possible to the point where one moves from the unnameable towards the nameable or the symbolic realm, from the underworld towards the world of language (hence the "Return of Orpheus"). The phantasm of esthetic creation involves both the eros of narcissistic identification with "fecund maternal power" and its displacement into words through the *agape* of paternal identification

(178).[46] The latter, Kristeva argues, is indispensable to artistic creation but only if it is paradoxically both unstable and rigid, sufficiently rigid to allow identification to take place but sufficiently unstable so that no identification is definitive, open to both symbolic stabilization and semiotic disturbance. This results in a permanent circulation between the maternal and the paternal, between eros and *agape*, and between the semiotic and the symbolic, ensuring that life becomes text but that the text also remains alive (cf. 178).[47] This transfusion from life into text, giving life to the text, is like a blood transfusion between the author and his work. Or like the fatherhood of the creator. If Joyce traces the story of Shakespeare and Hamlet, it is because the author's physical survival is his work. Shakespeare's son Hamlet dies, but the father is incarnated in the creation of *Hamlet* and becomes his own son (176). The author is incorporated into the "This is my body" of the text. The "legal fiction" of paternity is also this imaginary identification.

And we, the readers, up to a certain point we follow these constantly sliding identifications as we journey into *Ulysses*. We, too, pour our bodies into the lines of prose in constant flux, into the shifting characters, and we too are carried through innumerable metamorphoses. Exhilarating, terrifying, cathartic, the reading process swallows us up. But we can detach ourselves from it by dissociating the real and the imaginary: After all, it is only a book (JG 179). My identity finds its most important anchors elsewhere.

COMING TO TERMS WITH KRISTEVA AND DERRIDA

From these outlines of their arguments, "Joyce 'The Gracehoper'" and "Ulysses Gramophone" seem poles apart. The texts seem to confirm the common perception that, intellectually speaking, by the eighties, Kristeva and Derrida had gone their separate ways. The dividing line between their work here seems to coincide more or less with that between the disciplines of psychoanalysis and philosophy, even as these both intersect with other disciplines in the humanities. However, the parallel preoccupations of Kristeva and Derrida that we noted in the opening chapter of this book—the questions about self and other, inside and outside—continue to drive their texts or disseminate through them.

Derrida sees the movement of the text as an odyssey of circular reappropriation disturbing notions of inside and outside such that "everything is integrable in the 'this is my body' of the corpus" (UG 283, tr. mod.). Similarly, Kristeva describes an avid, unstoppable process of incorporation in *Ulysses* such that inside and outside swallow each other up. In Joyce's journey towards his work there is an

> assimilation of these external poles [of father and mother] which are captured in the fluid identity of an inconstant subject, lacking an interiority other than through the possibilities of assimilation (of people, text, memories, etc.). Neither interior nor exterior, but a constant transfer from one to the other. (JG 179, tr. mod.)

And just as the circle "can never be closed upon itself" (UG 283), identity can never be fixed by a definitive identification. It would appear that the circular movement of Derrida's text is also able to appropriate Kristeva's.

Both Kristeva and Derrida focus on the continuous bi-directional circulation between inside and outside that blurs any distinction between them. Whether it be the circulation of blood and the liquid self or of letters, dispatches and gifts, it is this ceaseless movement of renewal, through an other that is never really other, that provides the point of articulation between the work of the two theorists, here as elsewhere. In each case it is what sets the structure of structuralism in motion, such that the text is seen to be caught up in a movement without destination and cannot be quarantined either from what Kristeva calls biographical accidents[48] or from Derrida's potential car accidents (cf. UG 309).

There are some striking parallels between Derrida's work on *oui* and Kristeva's on identification. Although Derrida is not describing the constitution of the subject when he writes of "[t]he self-positing in the *yes* or the *Ay*," he outlines the argument that this *yes* is pre-ontological: it is presupposed by Being (UG 302). The "self-affirmation of the *yes*" is a circular movement between self and other, like a circulation of dispatches of oneself that never really leave or arrive at the self.[49] Saying *yes* necessarily indicates that there is an other or at least that there is otherness, but, as we saw in Chapter 1, the other can not be apprehended as such.

> *Yes*, the condition of any signature and of any performative, addresses itself to some other which it does not constitute, and it can only begin by *asking* the other, in response to a request that has always already been made, *to ask* it to say *yes*. (UG 299)

In Ulysses,

> Molly says to herself (apparently speaking to herself alone), she
> reminds herself, that she says *yes* in asking the other to ask her to say
> *yes*, and she starts or finishes by saying *yes* to the other in herself, but
> she does so in order to say to the other that she will say *yes* if the
> other asks her, yes, to say *yes*. (UG 303)

One can only say *yes* to the other by saying *yes* to oneself (to the other
in oneself). One can only say *yes* to oneself by saying *yes* to the other
(to the other in oneself). "A *yes* never comes alone, and we never say
this word alone" (UG 288). "*Yes* indicates that there is address to the
other" (299). What appears to be monologue is always-already
dialogue.

I do not wish to oversimplify, but it seems to me that the processes
of identification analyzed in Kristeva's text are also ways of affirming
the self through dispatching (or transferring) oneself to the place of the
other and receiving (incorporating) the other in oneself. And similarly,
in Kristeva's theory, any discourse on the subject or his Being is
necessarily derivative with respect to these continuous processes of
identification. Identification is also a form of saying *yes*, a form that
would enable Derrida to say *yes* to Kristeva's text.

To keep the play of identifications open, and to explore the
multiplicity of *yes*, both Kristeva and Derrida question the traditional
view of paternity. They write out the legal fiction of the father who
would guarantee either the identity of the text or identifications within
and with the text, the father of law who would stabilize or stop the text.
Derrida cannot recognize paternal authority in Joyce because the latter,
in fathering *Ulysses*, manages to father all texts, to say *yes* to all would-
be heirs. The concept of legitimacy dissolves. In focusing on the
imaginary father of love, Kristeva similarly moves away from a father
of law or legitimacy or authority. The father of *agape* bestows his love
without requiring me to deserve it, to legitimize my claim on it. Both
maternal and paternal, both unstable and rigid, this prototype of the
father, this intermediary figure before the advent of the symbolic father
allows for infinite identifications (those of Joyce, of his characters, of
his readers) that never stabilize definitively.

It is as if Derrida and Kristeva each use Joyce's work and his focus
on fatherhood to argue for a textual movement that is able to absorb
whatever one brings to it—what Joyce brings to it (his life, his loves)

and what his readers bring to it, whether our loves and psychical investments or our postcards and the lids of yoghurt containers (cf. UG 259). This movement not only gathers up and incorporates but disperses and dissolves, such that we read the text in a rhythm of appropriation and dissemination, of genesis and dissolution. Derrida and Kristeva use the "This is my body" of Joyce's text to show a body whose contours are as fluid as those of the imaginary body of the infant who does not yet see the breast as other, as impalpable as the veil or hymen that is both limit and passage.

What then does it mean to read a text according to these two readers? What does it mean to read a text with them? For Derrida, it is to countersign, to say *yes* to the text, to respond to it responsibly but in one's own idiom. For Kristeva, it is to identify with the text, to transfer one's body and the unnameable within one to a place where it becomes representable, where the text is able to represent it. For both theorists it is to bring something of one's own to the text, something that is paradoxically already there. This can be seen as the question of context, a (if not *the*) post-structuralist preoccupation. Derrida's and Kristeva's writings (on *or*, on *gl*, on Sollers, Mallarmé or Joyce) mobilize ways of thinking about context that disturb any dividing line between text and context, showing both to be unstable and mutually determining. Whether in the form of the geno-text working through the pheno-text, or of my body that I pour into the text, or of the history of Western philosophy, religion, languages, science and literature entailed by *Ulysses*: The other of the text is already within it and splits the text from itself. Rather than a boundary between text and reader, there is a multiple boundary dividing and fusing each repeatedly.

It is fittingly perverse that in these texts from the eighties, at a time when readers were ceasing to lump Kristeva and Derrida together unproblematically, I find so many reasons to focus on parallel moves they make. But as I hope this book indicates, there are multiple ways of articulating the moving parts of these two bodies of work, both separately and together. There are multiple ways of saying *yes*. If I have gathered the theories together here so that they make a similar point about reading, it is not to fix them in this position. "[I]t is only a question of rhythm": in a few pages, "the circle opens, reappropriation is renounced, the specular gathering together of the sending lets itself be joyfully dispersed in a multiplicity of unique yet numberless sendings" (UG 304). In the next chapter, Peter Cowley and I explore the dissemination of Derrida's name and the unstable identifications with Kristeva's in the various uptakes of their work to show the overwhelming productivity of their texts in the hands of so many others, those who pore over their theories and pour themselves into them. But first, a couple more words on my uptake.

The two texts on Joyce are the last ones I intend to put together from the Derrida + Kristeva corpus. I could have chosen the texts on *Romeo and Juliet* or those that play with memoirs and autobiography or those on sexual difference. I could have put together *Black Sun* and "White Mythology." But I didn't. And I have also neglected the texts that intersect around religion, time, forgiveness and paintings. I look forward to reading someone else's articulation of these some day. So why the Joyce texts? Largely a matter of chance of course: a neat conjunction in time and space. But in my reading/rewriting of them, in what I bring to them and find already there, I realize just how appropriate they are, how much they have to say about this book, about what has brought me thus far.

How I say *yes* to Derrida's work. Each time I read Derrida, I am thoroughly convinced by his arguments. It is not that he sews up all loopholes, for that would immobilize the texts. Rather the loopholes loop back to take in deconstruction: Derrida's texts are necessarily caught up in the circles he describes. Reading Derrida, I am often overwhelmed by the elegance of the arguments, by texts that already prefigure anything I could say about them, by a corpus "which a priori indebts you and in advance inscribes you in the book you are reading."[50] I can only say *yes*, add my name to the list of signatories subscribing to Derrida's work. Yes, the other is ungraspable; yes, the dividing line splits and twists together to make a mockery of the binary opposition; yes, the subject and presence are elusive and illusive; yes, texts and meaning are slippery in this way; yes, this is how words and sounds and ideas play together. And yet my reading speaks in its own idiom, carries the traces of my autobiography in its mundane but absolute singularity (my garden, my I's, the chance images that become my metaphors), a singularity among so many others.

I don't subscribe in the same way to all of Kristeva's arguments. The link between specific sounds and drives, the justifications for distinguishing between poetic language and metalanguage, or between drive investment and empty mimicry in wordplay require a certain leap of faith that I do not make. However, as I read Kristeva's texts, whether her theoretical work, her literary analyses or her patients' narratives, it often happens that I identify with the processes she describes. By this I do not merely mean that I recognize them in myself but that I take my body to the site of melancholy, abjection or revolt and accompany the text on the journey to the nameable. And if I manage to name some aspects of my underworld with terms like narcissistic identification and the inability to relinquish the maternal body, this is only a small part of my coming to terms with Kristeva. For writing this book with and partially from Kristeva's books has been a process of bringing my investment in my work into the sounds of the sentences. It has literally been a coming to terms as I grapple with my demons and manage a provisional victory by lining up words on the page. The writing of each chapter has required a kind of crisis of abjection and depression only resolved when what I cannot name or express otherwise becomes the occasional play of metaphors and music, of images and cadences. Kristeva's work speaks to me of my survival, takes me to it.

Thus escorted, I arrive at the term of this articulation of Kristeva's and Derrida's work. Its terms of reference were determined by questions that are still the motor for all my academic work: the need to find an alternative to the binary opposition as a way of understanding difference — sexual difference, cultural difference, my difference; the desire to understand relations of sameness as involving both sameness and otherness — same sex relations, sibling relations, my identifications with those I love. These are what I bring to the corpus and find already there. These are what bring me to read with Derrida and Kristeva.

Articulating Derrida's and Kristeva's work has led me to read them

- as the terms of an opposition, where the oppositional structure is always already compromised;
- as the terms of an agreement, an agreement between others;
- in terms of one another;
- in terms of a common object — literature.

What I hope to have achieved is to have placed the texts *on speaking terms*, such that they have something to say to and about each other and have different things to tell us in this situation than when separated by discipline or lumped together indiscriminately.

Change the terms of reference, however, and what we bring to these texts — and what we find there — changes too. The "Derrida" and "Kristeva" that emerge from my readings are not the only "Derrida" and "Kristeva" to be found. These two signatures are identified with different meanings when countersigned in different ways. In the following chapter we can see the diversity of ways in which the names "Derrida" and "Kristeva" are made to signify. Now, it is possible to say that some of the myriad uses to which the names are put are simply wrong, resulting from a careless or uninformed reading of their work. However, many dissimilar uses can claim legitimacy as "Derrida" and "Kristeva" are made to do work in reframing the questions of various disciplines or branches. Indeed all uses are potentially able to take on a life of their own as the names are repeated in the engendering-disseminating processes of textuality.

NOTES

1. Philippe Forest, *Histoire de Tel Quel* 259.

2. Rodolphe Gasché, *The Tain of the Mirror* 266.

3. Philip Lewis identifies "L'Engendrement de la formule" as marking a turning point in Kristeva's work, where her conceptual object shifts from the linguistic text to the semiotic process ("Revolutionary Semiotics" 30).

4. Quotations marked *Révolution* rather than RPL are from the latter half of the volume, which was not included in the published translation.

5. In fact, although Kristeva insists that "the text smashes [*brise*] the linearity of the sentence" (*Révolution* 288) and of the narrative, this does not mean that the linearity of communicable language is irretrievably destroyed. Just as the symbolic remains a necessary foil for semiotic attacks, the line is indispensable to its own transgression: "The text needs this line to absent itself from it; to slide into it, follow its movement, absorb it and suddenly take a 'vertical path' through which it unfolds into a multiplied elsewhere" (Σ 343). Absenting itself, sliding, unfolding: Kristeva's vocabulary is much closer to Derrida's in *Sèméiotikè* than in RPL and *Polylogue* where the struggle between law and transgression overtakes any slippage.

6. The "Mystic Pad" is a slab of wax with a celluloid sheet over it. When you write upon it, the writing is visible on the surface but only so long as the celluloid sheet remains in contact with the wax beneath. Raise the sheet from the wax and there is once again a clean, unmarked page on which to write. The trace of any previous writing, however, remains in the wax. Freud compares the wax and the celluloid to the functioning of the preconscious and the conscious. Cf. *The Standard Edition of the Works of Sigmund Freud* 19: 228-229.

7. When Kristeva occasionally writes of unfolding—unfolding the unary subject (PL 318) or the unicity of the thetic position (RPL 61)—there is not the idea of extension of the surface area so much as extension of a type of functioning. It is interesting to note that when, much later, Kristeva analyzes

folds and veils in *Sens et non-sens de la révolte* and even uses the term *différance* to do so, she is examining folds in three-dimensional art: eighteenth-century religious sculptures of veiled figures (186-195). Kristeva argues that the fold is a representation of representation: the sculpted folds of textile allow us to discern the form of a body that is not presented to us. Representation neither reveals nor hides a signified but infinitely defers it. Here the fold defers depth but without extending the surface.

8. Mallarmé, *Œuvres complètes*, 886-1053.

9. "Le texte dans le texte" appears in the same issue of *Tel Quel* as the first part of Kristeva's "L'Engendrement de la formule." Starobinski's presentation of Saussure's work is available in English as *Words upon Words: The Anagrams of Ferdinand de Saussure*.

10. For recent examples, see Kristeva's *Black Sun* 100, 161-162, *Proust and the Sense of Time* 34, SNR 254 and Derrida's "Two Words for Joyce," "*Che cos'è la poesia?*" (*Points . . .* 288-299), "Shibboleth" and "Fourmis." Not only literary texts are subject to this kind of fragmentation: patient discourse and philosophical texts are also fair game. Derrida argues that the words of Plato's text "communicate with the totality of the lexicon through their syntactic play and at least through the subunits that compose what we call a word" (Dis 130), as Plato's words "come apart, bits and pieces of sentences are separated, disarticulated parts begin to circulate through the corridors, becomes fixed for a round or two" (169).

11. *Révolution* 220-230 appears in translation as "Phonetics, Phonology and Impulsional Bases." The relevant quotations in this paragraph can be found 33, 36 (tr. mod.).

12. Cf. *Glas* 118.

13. "Phonetics, Phonology and Impulsional Bases" 33 (tr. mod.).

14. See Dis 262, 350-351, MP 247-248, 309-329.

15. "Phonetics, Phonology and Impulsional Bases" 33-34 (tr. mod.).

16. Cf. "Each syllable then becomes the support for a small portion of body" (DL 179).

17. I. Fonagy, "Les bases pulsionnelles de la phonation."

18. "Phonetics, Phonology and Impulsional Bases" 35 (tr. mod.).

19. "Phonetics, Phonology and Impulsional Bases" 34, 35 (tr. mod.).

20. Mallarmé, *Œuvres complètes* 938, cited *Révolution* 251.

21. Judith Butler makes a similar point with respect to the multiplicity of drives when she wonders "whether, ironically, multiplicity has become a univocal signifier" (*Gender Trouble* 89).

22. In her analysis of Kristeva's reading of "Prose," Leslie Hill argues that the semiotic is "colonized by the symbolic as a confirmation and extension of

the thematic meanings of the text" ("Julia Kristeva: Theorizing the Avant-Garde?" 149). But rather than the semiotic replicating the symbolic as Hill suggests, I would argue that the confirmation operates in the other direction. For example, according to Kristeva, the semanticization of *fr* and *vr* in terms of frigidity "tends to suggest that the renunciation of genital *jouissance* is the condition of its esthetic transposition, just as, conversely, esthetic production is a transposition of this *jouissance* into language" (*Révolution* 250). The thematic meanings confirm and extend the libidinal sublimation entailed in esthetic creation.

23. Cf. TP 171 where Derrida shows the supplementarity of *tr*.

24. Cf. "In order to speak of even the most intimate thing, for example one's 'own' circumcision, one does better to be aware that an exegesis is in process, that you carry the detour, the contour, and the memory inscribed in the culture of your body, for example." Thus the body is textual, but Derrida also makes the point that the text is bodily. He suggests "that these reading grids, these folds, zigzags, references, and transferences are, as it were, in our skin, right on the surface of our sex organ when we claim to be treating our 'own' circumcision'" (*Points . . .* 353). Derrida's "Circonfession" is written along the folds and zigzags of the uncertain and unstable dividing line between body and text. On the possibility of rethinking the relation between biology and textuality with respect to the body, see also *The Gift of Death* 55.

25. *Glas* 90-97, 149-160, cf. also 120, 231.

26. Cf. Derrida writes of "miming [. . .] a sort of more or less impersonal self-analysis" (*Résistances* 40).

27. Temptingly, Gayatri Spivak makes a connection between the recent death of Derrida's father at the time he was writing *Glas* and the analysis of the institution of the family he undertakes in the left-hand column of the text ("Glas-Piece" 22-23).

28. Cf. "there is no efficient deconstruction without the greatest possible pleasure" (Derrida and Attridge, "This Strange Institution Called Literature" 56).

29. In fact, Kristeva suggests that "It is probably necessary to be a woman" to take up this position (DL 146), a phrase repeated in the preface to *Desire in Language* (x). She gives the beginnings of an explanation in "Woman Can Never Be Defined" 138. These are not the only examples of a privileging of Kristeva's own position (woman, mother, analyst, foreigner). Cf. Jane Gallop's discussion in *Feminism and Psychoanalysis: The Daughter's Seduction* 115-120.

30. Derrida's texts repeatedly remind us of the overdetermination of the random, of the "interfacing of necessity and chance" ("My Chances/*Mes Chances*" 6). Cf. OG *passim*.

31. Introduction, *James Joyce: The Augmented Ninth* 8.

32. Cf. "Two Words for Joyce" 149-152.

33. Cf. "Two Words for Joyce" 147-149.

34. The literary network is, of course, not the only one to gather together the various threads of a culture: "In a minimal autobiographical trait can be gathered the greatest potentiality of historical, theoretical, linguistic, philosophical culture" (Derrida and Attridge, "This Strange Institution Called Literature" 42-43).

35. Introduction, *James Joyce: The Augmented Ninth* 4.

36. Cf. "I know that everything is in Shakespeare: everything and the rest, so everything or nearly. But after all, everything is also in Celan, and in the same way, although differently, and in Plato or in Joyce, in the Bible, in Vico or in Kafka, not to mention those still living, everywhere, well, almost everywhere . . ." ("This Strange Institution Called Literature" 67).

37. "Two Words for Joyce" 149.

38. *Ibid.*

39. "This Strange Institution Called Literature" 66-67.

40. Here echoes of Chapter 1 above can be heard: I respond to the otherness of the text by finding where this otherness resonates within me. There is no clear dividing line between the text and what I bring to it, just as "There is no simple distinction between what one says and how he is heard" (Llewelyn, *Derrida on the Threshold of Sense* 89).

41. Gasché's reading of *Ulysses Gramophone* emphasizes this point (*Inventions of Difference* 229-250). Regarding the ethical responsibility of the response, Attridge points out that the *singularity* of the response must be *repeatable* in order to be recognized by a community of readers (Introduction, *Acts of Literature* 20n). Cf. Derrida, *Points . . .* 384 on the responsibility of saying "yes" and "Passions" for a sustained discussion of the ethics of response.

42. Cf. "writing is also already a countersigning reading, looking at it from the work's side" ("This Strange Institution Called Literature" 69).

43. Kristeva's use of the terms "real," "symbolic" and "imaginary" in this essay approaches a Lacanian use without coinciding with it. Cf. Chapter 2 above.

44. Paragraph not translated JG 173 but present in both French texts available (*L'Infini* 8 1984, 8; *Les Nouvelles maladies de l'âme* 266). Cf. NMS 179.

45. Cf. Chapter 2 above ("Revisiting the Boundary: Kristeva's imaginary") and Oliver, *Reading Kristeva* 69-90.

46. Cf. "le déplacement de cette reduplication passionnelle dans les mots" (*L'Infini* 8, 1984, 12; NMS 186). JG 178 omits "into words" from the translation.

47. Kristeva suggests that Joyce's daughter, Lucia, who suffers from mental illness, bears the cost of his remaining so close to the limit between. Constantly engaged in fluid identifications, he cannot provide a sufficiently rigid support for her identifications with the imaginary father (JG 179).

48. The "mechanism" Kristeva refers to (JG 168) becomes the more explicit "biographical event" in Kristeva's revision of the text (NMS 174).

49. The argument is made more fully in, for example, "Envois" (PC 1-256) and "Envoi" (*Psyché* 109-143).

50. "Two Words for Joyce" 147.

PART IV

Reading with Kristeva and Derrida

CHAPTER 8

Uptakes: An A to Z of Debates and Disciplines

(co-authored with Peter Cowley)

A for Authenticity

The true, authentic and original, the one and only . . . ? Competing claims to represent the authentic Derrida and Kristeva abound. They tend to be made on the basis of context: Derrida and/or Kristeva need to be read in terms of French intellectual life, the history of philosophy, psychoanalysis and/or semiotics, in terms of their predecessors in these fields, their early work, the history of *Tel Quel*, French feminism, Russian formalism, Marxism, Judaism, Catholicism, etc. Readers making these claims tend to select their corpus from within the corpus of Derrida's/Kristeva's writings accordingly, favoring the philosophical or the literary, the early or the late, the semiological or the psychoanalytical. And alongside these claims there are often indications of other people's misappropriations.

It is certain that familiarity with any or all of these contexts can only assist in reading Derrida and Kristeva. As Derrida remarks, in order to read Rousseau,

> one must understand and write, even translate French as well as possible, know the corpus of Rousseau as well as possible, including all the contexts that determine it (the literary, philosophical, rhetorical

traditions, the history of the French language, society, history, which
is to say, so many other things as well). Otherwise, one could indeed
say just anything at all [. . .]. (LI 144)

An understanding of context can certainly be used to prove that a
particular reading is wrong. Context, however, can never be saturated.
The real, authentic and original specimen can never be presented as
such. However thoroughly we may steep ourselves in the innumerable,
overlapping formations shaping and shaped by Derrida's or Kristeva's
work, we cannot exhaust them. No matter how well informed, a
representation is an interpretation, one that usually has some kind of
agenda.[1]

This A to Z is an attempt to steer away from rating readings in
terms of their faithfulness to our vision of the true Kristeva or Derrida
(although we do occasionally feel compelled to point out
inconsistencies). After all, as Jonathan Culler remarks, there is a certain
irony in the concern to "separate orthodox deconstructive criticism
from its distortions or illicit imitations and derivations," an irony in the
desire for purity with regard to a theory emphasizing difference in
repetition.[2] Rather, the A to Z takes as its premise that the two theorists
are never simply read in terms of *their* context(s) but in terms of the
reader's contexts—her intellectual environment, personal history,
politics and passions, the debates in which she engages. It is an attempt
to look beyond the claims to authenticity to see what is at stake in any
given uptake of Kristeva or Derrida. The chapter therefore asks: Which
particular Derrida or Kristeva is being employed in this or that
instance? From which texts (and against which texts) is s/he
constructed and in order to do what job? The two theorists may be
invoked separately or together and for parallel, intersecting or
contradictory purposes, but they tend to be called on to intervene in
some way.

Derrida describes the readers he addresses as

people who, because they "like this stuff," signal their reception by
going off elsewhere, reading and writing in their turn altogether
differently. This is the generous response, always more faithful and at
the same time more ungrateful. (*Points* . . . 351)

Our A to Z is largely populated by such readers. As a list, it is open
ended, exhaustive neither of disciplines nor of debates within

disciplines. It represents a sampling of mostly Anglophone uptakes, and aims to give not an overview but an idea of range—from the flippant to the scholarly, from the local to the generalized, from A to Z.

B for Bodies: See G for Gender and E for Essentialism.

C for Critical Legal Studies

The term "deconstruction" frequently appears in association with Critical Legal Studies (CLS), an influential movement that arose in the mid-seventies among disaffected junior academics from the law schools of Yale and Harvard and quickly spread. The movement is far from unified but tends to be concerned with demystifying legal reasoning and doctrines through demonstrating their ideological presuppositions and their inherent contradictions.[3]

Derrida is by no means a reference for all those who identify themselves with CLS. Although precise links to Derridean texts and practices are made in some cases ("Devant la loi," "Force of Law" and "The Law of Genre" are frequently cited, together with the earlier *Of Grammatology*, *Writing and Difference* and *Margins of Philosophy*), deconstruction is commonly used as a synonym for critique, delegitimation, debunking and—that CLS speciality—"trashing."[4] Mark Kelman, a self-proclaimed practitioner, defines trashing thus:

> Take specific arguments very *seriously* in their own terms; discover they are actually *foolish* ([tragi]-*comic*); and then look for some (external observer's) *order* (*not* the germ of truth) in the internally contradictory, incoherent chaos we've exposed.[5]

Some of the fiery criticisms of trashing and of CLS in general are familiar to those who have followed the polemics around Derrida's work: It is said to be nihilist, non-serious, lost in relativity, unable to distinguish interpretation from misinterpretation, and it is said to propose no positive programme of reform.[6] But then again, it is true that some of the trashers within CLS see deconstruction as a form of complete skepticism, its critique of law's foundations equivalent to the destruction of these foundations. If, for some CLS "crits," deconstruction stands for

- undoing hierarchical oppositions between rival legal principles,
- undermining the foundational claims of law and

- indeterminacy of meaning (no meaning without interpretation),

for others (whom Drucilla Cornell dubs the "irrationalists" in CLS), these principles have been taken to the following not necessarily logical conclusions: Namely, that

- all distinctions are arbitrary;
- if irrationality or incoherence can be found at the foundation of law, then nothing in law is rational, coherent or justifiable;
- there is no shared communicable meaning.[7]

For these thinkers, there can be nothing but unjustifiable existential choices and personal meanings.

J. M. Balkin attempts to resignify "deconstruction" and distinguish it from the latter form of trashing. In "Deconstructive Practice and Legal Theory," Balkin reforges the link with Derrida's work and examines its pay-offs for legal theory. Deconstruction is thus described as an analytical tool that exposes what is privileged and what is excluded in legal thought (which tends in fact to be rather coherent). It does not demonstrate that all readings of a particular law are equally legitimate but rather "call[s] into question the ways in which we decide that a given interpretation [. . .] is illegitimate."[8]

For Cornell, however, it is too late for damage control regarding "deconstruction." She abandons the term and proposes another to refer to Derrida's philosophical project: "the philosophy of the limit." She sees Derrida's writings as working at the limit of idealism and at the limits constraining any system of meaning. In particular, she reads Derrida's understanding of justice as "the limit to any attempt to collapse justice into positive law."[9] In an attentive re-reading of Derrida together with Levinas that goes well beyond the scope of this entry, Cornell discusses the implications of such a philosophy for questions of ethics, justice and legal interpretation. She works to pose these questions together in a discipline that has tended to separate questions of interpretation from questions of ethics and justice.

D for Deconstructionism

The large-scale adoption of deconstruction has given rise to an avatar that is teachable and repeatable. Derrida labels it "deconstructionism."[10] This institutionalized and institutionalizing brand of deconstruction functions as a method or a set of theorems to be applied. It can come up with "the most conventional of readings."[11] Kristeva complains of American students who, when she interprets Mallarmé's work in relation to French history and the social context, ask why she speaks "about ethics and history when those notions already have been deconstructed."[12]

But we have no reason to smile smugly at such naivety. The price of deconstruction is eternal vigilance. Derrida cautions that the border between deconstruction as a questioning and destabilizing movement on the one hand and deconstructionism as an established methodology on the other is continually crossed, that deconstruction cannot immunize itself against the tendency to settle down.[13]

E for Essentialism

One site where Derrida and Kristeva continue to be regularly invoked in the one breath, footnote or line of text is the feminist polemic around essentialism. Here entire shelves in undergraduate libraries are occupied by texts from the last decade appealing to Derrida and Kristeva as anti-essentialist authorities. But then again, Kristeva is also regularly attacked for essentialism, and Derrida is less often cited in these instances.

If essentialism in the context of feminism can be described as "the belief that woman has an essence, that woman can be specified by one or a number of inborn attributes which define across cultures and throughout history her unchanging being and in the absence of which she ceases to be categorized as a woman,"[14] then both the work of Derrida and that of Kristeva undermine this position. Neither see "woman" in terms of an immutable given but rather as a more or less stable and largely social construct. They both question the very opposition woman/man in that it presupposes the unity and homogeneity of each category. In fact they challenge all notion of a unified subject. They write instead of multiple femininities, of multiple sexual markings dividing so-called individuals, such that "feminine" and "masculine" inhabit each other. But as we have seen, the differential relations within and between such categories, and the relations between the biological, the social and the linguistic do not necessarily coincide in their theories. Strategically, however, Kristeva's and Derrida's theories have been used together in this debate, perhaps more than in any other, and have often been conflated.

A major reason for this is that for those working in women's studies, the dissemination of these theories in anglophone universities was part of a wholesale importation of "French feminism" (see *F for French Feminism*). The debate around essentialism was, in fact, frequently framed in terms of anti-essentialist French feminism brought in to question and combat essentialist Anglo-American feminism.

A key text here was Toril Moi's *Sexual/Textual Politics*, published in 1985. "[C]ompact, cogent, readily accessible, widely circulated" (indeed the tattered library copy before me has to be read through layers of markings in pencil, biro, yellow and pink highlighter), the book "made (anti-)essentialism a household word."[15] It also gave very wide currency to a particular view of the relation between Kristeva and Derrida.

Like Irigaray and Cixous, Kristeva is seen by Moi as indebted to Derrida, but of the three she is said to be the most clearly and uncompromisingly anti-essentialist.[16] This is no doubt why Moi proposes a "combination of Derridean and Kristevan theory" as a promising tool for feminist readings.[17] Moi regularly quotes Derrida to explain Kristeva and her "'deconstructed' form of feminism."[18]

Moi's reading draws on a range of Kristeva's texts to give a complex picture of a complex theory. However, the schematic summary of "Women's Time" in the introduction to the book has been very influential in persuading readers that Derrida and Kristeva are interchangeable in their anti-essentialism:

1. Women demand equal access to the symbolic order. Liberal feminism. Equality.
2. Women reject the male symbolic order in the name of difference. Radical feminism. Femininity extolled.
3. (This is Kristeva's own position). Women reject the dichotomy between masculine and feminine as metaphysical.[19]

The short and fairly atypical text that has come to stand for Kristevan anti-essentialism is here represented as a text-book example of the mechanical application of deconstruction (or what Derrida would call "deconstructionism"): a binary opposition is reversed (phase 2) and displaced (phase 3).[20] In tandem with the interview "Woman Can Never Be Defined," this version of "Women's Time" is frequently taken as The Essential Kristeva-cum-Derrida.

But The Essentialist Kristeva also lurks. The prescription of French feminism as a cure for essentialism was of course not always well received. Anglophone feminists were, in fact, already questioning the homogeneity of the women they claimed to represent and, in turn, attacked the French feminists for *their* essentialism, often lumping Kristeva, Irigaray and Cixous together as proponents of an *écriture féminine* understood as women's writing.[21] More sophisticated critiques of Kristeva's work as essentialist also appeared and continue to appear,[22] but as Tina Chanter points out, these tend to view the semiotic/symbolic divide as absolute, such that the semiotic is seen as purely biological. Kristeva thus seems to repeat the nature/culture divide and, therefore, the sex/gender opposition. However, in associating the semiotic with the "feminine," she seems to privilege sex over gender, hence the charge of essentialism.[23]

The debate around essentialism, in which the encounter with "French feminism" played an important role, initially gave rise to an invigorating questioning of assumptions and a rethinking of politics among Anglophone and other feminists. Notions like "women" and "oppression" could no longer be taken for granted. Universalizing models for women's experience were undermined as their often class-based and ethnocentric premises came under scrutiny. What had appeared self-evident—the men/women opposition underpinning the feminist struggle—started to blur as it was argued that each of its terms was unstable and fragmented. The role of language in the construction of meaning and in the constitution of an object of study had to be addressed.

However, at some stage there ceased to be any debate over essentialism: Debate gave way to doctrine and a form of name-calling. "Essentialist" became a blanket insult, a way of contemptuously dismissing others. Teresa de Lauretis suggests that the triumph of anti-essentialism is partly due to its commitment to high theory, which has served as a way for feminism to improve its academic credentials.[24] Kristeva and Derrida have thus come to be used less to critique than as a form of academic legitimation.

Recently, however, the debate has been rekindled by prominent feminist theorists impatient with the "the policing of feminism by the shock troops of anti-essentialism."[25] In *The Essential Difference*, they note the use of some fairly crude binary oppositions and some very unified concepts in the way dogmatic anti-essentialism opposes essentialism. Naomi Schor suggests that "Anti-essentialism operates [. . .] by essentializing essentialism, by proceeding as though there were one essentialism, an essence of essentialism." In order to move on, "we must begin by de-essentializing essentialism" for it is not one and unified.[26] De Lauretis highlights "the pernicious opposition of low versus high theory."[27] Elizabeth Grosz argues that anti-essentialism appears to impose binary choices "between the goals of intellectual rigor (avoidance of the conceptual errors of essentialism and universalism) and feminist political struggles (struggles for the liberation of women as women)" and wonders whether we can't understand the linkages between theory and political practice differently.[28]

According to Gayatri Spivak, the problem with anti-essentialism is thinking it could possibly escape from essentialism. She understands the work of deconstruction, not as the promise of escape into a brave new world but as "the critique of something that is extremely useful, something without which we cannot do anything."[29] Essences may be fragmented but not done away with. There is always a remainder—"*ce qui reste*"—to be reckoned with.[30]

And Tina Chanter, in an essay published elsewhere, argues that anti-essentialism rests on a fairly rigid division between sex and gender. She suggests that Kristeva's semiotic/symbolic distinction unsettles sex/gender and nature/culture distinctions, questioning assumptions "about the ease with which gender can be siphoned off from sex."[31] For whilst Kristeva's notions of "masculine" and "feminine" are not about males and females, they are not independent of the relation to a sexed body.

. . . Which all goes to show that if uptakes of deconstruction and French feminism could give rise to axiomatic anti-essentialism, they can also provide tools for unsettling its hold on power.

F for French Feminism

1980 saw the publication of Marks and de Courtivron's *New French Feminisms* and Eisenstein and Jardine's *The Future of Difference*. In 1981 there were special issues of *Yale French Studies*, *Signs* and *Feminist Studies* focusing on French texts. And in 1982 came a special issue of *Diacritics* and Jane Gallop's *Feminism and Psychoanalysis*.[32] "French feminism" had arrived.

But did it arrive—or did it come into being as a recognizable set of texts, theorists and questions through its importation? Despite discriminating readings and presentations in these volumes and others, French feminism rapidly solidified into a coherent Kristeva-Irigaray-

Cixous borrowing from and/or influenced by Derrida+Foucault+Lacan, those in the first group appearing somewhat more interchangeable than those in the second. Through this form of packaging, Kristeva, Irigaray and Cixous (and also Derrida) were given a prominence they do not enjoy in French academic institutions, where they represent neither Frenchness nor feminism.[33]

French feminism was constituted through its difference from Anglo-American feminism. But of course Anglo-American feminism is just as discursively constructed, prone to reductive stereotyping and impossible to contain within geographical borders as French feminism. The tensions and exchanges within and between the two(?) strands of feminism are discussed at length by writers such as Spivak and Jardine.[34]

Such texts have not, however, been able to prevent cultural polarization, and this has resulted in a homogenization of French feminism in certain introductions to feminism and in surveys and overviews of feminist theory. Here a Kristeva constructed from "Women's Time" (from the *Signs* volume) and "Woman Can Never Be Defined" and "Oscillation Between Power and Denial" (from Marks and de Courtivron's anthology) descends from a Derrida with a somewhat less concentrated textual base (often including *Of Grammatology*, *Spurs* and "Choreographies"). Together they represent not only French feminism but also "feminist deconstruction," "post-structuralist feminism" and "feminist post-modernism." This Derrida/Kristeva intervenes strategically to reverse and displace binary oppositions, to deconstruct the category of "woman" and to focus on language as constitutive of the "I" rather than its tool.

I am struck by an index where, between "Dennett, David" and "Descartes, René," we find not "Derrida, Jacques" but "Derrida (French feminist)."[35] The entry is apt: this is one "Derrida" among others. But as this A to Z shows, the French feminist Kristeva is also one "Kristeva" among others.

G for Gender

In her work on gender and bodies, Judith Butler manages to avoid many of the pitfalls and oversimplifications of the essentialism debate described above. If, in *Gender Trouble*, she argues cogently against feminisms that presume the existing identity of a unified Woman and then purport to represent her, in *Bodies That Matter* she deconstructs the essentialism/constructivism opposition and disavows the kind of pure constructivism that her work had been read as supporting. In both texts she is also careful to avoid collapsing the work of Derrida and Kristeva. In fact, she even uses one against the other.

Gender Trouble includes an extended critique of Kristeva's theory and, in particular, her model of subversion.[36] The subversion of the symbolic by the semiotic is described as "doubtful," "self-defeating," "futile" and a "failure" (80-81). Butler argues that it cannot lay the basis for change: it cannot revolutionize paternal law and the binary system of gender roles imposed by that law. This is because any disruption by the semiotic depends on the stability of the symbolic. No "full-scale refusal" (86) of the existing hierarchy is possible, only a local, temporary dislodging before the symbolic "reasserts its hegemony" (80). Semiotic subversion even depends on its own failure, for were it to triumph over the symbolic, there would be no culture, only psychosis.

For Butler, the problem is that Kristeva describes the semiotic as pre-cultural, which precludes its subversion from becoming an effective cultural practice. Symbolic renewal is not enough. What is needed is a subversive practice operating within culture that can transform symbolic law in more sustainable ways. The alternative "more effective strategy of subversion" that Butler proposes involves "the law turn[ing] against itself and spawn[ing] unexpected permutations of itself" (93). In the conclusion to the book "From Parody to Politics," it becomes clear that gender as performance and repetition is the key to this strategy. Gender is a question of role-play: "The task is not whether to repeat but how to repeat or, indeed, to repeat and, through a radical proliferation of gender, to *displace* the very gender norms that enable the repetition itself" (148). And in *Bodies That Matter,* she spells out the Derridean premises of this argument: performativity as citationality, and the iterability that constitutes identity. Performing gender is like the citation of a citation or the imitation of an imitation without an original.

This is an interesting adversarial encounter between Kristevan and Derridean theory. Although Butler frames her chapter on Kristeva in terms of a Foucaldian critique, some of the questions she raises are similar to those of the Derridean reading proposed in Chapter 4 above (Is the *chora* conceived as a naturalized origin? Can we know drives other than through their effects and representations? Is the semiotic/symbolic distinction sustainable?). If these lead her to disagree with Kristeva, this is largely because she reads Kristeva's elaboration of the *chora* as unambiguously pre-cultural. To some extent, however, she is arguing against a straw case in equating the *chora* with a notion of unconstructed nature and a pre-cultural body. For (as we saw in Chapter 2) Kristeva herself describes her explanation of the semiotic preceding the symbolic as a heuristic ploy, a "*theoretical supposition* justified by the need for description" (RPL 68) and also points out that symbolic law has always-already left the imprint of its constraints on the semiotic through the mediation of the mother's body which is inscribed in social/family organization (RPL 27). In fact Kristeva herself problematizes the same simplistic before/after, biology/culture distinctions that Butler finds in her work.[37]

Despite these differences, Butler's critique does arrive at a similar challenge to Kristeva as Chapter 4 above: the Derridean challenge to accept revolt in the form of the mimicry of law or fetishism, that is to say, a subversion through repetition, a shift through drift rather than through the overturning and restoration of norms.

H for Hoax

An application of deconstruction in the field of quantum gravity? (You know, "the emerging branch of physics in which Heisenberg's quantum mechanics and Einstein's general relativity are at once synthesized and superseded.")[38] Alan D. Sokal does it tongue-in-cheek in "Transgressing the Boundaries," an impressive display of quasi-erudition in which French theorists are well represented. And he gets away with it in *Social Text*.

At first glance, what seems to bring together theorists including Althusser, Culler, Deleuze, Lacan, Lyotard, Schor and Serres in Sokal's article is a less than scientific use of scientific concepts. Irigaray is cited for her insights into fluid mechanics and Barbara Johnson for "an analysis of Derrida's and Lacan's efforts toward transcending the Euclidean spatial logic" (237n). It is strange that Sokal doesn't pick up on Kristeva's algebra in *Sèméiotikè* — but then again Kristeva was a serious student of mathematics in Bulgaria.

Derrida comes in for special attention. A remark he makes about Einstein's constant not constituting a center is interpreted thus:

In mathematical terms, Derrida's observation relates to the invariance of the Einstein field equation $G_{\mu\nu} = 8\pi G T_{\mu\nu}$ under nonlinear space-

time diffeomorphisms (self-mappings of the space-time manifold that
are infinitely differentiable but not necessarily analytic). (222)[39]

If the parody makes a point about jargon substituting for proof, clearly
the danger is not restricted to the humanities: The really opaque bits of
text are often composed of scientific tech-talk.

However, in revealing his spoof, Sokal declared that its target was
primarily those in cultural studies who critique science by ostensibly
denying the existence of objective reality. Apparently, Derrida and
company are perceived as colluding in this denial. And judging from
some of the letters to the Higher Education supplement to *The
Australian* following the hoax, this is neither an uncommon perception
of "French linguistic philosophy," nor one confined to physical
scientists.[40]

Now, whilst many of the theorists cited by Sokal may agree that
"scientific 'knowledge,' far from being objective, reflects and encodes
the dominant ideologies and power relations of the culture that
produced it" (217-218), unlike the legendary idealist, Bishop Berkeley,
they do not proceed from this argument to a claim that there is no
external world. Yet again, Derrida's "there is nothing outside the text"
has been taken as a form of radical idealism, according to which one
only stubs one's toe against words.

I for Intertextuality

An entry among others . . . or an entry that accounts for the others?

Kristeva is widely credited with coining the term intertextuality in
her 1966 article on Bakhtin, "Word, Dialogue, and Novel" (DL 64-91),
in which she wrote: "any text is constructed as a mosaic of quotations;
any text is the absorption and transformation of another. The notion of
intertextuality replaces that of intersubjectivity" (DL 66).

Of course the term itself does not govern or escape intertextual
transformations but is produced by and subject to them. Michael
Worton and Judith Still maintain that theories of intertextuality in a
broad sense can be found "wherever there has been discourse about
texts," citing Plato and Socrates, Cicero, Quintilian and Montaigne
among others.[41] And since 1966, the absorption of texts by one another
has led to the term "intertextuality" loosening its specific link with
Kristeva's work.[42] It has come to refer to a range of theories affirming
that texts cannot exist or function in isolation from other texts. These

include the work of Kristeva, Barthes, Foucault, Genette, Riffaterre and Derrida among others. What groups these latter together is that each in their own way has depersonalized intertextual encounters, moving away from talk of sources, influence, and the individual author in favor of anonymous networks of texts, and the role of language in the constitution of the subject/author. In Derrida's work a form of intertextuality is read through a series of terms including citation, graft, iterability, parasitism and supplementarity (that necessary supplement without which the text would not be itself).

The grouping together of these theories of intertextuality received momentum as they were pitted against the tenets of Harold Bloom's *The Anxiety of Influence*, in which literary texts were seen to be produced through the author's personal, Oedipal struggle with his (her?) predecessors. The debate became polarized between influence and intertextuality. Like all oppositions, however, this one is not as clear-cut as some would like to claim. Introductions to Kristeva's theory of intertextuality sometimes find it necessary to mention the influence of Derrida's work.[43] Certainly Kristeva writes of "writing" and the "*gram*" in the first paragraph of "Word, Dialogue, and Novel" (and her editor adds a footnote to Derrida in the English edition), but it may be more useful to read this precisely in terms of "a mosaic of quotations," the "absorption and transformation" of another text, or indeed in terms of citation, graft, etc.

Perhaps, however, there is an inevitable mutual parasitizing of pairs such as anonymous/personal and intertextuality/influence that the debate has worked to conceal and that can be profitably exploited. Jay Clayton and Eric Rothstein suggest that feminism has a stake in rehabilitating some form of influence by retheorizing intertextuality in terms of an embodied and gendered agent rather than an abstract network.[44] Worton and Still note a trend towards reinscribing passion and politics, loves and hates into intertextual relations.[45] And among the essays in their collection exemplifying the trend are Seán Hand's reading of transference as a form of intertextuality and Ross Chambers' analysis of the seduction of the reader who is persuaded to produce intertextuality (by perceiving discourse as part of a literary system) in complicity with the text.[46]

The term intertextuality has changed hands many times since its Kristevan coinage. The gradual effacing of the Kristevan imprint is a story of the intertextuality of intertextuality. It can be compared to

Nicholas Royle's utopian reading of the Derridean concept of signature — its dispersal, its invisible inscription:

> The best signature would be that which dissolves, no longer lets itself be read or lets itself be read only as a kind of ghost. [. . .] It would no longer be necessary to cite Derrida: the most effective kind of writing after Derrida would be that in which Derrida, the proper name, and everything ostensibly belonging to it, or presumed to enable a reader to read and identify the singularity of a corpus (even that of a sentence) signed "Derrida," had disappeared, passed into the language.[47]

J for Jurisprudence

For an uptake of Derrida in legal theory, see *C for Critical Legal Studies*. Uses of Kristeva in legal studies tend to be concerned with feminist jurisprudence and in particular with the question of the configuration of the subject before the law. Kristeva is invoked with other "French feminists" to problematize binary oppositions such as man/woman and to question the category of reason in a field where "the test of the reasonable man" still holds sway.

K for Kitty Kisses

Infinity Kisses is a series of photographs in which performance artist Carolee Schneemann and her cat Vespers are locked in passionate kisses. Rebecca Schneider reads it in terms of Derrida's discussion of sexual markings. Given that the cat's gender is unclear and irrelevant in the exhibit, Schneider suggests that "such art-bestiality is a multiplication of sexualities as much as an interruption of gender codes, that is, a multiplication of possibilities in the hope-filled vein of Derrida's 'incalculable choreographies.'"[48]

L for Lesbian Studies

One place where Kristeva and Derrida are rarely confused is in Lesbian Studies. Indeed in Queer Theory generally, Kristeva is berated for what appear to be some very orthodox psychoanalytical views supporting the regime of compulsory heterosexuality.[49]

Elizabeth Grosz protests against the exclusion of lesbianism in Kristeva's work: "the one category of love missing from *Tales of Love* is the love of a woman for women."[50] Kristeva effectively reduces female homosexuality to the relation between a mother and her own mother. But does this necessarily have anything to do with lesbianism? Judith Roof contrasts Kristeva's "heterosexual utopian vision of mother-daughter relations" with the denial of the mother in lesbian novels.[51]

Teresa de Lauretis condemns Kristeva's pathologization of homosexuality whereby "*any* form of lesbianism harks back to a pre-Oedipal maternal bond" and is destined to end up in psychosis or even death because it lacks the third term enabling symbolic access.[52] Similarly, Judith Butler criticizes Kristeva's association of homosexuality with a refusal to give up the mother as a libidinal object such that the loss is internalized and the girl's identity becomes a kind of self-loss. According to Butler, in Kristeva's account, "heterosexuality and coherent selfhood are indissolubly linked" and the unmediated realization of lesbian desire can only lead to "the psychotic unraveling of identity."[53] Female homosexuality is seen as a "culturally unintelligible practice" and its desires must be displaced onto the symbolically sanctioned practices of poetry and maternity.[54]

Kaja Silverman proposes a different and largely recuperative reading of Kristeva's propositions: "Kristeva's account of the maternal voice speaks to an erotic desire which is completely unassimilable to heterosexuality, and which functions in some very profound way as the libidinal basis of feminism."[55] The identification of the homosexual aspect of motherhood is to be celebrated: "I would even go so far as to argue that without activating the homosexual-maternal fantasmatic, feminism would be impossible."[56] Kelly Oliver echoes this reading. If Kristeva reduces lesbianism to the maternal, at the same time she makes lesbianism the basis for all feminine sexuality: "Within Kristeva's analysis, [. . .] feminine sexuality is fundamentally homosexual." Far from lamenting the exclusion of lesbianism in her texts, Oliver writes: "I see lesbian love pushed into every corner of *Tales of Love*."[57] Both Silverman and Oliver see Kristeva's defensiveness with regard to homosexuality as concealing her own desire for union with the mother: "Behind all of Kristeva's writing is a longing for her one true lesbian lover, her mother."[58]

De Lauretis, however, takes issue with Silverman's reading of Kristeva and indeed with a whole set of appropriations by feminist theory of lesbianism as a kind of metaphor for relations between women generally and even for feminism itself. Taking the sex out of homosexuality, they idealize lesbianism and erase its specific sexual and social difference.[59] If Silverman manages to read Kristeva's homosexual-maternal fantasy as enabling for feminism, it is as a homosexuality available to heterosexual women that has little to do with women having sex with women.

M for Medieval Studies

It is perhaps inevitable that where the movement of critical theory represented by Derrida and Kristeva (among others) is introduced into an established discipline, this tends to lead to internecine struggles for control of the disciplinary agenda. Established reputations are undermined; classic texts are thrown out the window; the young Turks are at the city gates.

Take, for instance, medieval studies, within which one can easily identify the rallying posts for the critical theory medievalists and their more traditional colleagues. The development of the debate can be traced in the journals *Speculum* and *Exemplaria*, twin goalposts in a game of disciplinary point-scoring. While the former defends the purity of the discipline, the latter contends that it was never pure in the first place. The names of these two journals are not only exemplary medieval terms but carry further resonances for recent theory. They reflect both the way in which critical theory has entered the fray . . . and the history of some of its concerns.

Can there be medieval studies after Derrida and Heidegger, asks R. A. Shoaf, the general editor of *Exemplaria*?[60] He answers resolutely in the affirmative—the Middle Ages were never exclusively literalist. Behold how Chaucer, Dante and Jean de Meun were concerned with forestalling the foreclosure of language and text. "Chaucer our Derridean Contemporary," then?[61] Not quite, suggests Andrew Taylor, identifying the trap whereby eager medievalists "plunge right in, embracing full intentionality and deconstructive rhetoric almost in the same breath."[62] In other words, the rhetoric of *Speculum* is reflected back by deconstructionist medievalists in an attempt "to serve two masters," Chaucer and Derrida (475).

On the other hand, Taylor argues, a certain unwillingness to abandon the traditions of medieval studies is perhaps not a bad thing. The desire of some deconstructionists to throw out all the conventions of the discipline leads to a certain "depressing sameness": "if our sense of the radical instability of the sign can be imposed with equal ease and without distinction on the works of Chrétien, Chaucer, Borges, and John Barth, then surely something is wrong" (479). The usefulness of deconstruction depends crucially on paying attention to the institutional and material conditions of the discipline within which it operates. There is no point in introducing deconstruction to medieval studies if it is simply to deny or remove the traditional constraints of the latter and blithely opt for a form of free-play instead. The challenge is "to free the game but still maintain it" (483). Although kicking the ball through the goalposts may be the objective, the game can only go on if the teams make contact on the playing field.

N for Nation

In "DissemiNation," Homi Bhabha seeks a way of "writing the nation" as a non-centered, hybrid form of living rather than as a historicized, homogeneous object. To do so, he uses the work of Derrida, Kristeva and others, however he does not conflate theories, nor does he simply apply them. Rather, in the image of his theory of hybridity, he offers a hybrid theory, where various texts are grafted into his own. Derrida's work is quoted in a discussion of supplementarity but is also heard throughout the essay: in the scattering-gathering of the title, and in the references to grafting, iterability, double writing, the limit within, and living on borderlines. Similarly, Kristeva's "Women's Time" and her writings on dissidence are discussed, and there is a sense of the transposing of discourses when Bhabha writes of our strangeness to ourselves and the foreignness of our own language.

Bhabha poses the question of "nation as narration": how does a nation tell itself and constitute itself in the telling?[63] This is the question of "the representation of the nation as a temporal process" (142), but what kind of temporality is involved? Bhabha sees the "fissures of the present" transformed into the "rhetorical figures of a national past" (*ibid.*) Whatever is unaccountable, uncanny or ambivalent, whatever doesn't fit into received notions of the nation is surmounted and structured into the temporality of past-present-future. The nation is narrated as history. Against this teleological mastering of strangeness, Bhabha pushes a wedge into the fissures, opens them up to produce a double time and a double writing that can narrate not just the solidification of the nation but its disturbance.

The two sorts of temporality wedged apart can be termed pedagogical and performative. The former ("continuist" and "accumulative") constitutes 'the people' as the historical object of an authoritative nationalist discourse (i.e., the notion of 'the people' becomes what is told). However the latter ("repetitious" or "recursive") positions 'the people' as the subjects of a process of signification, such that the nation is seen as constantly (re)producing itself through a process of iteration (i.e., 'the people' do the telling) (145). For Bhabha, writing the nation thus involves a double narrative movement, an ambivalence, a shifting between enunciative positions. The subject of narration is "graspable only in the passage between telling/told" (150). This splitting disturbs the inside/outside division that habitually defines nationhood and produces instead a border within the notion of nation. In doing this, it "provides both a theoretical position and a narrative authority for marginal voices" which are normally excluded from pedagogical representations (*ibid*.).

Bhabha draws an analogy between his two sorts of temporality and Kristeva's distinction between "cursive time" and "monumental time":

> The borders of the nation, Kristeva claims, are constantly faced with a double temporality: the process of identity constituted by historical sedimentation (the pedagogical); and the loss of identity in the signifying process of cultural identification (the performative). (153)[64]

Unlike most readers of "Women's Time," Bhabha emphasizes the fact that it is through a redefinition of the nation that Kristeva designates a space for feminist identifications to emerge. The point of his analogy is that Kristeva's essay forces us to think of the process whereby a nation or community becomes both "the subject of discourse and the object of psychic identification" (*ibid*.). This process occurs *within* a discourse of nationhood or culture. That is to say that there is no transcendental moment where the nation exists outside of its (split or double) enunciation. There is always a telling of what is told. Bhabha compares this to the structure of Derridean supplementarity: "The nation's totality is confronted with, and crossed by, a supplementary movement of writing" (154). The supplement (of performative writing) adds to (the writing of the nation) without adding up (to oneness and wholeness). Rather it disturbs the calculation (155). It disturbs the generalization of knowledge and the homogenization of experience implicit in the notion of nation as historicized object (163), enabling the nation to be narrated otherwise: "as a contentious, performative space of the perplexity of the living in the midst of the pedagogical representations of the fullness of life" (157).

By drawing Derrida and Kristeva together and bringing them to bear on the dividing line between same and other, subject and object, even self and self, Bhabha explores the possibility for nations to define themselves in terms of an otherness within rather than in terms of us and them.

O for Opera

If Derrida and Kristeva have become icons in the visual arts, they fall short of diva status in the field of opera. References to either are comparatively sparse, but they tend to occur in the same context: Derrida and Kristeva—along with various other theorists we could loosely term post-structuralist—are called on to unsettle the primacy of music over libretto in opera. Given the widespread acceptance of the notion of *prima la musica, dopo le parole*, this debate is somewhat marginal.

David J. Levin has, however, edited a collection of essays engaging specifically with this question. *Opera Through Other Eyes* (and pointedly not through ears) includes essays by theorists who have translated and/or published alongside Derrida over the years (Philippe Lacoue-Labarthe, Peggy Kamuf and Samuel Weber). In his introduction, Levin positions the book against a tradition whereby libretto—as "the embodiment of poetic banality"—serves to direct attention away from itself and towards the music.[65] And he positions it against Paul Robinson's polemical "Deconstructive Postscript," which encourages listeners and discourages readers of opera and which dismisses the libretto and indeed the notion of textuality in opera in favor of allowing oneself to be transported by the music.[66] There are signs that the rule of rapture over reading is being challenged. However Levin laments the fact that even books with such promising titles as *Analyzing Opera* and *Reading Opera*, although they draw on contemporary theory in order to engage with the poetry and drama of opera, still find it necessary to subordinate words to music.[67]

When Levin invokes theory to redress this imbalance, he tellingly refers to it as *literary* theory, for his purpose (not necessarily shared by the writers represented in the collection) is a literary one and, specifically, not a musicological one. Levin is in the business of promoting the libretto. If he admits that the operatic "text" encompasses "first and foremost the libretto, but also—and less concretely—those aspects of opera that can be read: for example, the music, the stage directions, and the preparation, presentation, and reception of the work," he quickly assures his readers that the "primary focus" of the essays presented is the libretto (4-5). Weber's and Kamuf's essays, however, work extensively on the visual and spatial aspects of opera. Although the book as a collection may function to rehabilitate the libretto, the essays themselves are far from homogeneous. Issues that are raised deconstructively include questions of referentiality, quotation and liminal spaces.

There are clear parallels between the celebration of operatic music in its throbbing vocal presence at the expense of the libretto and the repression of writing by the full presence of living speech denounced by Derrida, a point taken up by Carolyn Abbate in *Unsung Voices*. Abbate's book is informed by current theoretical debates on the production of meaning, and she makes a couple of strategic references to the work of Derrida and Kristeva. However, whilst both Abbate and Levin write against the swoon effect as a measure of operatic appreciation and promote the readability and textuality of opera to this end, their strategies are rather different. Levin confines the act of reading to the extra-musical aspects of opera, to the libretto as supplement (but a supplement that Levin virtually detaches from the music). Abbate, on the other hand, looks for a way of *reading music*.

Instead of perpetuating the opposition music/libretto or music/plot, she explores the idea of music as narration. By this, she does not mean that all music tells a story. Rather, she looks for a disjunction in opera between music as nonnarrative expanses acting out events (which she compares to "a sort of unscrolling and noisy tapestry that mimes actions not visually but sonically") and moments of musical narration ("respeaking an object in a morally distancing act of narration").[68] The latter moments interrupt like "musical voices that distance us from the sensual matter of what we are hearing, that speak across it" (xii). Leaning on contemporary narrative theory, she reminds us that narrative is not just plot structure and action sequences but "a way of speaking, of manipulating time, of using figural language, of constituting event, and the *context of performance* in which narrating occurs" (28). These are what she looks for in the music of opera.

By exploring the tensions in the relation between musicology and literary theory, Abbate manages to work at the very limit of the analogy 'music-is-a-language' and to open a space for reading the specificity of the production of meaning in opera. If theory enables Levin to reverse a hierarchical opposition between music and text, it enables Abbate to undo that opposition.

P for Play

"For years," writes Richard Rorty, "a quarrel has been simmering among Derrida's American admirers," a quarrel that Rorty himself has done his utmost to further. He summarizes the debate thus:

> On the one side there are the people who admire Derrida for having invented a new, splendidly ironic way of writing about the philosophical tradition. On the other side are those who admire him for having given us rigorous arguments for surprising philosophical conclusions. The former emphasize the playful, distancing, oblique way in which Derrida handles traditional philosophical figures and topics. The second emphasize what they take to be his results, his philosophical discoveries. Roughly speaking, the first are content to admire his manner, whereas the second want to say that the important thing is his matter—the truths which he has set forth. [69]

Rorty situates himself firmly in the first camp, together with Geoffrey Hartman. The second camp is said to include Christopher Norris, Rodolphe Gasché and Jonathan Culler. In fact this second group includes any who would argue for *both* play and rigour in Derrida's work, for the quarrelsome Rorty is "hostile" to those who think the two can be combined into a single activity (239). Rorty suggests that we need to "jettison the 'rigorous argument' part" (235), insisting that "you cannot have it both ways" (239). Obviously, Rorty is not particularly perturbed by binary oppositions: "I confess that I find the knee-jerk suspicion of binary oppositions among deconstructionists baffling."[70] Indeed he is happy to divide up Derrida's work into early, philosophical writings with a public mission and late, playful texts amounting to private jokes and fantasies, claiming that since *Glas* Derrida has abandoned his earlier seriousness.[71] Rorty's sympathy for clear-cut oppositions extends to his suggestion that he is doing newcomers to Derrida a favor in offering them "a choice between opposed readings."[72]

Rorty's arguments have given rise to a whole series of texts in conversation with each other.[73] Christopher Norris is probably the most tenacious of Rorty's opponents, citing Rorty in the acknowledgments to his *The Contest of Faculties* as being largely responsible for very existence of the book: "nearly all the ideas in this book have been arrived at through disagreement with Rorty" (vii). Texts by Norris and Rorty argue with one another in Dasenbrock ed., *Redrawing the Lines* and Wood ed., *Derrida: A Critical Reader*.

To fuel all this writing, however, the debate turns around more than the opinions of one man who, despite Derrida's note of caution regarding any choice between truth and play (WD 292-293), cheerfully chooses a play that claims to escape truth. And it concerns itself with more than the seriousness or otherwise of Derrida's texts from the seventies and eighties. In fact, Derrida's work is only the pretext for this debate: presumably Rorty would have to reject most of Derrida's writings from the nineties as selling out to philosophy. So beyond the claims to represent the authentic Derrida (see *A for Authenticity* above), what is at stake? The stakes seem to be primarily disciplinary ones: the status of various disciplines (but in particular "theory" and philosophy) and their claims to truth, and the relations between disciplines.

Rorty uses Derrida to undo philosophy as a discipline, seeking to topple it from its privileged position as queen of the humanities. He maintains that philosophy is just one kind of writing among others, that it is not more rigorous or closer to the truth than other disciplines and that it has no firm place from which to argue for it has invented its own foundations and has itself devised the rules by which it argues. Since truth in philosophy is a metaphysical delusion, we would do better to recognize the fact and start enjoying it, instead of pretending that reason can actually achieve something. We should therefore cease to maintain the division between philosophy and literary criticism and celebrate play.[74]

While some within literary studies (and American literary studies in particular) have taken their cue from Hartman, Rorty and selected passages from Derrida to embrace fun, frivolity and free-play euphorically, others have rejected the view that questioning a discipline's claims to truth means abandoning the search for truth entirely. Thus Culler explains that when deconstruction uncovers a consensus masquerading as a foundation for philosophy, it does not conclude that truth is merely a sham, but seeks what has been excluded from the consensus, and tries to go beyond what is demonstrable within the system.[75] Thus Norris defends the use of reason, arguing that we do not simply abandon philosophy by turning our back on it. Rather, in questioning the foundations of philosophy, and in particular the blind spot of its textual/rhetorical constitution, "deconstructive theory has uncovered certain problematic aspects of philosophy which can now be thought through in more rigorous fashion *without* losing sight of philosophy's distinctive concerns."[76] We can see that the arguments for free-play and those for rigor both use Derrida's questioning of the conditions of possibility and of the foundational gestures of branches of knowledge, but to different ends.

Dasenbrock notes the irony of "Norris —the literary theorist— [. . .] defending the continuing separateness of philosophy while Rorty—the philosopher—wants to abandon it."[77] However there is a certain logic in this if we consider the status of philosophy and literary theory as disciplines. For unlike the established disciplines of philosophy and literary criticism, "theory" has hardly been in a position to undo itself. Rather, as a somewhat nebulous field of inquiry asking an open set of questions across a number of traditional areas of study, and as a field whose existence was under attack from many quarters, it has used work like Rorty's (often as a foil) in order to constitute itself as a discipline.[78]

Now that literary theory is perhaps less threatening/threatened as a discipline, perhaps the concerns obscured by this debate can come to the fore. Attridge sets up his anthology *Acts of Literature* as a way of trying to get past the polarization between "sternly philosophical or playfully literary" visions of Derridean criticism (12), a polarization which "is quite out of keeping with the work itself" (13):

> Not only is the opposition [philosophy/literature] a philosophical one, it is an opposition by means of which philosophy produces, and thus constitutes itself against, its other. [. . .] The rejection of the "literary" Derrida can be seen as the repetition by philosophy, once again, of its founding move [. . .]. At the same time, any thought of expelling philosophy from the practices of writing in the name of literary "free play" or "textuality" is doomed [. . .]. The very notion of literature as ungoverned rhetoricity, as a practice safely "outside" philosophy, is a philosophical notion *par excellence*. (*ibid.*)

Attridge's aim, on the other hand, is "to grasp *together* the literature/philosophy couple, to gain a sense of their co-implication [. . .] as well as their distinctiveness" (*ibid.*).

The play versus rigor debate can be framed in other ways, but disciplinarity still seems to be the issue. Dasenbrock locates the debate as a site of exchange between two traditions that compete to represent philosophy: Anglo-American analytical philosophy and continental philosophy.[79] Certainly Rorty's admiration of Derrida meets up in a curious way with attacks by other analytical philosophers. As Norris writes, "what Rorty finds congenial in Derrida is exactly what offends a mainstream practitioner like Searle."[80] But then, Rorty's admirative comments are reflected in claims from all those who would attack Derrida as non-serious. A notorious attack of this kind, by philosophers seeking to protect the integrity of their discipline, was prompted by the proposal by Cambridge University to award Derrida an honorary doctorate. The two senses of integrity virtually coincide in their letter to the *Times*, for one of their main complaints seems to be that Derrida's influence has been felt beyond rather than within the bounds of philosophy.[81] But not only philosophers felt the need to protect their discipline from the corrupting effects of Derrida's work. A question put to Derrida by the editors of the *Cambridge Review* suggests that a number of scientists "felt that in opposing the award of the degree, they were in some way upholding the standards and procedures which constitute their disciplines."[82]

Q for Queer Theory

L for Lesbian Studies discusses readings of Kristeva's problematic assertions about homosexuality. Her work on abjection, however, has proved useful in theorizing the constitution of taboos against homosexuality and the repudiation and exclusion of the other implicit in homophobia.[83] Derrida is also used, but differently, to explain the hetero/homo divide and the exclusions it entails. Unlike Kristeva, however, he is also invoked to displace it. Eve Kosofsky Sedgwick refers to the undermining of the symmetry of binary oppositions such as heterosexual/homosexual and Diana Fuss takes up the deconstruction of the inside/outside opposition.[84]

Other uses of Derrida include Judith Butler's notion of gender as repeated and repeatable performance based on the explanation of iterability in "Signature Event Context" and Edelman's reading of the deconstruction of behind/before in the sodomitic scene of writing between Plato and Socrates in "Envois."[85] Derrida's allusion to the notion of a relationship "beyond bisexuality [. . .], beyond homosexuality and heterosexuality which come to the same thing" has also given rise to debate over essentialism and the possibilities for queer identity.[86] Heather Findlay, for example, in "Is there a Lesbian in this Text?" critiques Derrida's work for excluding the possibility of lesbian specificity and for scapegoating a position analogous to that of the lesbian separatist.

R for Rigor: See P for Play.

S for Screen

When it comes time for film theory to reinvent or renovate itself, to whom does it turn? Well, among others, to both Derrida and Kristeva but with different expectations.

When Peter Brunette and David Wills decide to read Derrida for film theory, it is with the express aim of extrapolating a new set of methodological tools for analyzing film. They begin by noting that "Lacan's work has been so much more influential than Derrida's in film studies, exactly reversing the situation that has prevailed, at least until very recently, in American literary criticism."[87] Lacan's work is seen to have been useful in challenging the myth of a unified coherent self and in emphasizing the importance of the visual in the construction of the subject, such that critics attend to the positioning and construction of the spectator-subject. However Lacanian film analysis is not without its shortcomings. In particular, there is said to be a tendency to focus on film reception at the expense of attention to the text, and to treat the symbolic and the imaginary as a rigid dualism. Other problematic propensities in film theory include assumptions about the wholeness of films and the integrity of generic categories and a tendency towards essentializing definitions of historical periods. Brunette and Wills introduce Derrida's work into the field as a way of nudging these and other trends off track. They suggest that in addition to reorienting questions of the subject and of the constitution of meaning, deconstructive film theory could reframe questions

- of framing (the complex folds between inside and outside),
- of the signature (the dissemination of the proper name or the mark of a director, cast or crew member within the text),
- of representational hierarchies (examining what escapes the visual or aural),

- and of the "right of inspection" (suggesting strategies for reading that avoid the positioning of the spectator by the images and challenge the institutions that determine readings).[88]

Unlike Brunette and Wills, who hope for a wholesale shift in the parameters of film criticism, Kaja Silverman and Barbara Creed propose more localized refinements of theory in their uptakes of Kristeva. And rather than applying Kristeva's work to film theory in a one-way transfer, they exploit intersections between feminism, psychoanalysis and cinema in order to reorient work in more than one discipline.

Silverman studies Kristeva's "*choric* fantasy" of union in/with the maternal *chora*, in which the mother's voice functions as a blanket of sound and (in an adaptation of Lacan) as "the acoustic mirror in which the child first hears 'itself.'"[89] Comparing this voice to the first voice-over or voice-off, she goes on to study the *choric* role of the mother's voice in films. However, if in Kristeva's work *choric* space engages the homosexual facet of maternity (the mother's desire for union with her own mother), Silverman finds that recent films open up the *choric* enclosure to embrace a whole community of women.[90] Silverman is thus able to move outward from Kristeva's texts to hypothesize the homosexual-maternal relation as the libidinal basis for feminist solidarity.[91]

Barbara Creed reads Kristeva to analyze a rather different fantasy of the mother, one far less idyllic and reassuring.[92] Kristeva's work on abjection enables Creed to launch an assault on the conventional portrayal of woman-as-victim in readings of the genre of (schlock) horror. Rather, Creed suggests, woman as the female reproductive body is the prototype of the monster, that abject creature, neither this nor that, who threatens the clean-and-proper body of the self (whether protagonist or spectator) and both attracts and repels us.

But it is not only the abject mother who inspires dread. Creed proposes a shift away from the Freudian theory of the castrated woman to a reading of woman as castrating when she identifies a widespread fantasy of the castrating mother, the *vagina dentata*. And her argument leads outwardly from her generic analysis to broader feminist debates. She issues a challenge to psychoanalytical theories that insist on a fear of castration focused on the father: They ignore the possibility that the mother can be identified with symbolic law. Now, Kristeva is said to go some way towards remedying this by recognizing the fundamental ambiguity of the figure of the mother and the necessity for her to be abjected as the child moves towards symbolic positioning. However Creed suggests that the founding link between the symbolic and patriarchy can be questioned further by examining the role played by the fantasy of the castrating mother.

T for Translation

Derrida's best-known contribution to translation theory is his essay "Des Tours de Babel." It first appeared in a bilingual presentation in *Difference in Translation*, a collection of essays taking up the question of translation within a deconstructive framework. Reviewing the essays in 1988, Christopher Norris concluded: "This is a fine volume of essays which should help to start up some genuine exchange between philosophers and literary theorists."[93] And what about the translation theorists? Have they nothing to offer? Their apparent absence here may have something to do with the fortunes of the would-be discipline of Translation Studies. Whatever exchange might occur, it would seem that translation theorists are either excluded from it, or invisible within it, possibly because their work does not constitute a recognizable discipline.

But if translation theorists are overlooked, "translation," on the other hand, pops up everywhere: almost anything can be seen as a kind of translation, including of course "genuine exchange." According to Eve Tavor Bannet, "Translation has traveled from the periphery to center stage, where it serves as a metaphor for the work of the academy."[94] It is now common to find translation, as concept, metaphor and/or critical lever, at work in feminism, postcolonialism, cultural studies, jurisprudence and of course philosophy, to name just the more obvious cases, and Derrida's work has been instrumental in this proliferation.[95]

It seems that the exchange between deconstruction and translation theory is heavily weighted to one side: deconstructive uptakes of translation theory seem far more prevalent than the reverse. If, until recently, deconstruction has received "little attention" from translation theorists, Kaisa Koskinen attributes this to the possibility that "it may at first sight appear to be hostile to translation" in that it declares translation to be impossible.[96] A more careful reading will of course show that Derrida declares translation to be *necessary and* impossible, in any case inevitable. On the other hand, if deconstruction is (more accurately) understood as undoing the classical opposition between translatability and untranslatability—an opposition which has determined the shape of two thousand years of translation theory—then it is equally threatening to a Translation Studies bent on finding its own incontrovertible disciplinarity.

But perhaps we are asking the question the wrong way in looking for uptakes of deconstruction *within* Translation Studies. For deconstruction is precisely what takes it out of itself. If we examine texts like Tejaswini Niranjana's *Siting Translation: History, Post-Structuralism, and the Colonial Context*, Yopie Prins' "Elizabeth Barrett, Robert Browning, and the *Différance* of Translation" and Christina Zwarg's "Feminism in Translation: Margaret Fuller's Tasso," we find that they overflow into other fields. Once translation theorists take up deconstruction, they tend to work at the cusp of disciplines and it is hard to continue to classify them as before. It is as if systematically taking deconstruction on board means engaging with wider theoretical issues and becoming invisible as a translation theorist. This seems to bear out Derrida's argument that "for the notion of translation we would have to substitute a notion of *transformation*" (Pos 20). Rethinking translation is a process whereby translation studies and its specialists are transformed.

U for Urban Planning

In fact this entry should more properly appear under *A for Architecture* as the story of deconstruction-and-architecture coincides with a move by architecture away from the sprawling field of Urban Studies and into the galleries in its own right, aspiring to a status similar to that enjoyed by Art. However, slipping it in here conveniently disposes of an awkward letter and appropriately locates it next to *V for Visual Arts*.

Although Derrida had already been collaborating with Peter Eisenman and Bernard Tschumi and had written three texts pertaining to architecture in 1986[97] and although some architects had been reading Derrida carefully for years before that, it was in 1988 that two events boosted the profile of the interdisciplinary connection: the Tate Gallery Symposium entitled "Deconstruction in Art and Architecture" and the *Deconstructivist Architecture* exhibition at the New York Museum of Modern Art. The latter title has a history of its own, being a replacement for "Violated Perfection" (refused by the museum) and giving rise to a great deal of controversy from the moment it was proposed. For the "deconstructivist" label is not merely an interesting variation on "deconstructionist" or "deconstructive." It both determines and is determined by a particular reading of the projects it groups together. The term effectively gives a nod in two directions: on the one hand towards Derridean philosophy and on the other hand towards the Russian constructivists of the 1920s. One room of the MOMA exhibition was given over to the "Russian precursors."[98] The rest of the exhibition was devoted to the projects of seven architects including Tschumi and Eisenman. The seven "deconstructivists" were seen as indebted to Derrida, the constructivists or preferably both. But what links the two? Tschumi and Eisenman may have been doing something like a deconstruction of constructivism, but elsewhere the connection was far from obvious.

Philip Johnson, curator of the exhibition, saw formal similarities between the constructivists and the deconstructivists such as the "diagonal overlapping of rectangular or trapezoidal bars."[99] However it was his associate, Mark Wigley, who linked the skewed geometry of both with philosophical deconstruction, pointing to the disturbance of the dream of pure form. Deconstructivist architecture was concerned with locating the dilemmas inherent within buildings, the flaws intrinsic to structure, the instability contaminating stability. It was about finding the unfamiliar within the familiar. The architects represented in the exhibition were seen to be employing the formal strategies of the Russian avant-garde in order to re-examine the radical possibilities of the latter and challenge ideas about the coherence and stability of form.[100]

Deconstructivist Architecture, then, is not about buildings falling down. Dislocation, not demolition, says Wigley.[101] Is it a style? Here opinion is divided. Charles Jencks answers "yes": "Like the clothing of *Esprit* and post-Punk music, it is an informal style appealing to a substantial taste for the discordant and ephemeral, the unpretentious and tough."[102] Others—including most of the practitioners—answer no: whilst there are some recognizable traits shared by many projects labelled deconstructivist, deconstruction is not a style, and certainly not just a style, in the pejorative sense.[103] Rather it is a different way of thinking about architecture, exploiting its paradoxes and insisting on what its conventions repress .[104]

But although such descriptions may echo Derrida's work, the intersection between deconstruction and architecture has not been an application of theory to practice. Eisenman's and Derrida's remarks are indicative in this regard:

> I have no doubt misread Derrida's work, but to misread is ultimately a way of creating, and it is by misreading that I manage to live in reality and to work with him. [105]

> So I gave this text [an earlier version of *Khôra*] to Peter Eisenman and in his own way he started a project that was correlated with but at the same time independent of my text. That was true collaboration— not "using" the other's work, not just illustrating or selecting from it . . . and so there is a kind of discrepancy or, I would say, a productive dialogue between the concerns, the styles, the persons too. [106]

One of the most interesting aspects of deconstruction-and-architecture is the extent to which the uptake has been a two-way process, deconstruction being unsettled by the architecture it unsettles. Mark Wigley has perhaps gone furthest in drawing out the implications of the mutual translation of architecture and deconstruction. Rather than a separate discipline, Wigley shows that architecture has never *not* been implicated in deconstruction. Using Heidegger's reading of the architectonic metaphor in philosophy, he shows architecture to be embedded in the very discourse of deconstruction. But it cannot be dismissed (in a classic philosophical gesture) as simply a metaphor. Derrida's work depends on a certain thinking of architecture that is written into his texts and cannot be detached from them.[107] Examining the towers in Derrida's essay on translation ("Des Tours de Babel"), Wigley argues that architecture "cannot simply translate deconstruction. It is so implicated in the economy of translation that it at once preserves and threatens deconstruction."[108]

V for Visual Arts

The visual arts cover a broad spectrum of disciplines including architecture, dealt with in the previous entry. The fact that Derrida and Kristeva have themselves written extensively on the visual arts, has facilitated uptakes of their work in these areas, pointing the way to some extent. [109]

In Derrida's case, this way has been followed in books like *Deconstruction in the Visual Arts* and *What Is Deconstruction?* [110]

which group the visual arts under one umbrella and attempt a deconstructive overhaul of their theoretical premises. The desire to tackle systematically the basis of a discipline is, however, absent from uptakes of Kristeva's work in the visual arts. As in cinema studies, Kristevan theory tends to be mobilized in the visual arts in order to intervene locally.[111]

Having concentrated on deconstruction in the previous entry and being unable to give more than a tiny taste of the uptakes of either theorist in this vast field, we shall focus on the use of Kristeva's work in this entry, and on one particular uptake that does not simply follow the way indicated by her readings of Giotto or Bellini. One of the most frequently recurring uses of Kristeva's work in the visual arts involves references to her theorizing of the abject in *Powers of Horror*. The care with which it is invoked, however, varies widely. On the one hand it has become a kind of catch-all term for "yucky" stuff. The inclusion of "yuckiness" in installation and performance art, in particular, is all too easily glossed as artistically worthwhile *because it's just like Kristeva's abject*. On the other hand, there are considered uptakes of this aspect of Kristeva's work, for example Frazer Ward's "Foreign and Familiar Bodies."

Ward's essay appears in the catalogue accompanying the exhibition *Dirt and Domesticity. Constructions of the Feminine*. In it, Ward contrasts several artistic uses of filth. Dirt can be transgressive of symbolic organization. As Kristeva shows, when we are confronted with our inability to exclude filth definitively, the stability of our borders and of our symbolic and social positioning is brought into question. Thus in modern installation art, Andres Serrano's photographs of menstrual blood and Cindy Sherman's images of bulimic vomit can provoke outrage or at the very least disquiet. At a certain ironic distance, they can also be read as theatrical representations of the feminine-as-abject.

However dirt is not simply transgressive of borders. In fact, certain representations of filth actually rehearse its expulsion to the margins of society and thus reinforce social organization. Ward examines documentary photos associating dirt and the cleaning up of dirt with working-class women, African American women and migrant women. Although femininity is traditionally associated with filth and abjection, here the middle-class white housewife is protected from domestic dirt which is projected onto the socially low, the racially other. The photo of the grimy *Migrant Mother* reflects the gesture of a culture constituting itself by pushing dirt to its borders.

W for Woolf

Virginia Woolf's writings are the site of an engagement between conflicting feminist readings, and in the quest to recuperate Woolf for feminism, Kristeva and Derrida are frequently invoked together.

Toril Moi opens *Sexual/Textual Politics* with the question "Who's Afraid of Virginia Woolf?"[112] Her point is to open out the intersection between feminism as a political practice and contemporary (French) literary theory. In this introductory chapter, Moi admonishes those feminists—exemplified by Elaine Showalter—who have taken Woolf to task for the lack of authentic representations of women's experience in her writing and for not sounding a clear and unmistakable political clarion call. Using Derrida, Moi argues instead that Woolf shows how "language refuses to be pinned down to an underlying essential meaning," and that her narrative strategies offer "playful shifts and changes of perspective" that unravel the kind of unified subject Showalter would prefer. In this way, Woolf "rejects the metaphysical essentialism underlying patriarchal ideology" (9). Then, using Kristeva, Moi points to the disruption of rational and logical language under the pressure of Woolf's drives and desires, and to the deconstruction of gender identity and of the masculine/feminine dichotomy in her work (11-12). Understood in these terms, Woolf is clearly an experimental writer, perhaps even a revolutionary one. Her politics of language make her a political writer and a feminist model.

Unproblematically synthesizing the work of the two theorists, Moi suggests that "A combination of Derridean and Kristevan theory [. . .] would seem to hold considerable promise for future feminist readings of Woolf" (15).[113] A number of critics have taken up this proposal. In particular, several texts have appeared tracing parallels between Kristevan theory and Woolf's novels—focusing on fluidity of identity or identifying the semiotic in the rhythms and sound patterns of *The Waves*—and alluding to Derrida's work in footnotes and in their critical vocabulary (dissemination, deconstruction, spacing).[114]

Miglena Nikolchina, in "Born from the Head: Reading Woolf via Kristeva," does much more than find parallels between Kristeva's literary theory and Woolf's literary practice, and the article is worth lingering on. It contrasts the Kristevan reading of Woolf urged by Moi with Kristeva's own comments on Woolf, which include the following:

> In women's writing, language seems to be seen from a foreign land; is it seen from the point of view of an asymbolic, spastic body? Virginia Woolf describes suspended states, subtle sensations and, above all, colours—green, blue—, but she does not dissect language as Joyce does. Estranged from language, women are visionaries, dancers who suffer as they speak. [115]

Nikolchina argues that both Showalter *and* Kristeva have silenced Woolf, the former by suggesting that Woolf is cut off from her body and the latter by contending that Woolf is cut off from language. In doing so, both Showalter and Kristeva relegate Woolf to a position that Woolf herself set out in *A Room of One's Own* —that of Shakespeare's mute sister. Meanwhile they fail to acknowledge the other position Woolf established and struggled successfully to occupy—a *speaking* position, that of the androgynous Shakespeare. In reproducing Woolf's topology, they displace Woolf from her position of speech to the position of silence.

However, far from rejecting the idea of the usefulness of Kristeva's work for Woolf studies, Nikolchina uses Kristeva to analyze Kristeva's own gesture. She sees this gesture as one that not only repeats moves by Woolf and Showalter but that is also to some extent a move repeated in work by Irigaray, Cixous and Spivak among others. This is the gesture of speaking via an ambiguous position (androgyny for Woolf, "the mother-oriented male artist" for Kristeva) about a silence that is gendered as feminine (Shakespeare's sister for Woolf, melancholy as the "silent sister" of philosophy in Kristeva's *Black Sun*). [116]

Nikolchina considers Showalter's and Kristeva's silencing of Woolf firstly as a form of matricide, whereby the mother is abjected. Woolf and/or her writing are interpreted as a body and then abjected from literary history. But if Kristeva is right and "our entry into language depends on the successful *loss* of the mother," then it seems that "the mother will always precede us as silence, absence, and deprivation." [117] Is it possible for us to speak other than by banishing our mothers to the position of silence?

A partial recovery of the mother is detected when Nikolchina examines Woolf's use of androgyny and compares it to Kristeva's use of the male mask: Kristeva "speak[s] via a male artist who speaks via a female double who further splits into a male/female couple" in her work on Nerval, Stendhal and Céline (39). The masquerade of the male artist allows a confrontation with the enigmatic maternal spaces visited in abjection, melancholy and *jouissance*. The mask can thus be seen as the means for the return of the mother but also as the space of separation protecting us from being engulfed by her. The mask is like the detour of translation;[118] it enables silence to be transformed into speech. The mask allows Woolf, Kristeva and others to take up a provisional position from which to speak (of) silence, for "what separates can always turn into a medium of transmission" (41). Thus the gesture that silences the mother in order to separate from her can also become the means of returning to her to translate her.

If Moi suggested reading Woolf via Kristeva in order to recuperate Woolf for feminism, Nikolchina suggests that reading Kristeva's reading of Woolf via Kristeva makes it possible, if not to recuperate Kristeva for feminism, at least to ask feminist questions about the circular repetition of a certain discourse of speech and silence.

XYZ...

And the list goes on. The uptakes are not grounded and centered by the writings of Kristeva and Derrida, although that is where they find their impetus. Rather, each reading shifts and revitalizes the possibilities for their use. We leave the last word to a medievalist and quote from—and gloss—a passage that is itself a palimpsest:

> The word "deconstruction," like other words, *[like "semiotic" and "symbolic," like "poetic language," like the proper names "Kristeva" and "Derrida"]* acquires its value only from its inscription in a chain of possible substitutions, in what is too blithely called a "context." Are there not those who might wish to say that for them, for what they have tried and still try to write, the word has its interest only within a certain context where it replaces and lets itself be determined by other words, other words such as "game," "integumentum," "gloss," "palimpsest," "speculum," or "jonglerie," etc.? *[and each reader-writer will select a series of substitutions to match her disciplinary concerns.]* By definition, such a list can never be closed, but always must be, and that for reasons of economy. [119]

NOTES

1. Cf. the end of the previous chapter for an indication of the agenda of this study.

2. *On Deconstruction* 227.

3. Cf. Margaret Davies, *Asking the Law Question* 143-166, for an overview of the history of CLS, its strands of thinking and the criticisms it has attracted. Cf. also Bronwyn Statham's *Figuring the Interdisciplinary in Critical Legal Theory*.

4. David Fraser, for example, makes both substantial and flippant references to Derrida in "What a Long, Strange Trip It's Been" and "The Owls Are Not What They Seem." Christine Husson, on the other hand takes deconstruction to mean critique in "Expanding the Legal Vocabulary."

5. "Trashing" 293. Kelman makes no reference to Derrida in this article.

6. See for example, Louis Schwartz, "With Gun and Camera Through Darkest CLS-Land."

7. Cf. Drucilla Cornell, *The Philosophy of the Limit* 100-103. Christopher Norris makes a similar point in "Law, Deconstruction, and the Resistance to Theory" 167.

8. J. M. Balkin, "Deconstructive Practice and Legal Theory" 776.

9. Cornell, *The Philosophy of the Limit* 2.

10. "Some Statements and Truisms" 72-76.

11. Derrida, "This Strange Institution Called Literature" 51.

12. Kristeva and Kurzweil, "An Interview with Julia Kristeva" 218-219.

13. Some Statements and Truisms" 76, 88.

14. Naomi Schor, "This Essentialism Which Is Not One" 42, but as the title of her piece indicates, Schor is not sure that it can be described as one unified concept. . . .

15. Schor, Introduction, *The Essential Difference* ix.

16. Moi, *Sexual/Textual Politics* 164, 166-167.

17. *Ibid.* 15.

18. *Ibid.* 13.

19. *Ibid.* 12. See *N for Nation* for a rather different take on Kristeva's "Women's Time."

20. Possibly as a corrective measure, Moi's Introduction to *The Kristeva Reader*, published the following year, stresses Kristeva's opposition to Derrida and deconstruction (15-18).

21. Cf. Oliver, *Reading Kristeva* 166-168.

22. Elizabeth Grosz, for example, critiques the paradox created by Kristeva's anti-essentialist problematization of "woman" on the one hand and

what Grosz sees as her essentializing of maternity as biological on the other (*Sexual Subversions* 81).

23. Tina Chanter, "Kristeva's Politics of Change" 183-185.

24. Teresa de Lauretis, "The Essence of the Triangle" 11. Cf. Schor, Introduction, *The Essential Difference* xii.

25. Schor, Introduction, *The Essential Difference* vii.

26. Schor, "This Essentialism Which Is Not One" 43. Diana Fuss also makes this point in *Essentially Speaking* 21.

27. De Lauretis, "The Essence of the Triangle" 11.

28. Elizabeth Grosz, "Sexual Difference and the Problem of Essentialism" 93-94.

29. Gayatri Chakravorty Spivak with Ellen Rooney, "In a Word" 156.

30. *Ibid.* 180.

31. Tina Chanter, "Kristeva's Politics of Change" 189.

32. The special issues were *Yale French Studies* 62, *Signs* 7.1, *Feminist Studies* 7.2, *Diacritics* 12.2.

33. Kelly Oliver (*Reading Kristeva* 163-167) details the production in non-Francophone contexts of what Toril Moi dubbed "the holy Trinity of French feminist theory" (*French Feminist Thought* 5).

34. Gayatri Spivak, "French Feminism in an International Frame" and Alice Jardine, *Gynesis* 13-28. See also Elaine Marks and Isabelle de Courtivron's introduction to *New French Feminisms*, Jane Gallop and Carolyn Burke, "Psychoanalysis and Feminism in France" and Dorothy Kaufmann-McCall, "Politics of Difference: The Women's Movement in France from May 1968 to Mitterrand."

35. Jane Duran, *Toward a Feminist Epistemology*.

36. Judith Butler, "The Body Politics of Julia Kristeva" (*Gender Trouble* 79-93). Further references to *Gender Trouble* are incorporated into the text.

37. Butler's reading of Kristeva also assumes that for subversion we must choose the semiotic over the symbolic, identifying wholly with one against the other. We can contrast this with Allison Weir's less binary reading whereby "Resistance to the given symbolic order requires that we identify with that order, learn its language. It requires, moreover, that we recognize and insist that the symbolic order is not purely 'phallic,' that it is not an unassailable monolith, but that it is a product of, and constantly changed by, conflicting, heterogeneous processes" ("Identification with the Divided Mother" 80).

38. Alan D. Sokal, "Transgressing the Boundaries" 218. Further references are incorporated into the text.

39. In a footnote, Sokal explains the striking affinity between Derrida's work and his own which "can be read as an exploration of how the orthodox

discourse [. . .] on scalar quantum field theory in four-dimensional space-time [. . .] can be seen to assert its own unreliability and thereby to undermine its own affirmations" (233n).

40. *The Australian*, June 5 and 12, 1996.

41. Michael Worton and Judith Still eds., *Intertextuality: Theories and Practices* 2.

42. In fact, early construals of intertextuality as merely concerned with source studies caused Kristeva to abandon the term in favor of "transposition" (RPL 59-60).

43. Michael Worton and Judith Still, eds., *Intertextuality: Theories and Practices* 23 for example. Similarly, Susan Friedman argues that "Kristeva's very use of Bakhtin to expound her theory of intertextuality embodies the principles of influence" ("Weavings" 154).

44. Jay Clayton and Eric Rothstein, eds., *Influence and Intertextuality in Literary History* 10-11, 28-29.

45. Worton and Still, eds., *Intertextuality: Theories and Practices* 2.

46. Seán Hand, "Missing You: Intertextuality, Transference and the Language of Love"; Ross Chambers, "Alter Ego: Intertextuality, Irony and the Politics of Reading."

47. Nicholas Royle, *After Derrida* 170.

48. Rebecca Schneider, *The Explicit Body in Performance* 49.

49. Key passages in Kristeva's work referring to lesbian desire and the homosexual-maternal link can be found TL 81 and DL 239-240.

50. Elizabeth Grosz "The Body of Signification" 94. Cf. *Sexual Subversions* 93.

51. Judith Roof, *A Lure of Knowledge* 12, cf. 90-118.

52. Teresa de Lauretis, *The Practice of Love* 72.

53. Judith Butler, *Gender Trouble* 87.

54. *Ibid.* 86.

55. Kaja Silverman, *The Acoustic Mirror* 102.

56. *Ibid.* 125.

57. Kelly Oliver, *Reading Kristeva* 140.

58. *Ibid.* 141. Cf. Silverman, *The Acoustic Mirror* 113, 119. Jane Gallop also identifies Kristeva's defensiveness with regard to lesbianism. She, however, associates it not with desire for the mother so much as fear of the phallic mother (*Feminism and Psychoanalysis: The Daughter's Seduction* 127-130).

59. De Lauretis, *The Practice of Love* 182-198.

60. R. A. Shoaf, "Medieval Studies after Derrida after Heidegger."

61. A not uncommon trend in literary studies consists in retrospectively construing past writers as Derridean before their time. Cf. the following titles: Martha Henn, "The Unseen Antagonist: Virginia Woolf as a Derridean Deconstructive Writer" and Ruth Porritt, "Surpassing Derrida's Deconstructed Self: Virginia Woolf's Poetic Disarticulation of the Self."

62. Andrew Taylor, "Chaucer Our Derridean Contemporary?" 476. Further references are incorporated into the text.

63. Homi Bhabha, "DissemiNation" 142. Further references are incorporated into the text.

64. Cf. KR 189.

65. David J. Levin ed., *Opera Through Other Eyes* 6. Further references are incorporated into the text.

66. Paul Robinson, "A Deconstructive Postscript: Reading Libretti and Misreading Opera."

67. Carolyn Abbate and Roger Parker, *Analyzing Opera: Verdi and Wagner*, Arthur Groos and Roger Parker eds., *Reading Opera*.

68. Carolyn Abbate, *Unsung Voices* xi-xii. Further references are incorporated into the text.

69. Richard Rorty, "Is Derrida a Transcendental Philosopher?" 235. Further references are incorporated into the text.

70. Rorty, "Two Meanings of 'Logocentrism': A Reply to Norris" 208.

71. See for example Rorty, "Is Derrida a Transcendental Philosopher?" 236.

72. *Ibid*. 243. And yet for all his oppositional rhetoric, Rorty blurs dividing lines: he is an analytical philosopher who engages productively with continental philosophy and seeks to abolish the divide between philosophy and literary criticism. Dasenbrock comments on his interdisciplinary professorship (*Redrawing the Lines* 18).

73. Major contributions to the debate are Rorty, "Philosophy as a Kind of Writing," "Deconstruction and Circumvention," "Two Meanings of 'Logocentrism': A Reply to Norris"; Hartman, *Saving the Text*; Norris, *The Deconstructive Turn, The Contest of Faculties*, "Philosophy as *Not* Just a 'Kind of Writing,'" "Deconstruction, Postmodernism and Philosophy"; Gasché, *The Tain of the Mirror*, "Infrastructures and Systematicity," *Inventions of Difference*; Culler, *On Deconstruction*.

74. Derrida replies to a question from Norris about this view by remarking that it sometimes "opens doors and spaces in the fields which are trying to protect themselves from Deconstruction. But once the door is open, then you have to make things more specific, and I would say, following your suggestion, that no indeed, philosophy is not *simply* a 'kind of writing'; philosophy has a

very rigorous specificity which has to be respected" ("Jacques Derrida in Discussion with Christopher Norris" 75).

75. Cf. Culler, *On Deconstruction* 153.

76. Norris, *The Contest of Faculties* 11.

77. Dasenbrock, Introduction, *Redrawing the Lines* 18.

78. On the status of "theory," cf. David Carroll, ed., *The States of "Theory."*

79. Dasenbrock, Introduction, *Redrawing the Lines* 1-26. Norris, on the other hand, locates his polemic with Rorty within continental philosophy as an extension of the debate between Habermas and Gadamer (cf. Norris, *The Contest of Faculties* and "Deconstruction, Postmodernism and Philosophy").

80. "Philosophy as *Not* Just a 'Kind of Writing'" 191.

81. Reprinted in Derrida, *Points* . . . 419-421.

82. *Ibid.* 413-414 .

83. Cf. Iris Young, *Justice and the Politics of Difference* 142-148, Judith Butler, *Gender Trouble* 133-134.

84. Eve Kosofsky Sedgwick, introduction to *Epistemology of the Closet,* Diana Fuss, introduction to *Inside/Out.*

85. Butler, *Gender Trouble* and *Bodies That Matter* (see *G for Gender* above); Lee Edelman, "Seeing Things."

86. Derrida and McDonald, "Choreographies" 76.

87. Peter Brunette and David Wills, *Screen/play: Derrida and Film Theory* 16.

88. These questions are all discussed in Chapter 4 of *Screen/play.*

89. Kaja Silverman, *The Acoustic Mirror* 100.

90. *Ibid.* 140.

91. *Ibid.* 125. See *L for Lesbian Studies* for a counter-reading.

92. Barbara Creed, *The Monstrous-Feminine. Film, feminism, psychoanalysis.*

93. Christopher Norris, Review Essay: *Difference in Translation* 58.

94. Eve Tavor Bannet, "The Scene of Translation: After Jakobson, Benjamin, de Man, and Derrida" 578.

95. For examples of such uses of translation, see U for Urban Planning and W for Woolf.

96. Kaisa Koskinen, "(Mis)Translating the Untranslatable: The Impact of Deconstruction and Post-Structuralism on Translation Theory" 446.

97. "Point de folie—maintenant l'architecture," "Why Peter Eisenman Writes Such Good Books," and "Fifty-two Aphorisms for a Foreword."

98. Similarly, a large section of Papadakis, Cooke and Benjamin eds., *Deconstruction: Omnibus Volume* is devoted to Catherine Cooke's analysis of "Constructivist Origins" (11-63).

99. Preface to Philip Johnson and Mark Wigley, *Deconstructivist Architecture* 7. Catherine Cooke's juxtaposition of images (*Deconstruction: Omnibus Volume* 11-19) highlights such affinities.

100. *Deconstructivist Architecture* 10-11, 17.

101. *Deconstructivist Architecture* 17.

102. Charles Jencks, "Deconstruction: The Pleasures of Absence" 119.

103. See, for example, the comments by Peter Eisenman and Mark Wigley (*Deconstruction: Omnibus Volume* 134, 146).

104. Valerie Tan identifies the disagreement here as not being over deconstruction but arising from different understandings of the concept of "style" ("A Dilemma of Deconstruction: The Paradox of Style").

105. Peter Eisenman in Papadakis, ed., *Deconstruction II* 63. John Macarthur, in "Experiencing Absence," examines the limits of such "misreading" in the case of Derrida's and Eisenman's exchange over the value accorded to absence in buildings ostensibly designed to deconstruct the subject.

106. "Jacques Derrida in Discussion with Christopher Norris" 72.

107. Mark Wigley, *The Architecture of Deconstruction* xiii.

108. *Ibid.* 32.

109. The principal texts are Derrida's essays in *The Truth in Painting, Right of Inspection*, Envois (PC 1-256), *Memoirs of the Blind*, his writings on architecture listed in the previous entry, and Kristeva's readings of Giotto and Bellini in *Desire in Language*, of Holbein in *Black Sun*, and of installation art and Baroque sculpture in *Sens et non-sens de la révolte*.

110. Peter Brunette and David Wills eds., *Deconstruction and the Visual Arts: Art, Media, Architecture*, Christopher Norris and Andrew Benjamin, *What Is Deconstruction?*

111. Of course Derrida's work is invoked in very localized ways as well (see *K for Kitty Kisses* for an example).

112. Toril Moi, *Sexual/Textual Politics* 1-18. Further references are incorporated into the text.

113. Cf. *E for Essentialism* above for a discussion of Moi's influential Derridean presentation of Kristeva.

114. Following Kristeva, Garrett Stewart identifies "the breakthrough of phonic play into the chain of symbolic or discursive continuity" (421), and relates his analysis of sound patterns to Derrida's notion of textual spacing ("Catching the Stylistic D/rift: Sound Defects in Woolf's *The Waves*" 421, 440). Makiko Minow-Pinkney finds the irruption of the semiotic in Woolf's

"oceanic aesthetics" and traces dialogism, polyphony and the dissemination of the ego in Woolf's novels ("Virginia Woolf 'Seen from a Foreign Land'" 174). Ellen Carol Jones uses the later Kristeva of *Tales of Love* in "The Flight of a Word: Narcissism and the Masquerade of Writing in Virginia Woolf's *Orlando*." She starts out from the idea of shifting identities and the mutually constitutive work of gender and language (with a footnote to Derrida's *Spurs*) and goes on to show how Woolf creates a narcissistic love object out of the self and out of language. Ruth Porritt's "Surpassing Derrida's Deconstructed Self: Virginia Woolf's Poetic Disarticulation of the Self" provides a counter-example to the usual use of Derrida and Kristeva in Woolf criticism. Porritt concludes that Woolf "not only anticipated Derrida's deconstruction of the self, but indeed even surpassed the limitations of his critique." (335). These limitations include a "myopic view of language" used to justify a longing for free-play (333) and a focus on splitting a singular self. In an interesting reversal of the Derridean Kristeva that Moi proposes, Porritt's Derrida is offered a cure that borrows if not Kristevan then at least Bakhtinian vocabulary: "the Derridean 'split self' can be more constructively interpreted as a 'dialogic self' which creates itself in creating relationships with other people" (335).

115. Kristeva, "Oscillation between Power and Denial" 166. Kristeva makes a similar statement in "About Chinese Women" (KR 157).

116. Miglena Nikolchina, "Born from the Head: Reading Woolf via Kristeva" 31. Musing on what seems like a repetition compulsion, Nikolchina wonders "whose silent sister Kristeva will be in a few decades" (*ibid*.). Given the way Kristeva's work is sometimes read as a mere offshoot of deconstruction, is there a danger that she might become Derrida's?

117. *Ibid.* 35. Further references are incorporated into the text.

118. It is in such phrases as "the circuiting of truth" (38), "the rigor required by playing" (39) and "the art of translation, the detour of the library" (41) that we hear the faint echo of Derridean theory being combined with Kristevan.

119. Andrew Taylor, "Chaucer Our Derridean Contemporary?" 486. The passage writes over a paragraph from Derrida's "Letter to a Japanese Friend" 5.

Works Cited

(Dates in parentheses following the title indicate dates of first publication where different)

WORKS BY JACQUES DERRIDA

Acts of Literature. Ed. Derek Attridge. New York and London: Routledge, 1992.

"Aphorism Countertime." (1986) *Acts of Literature*. Ed. Derek Attridge. Trans. Nicholas Royle, 1992. 414-433.

"At This Very Moment in This Work Here I Am." (1980) *Re-Reading Levinas*. Eds. Robert Bernasconi and Simon Critchley. Bloomington and Indianapolis: Indiana University Press, 1991. 11-48.

"Biodegradables, Seven Diary Fragments." *Critical Inquiry* 15.4 (1989): 812-873.

"Bonne volontés de puissance." *Revue Internationale de Philosophie* 38.151 (1984): 341-343.

"But, beyond . . . (Open Letter to Anne McClintock and Rob Nixon)." *Critical Inquiry* 13.1 (1986): 155-170.

Cinders. (1984) Trans. Ned Luckacher. Lincoln: University of Nebraska Press, 1992.

"Circonfession." Geoffrey Bennington and Jacques Derrida. *Jacques Derrida*. Paris: Seuil, 1991. 5-291.

"Des Tours de Babel." *Difference in Translation*. Ed. Joseph F. Graham. Trans. Graham. Ithaca: Cornell University Press, 1985. 165-207.

"Devant la loi." (1984) *Kafka and the Contemporary Critical Performance: Centenary Readings*. Ed. Alan Udoff. Trans. Avital Ronell. Bloomington: Indiana University Press, 1987. 128-149.

Dissemination. (1972) Trans. Barbara Johnson. Chicago and London: University of Chicago Press, Athlone, 1981.

"The Double Session." (1970) *Dissemination*. 173-285.

The Ear of the Other: Otobiography, Transference, Translation. (1982) Ed. Christie McDonald. Trans. Avital Ronell, Peggy Kamuf. Lincoln and London: University of Nebraska Press, 1988.

"Fifty-two Aphorisms for a Foreword." (1987) *Deconstruction: Omnibus Volume*. Eds. Andreas Papadakis, Catherine Cooke and Andrew Benjamin. Trans. Andrew Benjamin. London: Academy Editions, 1988. 67-69.

"Force of Law: The 'Mystical Foundation of Authority.'" (1990) *Deconstruction and the Possibility of Justice*. Eds. D. G. Carlson, D. Cornell and M. Rosenfeld. Trans. M. Quaintance. New York and London: Routledge, 1992. 3-67.

"Fors: The Anglish Words of Nicolas Abraham and Maria Torok." (1976) Nicolas Abraham and Maria Torok. *The Wolf Man's Magic Word: A Cryptonomy*. Trans. Barbara Johnson. Minneapolis: University of Minnesota Press, 1986. xi-xlviii.

"Fourmis." *Lectures de la différence sexuelle*. Ed. Mara Negron. Paris: des femmes, 1994. 69-102.

"Geopsychoanalysis—and 'the rest of the world.'" (1981) *American Imago* 48.2 (1991): 199-231.

"*Geschlecht*: Sexual Difference, Ontological Difference." (1983) *A Derrida Reader: Between the Blinds*. Ed. Peggy Kamuf. Trans. Ruben Bevezdivin. New York: Columbia University Press, 1991. 378-402.

The Gift of Death. (1992) Trans. David Wills. Chicago: University of Chicago Press, 1995.

Glas. (1974) Trans. John P. Leavey, Jr., Richard Rand. Lincoln: University of Nebraska Press, 1986.

"How to Avoid Speaking: Denials." (1987) *Languages of the Unsayable: The Play of Negativity in Literature and Literary Theory*. Eds. Sanford Budick and Wolfgang Iser. Trans. Ken Frieden. New York: Columbia University Press, 1989. 3-70.

"Interpretations at War." (1989) *New Literary History* 22 (1991): 39-95.

Khôra. (1987) Paris: Galilée, 1993.

"The Law of Genre." (1979) *Critical Inquiry* 7.1 (1980): 55-81.

"Letter to a Japanese Friend." *Derrida and Différance*. Eds. David Wood and Robert Bernasconi. Trans. David Wood and Robert Bernasconi. Coventry: Parousia Press, 1985. 1-5.

Limited Inc. Ed. Gerald Graff. Trans. Samuel Weber, Jeffrey Mehlman. Evanston: Northwestern University Press, 1988.

Margins of Philosophy. (1972) Trans. Alan Bass. Chicago: University of Chicago Press, 1982.

Memoirs of the Blind. (1990) Trans. Pascale-Anne Brault, Michael Naas. Chicago: University of Chicago Press, 1993.

"My Chances/*Mes Chances*: A Rendezvous with Some Epicurean Stereophonies." (1983) *Taking Chances: Derrida, Psychoanalysis and Literature*. Eds. William Kerrigan and Joseph H. Smith. Trans. Irene Harvey and Avital Ronell. Baltimore and London: Johns Hopkins University Press, 1984.

"A Number of Yes." (1987) *Qui Parle: Literature, Philosophy, Visual Arts, History* 2.2 (1988): 118-133.

Of Grammatology. (1967) Trans. Gayatri Chakravorty Spivak. Baltimore: Johns Hopkins University Press, 1974.

"Pas." *Parages*. Paris: Galilée, 1986. 19-116.

"Passions: 'An Oblique Offering.'" *Derrida: A Critical Reader*. Ed. David Wood. Oxford UK and Cambridge USA: Blackwell, 1992. 5-35.

"Point de folie—maintenant l'architecture." *AA Files* 12 (1986): 65-73.

Points . . . : Interviews, 1974-1994. Ed. Elisabeth Weber. Trans. Peggy Kamuf et al. Stanford: Stanford University Press, 1995.

Positions. (1972) Trans. Alan Bass. Chicago and London: University of Chicago Press, Athlone, 1981.

The Post Card: From Socrates to Freud and Beyond. (1980) Trans. Alan Bass. Chicago: University of Chicago Press, 1987.

"Post-Scriptum: Aporias, Ways and Voices." *Derrida and Negative Theology*. Eds. Toby Foshay and Harold Coward. Trans. John P. Leavey, Jr. Albany: State University of New York Press, 1992. 283-323.

"Préjugés: devant la loi." *La Faculté de juger*. Paris: Minuit, 1985. 87-139.

"The Principle of Reason: The University in the Eyes of its Pupils." *Diacritics* 13.3 (1983): 3-20.

Psyché: Inventions de l'autre. Paris: Galilée, 1987.

"Psyche: Inventions of the Other." (1987) *Reading de Man Reading*. Eds. Lindsay Waters and Wlad Godzich. Trans. Catherine Porter. Minneapolis: University of Minnesota Press, 1989. 25-65.

"Racism's Last Word." (1983) *Critical Inquiry* 12 (1985): 290-299.

Résistances: de la psychanalyse. Paris: Galilée, 1996.

"Right of Inspection." (1985) *Art & Text* 32 (1989): 19-27.

"Shibboleth: For Paul Celan." (1986) *Word Traces*. Ed. Aris Fioretis. Trans. Joshua Wilner. Baltimore and London: Johns Hopkins University Press, 1994. 3-72.

"Some Statements and Truisms about Neologisms, Newisms, Postisms, Parasitisms, and Other Small Seismisms." *The States of "Theory."* Ed. David Carroll. Trans. Anne Tomiche. New York: Columbia University Press, 1990. 63-94.

Speech and Phenomena, and Other Essays on Husserl's Theory of Signs. (1967) Trans. David B. Allison. Evanston: Northwestern University Press, 1973.

Spurs: Nietzsche's Styles. (1976) Trans. Barbara Harlow. Chicago: University of Chicago Press, 1978.

"Structure, Sign and Play in the Discourse of the Human Sciences." (1966) *Writing and Difference.* 278-293.

"The Time of a Thesis: Punctuations." *Philosophy in France Today*. Ed. Alan Montefiori. Trans. Kathleen McLaughlin. Cambridge: Cambridge University Press, 1983. 34-50.

"TITLE (to be specified)." *SubStance* 31 (1981): 5-22.

The Truth in Painting. (1978) Trans. Geoffrey Bennington and Ian McLeod. Chicago: University of Chicago Press, 1987.

"Two Words for Joyce." *Post-structuralist Joyce: Essays from the French.* Eds. Derek Attridge and Daniel Ferrer. Trans. Geoff Bennington. Cambridge: Cambridge University Press, 1984. 145-159.

"Ulysses Gramophone: Hear Say Yes in Joyce." (1985) *Acts of Literature.* Ed. Derek Attridge. Trans. Tina Kendall and Shari Benstock, 1992. 253-309.

"Why Peter Eisenman Writes Such Good Books." (1987) *Restructuring Architectural Theory*. Eds. Marco Diani and Catherine Ingraham. Trans. Sarah Whiting. Evanston: Northwestern University Press, 1989. 99-105.

Writing and Difference. (1967) Trans. Alan Bass. Chicago and London: University of Chicago Press, Routledge & Kegan Paul, 1978.

Derrida, Jacques, and Derek Attridge. "'This Strange Institution Called Literature': An Interview with Jacques Derrida." *Acts of Literature.* Ed. Derek Attridge. Trans. Geoffrey Bennington and Rachel Bowlby. 33-75.

Derrida, Jacques, and Richard Kearney. "Deconstruction and the Other." *Dialogues with Contemporary Continental Thinkers: The Phenomenological Heritage.* Ed. Richard Kearney. Manchester: Manchester University Press, 1984. 105-126.

Derrida, Jacques, and Christie V. McDonald. "Choreographies." *Diacritics* 12.2 (1982): 66-76.

Derrida, Jacques, and Christopher Norris. "Jacques Derrida in Discussion with Christopher Norris." *Deconstruction: Omnibus Volume*. Eds. Andreas Papadakis, Catherine Cooke and Andrew Benjamin. London: Academy Editions, 1989. 71-75.

WORKS BY JULIA KRISTEVA

Black Sun. (1987) Trans. Leon Roudiez. New York: Columbia University Press, 1989.

Desire in Language. Ed. Leon S. Roudiez. Trans. Thomas Gora, Alice Jardine, Leon Roudiez. New York: Columbia University Press, 1980.

"Evénement et révélation." *L'Infini* 5 (1984): 3-11.

"Joyce 'The Gracehoper' or the Return of Orpheus." (1984) *James Joyce: The Augmented Ninth*. Ed. Bernard Benstock, 1988. 167-180.

"Julia Kristeva in Conversation with Rosalind Coward." *Desire, ICA Documents*. London: Institute of Contemporary Arts, 1984. 22-27.

The Kristeva Reader. Ed. Toril Moi. Oxford UK, Cambridge USA: Blackwell, 1986.

Language: The Unknown. (1969) Trans. Anne M. Menke. New York: Columbia University Press, 1989.

"My Memory's Hyperbole." (1983) *The Female Autograph*. Ed. Domna C. Stanton. Chicago: University of Chicago Press, 1984. 219-235.

New Maladies of the Soul. (1993) Trans. Ross Guberman. New York: Columbia University Press, 1995.

The Old Man and the Wolves. (1991) Trans. Barbara Bray. New York: Columbia University Press, 1994.

"Oscillation between Power and Denial." *New French Feminisms: An Anthology*. Ed. Elaine Marks and Isabelle de Courtivron. Trans. Marilyn A. August. Brighton, Sussex: Harvester Press, 1981. 165-167.

"Phonetics, Phonology and Impulsional Bases." *Diacritics* 4.3 (1974): 33-37.

Polylogue. Paris: Seuil, 1977.

Possessions. Paris: Fayard, 1996.

Powers of Horror. (1980) Trans. Leon Roudiez. New York: Columbia University Press, 1982.

Proust and the Sense of Time. Trans. Stephen Bann. New York: Columbia University Press, 1993.

La Révolution du langage poétique. Paris: Seuil, 1974.

Revolution in Poetic Language. (1974) Trans. Margaret Waller. New York: Columbia University Press, 1984.

The Samurai. (1990) Trans. Barbara Bray. New York: Columbia University Press, 1992.

Sèméiotiké: Recherches pour une sémanalyse. Paris: Seuil, 1969.

Sens et non-sens de la révolte. Paris: Fayard, 1996.

Strangers to Ourselves. (1988) Trans. Leon Roudiez. New York: Columbia University Press, 1991.

Tales of Love. (1983) Trans. Leon Roudiez. New York: Columbia University Press, 1987.

"Woman Can Never Be Defined." (1979) *New French Feminisms: An Anthology*. Eds. Elaine Marks and Isabelle de Courtivron. Trans. Marilyn A. August. Brighton, Sussex: Harvester Press, 1981. 137-141.

Kristeva, Julia, Elaine Baruch, and Perry Meisel. "Two Interviews with Julia Kristeva." *Partisan Review* 51.1 (1984): 120-132.

Kristeva, Julia, Alice Jardine, and Anne Menke. "Julia Kristeva." *Shifting Scenes: Interviews on Women, Writing and Politics in Post-68 France*. Eds. Alice Jardine and Anne Menke. New York: Columbia University Press, 1993. 113-124.

Kristeva, Julia, and Edith Kurtzweil. "An interview with Julia Kristeva." *Partisan Review* 53.2 (1986): 216-229.

Kristeva, Julia, Josette Rey-Debove, and Donna Jean Umiker, eds. *Essays in Semiotics : Essais de Sémiotique*. The Hague, Paris: Mouton, 1971.

Kristeva, Julia, and Françoise van Rossum-Guyon. "Talking about *Polylogue*." *French Feminist Thought*. Ed. Toril Moi. New York, Oxford: Blackwell, 1987. 110-117.

Kristeva, Julia, et al. *La Traversée des signes*. Paris: Seuil, 1975.

OTHER WORKS CITED

Abbate, Carolyn. *Unsung Voices: Opera and Musical Narrative in the Nineteenth Century*. Princeton: Princeton University Press, 1991.

Abbate, Carolyn, and Roger Parker. *Analyzing Opera: Verdi and Wagner*. Berkeley: University of California Press, 1989.

Attridge, Derek. Introduction. *Acts of Literature*. Ed. Derek Attridge. New York and London: Routledge, 1992. 1-29.

Balkin, J. M. "Deconstructive Practice and Legal Theory." *Yale Law Journal* 96 (1987): 743-786.

Bannet, Eve Tavor. "The Scene of Translation: After Jakobson, Benjamin, de Man, and Derrida." *New Literary History* 24.3 (1993): 577-595.

Benjamin, Andrew, and John Fletcher, eds. *Abjection, Melancholia and Love: The Work of Julia Kristeva*. London: Routledge, 1989.

Bennington, Geoffrey, and Jacques Derrida. *Jacques Derrida*. Paris: Seuil, 1991.

Benstock, Bernard, ed. *James Joyce: The Augmented Ninth. Proceedings of the Ninth International James Joyce Symposium, Frankfurt 1984*. Syracuse: Syracuse University Press, 1988.

Bernasconi, Robert. "Deconstruction and the Possibility of Ethics." *Deconstruction and Philosophy: The Texts of Jacques Derrida*. Ed. John Sallis. Chicago & London: University of Chicago Press, 1987. 122-139.

Bhabha, Homi. "DissemiNation: Time, Narrative and the Margins of the Modern Nation." *The Location of Culture*. London and New York: Routledge, 1994. 139-170.

Bloom, Harold. *The Anxiety of Influence: A Theory of Poetry*. Oxford and New York: Oxford University Press, 1973.

Brunette, Peter, and David Wills, eds. *Deconstruction and the Visual Arts: Art, Media, Architecture*. Cambridge: Cambridge University Press, 1994.

Brunette, Peter, and David Wills. *Screen/play: Derrida and Film Theory*. Princeton: Princeton University Press, 1989.

Butler, Judith. *Bodies That Matter*. New York and London: Routledge, 1993.

Butler, Judith. *Gender Trouble: Feminism and the Subversion of Identity*. New York and London: Routledge, 1990.

Carroll, David, ed. *The States of "Theory"*. New York: Columbia University Press, 1990.

Caws, Mary Ann. "*Tel Quel*: Text and Revolution." *Diacritics* 3.1 (1973): 2-8.

Chambers, Ross. "Alter Ego: Intertextuality, Irony and the Politics of Reading." *Intertextuality: Theories and Practices*. Ed. Michael Worton and Judith Still, 1990. 143-158.

Chanter, Tina. "Kristeva's Politics of Change: Tracking Essentialism with the Help of a Sex/Gender Map." *Ethics, Politics and Difference in Julia Kristeva's Writing*. Ed. Kelly Oliver, 1993. 179-195.

Clayton, Jay, and Eric Rothstein, eds. *Influence and Intertextuality in Literary History*. Madison: University of Wisconsin Press, 1991.

Cooke, Catherine. "Constructivist Origins." *Deconstruction: Omnibus Volume*. Eds. Andreas Papadakis, Catherine Cooke and Andrew Benjamin, 1989. 11-63.

Cornell, Drucilla. *The Philosophy of the Limit*. New York and London: Routledge, 1992.

Coward, Harold, and Toby Foshay, eds. *Derrida and Negative Theology*. Albany: State University of New York Press, 1992.

Creed, Barbara. *The Monstrous-Feminine: Film, Feminism, Psychoanalysis*. London, New York: Routledge, 1993.

Critchley, Simon. "The Chiasmus: Levinas, Derrida and the Ethical Demand for Deconstruction." *Textual Practice* 3 (1989): 91-106.

Culler, Jonathan. *On Deconstruction: Theory and Criticism after Structuralism.* London, Melbourne & Henley: Routledge & Kegan Paul, 1983.

Dasenbrock, Reed Way, ed. *Redrawing the Lines: Analytic Philosophy, Deconstruction, and Literary Theory.* Minneapolis: University of Minnesota Press, 1989.

Davies, Margaret. *Asking the Law Question.* Sydney: The Law Book Company Ltd, 1994.

de Lauretis, Teresa. *Alice Doesn't: Feminism, Semiotics, Cinema.* Bloomington: Indiana University Press, 1984.

de Lauretis, Teresa. "The Essence of the Triangle or, Taking the Risk of Essentialism Seriously: Feminist Theory in Italy, the U.S., and Britain." *The Essential Difference.* Eds. Naomi Schor and Elizabeth Weed, 1994. 1-39.

de Lauretis, Teresa. *The Practice of Love: Lesbian Sexuality and Perverse Desire.* Bloomington and Indianapolis: Indiana University Press, 1994.

de Nooy, Juliana. "The Double Scission: Dällenbach, Dolezel and Derrida on Doubles." *Style* 25.1 (1991): 19-27.

Descombes, Vincent. *Modern French Philosophy.* Trans. L. Scott-Fox, J. M. Harding. Cambridge and New York: Cambridge University Press, 1980.

Duran, Jane. *Toward a Feminist Epistemology.* Savage, Md: Rowman and Littlefield, 1991.

Edelman, Lee. "Seeing Things: Representation, the Scene of Surveillance, and the Spectacle of Gay Male Sex." *Inside/Out.* Ed. Diana Fuss, 1991. 93-116.

Findlay, Heather. "Is There a Lesbian in This Text? Derrida, Wittig, and the Politics of the Three Women." *Coming To Terms: Feminism, Theory, Politics.* Ed. Elizabeth Weed. New York: Routledge, 1989. 59-69.

Fisher, David. "Kristeva's *Chora* and the Subject of Postmodern Ethics." *Body/Text in Julia Kristeva: Religion, Women, and Psychoanalysis.* Ed. David R. Crownfield. Albany: State University of New York Press, 1992.

Fonagy, Ivan. "Les bases pulsionnelles de la phonation." *Revue Française de Psychanalyse,* Jan. 1970: 101-136; July 1971: 543-591.

Forest, Philippe. *Histoire de Tel Quel: 1960-1982.* Paris: Seuil, 1995.

Fraser, David. "The Owls Are Not What They Seem: David Lynch, The Madonna Question and Critical Legal Studies." *Queen's Law Journal* 18 (1993): 1-70.

Fraser, David. "What a Long, Strange Trip It's Been: Deconstructing Law from Legal Realism to Critical Legal Studies." *Australian Journal of Law and Society* 5 (1990): 35-43.

Freud, Sigmund. *The Standard Edition of the Complete Psychological Works of Sigmund Freud*. Ed. James Strachey. Trans. James Strachey. London: The Hogarth Press, 1953-1974.

Friedman, Susan Stanford. "Weavings: Intertextuality and the (Re)Birth of the Author." *Influence and Intertextuality in Literary History*. Eds. Jay Clayton and Eric Rothstein, 1991. 146-180.

Fuss, Diana. *Essentially Speaking: Feminism, Nature and Difference*. New York and London: Routledge, 1989.

Fuss, Diana. *Inside/Out: Lesbian Theories, Gay Theories*. New York and London: Routledge, 1991.

Fynsk, Christopher I. "A Deceleration of Philosophy." *Diacritics* 8.2 (1978): 80-90.

Gadamer, Hans-Georg. "Et pourtant: puissance de la bonne volonté." *Revue Internationale de Philosophie* 38.151 (1984): 344-347.

Gadamer, Hans-Georg. "Le Défi herméneutique." *Revue Internationale de Philosophie* 38.151 (1984): 333-340.

Gallop, Jane. *Feminism and Psychoanalysis: The Daughter's Seduction*. London and Basingstoke: Macmillan, 1982.

Gallop, Jane, and Carolyn Burke. "Psychoanalysis and Feminism in France." *The Future of Difference*. Eds. Hester Eisenstein and Alice Jardine. New Brunswick, London: Rutgers University Press, 1985. 106-121.

Gasché, Rodolphe. "Infrastructures and Systematicity." *Deconstruction and Philosophy: The Texts of Jacques Derrida*. Ed. John Sallis. Chicago & London: University of Chicago Press, 1987. 3-20.

Gasché, Rodolphe. *Inventions of Difference: On Jacques Derrida*. Cambridge USA & London UK: Harvard University Press, 1994.

Gasché, Rodolphe. *The Tain of the Mirror: Derrida and the Philosophy of Reflection*. Cambridge Mass., London: Harvard University Press, 1986.

Groos, Arthur, and Roger Parker, eds. *Reading Opera*. Princeton: Princeton University Press, 1988.

Gross, Elizabeth. "The Body of Signification." *Abjection, Melancholia and Love: The Work of Julia Kristeva*. Eds. Andrew Benjamin and John Fletcher, 1989. 80-103.

Grosz, Elizabeth. "Ontology and Equivocation: Derrida's Politics of Sexual Difference." *Diacritics* 25.2 (1995): 115-124.

Grosz, Elizabeth. "Sexual Difference and the Problem of Essentialism." *The Essential Difference*. Eds. Naomi Schor and Elizabeth Weed, 1994. 82-97.

Grosz, Elizabeth. *Sexual Subversions: Three French Feminists.* Sydney: Allen & Unwin, 1989.

Hand, Seán. "Missing You: Intertextuality, Transference and the Language of Love." *Intertextuality: Theories and Practices.* Eds. Michael Worton and Judith Still, 1990. 79-91.

Handelman, Susan. "Parodic Play and Prophetic Reason: Two Interpretations of Interpretation." *Poetics Today* 9.2 (1988): 395-423.

Hart, Kevin. *The Trespass of the Sign: Deconstruction, Theology, and Philosophy.* Cambridge: Cambridge University Press, 1989.

Hartman, Geoffrey. *Saving the Text: Literature/Derrida/Philosophy.* Baltimore: Johns Hopkins University Press, 1981.

Henn, Martha. "The Unseen Antagonist: Virginia Woolf as a Derridean Deconstructive Writer." *Proceedings of the Louisiana State University/Texas A & M University Conference on Languages and Literature, 1991.* Ed. Scott Peeples. Baton Rouge: Dept. of English, Louisiana State University, 1992. 68-75.

Hill, Leslie. "Julia Kristeva: Theorizing the Avant-Garde?" *Abjection, Melancholia and Love: The Work of Julia Kristeva.* Ed. Andrew Benjamin and John Fletcher, 1989. 137-156.

Houdebine, Jean-Louis. "Lecture(s) d'une refonte." *Critique* 287 (1971): 318-150.

Husson, Christine A. Desan. "Expanding the Legal Vocabulary: The Challenge Posed by the Deconstruction and Defense of Law." *Yale Law Journal* 95 (1986): 969-991.

Jardine, Alice. *Gynesis: Configurations of Woman and Modernity.* Ithaca: Cornell University Press, 1985.

Jardine, Alice. "Opaque Texts and Transparent Contexts." *Ethics, Politics and Difference in Julia Kristeva's Writing.* Ed. Kelly Oliver, 1993. 23-31.

Jencks, Charles. "Deconstruction: The Pleasures of Absence." *Deconstruction: Omnibus Volume.* Eds. Andreas Papadakis, Catherine Cooke and Andrew Benjamin, 1989. 119-131.

Johnson, Philip, and Mark Wigley. *Deconstructivist Architecture.* New York: Museum of Modern Art, 1989.

Jones, Ellen Carol. "The Flight of a Word: Narcissism and the Masquerade of Writing in Virginia Woolf's *Orlando.*" *Women's Studies* 23.2 (1994): 155-174.

Kaufmann-McCall, Dorothy. "Politics of Difference: The Women's Movement in France from May 1968 to Mitterrand." *Signs* 9.2 (1983): 282-293.

Kelman, Mark. "Trashing." *Stanford Law Review* 36 (1984): 293-348.

Kofman, Sarah. *Lectures de Derrida.* Paris: Galilée, 1984.

Koskinen, Kaisa. "(Mis)Translating the Untranslatable: The Impact of Deconstruction and Post-Structuralism on Translation Theory." *Meta* 39.3 (1994): 446-452.

Lacan, Jacques. *Ecrits: A Selection*. Trans. Alan Sheridan. London: Tavistock, 1977.

Leavey, Jr., John P. "This (then) will not have been a book . . ." *Glassary*. Lincoln: University of Nebraska Press, 1986. 22-128.

Lechte, John. "Art, Love and Melancholy in the Work of Julia Kristeva." *Abjection, Melancholia and Love: The Work of Julia Kristeva*. Eds. Andrew Benjamin and John Fletcher, 1989. 24-41.

Lechte, John. *Julia Kristeva*. New York, London: Routledge, 1990.

Levin, David J., ed. *Opera Through Other Eyes*. Stanford: Stanford University Press, 1993.

Lewis, Philip E. "Revolutionary Semiotics." *Diacritics* 4.3 (1974): 28-32.

Llewelyn, John. "At a Point of Almost Absolute Proximity to Hegel." *Deconstruction and Philosophy: The Texts of Jacques Derrida*. Ed. John Sallis. Chicago & London: University of Chicago Press, 1987. 87-95.

Llewelyn, John. *Derrida on the Threshold of Sense*. London: Macmillan, 1986.

Llewelyn, John. "Responsibility with Indecidability." *Derrida: A Critical Reader*. Ed. David Wood, 1992. 72-96.

Lucy, Niall. *Debating Derrida*. Melbourne: Melbourne University Press, 1995.

Macarthur, John. "Experiencing Absence: Eisenman and Derrida, Benjamin and Schwitters." *Knowledge and/or/of Experience*. Ed. John Macarthur. Brisbane: Institute of Modern Art, 1993. 99-123.

Mallarmé, Stéphane. *Œuvres complètes*. Paris: Gallimard, 1945.

Marks, Elaine, and Isabelle de Courtivron, eds. *New French Feminisms: An Anthology*. Brighton, Sussex: Harvester Press, 1981.

McClintock, Anne, and Rob Nixon. "No Names Apart: The Separation of Word and History in Derrida's 'Le Dernier Mot du Racisme'." *Critical Inquiry* 13.1 (1986): 155-170.

Minow-Pinkney, Makiko. "Virginia Woolf 'Seen from a Foreign Land'." *Abjection, Melancholia and Love: The Work of Julia Kristeva*. Eds. Andrew Benjamin and John Fletcher, 1989. 157-177.

Moi, Toril, ed. *French Feminist Thought: A Reader*. New York, Oxford: Blackwell, 1987.

Moi, Toril. Preface. *The Kristeva Reader*. Ed. Toril Moi. Oxford UK, Cambridge USA: Blackwell, 1986. vi-vii.

Moi, Toril. *Sexual/Textual Politics*. London and New York: Methuen, 1985.

Nikolchina, Miglena. "Born from the Head: Reading Woolf via Kristeva." *Diacritics* 21.2-3 (1991): 30-42.

Niranjana, Tejaswini. *Siting Translation: History, Post-Structuralism, and the Colonial Context*. Berkeley: University of California Press, 1992.

Norris, Christopher. *The Contest of Faculties*. London & New York: Methuen, 1985.

Norris, Christopher. "Deconstruction, Postmodernism and Philosophy: Habermas on Derrida." *Derrida: A Critical Reader*. Ed. David Wood, 1992. 167-192.

Norris, Christopher. *The Deconstructive Turn*. London & New York: Methuen, 1983.

Norris, Christopher. "Law, Deconstruction, and the Resistance to Theory." *Journal of Law and Society* 15.2 (1988): 166-187.

Norris, Christopher. "Philosophy as *Not* Just a 'Kind of Writing'." *Redrawing the Lines: Analytic Philosophy, Deconstruction, and Literary Theory*. Ed. Reed Way Dasenbrock. Minneapolis: University of Minnesota Press, 1989. 189-203.

Norris, Christopher. "Review Essay: *Difference in Translation*." *Comparative Literature* 40.1 (1988): 52-58.

Norris, Christopher, and Andrew Benjamin. *What Is Deconstruction?* London, New York: Academy Editions, St. Martin's Press, 1988.

Oliver, Kelly, ed. *Ethics, Politics and Difference in Julia Kristeva's Writing*. New York, London: Routledge, 1993.

Oliver, Kelly. *Reading Kristeva: Unraveling the Double-bind*. Bloomington & Indianapolis: Indiana University Press, 1993.

Papadakis, Andreas, ed. *Deconstruction II*. London: Academy Editions, 1989.

Papadakis, Andreas, Catherine Cooke, and Andrew Benjamin, eds. *Deconstruction: Omnibus Volume*. London: Academy Editions, 1989.

Payne, Michael. *Reading Theory: an introduction to Lacan, Derrida and Kristeva*. Oxford: Blackwell, 1993.

Porritt, Ruth. "Surpassing Derrida's Deconstructed Self: Virginia Woolf's Poetic Disarticulation of the Self." *Women's Studies* 21.3 (1992): 323-38.

Prins, Yopie. "Elizabeth Barrett, Robert Browning, and the *Différance* of Translation." *Victorian Poetry* 29.4 (1991): 435-451.

Rajan, Tilottama. "Trans-Positions of Difference: Kristeva and Post-structuralism." *Ethics, Politics and Difference in Julia Kristeva's Writing*. Ed. Kelly Oliver, 1993. 215-237.

Riffaterre, Michael. "The Self-Sufficient Text." *Diacritics* 3.3 (1973): 39-45.

Robinson, Paul. "A Deconstructive Postscript: Reading Libretti and Misreading Opera." *Reading Opera*. Eds. Arthur Groos and Roger Parker. Princeton: Princeton University Press, 1988. 328-346.

Roof, Judith. *A Lure of Knowledge: Lesbian Sexuality and Theory*. New York: Columbia University Press, 1991.

Rorty, Richard. "Deconstruction and Circumvention." *Critical Inquiry* 11 (1984): 1-23.

Rorty, Richard. "Is Derrida a Transcendental Philosopher?" *Derrida: A Critical Reader*. Ed. David Wood, 1992. 235-246.

Rorty, Richard. "Philosophy as a Kind of Writing." *Consequences of Pragmatism*. Minneapolis: University of Minnesota Press, 1982. 89-109.

Rorty, Richard. "Two Meanings of 'Logocentrism': A Reply to Norris." *Redrawing the Lines: Analytic Philosophy, Deconstruction, and Literary Theory*. Ed. Reed Way Dasenbrock. Minneapolis: University of Minnesota Press, 1989. 204-216.

Roudiez, Leon. Introduction. Julia Kristeva. *Nations Without Nationalism*. New York: Columbia University Press, 1993. ix-xii.

Roudiez, Leon S. "Twelve Points from *Tel Quel*." *L'Esprit créateur* 14.4 (Winter) (1974): 291-303.

Royle, Nicholas. *After Derrida*. Manchester, New York: Manchester University Press, 1995.

Ryan, Michael. *Marxism and Deconstruction: A Critical Articulation*. Baltimore: Johns Hopkins University Press, 1982.

Schneider, Rebecca. *The Explicit Body in Performance*. London and New York: Routledge, 1997.

Schor, Naomi. "This Essentialism Which Is Not One: Coming to Grips with Irigaray." *The Essential Difference*. Ed. Naomi Schor and Elizabeth Weed, 1994. 40-62.

Schor, Naomi, and Elizabeth Weed, eds. *The Essential Difference*. Bloomington and Indianapolis: Indiana University Press, 1994.

Schwartz, Louis. "With Gun and Camera Through Darkest CLS-Land." *Stanford Law Review* 36 (1984): 413-464.

Searle, John R. "Reiterating the Differences: A Reply to Derrida." *Glyph* 1 (1977): 198-208.

Sedgwick, Eve Kosofsky. *Epistemology of the Closet*. Berkeley: University of California Press, 1990.

Shoaf, R. A. "Medieval Studies after Derrida after Heidegger." *Sign, Sentence, Discourse: Language in Medieval Thought and Literature*. Ed. Julian N. Wasserman and Lois Roney. Syracuse: Syracuse University Press, 1989. 9-30.

Silverman, Kaja. *The Acoustic Mirror: The Female Voice in Psychoanalysis*. Bloomington and Indianapolis: Indiana University Press, 1988.

Sokal, Alan D. "Transgressing the Boundaries: Towards a Transformative Hermeneutics of Quantum Gravity." *Social Text* 14.1&2 (1996): 217-252.

Sollers, Philippe. *Nombres*. Paris: Seuil, 1968.

Spivak, Gayatri Chakravorty. Translator's Preface. Jacques Derrida. *Of Grammatology*. Baltimore: Johns Hopkins University Press, 1974. ix-lxxxvii.

Spivak, Gayatri Chakravorty. "French Feminism in an International Frame." *Yale French Studies* 62 (1981): 154-184.

Spivak, Gayatri Chakravorty. "Glas-Piece." *Diacritics* 7.3 (1977): 22-43.

Spivak, Gayatri Chakravorty, and Ellen Rooney. "In a Word. Interview." *The Essential Difference*. Eds. Naomi Schor and Elizabeth Weed, 1994. 151-184.

Starobinski, Jean. "Le Texte dans le texte." *Tel Quel* 37 (1969): 3-33.

Starobinski, Jean. *Words upon Words: The Anagrams of Ferdinand de Saussure*. Trans. Olivia Emmet. New Haven: Yale University Press, 1979.

Statham, Bronwyn. *Figuring the Interdisciplinary in Critical Legal Theory*. University of Queensland, doctoral thesis (in preparation).

Stewart, Garrett. "Catching the Stylistic D/rift: Sound Defects in Woolf's *The Waves*." *ELH* 54.2 (1987): 421-461.

Tan, Valerie. "A Dilemma of Deconstruction: The Paradox of Style." Bachelor of Architecture Thesis. University of Queensland, 1992.

Taylor, Andrew. "Chaucer Our Derridean Contemporary?" *Exemplaria: A Journal of Theory in Medieval and Renaissance Studies* 5.2 (1993): 471-486.

Tel Quel. "Positions du mouvement de juin 71." *Tel Quel* 47 (1971): 135-141.

Tel Quel, ed. *Théorie d'ensemble*. Paris: Seuil, 1968.

Ward, Frazer. "Foreign and Familiar Bodies." *Dirt and Domesticity: Constructions of the Feminine*. Ed. Jesús Fuenmayor, Kate Haug and Frazer Ward. New York: Whitney Museum of American Art, 1992. 8-37.

Weir, Allison. "Identification with the Divided Mother." *Ethics, Politics and Difference in Julia Kristeva's Writing*. Ed. Kelly Oliver, 1993. 79-91.

Wigley, Mark. *The Architecture of Deconstruction: Derrida's Haunt*. Cambridge, Mass and London: MIT Press, 1993.

Wood, David, ed. *Derrida: A Critical Reader*. Oxford UK & Cambridge USA: Blackwell, 1992.

Worton, Michael, and Judith Still, eds. *Intertextuality: Theories and Practices*. Manchester and New York: Manchester University Press, 1990.

Wyatt, Jean. "Avoiding Self-Definition: In Defense of Women's Right to Merge (Julia Kristeva and *Mrs. Dalloway*)." *Women's Studies* 13.1-2 (1986): 115-126.

Young, Iris Marion. *Justice and the Politics of Difference*. Princeton: Princeton University Press, 1990.

Ziarek, Ewa. "Kristeva and Levinas: Mourning, Ethics, and the Feminine." *Ethics, Politics and Difference in Julia Kristeva's Writing*. Ed. Kelly Oliver, 1993. 62-78.

Zwarg, Christina. "Feminism in Translation: Margaret Fuller's Tasso." *Studies in Romanticism* 29.3 (1990): 463-490.

Index